H
C
C
S

Harvard Contemporary China Series, 12

The Harvard Contemporary China Series, now under the editorial direction of Harvard University Press, is designed to present new research that deals with present-day issues against the background of Chinese history and society. The focus is on interdisciplinary research intended to convey the significance of the rapidly changing Chinese scene.

The Paradox of China's Post-Mao Reforms

Edited by

Merle Goldman

Roderick MacFarquhar

Harvard University Press
Cambridge, Massachusetts
London, England   1999

Library of Congress Cataloging-in-Publication Data

The paradox of China's post-Mao reforms / edited by Merle Goldman and
   Roderick MacFarquhar.
     p.   cm. — (Harvard contemporary China series ; 12)
   ISBN 0-674-65453-6 (cloth : alk. paper).
   ISBN 0-674-65454-4 (paper : alk. paper)
   1. China—Politics and government—1976—Congresses.   2. China—
Economic conditions—1976—Congresses.   3. China—Economic
policy—1976—Congresses.   4. China—Social conditions—1976—
Congresses.   I. Goldman, Merle.   II. MacFarquhar, Roderick.
III. Series.
JQ1510.P37   1999
320.951—dc21
98-43096

Contents

III Fragmenting Society

Conclusion

Preface

This volume derives from a conference entitled "The Unintended Consequences of the Post-Mao Reforms," examining the impact of China's economic reforms on Chinese politics, culture, and society. The conference was held at the Fairbank Center for East Asian Research at Harvard University in September 1996. The participants, ranging from senior scholars to recent Ph.D.s from a variety of disciplines, presented different, sometimes conflicting perspectives. Despite the large number of participants, it was quickly apparent that it would be impossible to deal with the various facets of this question in just one conference. Thus the organizers decided that this would be the first of a series on the unintended consequences of China's economic reforms. The second conference was organized by William Hsiao at the Harvard School of Public Health and held in May 1997. It focused on the consequences of the economic reforms for demographics, income distribution, education, social security, and health. There are other areas—religion, the family, gender, values, popular culture, the media, environmental pollution, the law—that will be the subject of future conferences and subsequent volumes.

A number of people and institutions made this volume possible. Joseph Fewsmith, one of the contributors, also played an important role in planning and writing the initial proposal that solicited funding for the conference. We received generous support from the Joint Committee on Chinese Studies of the American Council of Learned Societies and the Social Science Research Council, with additional funds provided by the Henry Luce Foundation and from the American Academy of Arts and Sciences. The Fairbank Center for East Asian Research at Harvard provided the staff assistance for both convening the conference and preparing the book for publication. Our editor at Harvard University Press, Elizabeth Gretz, used her knowledge of the field as well as her editorial skills to make a complicated topic more accessible. And as always, Nancy Hearst, the librarian of the Fairbank Center Library, edited, proofread, and checked notes with the dedication and care she brings to so many of us in the field of Chinese studies.

Merle Goldman
Roderick MacFarquhar
September 1998

1 | Introduction

MERLE GOLDMAN
RODERICK MACFARQUHAR

1 | Dynamic Economy, Declining Party-State

Is the Deng Xiaoping program of reforms in the post-Mao Zedong era, called "socialism with Chinese characteristics," just another one of the many vain efforts since the Opium War of 1839–1842 to modernize China, or has it finally brought China into the modern world? For over 150 years, China's reformers have sought to make China "rich and powerful" (*fuqiang*) and restore its former greatness. In this endeavor, they launched a bewildering succession of reforms based on a variety of principles: self-strengthening; "Chinese studies for the base; Western studies for use"; the Hundred Days of Reform; constitutionalism; the May Fourth movement; Sun Yat-sen's Three Principles of the People; Chiang Kai-shek's New Life Movement; Marxism-Leninism-Mao Zedong Thought; "the Soviet Union today is our tomorrow"; the Great Leap Forward; and the Great Proletarian Cultural Revolution. These programs veered from conservative to radical, attempting either to save the existing political and social order or to transform it thoroughly or even to discard it. Economic development was seen as vital to their efforts and foreign practices were often the model, but reformers always sought a doctrinal framework to define the civilization they were shaping.

All of these reform efforts failed, some disastrously, until Deng's program of "socialism with Chinese characteristics," which beginning in December 1978 sought to combine a market economy with the centralized Leninist party-state. Unlike his predecessors, Deng had no overarching vision. Provided the party stayed in power, he was prepared to sanction any means of catapulting China out of poverty: the cat could be any color, he said, as long as it caught mice. His program has achieved spectacular economic success, with China's GNP growing an average of 9 percent per year for over two decades. China at the close of the twentieth century was the fastest-growing economy in the world. Even if the Asian economic crisis should slow China's pace over the next few years, there is no question that the "sleeping giant," whom Napoleon cautioned against disturbing, has finally awakened.

Precisely because the Deng reform program—continued by his successor, Jiang Zemin—is so pragmatic, it has triggered changes in state and society far more radical than preceding programs. The forces unleashed by the reforms have challenged not only China's command economy but also the party-state itself. Barry Naughton analyzes the economic reforms that paved the way for China's increasingly developed and prospering economy. But because the market reforms that sparked China's economic dynamism were accompanied by only limited political reforms and lacked a legal and regulatory framework, they gave rise to bouts of inflation, rampant corruption, growing social and regional disparities, and economic and political decentralization. Although the economic growth and rising incomes generated by the reforms were meant to enhance the authority of the party-state, they have actually undermined it.

Nevertheless, the bold reforms of the post-Mao leadership ended the political chaos and economic stagnation of the Cultural Revolution and sparked China's unprecedented economic boom. Because of the Cultural Revolution's destructiveness (1966–1976) and the resultant decimation of the Chinese Communist Party, Deng and the other surviving party elders, who were returned to power after Mao's death in 1976, sought to abandon Maoist policies that they had previously supported. After the Third Plenum of the Eleventh Central Committee in December 1978, most of the elders rejected not only Mao's utopian visions of the egalitarian society of the Great Leap Forward and the unending class struggle of the Cultural Revolution but also the Stalinist model of state control of the economy, collectivization of agriculture, and emphasis on heavy industry that China had followed since the 1950s. By the late 1970s this model had produced faltering economies both in China and throughout the rest of the Communist world.

Because of the failures of the Mao era, Deng believed that the only way for the party to hold on to its weakened mandate was to improve the standard of living for the majority of the population. Specifically, because several of the elders and/or their families had been sent to the countryside during the Cultural Revolution, where they encountered the harshness and marginal existence of peasant life, they were determined to introduce reforms in the rural areas. By the late 1970s they were also becoming increasingly aware of the economic dynamism of their post-Confucian and ethnic cousins in East Asia—Taiwan, South Korea, Hong Kong, Singapore, and Japan. As China moved away from the Stalinist model, it turned to the East Asian example. Consequently, party leaders sought to regain their mandate by promoting the family farms, market economy, consumer goods industry, and engagement in international trade of their East Asian neighbors.

However, whereas the leadership was relatively united in the move away from Mao's policies and the introduction of the rural reforms, differences soon emerged over the speed and direction of the reforms. The more conservative elders wanted a controlled gradual reform, restricted to the economy; another group, led by Deng Xiaoping and his reformist disciples, Hu Yaobang and Zhao Ziyang, as well as a few of the elders, moved beyond economic reforms to implement several limited political reforms. These reforms not only made China more open to the outside world than at any other time in the twentieth century, but also decentralized both political and economic power as China moved toward a market economy. For the first time since the 1949 revolution, individuals, collectives, and local areas were empowered to make their own decisions and pursue their own interests. After the June 4, 1989, crackdown on demonstrators in Tiananmen Square, when the conservative elders and remnant Maoists reasserted their authority, the economic reforms virtually stopped. But with the collapse of the Soviet Union in 1991, Deng in early 1992 embarked on a highly publicized tour of South China to call attention to and reinvigorate the economic reforms in order to stave off a Soviet-style collapse.

Deng's replacement of Mao's dictum "politics in command" with "economics in command" put China on a course that neither he nor his colleagues anticipated. As the reforms took off, Beijing's role as the country's economic decision maker declined. In part, this decline reflected a conscious decision by the reformers to replace the central government's direct involvement in economic affairs with more indirect levers of macroeconomic control and with more local decisionmaking. The party-state's loosening grip over the economy, however, also set in motion processes in the society, the political structure, and the cultural arena that it could not control. At the same time, China's opening to international trade was accompanied by an influx of Western influences in politics and culture as well as in the economy that challenged official values and official culture and moved beyond urban circles to influence rural areas by means of radio, television, telephone, fax, film, and e-mail.

The party's more limited role may also be attributed to Deng and his allies' deliberate withdrawal of the party from most nonpolitical areas. The party no longer monopolizes virtually all aspects of life as it did during the Mao era. Except for the areas of birth control and politics, Deng relaxed party control over personal and cultural life—not only because of the move to the market, but also because he wanted to repair the damage caused by the all-encompassing politicization of everyday life under Mao. Even in the political arena, which the post-Mao regime controls more tightly than other areas, relations within the party and the relationship of the party-state to society have been transformed by economic reforms, outside influences, and limited political reforms. Although the structures of the Leninist party-state remain, the leadership's ability to ensure obedience to its commands has waned. The National People's Congress (NPC), hitherto China's rubber-stamp legislature, no longer invariably obeys party directives. Marxism-Leninism and Mao Zedong Thought continue to be invoked, but few still believe in them and even fewer act upon them. Chinese society has become pluralistic and its culture diverse. For the first time since 1949, individuals and groups voice their own views and pursue their own interests rather than echo and follow the dictates of the party-state.

Forces Unleashed by the Economic Reforms

Deng Xiaoping and his colleagues had no blueprint for the post-Mao economic reforms. In the aftermath of the Cultural Revolution, they first responded to demands from below, relying initially on reformist policies that had been tried during the Mao era or during the late Qing reforms. Following the economic disaster of the Great Leap Forward, the "household responsibility system," which devolved production decisions from the commune to the family, suddenly appeared in several areas. When by September 1962 this system had led to some dismantling of the communes and a return to market forces and material incentives, Mao stopped it. But after Mao's death, peasants once again returned to the household responsibility system, particularly in Anhui and Sichuan provinces, where productivity quickly increased. At the same time, Deng and his colleagues observed that their East Asian neighbors' land reform and increasing prosperity among farmers had sparked the development of a consumer goods industry and involvement in international trade. Consequently, without a leader of Mao's stature to oppose them, in the early 1980s Deng and his colleagues made the household responsibility system national policy. Within just a few years, virtually all the communes were decollectivized and millions of Chinese peasants returned to family farming.

Similarly, the development of village and town industries, first begun during the Great Leap Forward, resumed and accelerated in the post-Mao era. Before the reforms, collective units within the communes had set up and run these industries. This collective sector had been the nonsubsidized part of the public economy and was not governed by the state plan. Consequently, as China moved to the market, this sector was better able to respond to market pressures because it had more flexibility and was without the higher labor costs and larger overheads—housing, health care, pensions, and education—of the state industries. The collectives also paid relatively fewer taxes and were subjected to fewer administrative regulations. In the post-Mao era, the collectives, primarily in the towns and villages, were able to turn underutilized labor resources to more productive uses. Initially they began with agricultural machinery repair shops, transport, and small light industry for domestic markets, but gradually they expanded into larger factories, producing consumer goods for international markets.

Deng's slogan "to get rich is glorious" inspired the growth of private enterprises, which were primarily small-scale and involved in retail and service trades. When private entrepreneurs sought to grow and become more technologically advanced, they usually set themselves up as collective enterprises. Even though some of these collectives actually remained private, they were better able as collectives to obtain the local government's help in securing land, buildings, market opportunities, and access to resources and loans. Although many failed because such ventures were so risky, the nonstate collectives and private enterprises became the most dynamic sector of China's reform economy. They grew at a rate of 20–30 percent per year until the late 1990s, when their pace began to slow. As Deng himself noted, this was a development they had not anticipated.[1] The reformers aptly described their strategy as "feeling for the stones as one crossed the river."[2]

Yet while these economic reforms led to China's accelerating economic growth, they also led to increasing political and economic decentralization as local governments made economic decisions, used tax revenue for local projects, and received less financial support from higher levels. Furthermore, as the local governments facilitated the money-making capacities of the collective-private enterprises, they formed alliances with these enterprises that benefited both sides materially. It was often in the economic interests of local authorities to disregard central government injunctions against corruption, labor exploitation, product duplication, tax overcharges, and payment for grain production with IOUs. As their interests diverged from those of the central government, local political authorities and nonstate entrepreneurs gradually formed a united front against the center's commands.

The growth of the collective-private sector thus not only helped increase the livelihood of the majority of the population, but also shifted political as well as economic power to the officials in the provinces and localities. Whereas Deng and his colleagues had realized that in order to move to the market, it was necessary to have a degree of decentralization and to reduce the overconcentration of political power at the top, they did not foresee the extent to which the economic and political decentralization that accompanied the move to the market would diminish the reach of the party-state's authority and would decrease the flow of taxes to the center.

The special economic zones and foreign joint ventures also enhanced and accelerated China's economic modernization, while reducing the party-state's control. The zones, which were first established in the early 1980s, were to attract foreign investments by offering special tax benefits and involving less red tape than in the rest of China. Initially the zones sputtered along, but propelled by Deng and his colleagues, they took off in the late 1980s just as their East Asian neighbors, particularly Hong Kong, began moving industries to China because of lower labor costs. Deng simultaneously encouraged overseas Chinese business communities in Hong Kong, Thailand, Malaysia, the Philippines, Indonesia, Singapore, and Taiwan to invest in and trade with China. Their capital, entrepreneurial instincts, and management skills helped make China's coastal provinces the most dynamic region not only in the country but in Asia.

The competitiveness of the zones and foreign joint ventures as well as the flexibility of the private and collective enterprises underscored the bankruptcy or stagnation of over 60 percent of China's relatively inefficient and obsolete state industries. Although state industries employed over two thirds of the work force, the state sector's share of economic activity gradually decreased so that by the mid-1990s it made up less than half of China's economic production and was shrinking at an accelerating rate. Because the central government formerly received 60 percent of its revenue from state-owned enterprises[3] and its tax returns from the provinces are diminishing, its economic base is eroding. Its ability to wield political authority, let alone economic power, is therefore weakened.

The Impact of Limited Political Reform

China is generally contrasted with the former Soviet Union in terms of initiating economic reforms without political reforms, but such a description is not completely accurate. In the 1980s, China's reform leaders introduced limited political reforms that sparked unexpected changes in China's party-state. Though weakened, the Leninist structure remains intact and can suppress any direct challenge that party leaders see as a political threat. In addition to the purges of two party general secretaries, Hu Yaobang in 1987 and Zhao Ziyang in 1989, for views and actions that antagonized the party elders, campaigns against political dissidents have continued during the Deng and Jiang eras. Nevertheless, with the glaring exception of the Tiananmen June 4 military crackdown, these campaigns have lacked the zeal, threat of violence, and mass movements of the Mao period, and they no longer target dissidents' families, colleagues, friends, and profession. Most important, after brief periods of silence, dissidents throughout the 1980s continued to express their ideas publicly, some even more strongly than before. Because the party restrained its power, its victims were no longer frightened into silence. After June 4, however, the most outspoken nonestablishment political activists were imprisoned or reimprisoned, and by the mid-1990s even most establishment dissidents were either in exile or silenced. However, when Jiang Zemin renewed the call for political reform at the Fifteenth Party Congress in the fall of 1997, a number of prominent intellectuals once again called publicly for political reforms to accompany the economic reforms. But at the close of the century, political reforms still lagged far behind reforms in the economic sector.

Nevertheless, though Deng's overriding concern was with the economy, he and his disciples, Hu Yaobang and Zhao Ziyang, and a few of the elders, such as Peng Zhen and Bo Yibo, played pivotal roles in promoting a number of limited political reforms in the 1980s. Deng blamed the party's loss of legitimacy less on economic stagnation than on the instability, arbitrariness, and overconcentration of personal political power during the Mao years that led ultimately to the violence and chaos of the Cultural Revolution. Therefore, despite his own decisive political role, Deng eschewed the highest offices. He sought to reestablish the party's legitimacy by emphasizing collective rule, regularizing procedures, and reforming political institutions. To that end, he and his colleagues called for "socialist democracy" and "socialist legality." Their definitions, however, were vague; they clearly did not mean a system of checks and balances, as advocated by some Chinese intellectuals. Nevertheless, they acknowledged the need to reform the political system that had allowed the unbridled expansion of one leader's political power. As Deng stated in a 1980 speech to an enlarged meeting of the Politburo, the excesses of the Cultural Revolution were the fault not just of the leader but of the party structure that gave him unlimited power: "Even so great a man as Comrade Mao Zedong was influenced to a serious degree by certain unsound systems and institutions which resulted in grave misfortunes for the party, the state and himself."[4]

Thus Deng and his disciples, early in the post-Mao era, introduced institutional procedures that were supposed to limit the concentration of political power in the hands of one or a few individuals. They replaced the life-long tenure of government leaders, though not party leaders, with fixed terms. They also tried to separate the activities of the government and the party; they proposed that the party formulate overall national goals and priorities, while the government make and implement policies to carry them out. Although Deng never questioned the overriding role of the party and its leadership, this separation had the potential gradually to diffuse the party's power by shifting some of its functions to the government administration. But Zhao Ziyang's cautious moves in that direction, beginning in mid-1986, came to an abrupt end when Zhao was blamed for the Tiananmen Square demonstrations and was put under a form of house arrest in May 1989. The Jiang Zemin era brought a return of overlapping functions of government and party officials, though there was renewed talk of separation after the 1997 Fifteenth Party Congress The establishment of procedures and rules of the game, such as convening regular party meetings and formulating civil and criminal codes, as Joseph Fewsmith details, continued after June 4.

Equally significant, members of the hitherto irrelevant National People's Congress began to exert a relative degree of independence. Deng repeatedly called attention to Article 57 of the Chinese Constitution, which states that the NPC is the "highest organ of the government." Murray Scot Tanner describes the increased assertiveness of the NPC owing to the efforts of three successive heads, the important party elders Peng Zhen, Wan Li, and Qiao Shi. They sought to strengthen the NPC's powers and its bureaucracy not only to enhance their own power but, as Tanner points out, to enhance the NPC's authority, by putting technocrats on the NPC's Standing Committee and establishing a committee system to buttress NPC work. The NPC could not set its agenda, which was established by the party leadership, but it did modify, revise, and on certain issues, withhold approval of party programs. Even after Jiang Zemin reestablished party committees in the government administration in the 1990s, the NPC and its local equivalents continued to develop a degree of independence from party control.

Gradual empowerment of the legislative branches occurred at the local levels as well as at the center. Beginning in 1980 in place of party appointment, representatives to some local people's congresses were chosen by direct vote in multicandidate elections. Although all the candidates had to be vetted by the party, for the first time in the history of the PRC the local population was given the opportunity to choose its own representatives. While this practice came to an end in the urban areas after the 1980 elections brought results that the party disliked, in the rural areas it continued and even accelerated after June 4. In an effort to rebuild authority in the countryside that had begun to erode with the Great Leap Forward famine, had deteriorated further with the Cultural Revolution, and had virtually disappeared with the end of the communes in the post-Mao era, the party, with the prompting of the party elders Peng Zhen and Bo Yibo, started to experiment with local elections.

As described by Kevin O'Brien and Li Lianjiang, beginning in the late 1980s villagers in a number of areas were given the right to choose their own village leaders and village assemblies in multicandidate elections. Despite the vetting of the candidates by officials from the Ministry of Civil Affairs, the process of multicandidate elections for village leaders instead of their appointment by the upper levels further devolved central power to the local areas. Though in many cases the elections miscarry or are rigged, in other cases, as O'Brien and Li show, the elections not only make it possible for villagers to remove predatory, corrupt village leaders, but also make the local leaders more accountable to their constituents. Evidence also suggests that democratically elected village cadres are relatively successful in securing popular compliance with state policies in return for defending villagers against the illegal predatory exactions of township and county officials, on whom they no longer need to depend for their positions. There is debate about the number of villages involved in local elections. The estimates range from 10 percent, provided by a knowledgeable high party official, to the one-third estimate of the International Republican Institute, which has helped train villagers in democratic practices, to the 80 percent estimate of the Ministry of Civil Affairs, which is in charge of the village elections.[5]

Although multicandidate elections have not yet reached the provincial level, the increasing devolution of political power recalls a similar process in the late nineteenth and early twentieth centuries. At that time, local and provincial assemblies grew in power and dominated the local scene at the expense of a weakening center. At the turn of the century, counties and provinces produced new political leaders, who, in time, gradually moved up to the national level. A similar process seems to be under way in the People's Republic, primarily for economic reasons. Leaders of the economically stronger coastal provinces have increasingly become important figures at the center as well as in their regions. Yet even though some have been placed on the Politburo, they are still likely to identify with their local interests. Jiang Zemin and his Shanghai group, who have dominated the party-state in the 1990s, favor their local interests with high-level appointments and beneficial economic policies. While the growing power of regional leaders further dilutes the center's power, Yasheng Huang has stressed that the center still retains leverage in its continuing capacity to make important provincial appointments.[6]

In the mid-1980s some intellectuals and technocrats, who had been rehabilitated by Hu Yaobang and placed in high government, media, and academic positions, called for a radical revision of Marxist-Leninist ideology and demanded a more Western-style democracy than that sought by Deng. The senior leaders, particularly the party elders, persuaded Deng to redefine "socialist democracy" to mean an improvement in the functioning of the bureaucracy rather than in the creation of institutions to curb political power. Zhao Ziyang promoted a civil service exam system in 1986 as one way to improve the bureaucracy. Although the exam represented a return to Chinese tradition, it was a new political institution in the People's Republic, where appointment generally had been based on political loyalty rather than on merit. Another reform introduced to make the bureaucracy function more fairly was the Administrative Procedure Law, which went into effect in October 1990. It gave ordinary people the right to bring suit against rapacious, arbitrary officials. Villagers, for example, began bringing suit against local officials who had confiscated their land for village industries or projects. In 1995 alone it was reported that 70,000 citizens filed suit against government agencies and officials.[7]

Nevertheless, despite this law, the slow resurrection of a civil service system, and some progress in developing property and business law, efforts to clean up the rampant corruption that accompanied China's move to the market have been ineffectual. No matter how many campaigns are launched against corruption, without the introduction of a regulatory system, a rule of law, and an independent judiciary, and with the party's continuing control over law enforcement, official directives against corruption produce minimal results. The officials assigned to clean up corruption are often the very ones who engage in it. Some corruption may facilitate the move to the market, but in China the general perception is that widespread corruption historically spelled the end of the dynasties as well as of the Guomindang. The party-state's inability to control corruption undermines its legitimacy.

Deng's death in February 1997 further weakened the party's authority. Even though the reforms aimed at checking the concentration of political power at the top, Deng had continued to rely on his personal prestige to carry out his policies, especially during the 1989 Tiananmen Square demonstrations. The organizations and procedures that Deng and his disciples introduced were never sufficiently institutionalized to replace personal rule. Since Jiang Zemin and his colleagues were already governing the party-state more than seven years before Deng's death, his passing did not leave a vacuum in formal terms. But his death marked the end of the revolutionary generation of leadership. When the history of China's tortuous road to political as well as economic modernization is written, Deng will be seen as the one who finally found the right way, even if he hesitated to go the full distance.

None of China's present leaders has played Deng's historic role. Moreover, they lack his deep roots in the military, whose support is still crucial for holding on to power in China. Jiang and his colleagues are technocrats who have made their way up the political ladder via state industry or the bureaucracy. Their right to rule comes primarily from Deng's blessing. Jiang has tried to build personal ties to the generals by promotions and by increasing the percentage of the state budget going to the military, but such actions do not necessarily mean that he has their support. Because of cuts in military spending during the Deng years, as Paul Godwin points out, units of the People's Liberation Army (PLA) began producing for the market economy to enrich both the military budget and themselves. PLA units have established a large number of enterprises for the civilian market at home and abroad. Indeed, the PLA is perhaps the largest business conglomerate in China in the post-Mao era, though in 1998 pressure was put on the PLA to divest itself of its business empire. In addition to its expanding business empire, Godwin suggests that the passing of politicized military elders, the military's increasing professionalization, and further reductions in its size might also help limit the military's political role. Nevertheless, even if these factors decrease the military's involvement in politics, at the end of the twentieth century the PLA is the only organization other than the party that is able to play a major political role in China.

Several Chinese intellectuals have bemoaned the fact that among the casualties of the June 4 tragedy was any opportunity for gradual political democratization within the party-state framework. In the aftermath of June 4, the intellectuals and ex–Red Guard organizations concerned with political issues in the 1980s, as described by Merle Goldman, were crushed and their leaders imprisoned or exiled. Unlike Czechoslovakia and Poland in the 1980s, all efforts to establish independent groups and trade unions outside party control have been thwarted and their intellectual and worker leaders have been imprisoned. Although hundreds of supposedly nongovernmental associations have sprung up in the 1990s to deal with a wide range of social, environmental, and intellectual questions,[8] they can survive only as long as they stay away from political issues. Chinese in the 1990s can change jobs, travel abroad, criticize the potholes in the street on talk radio, and vote their village leaders out of office, but they cannot express political criticism of the party-state or its leaders publicly. Those who do are put in prison. Although China at present has an incipient civil society, as described in several essays, it is so diverse, fragmented, and fluid that it is potentially a destabilizing rather than a stabilizing force. Nevertheless, even those who seek more democratic political change share with the party and the business community the fear of social disorder. There is a common apprehension that too rapid political change may produce chaos, such as that in the former Soviet Union, and thus jeopardize the gains in the standard of living of the post-Mao era.

Only a few intellectuals dare publicly express the fear that too slow political change may also be destabilizing because of the obsolescence and weakening of the central government. Yet without a Deng-like paramount leader or strong political institutions, weakening party-state controls and the accompanying accelerating shift of political power from the center to the regions and local areas will continue to erode the center's authority. A kind of informal federalism has emerged in post-Mao China, but without the political and civil institutions to hold it together. Thus the paradox of the post-Mao era is that an expanding, dynamic economy has undermined the authority of the political leaders who made it possible. Despite some limited political and legal reforms, there is an increasing dichotomy between China's economic growth and its increasingly fragile party-state. As long as such a contradiction exists, China will be haunted by the specter of political instability.

Fragmented and Fragmenting Society

There is also a dichotomy between the leadership's outdated and unheeded emphasis on centralized control and social conformity and its increasing social pluralism. The social scientist Gordon White has characterized the social changes kindled by the post-Mao reforms as "fragmented and fragmenting."[9] The introduction of market forces and individual and collective economic initiatives, as well as the political and economic devolution of power to the local levels, has produced far-reaching social changes throughout Chinese society. Some of these changes can be seen in the alliances formed between local officials and heads of local enterprises in Shanxi province, as described by David Goodman. While the alliances improved the livelihood of the nonstate entrepreneurs and workers, they enriched the local officials even more by giving them ultimate control. In some respects, the alliances appear to be revivals of traditional social configurations. They resonate with the late Qing enterprise structure of "officials supervise, merchants manage" *(guandu, shangban)*.

In the relationship between officials and entrepreneurs in the post-Mao era, which has been dubbed corporatism,[10] the line between state and society is blurred. Because the newly rich either spring from officialdom or are dependent on officials for their increasing wealth, they generally support the political status quo rather than challenge official authority. So far, China's expanding business class is seemingly unconcerned with political reform, because its interests are served by maintaining its present relationship with officials. The subordinate status of the rising economic forces—the self-employed, collectives, clans, and small and large-scale private businesses—has been reinforced by the party's efforts to coopt their associations and head off any challenge to the political system. Even the nongovernmental associations, which are self-financing, function under some sort of official supervision. Professionals and academics, some of whom—lawyers, doctors, engineers, and educators—are establishing private practices, also have set up smaller, more flexible groups, which have replaced the official professional federations as their main source of association. Yet the degree of autonomy of even influential nongovernmental groups of professionals and academics is delineated and policed by officials. Although China's business and professional classes are becoming richer and more numerous, at the end of the twentieth century they have not yet developed into an independent capitalist or middle class able to assert itself in its own right.

Nevertheless, even associations established under official supervision have helped to open up spaces in society where they can express the interests of their constituencies rather than only the views of their official sponsors. These spaces resemble those opened up in late nineteenth century China, where various groups and individuals gradually shifted from expressing the official views of the Qing to expressing their own or their group's views and by doing so gained greater political influence. In fact, the party's efforts to supervise this emerging intermediary realm have in some areas been outpaced by informal alliances outside the party's purview. In his study of Tianjin, Christopher Nevitt points out that although associations of small-scale merchants remain subservient to officials, associations of large-scale entrepreneurs, as they acquire more wealth and grow less reliant on state resources, have become more assertive about their own interests.[11] Tianjian Shi argues that as the economy and social structures develop, individuals and groups become bolder in asserting their interests. Kristen Parris describes private entrepreneurs in specific local areas, such as Wenzhou, for example, who have become influential in shifting the balance between the public and the private sectors. Furthermore, while some informal alliances of officials and nonstate entrepreneurs foster corruption and clientelism, Parris points to other alliances that promote more constructive causes, such as improving education and social services, that further the partners' interests as well as those of their workers. As several essays suggest, political leaders increasingly feel more pressure from below.

Another manifestation of the social fragmentation caused by the move to the market is the growing gap between the rich and poor. Whereas under Mao the workers in state industries had high status and were the highest paid, in the post-Mao era, as described by Martin Whyte, their status has rapidly declined. While their salaries have been frozen, reduced, or left unpaid and millions have been laid off, the salaries of those who work in nonstate and joint enterprises with foreign investors have increased. The loosening of controls combined with the unsettling effects of economic change, as Elizabeth Perry reveals, has sparked an explosion of collective resistance in the form of tax riots, industrial strikes, and street demonstrations. In the rural areas, an increasing gap is found between the prospering managers and workers in rural industries and farmers who work in the fields. In addition, there have been growing economic and social disparities between urban and rural areas as the urban rate of growth has increased and quickly surpassed the early rural growth, which began to stagnate in the mid-1980s. These economic and social disparities are intensified by the accelerating geographic disparities between the coastal areas, involved in international trade, and the inland provinces, which focus on domestic trade.

Although the urban-rural gap of the pre-Communist period was somewhat mitigated during the Mao years, especially in the areas of health care, gender inequality, and education, the market reforms have once again widened the gap. In addition, expenditure on education has barely risen in the urban areas and has fallen in the rural areas since the communes, which bore the cost of education and health care in the Mao era, were dismantled. There have been some increases in educational spending at the most advanced end of the spectrum—in the universities and research institutes—but there has been a relative decline at the elementary and secondary level, particularly in the countryside, and this has added further to social disparities, particularly between rural and urban areas. The bankruptcy and stagnation in state industry, which until the post-Mao era was the major source of the party-state's revenue, along with the fact that the center is receiving an increasingly smaller share of provincial and local tax levies, mean that the party-state has fewer resources to ameliorate these intensifying and potentially destabilizing trends of the post-Mao period.

The disparities are further widened by the easing of restrictions on the movement of workers off the farms. By the mid-1990s, China's internal migration was estimated at over 100 million.[12] Migrants are moving everywhere in China, but mostly to work in the new enterprises and joint ventures in the fastest-growing areas along the coast. Nonstate and joint enterprises recruit youth and males from poorer localities to work for low wages, though their wages are high relative to their earnings in their home areas. Although the migrant workers send a portion of their pay back to their families, lessening the inequalities somewhat in the rural areas, overall these developments have further intensified rural and urban disparities. Farming villages are increasingly populated by the elderly and females. In addition, farmers who are paid in IOUs for their grain quotas and subjected to additional taxes to finance rural industries have registered their discontent by protesting, sometimes violently, at the offices of the local tax collectors. A more peaceful form of peasant protest, Thomas Bernstein points out, is expressed in articles and editorials about the peasants' plight in official newspapers representing the peasants' interests. Another nonviolent expression of peasant discontent takes place through the election of village heads and village assemblies, described by Li and O'Brien.

China's accelerating internal migration has also increased tensions in the urban communities in which migrants settle. Dorothy Solinger analyzes the disruptive nature of and alienation caused by the influx of large numbers of economic migrants into the cities and towns in search of jobs and economic benefits. Urban dwellers, fearing that they may lose the entitlements that come with their household registration, discriminate against and isolate the encroaching migrants. Although Solinger tells of migrants from the same area setting up their own communities, where they conduct primitive educational, policing, and welfare programs, the migrants have experienced little integration into the urban areas in which they work. Most live close to the margin of existence. In addition to the millions of migrants in search of jobs are millions more, perhaps as many as half of all state workers, whom Whyte reports as either being fired or not paid. Although the government continues to subsidize the social benefits of workers in state industry for fear of a social explosion, the Fifteenth Party Congress decision in September 1997 to move toward privatization of state industries may add millions more workers to the ranks of the unemployed and unpaid.

These increasing disparities in urban areas are revealed in a survey, reported in the *China Daily*,[13] of financial assets per household in Beijing. It shows that the average property value of the richest household was 7.85 times that of the poorest. Typical top income earners are managers working for private and foreign joint ventures; families of the unemployed and retired are at the bottom. Although the official government figure for those who lived below the poverty line was 58 million in 1996,[14] representing less than 5 percent of the population compared with 26 percent at that level in 1979, the accelerating societal change, unaccompanied by the establishment of a social welfare system and exacerbated by bouts of inflation, has had a profound psychological impact. Without the social security safety network of the Mao era for people in the unemployed and nonstate sector, those who have suffered the most have been women and the elderly in the countryside. Women's suicide rates have shot up. The anthropologist Arthur Kleinman estimates that China has the highest per capita rate of suicide among women in the world.[15] The official trade unions and the women's federation, as well as the new nongovernmental associations, have begun to address these problems. They provide consulting and legal education programs to make their constituents aware of ways to express and deal with their distress other than through protests or suicide. These services, however, are in their infancy. Moreover, the magnitude of such problems and the financial resources needed to deal with them are so large that they cannot possibly be handled by the federations or the nonstate sector alone. But the weakening party-state is less able to provide help, let alone solutions, for these problems.

Virtually all the authors reveal that the party has difficulties regulating this increasingly complex and fluid society in which the relationships between state and society are in flux. While a civil society may not yet have emerged, post-Mao China has developed a public sphere that resembles that of the late nineteenth and early twentieth centuries, in which the increasingly autonomous intellectuals, professionals, and business communities are likely to become more influential. At the same time, peasants, state workers, and nonstate entrepreneurs and collectives are moving into new economic and social spaces and expressing diverse views. Whether these various groups will be able to find regularized channels to express their interests and whether the waning party-state will find a way to accommodate their diverse interests may spell the difference between a China experiencing constructive institutional change, stalemate, or chaos.

Cultural Pluralism

The paradoxes in the economic, political, and social spheres also exist in the cultural realm. At the same time that China has become economically and intellectually interdependent with the rest of the world, its political leadership increasingly stresses nationalism; as China has become more regionalized and diverse, the leadership reemphasizes ideological and political unity. Inevitably, China's participation in the international community has been accompanied by the penetration of foreign cultures. The influx of Western economic practices, technology, and trade into China in the post-Mao era has also brought Western political ideas and values, as well as pornography and pop culture, especially from Hong Kong and Taiwan. Western and overseas Chinese culture has poured into China through books, travel, telephone, film, radio, television, fax, e-mail, tourism, and advertising. By 1983, party elders and Maoists began to put pressure on Deng to stop the swelling influx of heterodoxy. Labeling this inflow "spiritual pollution" and "bourgeois liberalization," they warned that the relaxation of controls over culture and everyday life would lead to political pluralism and an end to the party's absolute monopoly of power and ideology.

In response to pressure from the party elders, Deng launched a series of campaigns—against "spiritual pollution" in 1983–84, against "bourgeois liberalization" in 1987, and against "peaceful evolution" in the early 1990s. Despite these campaigns, however, as described by Merle Goldman, the attempts of intellectuals to work for gradual political change within the party-state and of former Red Guards to work for change outside the party-state continued throughout most of the 1980s. Until June 4, it was possible to engage in political debates in the public sphere and even establish relatively independent think tanks to formulate alternative political as well as economic policies. Deng initially also allowed his protégé, Hu Yaobang, to preside over a major effort to revise and update Marxism-Leninism to make it more relevant to the reforms, but these efforts were blocked by the party elders. After June 4, however, except for brief periods such as the calls for political reform following Deng's 1992 effort to resuscitate the economic reforms and after the Fifteenth Party Congress, public political dissent was suppressed. Those brave enough to criticize or suggest political alternatives were silenced, imprisoned, exiled, or sent away for labor reform. Furthermore, there was an effort to revitalize Mao worship and reindoctrinate the population in Marxism-Leninism. In the mid-1990s, Deng Liqun, former head of the Propaganda Department, together with a group of professional ideologues allied with former central planners, sought once again to make class struggle the core of propaganda work and to recentralize economic and regional state authority.

Neither the campaigns nor the efforts to revitalize ideology and recentralize power, however, could stop the influx of ideas, values, and culture from the West, Hong Kong, and Taiwan. Once the door was opened to the outside world, it was impossible to close it again as long as the regime wanted to be involved in international trade and a market economy. Moreover, unlike during the Mao period when China did not care what the rest of the world thought of its actions, in the Deng-Jiang eras China has sought acceptance by the world community both culturally and economically. Therefore, because foreigners visit and conduct business in China and foreign journalists report on events there, the regime's ability to act ruthlessly to suppress anyone attracted to Western or overseas Chinese culture is restrained, even as China's harsh treatment of political dissidents continues. Unquestionably, at the end of the twentieth century, though the Chinese still do not experience political freedom, they enjoy more artistic, academic, cultural, professional, economic, and individual freedom than at any time during the Mao period.

Despite Deng Liqun and his allies, the post-Deng leadership merely pays lip service to the efforts of the aging conservative ideologues to revive ideology. Because of Mao's ideological distortions and the fall of the former Soviet Union, Marxism-Leninism in China is bankrupt. To fill the ideological vacuum, Jiang and his associates, like Deng before him, stress "socialist spiritual civilization," a concept that implicitly rejects Western liberal ideas and affirms nationalistic values. They call for a revival of China's great civilization and hail the authoritarian aspects of Confucianism as relevant for the present. In the 1990s the dominant discourse avoids other aspects of Confucianism, such as the obligation of the educated to criticize officials or leaders who abuse power or engage in unfair treatment of the population. As Lucian Pye has pointed out, this form of nationalism has little meaning to a population that has virtually no knowledge of its own history and traditional culture. A nationalism without substance, Pye asserts, cannot be a unifying force.[16]

While the leadership pushes the Chinese people in one direction, the new economic realities push them in the opposite direction. The leaders and intellectuals decry the moral decay and commercial crassness that has accompanied China's move to the market. Although they have different reasons—the leadership's concern is with the rampant corruption and potential challenges to its authority, the intellectuals' concern stems from their traditional disdain for "selfish" activity and their own increasing impoverishment—both groups berate their countrymen for caring only about making money. In response to these complaints, Kristen Parris notes that the newly rich entrepreneurs have tried to redefine "private interests" as part of, rather than in opposition to, the public good. Moreover, the ordinary person increasingly defines the public good less in terms of public spiritedness and nationalism than in terms of material well-being and consumerism. As Geremie Barmé has noted, ordinary Chinese, unable to act as citizens, are absorbed in the pursuit of consumerism.[17] This pursuit, together with the inflow of heterodox views, undermines both the party's efforts to impose its ideological view, whatever it may be, on the populace and the intellectuals' desire to regain their status as value-setters for society. As

China's economic reforms shift the balance of power from the state to the nonstate sector, they also shift the balance from officials and intellectuals to consumers and audiences as the shapers of China's cultural life.

Significance of the Paradoxes of Reform for China's Future

The post-Mao economic reforms and the opening to the outside world have finally begun to fulfill the wish of China's reformers since the late nineteenth century to make China "rich and powerful." China has a greater international presence than at any other time in the twentieth century, and a majority of Chinese have seen an improvement in their standard of living. As these essays indicate, however, China's success has been at a cost to both the Leninist party-state and various segments of society. Thus the very success of China's economic reforms has created new problems. The shift to the market and the accompanying disintegration of the command economy released suppressed energies and entrepreneurial skills, as Deng and his colleagues had anticipated. But as Perry, Solinger, Bernstein, and Whyte show, these forces also engendered a discontent lying beneath the surface, which periodically expresses itself in workers' strikes, farmers' protests, and the disruptions of migrant laborers. Although the reforms have given members of the population more control over their economic, cultural, and personal activities, they have weakened the party-state's capacity to deal with society's ills.

Because Deng and his associates recognized that economic reform required granting more economic power to local authorities, they tolerated a degree of regional autonomy. But they probably did not anticipate that diffusion of economic decisionmaking to the local areas and regions would concentrate less political power in Beijing. The efforts of the Jiang Zemin leadership to reestablish strong centralized control and to slow the dynamic of regionalism have been thwarted, because China's continued economic growth depends on decentralization, privatization, and openness. In fact, the regions have become increasingly less responsive to central directives. This is especially true of the wealthier provinces along the coast, involved in international trade. These provinces have closer economic relations with neighboring areas—Guangdong with Hong Kong, Fujian with Taiwan, Shandong with South Korea, and Heilongjiang with Russia—than they have with Beijing. They are less willing to follow Beijing's directives on issues such as taxes and trade when they conflict with their own regional economic interests.

Except for the areas along China's borders, such as Tibet, Inner Mongolia, and Xinjiang, the Chinese population is over 90 percent Han or ethnic Chinese. Therefore, unlike the former Soviet Union where Russians make up just over 50 percent of the population, China's decentralization does not so much threaten China as a nation as it weakens the effectiveness of its Leninist structure. The party-state can still repress anyone or any group that it believes threatens the party or its leaders; but it has been unable to handle, let alone stop, other perceived threats. As these essays point out, party directives and ideological exhortations on matters such as rampant corruption, increasing social and geographic disparities, agricultural stagnation, increasing lawlessness, and worsening environmental pollution are ignored or only superficially followed. So far, Beijing has been able to moderate repeated bouts of inflation, but each time it has had to rely on crude administrative intervention rather than macroeconomic controls of the money supply or interest rates. As the center's control over the regions and individuals continues to weaken, its ability to intervene administratively may also lessen its ability to control inflation, a task crucial to China's continuing economic dynamism.

Deng has unleashed such compelling forces of change that any successors, let alone Jiang and his associates, may be unable to manage these forces without redefining or even changing the Leninist structure. At present, the party-state lacks the political institutions and infrastructure to regulate China's accelerating informal federalism. There are no procedures or institutionalized structures through which the regions can interact regularly with the center on policy issues. Yet unless the party-state establishes and institutionalizes a new relationship between the center and the regions, it is likely that its authority will further wane. The disintegration of the former Soviet Union, however, has instilled a common belief among China's intellectual elite as well as its leadership that political change will lead to instability and will undermine the gains in the standard of living and economic growth. Although—as discussed in the essays that follow—some political reforms within the party-state have taken place, without more accommodation of the political structure to the accelerating economic and political decentralization, cultural pluralism, fragmenting society, and sprouting democratization in the localities and in the NPC, the party-state may well face even greater disorder. Indeed, the party-state may only be able to survive if it recognizes and adjusts to these changes; any such adjustments, however, will mark the end of the Leninist party-state. As Richard Baum and Alexei Shevchenko point out in the concluding essay, without a formal reconstitution of the Chinese polity, it is uncertain whether the party-state will be able to cope with the effects of the move to the market. They argue that no Leninist system under Communist Party leadership has carried out successful institutional transformation.

The party leadership has yet to acknowledge the need for such a transformation. It would prefer to follow the Singapore model of economic modernization, without major political change. But that which can be done in a city-state of 3 million cannot be replicated in a population of over 1.2 billion that is growing by 13 million each year. Even the experience of China's Confucian and ethnic neighbors, Japan, South Korea, and Taiwan, does not offer a realistic alternative. After several decades of economic growth and modernization, guided by an authoritarian political system and supported by a burgeoning middle class, these countries have gradually and peacefully evolved into democratic polities. China's huge size, massive population, greater economic regionalization, and social disparities make it much more difficult to guide China politically in any direction. China's modern history and experience are also different from those of its East Asian neighbors in ways that will influence its development. It does not have the 100 percent literacy rates and Western-trained bureaucracy of its neighbors. In addition, the diffusion of state power has already gone much further in China than in these still relatively centrally governed nations.

Jiang and his Shanghai associates, who rose through the com-

mand economy and the bureaucracy, lack the tradition and authority to sustain the already hollowed-out party-state. Moreover, there is
no legitimizing institution, such as elections, to grant them authority
and power. A factional leadership struggle, an economic downturn,
or an international crisis could further undermine the authority of
the present leaders and even the present system. But who and what
can replace them? There are other party leaders who may replace
the Jiang leadership, but at present there is no alternative to the
Communist Party. The military, with representatives at the highest
levels of the party-state, could wield influence in a factional struggle,
but it may be too busy tending to or, as Jiang Zemin demanded in
1998, selling off its business empire to put pressure on the government to provide additional funds for arms modernization to take on
a political role again. Short of a systemic collapse, it is also unlikely
that new leadership will come from members of China's dissident
community. Unlike the East European and the former Soviet dissidents, Chinese dissidents lack an organization, such as the Solidarity
movement in Poland or Charter 77 in Czechoslovakia, or a platform
of political reform to challenge the party-state or to present an
alternative.

Yet the history and experience of other countries, including
China's East Asian neighbors, have shown that a growing middle
class with rising incomes and educational levels will in time demand
a greater voice on political issues. Although several essays point out
that China's emerging middle class is not yet large enough or independent enough to exert much pressure on political issues in the
near future, the country's neighbors have demonstrated that political pluralism can gradually emerge from economic and cultural
pluralism and shift the balance of power from state to society. Other
essays reveal that in some local areas and in a variety of associations,
new groups have taken advantage of the weakening party-state to
move into the spaces from which the party-state has withdrawn or
which it can no longer occupy. In time, as the party-state continues
to decline and as these spaces expand further, a growing and diverse
middle class may organize itself politically as an alternative to the
party-state.

In the aftermath of the Cultural Revolution, the impulse for the post-Mao political and economic reforms came from pressures from below as well as from officials who had been persecuted. Thus the move to the market and the open-door policies that have led to a weakening party-state could in time lead to a freer, more democratic society as China's huge population becomes more prosperous and demands greater rights. At the same time, as these essays also reveal, China's increasing geographic and social inequalities, coupled with rising expectations, also have the potential to lead to massive social upheaval and political instability. Such is the paradox of China's reforms.

BARRY NAUGHTON

2 | China's Transition in Economic Perspective

Chinese economic reform is far more than simply an economic process. Nearly everything about China is changing, and our increasingly specialized disciplinary vocabularies are not well suited to cover the scope and interconnectedness of change of this magnitude. The channels of influence from economic changes to non-economic impacts are too numerous to be surveyed comprehensively. Yet two broad processes of economic change stand out as critically important in shaping contemporary Chinese society. The first is China's transition to a market economy according to its own distinctive transition strategy; the second is China's transformation from a predominantly agrarian economy to an increasingly urbanized, industrializing economy. The pace of change in contemporary China is so rapid precisely because China is undergoing both of these dramatic transformations simultaneously.

I will refer to these two processes by the labels "market transition" and "structural transformation." Market transition in China includes elements that are common to all market transitions, most prominently the shift from bureaucratic control of resources to market-determined allocation, and the corresponding shifts in the nature of political and economic power. While acknowledging the importance of such fundamental shifts, the discussion here focuses on aspects of China's market transition that are distinctive to China. The first section of the chapter describes the distinctive elements of China's market transition during the first decade or so of transition, and then develops some of the noneconomic implications of the approach. The second section describes the ways in which the strategy of transition inevitably shifted during the 1990s, and brought transition more in line with the demands and processes of structural transformation. The third section focuses on the structural transformation and shows that it reinforces many of the social changes associated with market transition. The chapter concludes with speculations about the ongoing impact of reform.

China's Transitional Strategy and Its Social Impact

It is now broadly recognized that China followed a dual-track transition strategy, and "grew out of the plan."[1] I will characterize China's strategy by drawing contrasts with a stylized and simplified "East European" strategy of transition. In Eastern Europe, the predominant objective of the most committed reformers was to move as rapidly as feasible to a modern market economy.[2] Models of what that economy ought to look like were readily available and close at hand: reformers saw their own economies as potentially similar to those in neighboring Western Europe, and in need above all of a rapid and profound institutional transformation to quickly shed the legacy of communism. For these reformers, it was of critical importance to free prices so they could be determined by market forces as quickly as possible. With freely determined prices, all comers would have an equal opportunity to compete on a level playing field in all forms of economic activity. The objective was to eliminate as many distortions as possible as quickly as possible: it was felt that these economies were so distorted by government misallocations and misleading signals that it would be impossible for governments to successfully correct individual distortions. It was better to smash the entire edifice, eliminating as many distortions and privileges and the resulting rent-seeking opportunities as possible, and start all over from the bottom up. If in the process there was some short-term loss of output, so be it. Reformers thought it better to undergo the costs early, in order to lay the foundation for healthy long-term growth later.

China's approach was quite different. In the first place, the imperative of economic development was constantly on the minds of reform policymakers. It was never conceivable to Chinese policymakers that their economy would "mark time," postponing economic development until after an interlude of system transformation. It was always assumed that system transformation would take place concurrently with economic development and, indeed, that the process of economic development would drive market transition forward and guarantee its eventual success. Partial system reforms were frequently judged to be effective or not depending on whether they contributed to the goal of short-run economic growth. Completion of market transition was not anticipated before the economy reached a moderate level of development.

The distinctiveness of the Chinese market transition derived partially from this growth imperative. Early reforms almost never eliminated distortions. Instead, early reforms created pockets of unregulated and lightly taxed activity within the system. Reformers allowed such pockets to open up because they were seen as contributing to developmental objectives. If rural collectives were allowed to run township and village enterprises they would be encouraged to invest more, leading to more rapid growth. If foreign businesses were allowed to operate freely in special economic zones (SEZs) they would invest in China, bringing additional capabilities. Such policies were seen as contributing to growth while not initially threatening the overall ability of the government to manage and direct the economy.

As a result, huge distortions remained in the system, but those distortions, on balance, tended to encourage resources (people, money, initiative) to flow into these less regulated "pockets." Individuals or communities saw "niches" available that they could exploit. First movers made high profits. There was almost never equal and fair competition: rarely did one see a "level playing field." The overall level of distortions in the system probably did not decrease very much in the initial stages of reform, but as dual price systems sprang up, distortions became more visible, because they could be measured by the difference between market prices and plan prices for the same goods.

Almost all of the most important early reforms fit into this pattern. Township and village enterprises were allowed to sell a wide range of products beginning in 1979. With few price controls and limited competition, they were initially remarkably profitable. Because of pervasive market shortages, they were able to charge relatively high prices even for goods of dubious quality. In 1980 the average total rate of return to capital for China's township and village enterprises (TVEs) was an enormous (and unsustainable) 32 percent per year. The dual-track system for state-owned enterprises (SOEs), in which SOEs were allowed to sell above-plan output at market prices, had a similar orientation. While SOEs were still required to fulfill planned output and delivery targets at planned prices, they were allowed to use whatever surplus capacity they had to produce market goods to be sold at unregulated prices. The foreign trade strategy based initially on the special economic zones and subsequently expanded to the coastal development strategy in 1987–88 also implied the granting of numerous exemptions from regulations and taxes for export-oriented producers. In each of these cases, producers were given access to profitable opportunities, the high profitability of which was at least partly contingent upon the maintenance of the rest of the planned economic system.

Alert individuals began to move resources into the unregulated pockets. Returns were higher, and so was risk. In the unregulated pockets of activity, prices were set by market forces, but these prices were initially a long way from their equilibrium values. Profitability was strongly conditioned by what was happening in the regulated (state) sector, and also by the level of taxation. The result was a kind of Swiss cheese economy, in which the regulated sector provided the matrix for all economic activity, while holes were opened up to provide space for private activity.

It is natural to see the Chinese approach as being distinctively Chinese, perhaps reflecting traditional Chinese culture. But in fact this approach to policy reform is also used in the developed market economies. For example, telecommunications reform in the United States began not with broad price deregulation but, rather, with the entry of new service providers. Regulators allowed MCI to compete with AT&T to provide long-distance services. Previously, long-distance rates had been set high in order to give AT&T a financial resource to subsidize local telephone service. MCI understandably wanted to enter the high profit areas, if possible, to "cherry pick." Selective entry is, in a sense, "unfair," but has the merit of initiating change with a minimum of disruption and increasing competition immediately. Moreover, the new competitor could be counted on to articulate his own interests and, to a certain extent, the interests of other potential competitors. The same considerations applied in China. Reforms began smoothly; information about effective changes was elicited; and interest groups supporting further reforms were created.

Gradually, the process of attracting new entrants into "pockets" in the planned economy proceeded sufficiently far that the overall balance between plan and market began to shift. The plan, from having been the solid material out of which a few pockets were excavated to provide space for entrepreneurial activity, became more like a sponge floating in a sea of predominantly market activity. From this point, approximately 1991–92, a new phase of economic reform could begin. The focus of reforms shifted toward dissolving the compulsory plan and creating uniform rules and tax rates for all sectors of the economy. The dual-track plan and market system was phased out, and most prices were unified at market prices. This later phase of reform will be discussed in a subsequent section. Here, I note some of the implications of the initial transitional strategy for the noneconomic outcomes of the transition. Four are most important.

(1) The strategy worked, and worked surprisingly well. As a result, reforms began smoothly, without a significant drop in output. Over time, growth accelerated. When the time came to abolish the plan, in 1992–93, it disappeared without incident. Planning ended not with a bang, but with a whimper. The contrast with Eastern Europe is great, where the Big Bang created a large drop in output and a smaller but still significant drop in consumption. In China, development continued and growth accelerated. People were better off, and took advantage of improved conditions to acquire improved

skills and enhanced capabilities. Successful development eased bottlenecks and permitted a broader process of change to unfold.

The opportunities presented to those who first took advantage of opportunities in the lightly regulated pockets were significant. Savings, investment, and entrepreneurship were forthcoming to take advantage of those opportunities. Household savings increased, and local government entrepreneurship surged. It was not merely that growth did not collapse: it accelerated. The plan framework provided some stability for future expectations and allowed many profitable undertakings to proceed. Export enclaves succeeded in expanding exports, relaxing the constraint on foreign exchange, and allowing China to import a broader range and greater amount of investment goods and production inputs, also fueling growth acceleration. Growth acceleration contributed to structural transformation.

(2) The process was Pareto-improving in its early stages, and provided opportunities to buy off opponents.[3] Influential and powerful people at both central and local levels took advantage of opportunities, along with others who were simply more alert or better equipped for a market economy. These individuals were made clearly better off, while nobody was made obviously worse off. There were surprisingly few diehard opponents of reform, and those who were initially opponents were generally bought off. After Zhao Ziyang was removed from power by conservative Communist Party leaders, it did not take the new leaders very long to adopt the main elements of Zhao's approach to reform. They then found that this approach to reform was extremely well adapted to a neo-authoritarian approach to political relations.

(3) During the transition, complex interdependencies developed between the waning but still predominant state-owned economy and the less regulated individual and collective (or community-owned) economy. Individuals learned to "work the system," taking what they could get from the old system while simultaneously exploiting new opportunities. While some individuals who were willing to bear risk took the plunge into unregulated sectors, many individuals maintained links with the regulated sector for insurance purposes. The "one household, two systems" model was a particular version of this:

one family member stayed in the state sector in order to obtain subsidized housing, medical care, and social insurance, while his or her spouse launched a market-oriented enterprise. In that sense, the two "tracks" of the economy had a mutually supportive relationship. Another example of a mutually supportive relationship was the commercial relationship between TVEs (especially in Jiangsu) and SOEs (especially in Shanghai). TVEs often got their start working for urban SOEs, which would subcontract activities to rural TVEs to expand output despite their own space constraints. Competitive relationships were important as well. As the market sector expanded relative to the bureaucratic sector, SOEs increasingly felt the pressure of market competition.

(4) Government revenues eroded. Even with economic growth, there had to be some loser for all the winners, and that loser, generally speaking, was the "public treasury." As nonstate actors were allowed into more and more of the protected niches previously monopolized by state agents, the state's ability to earn and harvest monopoly revenues declined. This can be seen by examining patterns of fiscal revenues and expenditure. Total budgetary revenues were 35.2 percent of GDP in 1978, on the eve of reform. After 1978, revenues as a share of GDP declined every year until 1995, when they reached a minimum of only 11.2 percent of GDP. Subsequently—and only after a major tax reform was finally implemented during 1994—revenues finally stabilized. According to preliminary figures announced as part of the finance minister's budget report, total revenues in 1997 equaled 12 percent of GDP, a small but significant recovery from the 1995 minimum. Since budget deficits have been maintained at around 2 percent of GDP or below, expenditures show the same basic trend as revenues. There are four broad categories of budgetary expenditure. Overt subsidies have been a major component of spending since the late 1970s, but have been cut back substantially since their peak in 1981–1983. Military spending has declined fairly steadily since 1978. Investment outlays have accounted for the largest share of the reduction in budgetary expenditures, dropping from about 16 percent of GDP to less than 3 percent. Finally, civilian current expenditures have shown relatively little change, particularly through the early 1990s. Throughout the

1980s, current expenditures hovered around 10 percent of GDP. Since the early 1990s, however, they have begun to slip below the level previously sustained, and by 1995 civilian current expenditures amounted to only 8.4 percent of GDP. Fiscal decline was reinforced by the dissolution of the agricultural collectives, which in 1978 had controlled funds—drawn from net collective income—equal to another 2.8 percent of GDP. Overall, there was a huge decline in the size of the public sector.

These four implications together have complex and ambivalent implications for the social impact of reform. On the one hand, reform fed development and growth so there were increasing real benefits provided to the general population. Living standards improved, with more than just material implications. Demands for information, for new kinds of cultural products, for new careers, and for new kinds of political participation increased. Moreover, groups were created with a powerful vested interest in reform, and these groups helped to ensure that economic reforms did not expire after Tiananmen, but rather, after a brief pause, resumed with undiminished intensity.

On the other hand, the distribution of these gains was "unfair." Crony capitalism was prominent. In localities, enormous power was amassed by some local officials. New combinations of economic power linked emergent entrepreneurs with established bureaucrats. New configurations of economic power are hardly unique to China. In Russia, for example, one of the new capitalists has recently boasted that he and six other businessmen control half of the Russian economy.[4] The Chinese economy is vast and quite competitive, and the devolution of very large state-owned industries has remained limited, so there are not yet private Chinese business groups of a scale comparable to the largest Russian groups. But one may hypothesize that there is greater continuity in China between the former political elites and the new business elites. It is only in China that the children of the former top political elites—the so-called princelings—have emerged as key economic elites. It would be interesting to know whether such continuity is as apparent at local levels as in Beijing.

Political and social issues have played out amid the backdrop of

continuous fiscal shortage. Over the long run, the erosion in government revenues is likely to cause some reduction in the quality of
basic human capital (health and education) that is one of the important preconditions of sustained economic development. As of
1978, China had invested a great deal in public health and education
(relative to its income level at that time), and also in certain kinds
of public infrastructure. These expenditures have slipped, however,
along with the general erosion in budgetary resources. For example,
total government health expenditures (excluding outlays for the
government insurance program that covers government employees
only) were still 0.8 percent of GDP in 1986, but declined to only 0.5
percent in 1993. Current outlays for education were still over 2
percent of GDP in 1985, but had declined to 1.66 percent in 1994.
There is some evidence that we are seeing the effects of these problems in measurable nonfiscal indicators. The mortality rate of children through the age of five has ceased declining since 1985, not-
withstanding continued gains in income. There is evidence of
deterioration in infant mortality rates in some of China's poorer
inland provinces.

Government interventions in the economy to limit the growth of
inequality, and even to enforce the rules against its own agents, have
become increasingly problematic. With fiscal resources in decline,
there have been ongoing struggles over the definition of the public
interest and over the division of revenues between center and locality. Deprived of formal taxation authority by the central government,
local officials resorted to various informal and often illegal practices
in order to replace lost revenues. In some cases these informal
practices were local attempts at self-taxation to provide desperately
needed public goods; but in other cases they were just corruption.
In response, the government in some respects tightened its control
over its agents in other ways, with ambiguous outcomes, as discussed
in Chapter 6.

Change within Transition: Reform since 1992

Since 1992 the focus of Chinese reform policymaking has shifted
away from the previous strategy of creating pockets of decontrol in

which entrepreneurship can flourish. The thrust of policymaking has shifted toward the creation of general rules that govern the entire economy and permit competition across a broad range of activities and on a level playing field. This process is far from complete, and there are many regulations and barriers that protect different parts of the Chinese market, but the direction of change is clear.

The transformed transitional strategy was clearly evident by 1993, when the compulsory plan and most of the remnants of the dual-track system were abolished. In the same year, a decision was made in principle to extend equal treatment to enterprises under different ownership systems. Two major unifying reforms were subsequently adopted on January 1, 1994. The first was the unification of the exchange rate, which was followed by a gradual shift to current account convertibility; the second was the creation of a new fiscal system with a broader tax base and lower, nearly uniform rates primarily based on a value-added tax.

Just as important—though less obviously successful—have been the efforts to push forward with the restructuring of state-owned industrial enterprises and commercial banks. Limited conversion of SOEs to joint stock companies began in 1992–93, but was then scaled back until a uniform company law could be promulgated. After the company law and a related banking law were passed in 1994 and 1995, restructuring picked up again in 1996 and 1997. SOE restructuring was very much on the agenda by mid-1997, and although it is too soon to determine the outcome of this latest reform initiative, it is clear that the conversion of SOEs to a modern, uniform commercial form—along with significant distribution of ownership shares to private parties—will be a primary element of the reforms. These changes share the characteristic that they envision systems in which all firms are treated equally, subject to essentially the same rules, tax rates, and price-setting mechanisms.

When market transition reached this stage, it began to interact in explosive ways with the process of structural transformation. Market transition measures of this kind have in common with structural transformation the fact that both involve much more factor mobility than before, and both create a demand for a much stronger set of

administrative institutions in order to regulate and order the interactions between these increasingly fluid and equal economic agents.
Market transition and structural transformation both imply a greater
mobility of labor between sectors and jobs, and of capital among
various competing uses. Structural transformation in general implies
the evolution of increasingly complex and sound institutions in order to regulate an increasingly anonymous mass society, replacing
the former face-to-face interactions that governed smaller-scale rural
society. As market transition moves to a new phase it tends to create
the same demands.

The initial approach to economic reform, whatever its merits, did
not fully conform to the demands of structural transformation. Access to pockets of opportunity was limited to "locals." Nothing was
more emblematic of this aspect of early reforms than policy toward
rural enterprises. Throughout the 1980s, the policy was *"litu bu-
lixiang"*—to have peasants move out of agriculture without leaving
the local area. Peasants were encouraged to stop farming and work
in local township and village enterprises, but strongly discouraged
from leaving the locality. In particular, rural to urban migration was
strongly discouraged by the system of residence permits. In the
cities, labor mobility increased very slowly during the 1980s, and by
the end of the decade nearly all urban workers were in the same
enterprises to which they had originally been assigned. Despite the
progress made in the 1980s, the basic framework of socioeconomic
segmentation was maintained in place. Generally speaking, since
1992, those controls have been very substantially reduced. Ironically,
explicitly political controls have often been strengthened, and can
in some senses be seen as a replacement for reduced economic
segmentation (see Chapter 6).

Since 1992 the system has increasingly begun to permit—or even
encourage—substantial labor mobility. Instead of only being allowed
to operate in the nearest free-market pocket, individuals have increasingly been able to move long distances and dramatically change
their status and occupation. The ultimate unification of rules in
Chinese society would of course be the abolition of urban residence
permits. This would permit the longest-lasting and most pervasive
form of dualism in Chinese society to be substantially reduced. However, while this process has begun, it is still far from completion.

Structural Transformation

Structural transformation is perhaps best examined by focusing on its single most significant process: the transformation of the labor force from agriculture to industry and other nonagricultural occupations. Through 1991, the pressure of population on employment opportunities was great, and policy did not encourage poor farmers to leave their localities. As a result, the absolute number of people employed in agriculture increased steadily, by over 5 million a year. Agricultural employment peaked in absolute terms in 1991, with a total employment of 387 million. Since then, agricultural employment fell to 348 million in 1996, shedding just under 8 million jobs annually over the intervening five years.[5] From a peak above 70 percent at the beginning of the reform process, agricultural employment dropped to 60 percent of the total labor force in the thirteen years to 1991, and then to 50 percent in the five years to 1996.

Agriculture was able to shed labor after 1991 because the modern nonagricultural sector had finally grown large enough to soak up a substantial part of long-standing rural labor surpluses. Nonagricultural employment growth jumped from under 10 million jobs a year before 1991 to almost 17 million a year after 1991. Some of the nonagricultural growth was due to the ongoing structural transformation of the economy, but some reflected the steady growth of nonstate employers. By the 1990s private employers had become large enough that their rapid proportional growth was able to absorb significant numbers of people for the first time. Indeed, during the period up through 1991, most employment was provided by publicly owned enterprises (state or collectively owned) or by the government. After 1991, the "private sector" accounted for two thirds of nonagricultural job creation.[6] Thus the liberalization in attitude toward different ownership forms that took place in the early 1990s quickly paid off in providing an additional source of employment growth.

Changes in the rate of growth of nonagricultural employment and in its ownership composition are emblematic of a whole series of changes reflecting a more mobile labor force. Jobs in state-owned enterprises, once held for life, are increasingly uncertain. The pace of quits and fires has accelerated: whereas less than one SOE employee in a thousand left the state sector in 1978 (for reasons other than death or retirement), the figure in 1996 was about one in fifty. Even this is a small part of job change, most of which occurs through layoffs in the financially troubled state sector. Laid-off workers usually continue to receive some minimal salary support, but no longer report to work. An official figure for laid-off urban workers at the end of 1996 was 8.2 million, almost twice the number of fully unemployed.[7] As job mobility increases, there is some recent evidence that returns to education and other skills are increasing, even as political connections retain value as well.[8]

Urbanization causes major social changes everywhere, and the influence of urbanization, and to a lesser extent internationalization, is affecting every aspect of Chinese society. Again, reforms have heightened the impact of a change occurring because of structural transformation. Urbanization everywhere is associated with increased diversification and social freedom for individuals. During the 1990s reforms transformed the urban retail sector, increasing the diversity of goods and services available to urban residents and improving their quality. Such diversification of consumption contributes to an increasing voluntary diversification of individuals. More specialized service providers have sprung up, at least in the big cities, that are willing to respond to increasingly specialized demand segments (in part because they are privately run and can survive on smaller sales volumes). Whether or not one chooses to attribute political importance to such changes, it is clear that it is easier for individuals to sort themselves into lifestyle subgroups. At the very least, this reduces the monotony of city life, and may contribute to the emergence of new social groups.

Finally, there is one additional factor associated with structural transformation that must be mentioned: the demographic transition. Developing countries regularly experience major changes in the age composition of their population as birth rates drop and people live longer. In China, the impact of those changes is particularly strong because of China's draconian birth control policies, which have led China into a precocious demographic transition. There are few elderly—since life expectancies were low until recently—but also few children—because of strict limits on births. As a result, the share of the population in the young adult age bracket is quite high. China's population is unusually adaptable, active, and resilient, because it is so young yet lacking a huge population of dependent children. Individuals under forty are much more willing and able to adapt to major work changes than workers over forty. The *median* age of the Chinese work force is now only thirty-two (it will increase steadily to forty in 2025). That means it is well positioned to cope with the dramatic social and economic changes occurring all around. Arguably, it makes the next stages of economic reform more feasible as well, since a young work force should be able to adapt to the necessary frictional unemployment caused by the restructuring of the state sector, which looms unavoidably on the horizon.[9]

Conclusion

The preceding discussion has helped explain why China's social transformation appears so broad and multifaceted today. Economic reform strategy was the crucial factor driving economic and social change during the 1980s. But successful reforms in that decade led to the exhaustion of that strategy in the 1990s and the need to progress to a different strategy. Inevitably the new approach to economic transition merged with the structural transformation of the economy to create intensified social change. In the 1990s, it is increasingly urbanization, migration, and career mobility that are driving economic change, instead of government economic reform policy. At the end of the 1990s, ironically, China looks perhaps less like a country in transition from socialism and more like an industrializing country in transition from its agrarian past.

This approach may help explain why China seems sometimes to be falling apart, or "deconstructing." Reform strategy as formulated in the 1980s led inevitably to a kind of deinstitutionalization. Resources were diverted away from the building of institutions, and given ample opportunity to earn private returns in the less regulated sectors of the economy. Now, as population mobility and structural change accelerate, institutions often appear insufficiently strong to cope with the social forces unleashed. The government has responded to its declining direct control over resources, and to perceptions and fears of diminishing social order, by strengthening police forces and propagating a tough set of political rules that everyone is supposed to know. But whether this process of "government by law" and rule strengthening is leading to a stable process of institutionalization is difficult to judge.

The early phases of reform created numerous groups with an interest in seeing reform survive. A crucial unanswered question today, however, is to what extent these emergent interest groups may obstruct the implementation of further reforms. To what extent have the Chinese lost the ability to enforce publicly recognized standards of behavior on their own officials? To what extent is China undergoing a process of deinstitutionalization that may be difficult to reverse? More concretely, one worries that the process of actually subjecting the economy to a uniform and impartial set of rules (taxation, import-export, corruption) has made relatively little progress in the last three or four years. It is easy to worry that if a process of building legitimate institutions does not take hold more robustly, then in the long run (certainly not tomorrow), the foundations for growth might be severely undermined, and the growth and development process will falter. In those moments, it is easy to see China as entering a phase of its history in which it once again resembles a "sheet of loose sand." It is important to recognize, however, that this deinstitutionalization is itself a by-product of an astonishing economic success. In the process of fashioning that success, Chinese institutions, however faulty, have repeatedly been capable of confronting and resolving their most serious challenges, while deferring additional tasks to an uncertain future. China today seems everywhere in motion, and often appears unstable. Yet we can take some comfort in the fact that the turmoil is a manifestation of the ceaseless striving of an intensely competitive and creative society.

II | Limited Political Reforms

3 | Elite Politics

The changes that have swept Chinese society over the past two decades have stirred hopes for the future just as continued repression has conjured visions of renewed despotism and fears of a more aggressive China. There is no question about the breadth or profundity of the social change that has occurred in China, much of which is chronicled in the pages of this volume, but there is a great deal of uncertainty and debate about its meaning for the present and future of China. Specialists who follow China closely remain deeply divided over whether China, as it begins the post-Deng era, is emerging as the latest instance of the East Asian developmental state, imploding like other socialist states, verging on democratic transition, or rising as a threat to East Asia and the United States.[1] People differ in their assessments of China, at least in part, because they make different assumptions about the impact of broad economic, social, and intellectual changes on the political system. That impact will indeed be critical, for politics, particularly elite politics, will be central to China's transition.[2] As Andrew Walder recently put it, the "ultimate question" about the sustainability of China's economic growth is whether China can maintain social stability and the coherence of its political institutions, "or whether they will become so weakened that growth will stall amidst corruption and political strife."[3]

One cannot assume either that the political system will remain stagnant in the face of the vast social changes that have taken place or that benevolent political changes will follow as a matter of course.

In thinking about the relationship between social and political change, it is useful to juxtapose two different approaches to state-society relations. One approach emphasizes the relative autonomy of the state.[4] In terms of the "rules of the game" by which elite politics are played, there is every reason to believe that elite politics (at least in China) are relatively autonomous from society and hence resistant to change. The rules of the game of the political system are not the written constitution or even the formal institutional arrangements at the top of the system but, rather, the assumptions that elite political actors bring with them about the nature of the game that they are playing. Such assumptions are deeply influenced by history ("history matters," as Douglass North reminds us), both in general and in personal terms. If political systems are "path dependent" they are so largely because political actors tend to internalize and replicate the patterns of behavior they have learned in the course of their own careers.[5]

The second approach emphasizes the mutual penetration and interaction between state and society.[6] This approach looks at the expansion of the realm of elite politics in the broad sense, at the various linkages that have developed between state and society, and indeed at the very duality ("amphibiousness," in the terms of one observer)[7] of various organs of the state. In this perspective, the distinction between state and society is not so sharp or clear cut. Changes in society do have an effect on politics because the various organs of the state are not hermetically sealed off from society and, sooner or later, absorb some of the perspectives and attitudes being adopted by nonstate actors.

As different as these perspectives are, both are useful to our consideration of contemporary PRC politics. The first approach is useful because of the particular *leitmotif* of modern Chinese politics, namely the quest for total dominance, that has characterized elite politics throughout the twentieth century.[8] Over the course of recent decades, political actors, often of quite different ideological persuasions, have nevertheless shared the perception that political power is "monistic, unified, and indivisible." The result of this conception has been that the game of politics has been played as a game to win all.[9] As the Chinese frequently if inelegantly put it, "You die, I live" *(nisi wohuo)*. The influential philosopher Li Zehou and prominent literary critic Liu Zaifu have recently reflected on this tradition, arguing that China "lacks a spirit of compromise" and that "in every political game everyone wants the result of 'I get 100 points and you get zero.'"[10]

This conception of politics, no doubt rooted in the emperor system of traditional China, was greatly strengthened by the end of the dynastic system in 1911, the humiliation China suffered at the hands of foreigners, the ravages of internal conflict, the revolutionary ideologies (with their privileged claims to truth) of the Guomindang (GMD) and the Chinese Communist Party (CCP), and the struggle for power between those two political parties.[11] The quest for "national salvation" and revolution (to "solve problems at their root," as CCP cofounder Li Dazhao put it) led to an emphasis on ideological purity and political struggle. As the political scientist Tang Tsou has argued, "the basic assumption of CCP politics has been that a group or a coalition of groups can and does decisively defeat a major rival group or coalition, and eliminate it."[12] If we assume that this winner-take-all conception of politics has been a hallmark of CCP politics, the critical question is whether the social, economic, and intellectual changes generated by some two decades of economic reforms are leading to the construction of institutions that can temper, constrain, and perhaps change this conception of politics.

The second approach to state-society relations (that is, the state-in-society approach) is thus useful because, even though elite political actors may share certain assumptions about the rules of the game, they must still act within the context of the broader society. It appears that the societal, economic, and intellectual pressures generated by nearly two decades of reforms have begun to challenge the conduct of elite politics, but whether such pressures can result in the growth of new institutions, both formal and informal, that can transform the rules by which politics are conducted or whether those same pressures will touch off a new round of "total conflict," thus reproducing and reinforcing the old rules of the game, is the critical question. Li Zehou and Liu Zaifu note, "If this train of thought [of 'you die, I live'] is not changed, China in the twenty-first century could still replay the extremely violent and painful political game of the twentieth century."[13]

In the short run, it appears that elite political actors have reacted to the rapid economic and social changes affecting Chinese society primarily in accordance with the old rules of the game, thus generating debilitating leadership conflict. This process was apparent in the conflict between "reformers" and "conservatives" that developed as reforms deepened in the 1980s. These tensions were partly responsible for the political meltdown the CCP experienced in the spring of 1989, suggesting the persistence of dysfunctional patterns of elite politics. Nevertheless, over the longer term, there is reason to believe that these social and economic pressures may yet temper or change the rules of the game. Although it is still too early to say with confidence which way Chinese politics will evolve, it is possible to outline the areas in which the past understanding of politics (as a struggle to win all) has influenced the progress of reform, where the changes produced by reform have influenced the conduct of politics, and how the interaction between these two factors is shaping China's political transition.

Impact of Elite Politics on Reform

Two aspects of elite politics appear to have had a particularly important impact on the development of reform in the late 1970s and early 1980s. The first was the winner-take-all assumption. Not only was this assumption apparent in the decision to eliminate the Gang of Four (Jiang Qing, Zhang Chunqiao, Yao Wenyuan, and Wang Hongwen) by arresting them and putting them on trial, but it was also important in the struggle for power between Hua Guofeng and Deng Xiaoping. This struggle, which unfolded in stages between 1977 and 1981, ended with the complete elimination of Hua Guofeng and his supporters from the political scene. These struggles, it should be noted, were not simply over power, but also over policy. Thus, the Gang of Four, Hua Guofeng, and Deng Xiaoping all articulated different ideological rationales that justified their quest for power and the policy goals that they pursued. These were struggles between competing political "lines."[14]

In the power *cum* policy conflict between Hua Guofeng and Deng Xiaoping, Deng and his supporters articulated a different political line *prior* to Hua's ouster. Hua was Mao's designated successor, and his removal and the inauguration of reform had to be legitimated in ideological and policy terms. Thus Deng Xiaoping and his followers explored significantly different approaches to ideology, agricultural and industrial policy, and the opening to the outside world. Of these the most important was ideology, for without putting his own reform efforts on a substantially different ideological basis, Deng and his reforms would have been vulnerable to political challenge.[15] The discussion on "practice as the sole criterion of truth" that began in the spring of 1978 and Deng's emphasis on "seeking truth from facts" were critical in Deng's defeat of Hua at the watershed Third Plenum in December 1978.[16] Ironically, although the reforms themselves aimed at a diminution of the role of ideology in Chinese society, that change itself had to be justified through ideology.

Deng did not win his struggle with Hua simply because he offered a more persuasive political vision. On the contrary, Deng's seniority in the party, his high-level administrative experience, the high opinion in which he was held by Mao Zedong, Zhou Enlai, and other party veterans (despite Mao's purging him twice), and, most important of all, his standing in the military were critical factors in Deng's emergence as the supreme leader (the political "core").[17] It is, however, precisely the existence of these elements of substantive power that underscore the importance of articulating a different "line" in this political struggle. Deng did not replace Hua as a result of back-room political maneuvers; he championed a different ideological vision publicly before defeating Hua and his followers at the Third Plenum.

If Chinese politics had operated with different assumptions about the rules of the game—if, for instance, Chinese politics had been more institutionalized at the time, and if there had been more of a tradition of political compromise—Deng might have been brought into a coalition leadership with Hua. The result of that type of politics might have been a much more incremental process of change; Deng's reform ideas might have been significantly diluted or compromised. In other words, there is every reason to believe that the implicit rules of the game of elite politics in China played a substantial role in pushing the reforms forward by forcing Deng Xiaoping and his followers (as outsiders and challengers) to articulate a substantially different vision of ideology and policy than that of Hua and his followers (the incumbents).

This is not to suggest that Deng and his supporters did not have significantly different ideas about the direction the country should take in the wake of Mao's death. Deng represented a major constituency of veteran cadres within the party who had been victims of the Cultural Revolution. Many of them had long harbored doubts about Mao Zedong's subordination of practical policy to ideological purity. Deng himself had raised his pragmatic slogan "yellow cat, black cat, whichever catches mice is a good cat" in 1962 as peasants in local areas began adopting forms of individual household contracting following the disaster of the Great Leap Forward.[18] In rejecting such practical approaches to governance in pursuit of revolutionary romanticism, Mao had ultimately undermined his own ideological vision and reconfirmed the pragmatic convictions of Deng and other veteran cadres. Nevertheless, the implicit rules of political conflict placed a premium on Deng and his followers' defining their differences with Hua Guofeng more sharply so as to legitimate the ouster of Hua and the refutation of the policy line he represented. This political process gave the early reforms a momentum they might not otherwise have had.

A second implicit understanding of politics that had an important impact on the inauguration and subsequent evolution of reform was the role of informal, personal relations.[19] Personal relations have always existed uneasily alongside formal institutions and party norms in CCP politics. Whereas party rules demand that personal relationships be based on party discipline and that personal feelings not deviate from abstract party principles, informal relations and personal networks have always been an important part of political practice. Moreover, because reform was proceeding in a political atmosphere that was uncertain, uninstitutionalized, and highly contested, it was necessary to rely on the use of personal networks to solidify the new leadership and to oversee the implementation of reform.

Thus as Deng fought to return to power and then to secure support for his reforms, he turned naturally to those he trusted. These associates included Hu Yaobang as head of the Organization Department and deputy head of the Central Party School, Wan Li in Anhui province, and Zhao Ziyang in Sichuan province. This role of informal politics has continued to be important throughout the reform period.[20] When Hu Yaobang, then general secretary of the party, was trying to consolidate his power following the Twelfth Party Congress of 1982 and to prepare the country for another round of reform, he, too, placed many of his trusted protégés in important central and provincial leadership positions. Many of these people were drawn from the Communist Youth League (CYL), which Hu had headed for many years. Whereas Deng was able to get away with building such personal networks, Hu was later tagged with engaging in "factionalism," one of the charges that led to his downfall. In the current period, party head Jiang Zemin seems to be following the same pattern, promoting people whom he has known from his tenure as CCP secretary of Shanghai and elsewhere.

This use of informal politics has sometimes involved the creation of "factions" (the clearest case may be Deng Xiaoping's use of people from the Second Field Army, which he had co-led during the Civil War, to secure his control of the military) or the use of trusted followers (as in Deng Xiaoping's use of such people as Wan Li and Zhao Ziyang), but sometimes it has meant putting together people who seem to have little relationship either with the leader or with one another but whom the leader thought could do the job and be trusted (Hu Yaobang's use of Wu Jiang and Ruan Ming, two of Hu's followers at the Central Party School, appears to fit in this category). Although one of the objects of reform has been to promote the regularization of personnel administration, the inauguration and development of reform have also thus involved, perhaps necessarily, the politics of personalism.

Reform as a Challenge to the Rules of the Game

If implicit understandings of the conduct of elite politics had an important impact on the unfolding of reform, it is also true that the inauguration of reform challenged the conduct of politics in a variety of ways, both direct and indirect. The essence of the Leninist approach to politics, Kenneth Jowitt argues, lies in the fusion of charismatic authority and impersonal organization.[21] The result is an organization, the party, that is organized around impersonal norms ("comradeship" rather than "friendship," in the terms of Ezra Vogel's well-known article)[22] but which exercises a type of charismatic authority vis-à-vis society. Rather than regularizing its relations with society and conducting itself in accordance with law (as in legal-rational authority), the party governs society through campaigns and considers itself to be above the law. Many Chinese observers, looking at the development of the CCP, have expressed this same thought by saying that the party has not made the transition from a revolutionary party to a ruling party.[23] This transition is a major focus of reform, and a major reason why reform encounters problems in Leninist systems is precisely because the requisites of being a "ruling" party (adhering to legal-rational norms and regularizing relations with society) clash with the charismatic impersonalism of Leninist systems.

The Third Plenum of the Eleventh Central Committee, which inaugurated reform in December 1978, opened a major breach with the preceding history of the CCP by announcing that the "period of large-scale class struggle" had come to a close.[24] Despite the important qualification that class struggle continued to exist and could, under certain circumstances, expand in scale (a sentence that has provided a basis for various efforts to hamper the development of the reforms), it was nevertheless clear that the party was renouncing the ideological justification for its repeated campaigns and seeking to regularize its relationship with society. However elusive a regularized relationship with society would prove to be, it was nevertheless clear that a major turning point had been passed and the Maoist order was over. There could be no turning back.

A second benchmark in this turn away from Leninist charismatic impersonalism was the discussion on practice as the sole criterion of truth that took place from May to December 1978. Whereas Mao's invocation of the criterion of practice during the revolution had marked his well-known effort to define an ideology that would work in China (what is often referred to as the Sinification of Marxism),

Deng's evocation of the same principle in 1978 marked a retreat from ideology. Deng was saying, in effect, that the party did not have the answers and that it would have to allow a variety of experiments and see which ones worked. The CCP, like most other revolutionary movements, had based its claim to power on solipsistic knowledge. Deng's invocation of the criterion of practice marked the end of the party's privileged claim to truth.

The end of the party's privileged claim to truth was apparent in Hu Qiaomu's July 1978 report to the State Council. Hu, Mao Zedong's former secretary and the party's leading ideological authority, stated that economic laws are "objective" and that violating them, as the party had in the Great Leap Forward and the Cultural Revolution, could lead to a "national crisis."[25] The party obviously needed to discover those objective economic laws and learn to obey them. Such an admission suggested that the party had no privileged claim on truth and that professional economists might be better equipped than party ideologues to discover objective economic laws. It soon became apparent that Hu's observations about objective economic laws were being extended to every other field of endeavor as practitioners inevitably claimed that objective laws governed their fields as well. Such efforts were, and are, the subject of intense conflict as the party has resisted giving up control over various fields. Nevertheless, practitioners from the hard sciences through the social sciences and the humanities have persisted in stressing the objective laws in their fields, trying to squeeze party bureaucrats out.[26]

A third benchmark was the 1982 State Constitution, which declared that "all political parties" must "take the Constitution as the basic norm of conduct."[27] Although this commitment to operate within the framework of the law has been upheld inconsistently at best, it nevertheless marked a conscious break with Mao's declaration that he was a "monk holding an umbrella," unrestrained by law or heaven.[28] The recognition, even in principle, that there were laws and principles that even the party had to obey implied the end of solipsistic knowledge as a legitimating principle. It also laid the basis for later efforts to separate the party from the government, an effort that has gone forward only with great conflict and tension precisely because the principle inherent in bureaucratic rationality conflicts with the privileged claim on truth on which the party originally based its legitimacy.

Such changes suggest the degree to which the inauguration of reform undermined the party's claim to authority, diminished the role of ideology, and altered the party's relationship to society. In giving up its privileged claim to truth, the party turned naturally to economic performance to bolster its claim to rule. Performance legitimacy—the ability to deliver the goods—replaced the utopian ideological vision that Mao had used to control and mobilize society. Ideology could no longer be the fulcrum for political action. The "four cardinal principles" (the socialist road, the dictatorship of the proletariat, the leadership of the CCP, and Marxism-Leninism-Mao Zedong Thought) could only mark a boundary (albeit an ambiguous and shifting one) beyond which speech and action were not to go. Boundaries do not elicit belief and mobilize actions.

The changing nature of the party's authority and of the role of ideology had ramifications both for the organization of the party and for the relations between the party and state on the one hand and society on the other. Ideology was abandoned as a mobilizing device, reducing the center's ability to ensure ideological compliance within the party, before administrative rationality could provide an alternative mechanism of control. Existing in an uncertain realm between an ideological system that no longer provided guidance or commanded respect and a bureaucratic order that remained undeveloped, individual units *(danwei)* began to assert themselves. Those with a stake in the old system pressed for its preservation; other units explored the limits of reform. Over time, counterelites—those who held privileged party and bureaucratic positions but held views different from these of the party leadership—were able to use the very structure that had been established to control society, the *danwei* system, to resist ideological conformity and to propose far-reaching changes in orthodox understandings of Marxism-Leninism, thus further undermining the state's ideological legitimacy.[29]

The same turn from mobilization to administration that undermined compliance within the party was reflected in the state's pulling back from society (without, it should be noted, giving up its residual right to reintroduce its power whenever and wherever it chose). The "zone of indifference" that emerged around individual activity had the salutary effect of restoring normal family life to China's citizens, allowing them control unprecedented in PRC history over their leisure time (which was increased dramatically by the reduction of political demands).[30] Inevitably, some citizens turned their attention to political activities, making demands on the political system and pressing for greater participation in the political process.

These tendencies were strongly reinforced by a reform strategy that effectively circumvented the state apparatus to devolve greater decisionmaking authority to local levels. In part because of uncertainty or opposition to reforms and in part because the central state itself was quite weak in the aftermath of the Cultural Revolution, reformers adopted a strategy known as *fangquan rangli* (devolving authority and granting benefits), in which the center provided incentives for local areas to undertake reforms. These were enabling reforms that allowed localities the latitude to pursue policies that had been prohibited in the previous history of the PRC. Supported by a revised tax system that allowed localities to garner benefits by developing their economies, the reforms, particularly in the rural areas, took off.[31] This approach to reform allowed China to avoid the titanic institutional struggles that paralyzed reform in the Soviet Union, but it did bring into being a sector of the economy, that of the township and village enterprises, that eventually eroded the profits of state-owned enterprises, constrained the financial position of the central state itself, and gave new vigor to local society.[32]

Reform also challenged the conduct of politics in more direct ways. The common demand of veteran cadres returning to power was that party norms be "restored." Party norms, it should be noted, stand in an ambivalent relationship with the "rules of the game" of the political system, particularly the assumption that political conflict ultimately results in either total victory or total defeat. After all, Mao had clearly established his dominance at least by the mid-1940s, but the concentration of power in Mao's hands did not, at least immediately, mean that there were no norms in the party. On the contrary, the CCP was at its most effective when Mao's dominance was complemented (*not* balanced) by the coexistence of such norms as democratic centralism and "curing the illness to save the patient" (that is, the practice of limiting the cost of deviance by allowing the offending person to be restored to political good standing after self-criticism and a period of contrition). As Mao's tolerance for the expression of differing views declined—Mao's denunciation of Peng Dehuai at the Lushan Plenum of 1959 for the latter's criticisms of the Great Leap Forward marked the critical turning point—inner-party norms were destroyed and the vetting of different views within the party was effectively curtailed for the next twenty years. The destruction of inner-party norms was widely believed by veteran party cadres to have been one of the root causes of the Cultural Revolution, so they were determined to restore important party norms in its aftermath.

The effort to restore party norms was reflected in the establishment of the Central Discipline Inspection Commission in January 1979, in the adoption of the "Guiding Principles for Political Life within the Party" at the Fifth Plenary Session of the Eleventh Central Committee in February 1980, and the adoption of new party and state constitutions (which emphasized that the party must operate within the scope of the law).[33] This effort to reassert the prerogatives of the party as an institution was an understandable organizational response to the destruction the party suffered at Mao's hands during the Cultural Revolution, and it resembles similar efforts in the Soviet Union following Stalin's death.

In important ways, however, this effort to restore party norms went beyond a restoration of the *status quo ante*. Indeed, the party's 1982 decision to abolish the post of party chairman reflected a sensitivity to widespread feelings that too much power had been concentrated in the hands of one person, and Deng's diminution of the personality cult was his acknowledgment of such feelings. But "collective leadership," as the restored norms demanded, conflicted with traditions of personal dominance, and one finds Chen Yun frequently voicing concerns about the need for collective leadership as Deng consolidated his own authority.

Of greater import than the tension inherent in such efforts to "restore" party norms was the effort to implement new norms. One such norm concerned retirement. Over the decade from 1978 to

1988, the party gradually ended (with a few notable exceptions) the system of life-long tenure and implemented an effective retirement system. By the end of the decade, it appears that most cadres had come to accept the system and agreed to step down from power on time.[34] The institution of the retirement system was an important step in turning the party from a revolutionary party based on "charismatic impersonalism" to a bureaucratic party, now more authoritarian than revolutionary.

The implementation of the retirement system coincided with efforts to promote younger and better-educated cadres. Hong Yung Lee, who has exhaustively studied the transformation of China's cadre structure, states that by the time of the Thirteenth Party Congress in 1987 the "process of elite transformation was nearly completed" and that "almost all leading positions, from the highest level to the basic level, were filled by the bureaucratic technocrats."[35] This transformation has profound implications for China's political future. As Hong Yung Lee notes, in Western Europe the creation of an efficient state bureaucracy was "the first step toward reducing the patrimonial power of the monarchy."[36]

Further evidence that China's cadre system is becoming more bureaucratic (in the Weberian sense) comes from Yasheng Huang. Contrary to the conventional wisdom, Huang argues that institutional changes made in the 1980s have improved the party center's ability to manage personnel and monitor their behavior. He argues that "Chinese central authorities have retained a firm grip over the vital aspects of personnel allocations: selection, promotion, and removal."[37] In other words, China's bureaucracy is behaving more like a bureaucracy.[38]

Finally, one should note the simple but, given CCP history, extraordinary fact that party meetings throughout the post-Mao period have been convened regularly. Given the party's poor record of holding party meetings in accordance with constitutional provisions in the years before reform, it is impressive that party congresses have been held every five years since the Eleventh Congress in 1977, and that plenums have been held at least yearly—and frequently more often—despite the evident conflicts within the party over the years, including the trauma of Tiananmen. It seems that no matter how serious the disputes may be within the party, there is now an expectation that issues will be dealt with through some combination of compromise, avoidance (that is, delaying the more controversial issues), and authoritative decision. Purging of leaders is still apparently an acceptable tactic in inner-party struggle, but delaying a party conclave is not. The regular convening of party meetings suggests that there is a process of institutionalization at work that constrains party conflict at least to a certain extent.

The first decade of reform reflected the contradictory tendencies of the period. The traditions of personal dominance and the struggle to win all coexisted with restored norms and new norms, while at the same time the role of the political system vis-à-vis society was changing dramatically. A brief overview of reform in the 1980s reveals these contradictions as well as the continuing importance of the game to win all.

Politics in the Era of Reform

The period of reform, as one would expect, has witnessed an intermingling and interaction between, on the one hand, the continuing legacies of previous understandings of the conduct of politics—understandings derived from China's traditional political culture, its revolutionary history, and the practice of politics at the highest levels of the party—and, on the other hand, the reassertion of old norms with new content, the emergence of new norms, and the rapidly changing environment in which politics take place. Indeed, it is this interaction that shaped the conflict between "conservatives" and "reformers" within the party on the one hand and between state and society on the other.

Broadly speaking, political conflict in the 1980s revolved around different understandings of the meaning of "reform." There were those, generally identified as "conservatives," who saw no fundamental problem with the CCP's traditional political structure and practice. Headed by such leaders as the economic specialist Chen Yun and the ideologues Hu Qiaomu and Deng Liqun, conservatives generally attributed the problems of the past to the various political movements launched by Mao Zedong. Once the extreme "leftism" identified with Mao's latter years and with his campaign-style politics was eliminated, they believed, *scientific* socialism could finally come into being. This understanding of reform was strongly supportive of the "restoration" of such party norms as democratic centralism and collective leadership and of the emergence of new norms such as retirement. After all, it was Chen Yun who first expressed concern about the problem of an aging cadre force and the need to rejuvenate the ranks.[39] Nevertheless, conservatives thought that reforms should not challenge the central tenets of the party-state system: the planned economy should be primary, Marxist-Leninist ideology should be actively propagated, and party building should stress the promotion of "loyal" Marxist-Leninists.[40]

In contrast, reformers, led by Deng Xiaoping, Hu Yaobang, and Zhao Ziyang, believed (or came to believe) that there *were* fundamental problems with the party-state system. Generally speaking, they saw "leftist" interferences not as exogenous to the system, as conservatives did, but as responses to the inherent contradictions of the system. For reformers, it was thus not sufficient to eliminate "leftism"; it was necessary to eliminate the causes of leftism. In the opinion of many reformers, the excesses of the Mao years were rooted in the ideological system. It was not enough, in their opinion, to curtail political movements; "leftism" would be a recurrent danger if Marxist-Leninism were not fundamentally reinterpreted in ways that were compatible with economic reform, political democratization (however understood), and intellectual freedom. Such views were pressed strongly at the Theory Conference of early 1979, provoking the first of several reactions against "deviating" from the tenets of Marxism-Leninism.[41]

The difference between conservative and reformist approaches was reflected in an early debate over the question of whether the cycles of centralization and decentralization that had been repeatedly experienced in PRC history were caused by "leftism" or were inherent in the planning system itself. Conservatives argued that there was nothing fundamentally wrong with the planned economy as it had been conceived in the early years of the PRC. The problem, in their opinion, was that the various political movements launched by Mao had interfered with the proper functioning of the planning system. Consequently, they argued that it was necessary to restore and revitalize state organs such as the State Planning Commission and to make their operation more scientific. Markets should be allowed, but they should exist around the fringes of the planned economy and not interfere in its operation. In contrast, reformers saw the planning system itself generating such cycles, forcing policymakers either to loosen up the centralized vertical controls *(tiao)* that stifled the economy or to overcome the chaos produced by decentralized horizontal coordination *(kuai)*. Reformers argued that the planning system needed to be reformed by incorporating the market mechanism *within* it, and thus they called for "integrating the planned and market *economies*," not just "integrating the planned economy with market *regulation*" as the conservatives called for.[42]

The question that must be addressed is why such differences of understanding and approach hardened over time, leading to a polarization of opinion within the party, to increasingly harsh campaigns, to the purge of Hu Yaobang in 1987, and finally to the inner-party crisis of spring 1989. I would contend that despite the development of norms and the increasing institutionalization (bureaucratization) of the party organization, political conflict was still conditioned by the perception that the rules of the game revolved around the struggle to win or lose all. This is not to say that there was not compromise throughout the first decade of reform, but that such compromise was tactical in nature, premised on the belief that sooner or later there would be a final "game" in which one side would win and the other would lose. In other words, compromises were made to gain temporary advantage (or, conversely, to minimize political damage); they were efforts to position oneself for the final game that would have to be played sooner or later. This understanding of the political game allows us to understand many aspects of the development of reform in the 1980s that are otherwise not comprehensible.

First, it allows us to understand the political importance of debates such as that between "integrating the planned and market *economies*" and "integrating the planned economy with market *regulation*." Such expressions were not, contrary to appearances, arcane exercises in Marxist-Leninist jargon without real consequences. On the contrary, such phrases were metaphors that encapsulated very different perceptions of the goals of reform. Political battles were fought over such terminology, harsh criticisms launched, self-criticisms made, and victories and losses recorded in the changing vocabulary of official party documents. One cannot understand the political importance of the 1984 "Decision on the Reform of the Economic Structure," which reflected the growing differences between Chen Yun and Deng Xiaoping, without reference to such debates.[43]

Second, reference to the political game being played allows us to better understand the importance of the structural conflict that underlay the evolution of reform. Generally speaking, conservatives in the 1980s controlled the bureaucracies most closely identified with CCP rule, particularly the State Planning Commission (which was central to the management of the planned economy) and the Propaganda Department (whose mission was to defend Marxism-Leninism). Because conservatives dominated such bureaucracies (something to which Deng Xiaoping clearly acquiesced), reformers had to depend largely on extra-bureaucratic networks. Hu Yaobang thus had his "intellectual network" (as well as his CYL network), and Zhao cultivated his economic "think tanks."[44] These networks tended to rely less on formal structures than on informal politics. They tended to be composed of a relatively small number of individuals, often concentrated in research organs. In general, their bureaucratic heft did not match their intellectual firepower. This pattern of authority helps explain why reform followed the course of enabling reforms that allowed latitude to pursue policies heretofore prohibited.

This structural dimension helps us to understand the pattern of conflict that emerged in the 1980s. It is hardly surprising that conservatives in orthodox bureaucracies such as the Propaganda Department would fight ferociously against independent-minded intellectuals, supported directly or indirectly by the general secretary, who developed ideological approaches that undermined the authority of the Propaganda Department. It is also not surprising that bureaucrats in the State Planning Commission and other conservative ministries objected to reform measures that made their jobs more difficult (by creating enterprises that competed with state-owned enterprises, eroding the profits of the latter and creating financial difficulties for the state) and diminished their relevance.

As reform proceeded, the problems associated with partial reform inevitably occurred. On the one hand, economic problems such as excessive investment, redundant industrial construction, local blockades, and inflation developed; on the other hand, reformers blamed the failure to open up the ideological atmosphere and reform the political system for creating obstacles for deepening reform. As such conflicts developed, there was a natural tendency for reformers to push for more reform even as conservatives sought solutions in reinforcing the old system, both by tightening administrative controls over the economy and by tightening the party's control over ideology. In some instances, reformers pushed ahead even when doing so was not advisable, because slowing down or turning back implied an admission of error, opening them to political attack. A classic instance of this logic occurred in early 1987 when Zhao Ziyang, facing conservative demands to tighten the money supply and strengthen central controls, decided to push ahead and urged a loosening of the money supply, thus fueling inflationary pressures.[45] It seems that Zhao feared that yielding to conservative criticisms on monetary policy would force him to cede greater influence over policymaking to his conservative critics. The calculus appears directly rooted in an intuitive understanding of the rules of the game, and Zhao, it seems, had a better understanding of the politics of the time than of the economics.

In this and similar instances, the dispute was not simply over policy but over power. The political game being played was not one of compromise but one of gradually forcing one's opponent into an indefensible position where he could be destroyed politically. Zhao Ziyang often used the metaphor of a boat being rowed upstream to describe reform—if it is not going forward then it will be pushed backward. This was at least as true politically as it was economically. Had Chinese politics been one of compromise, Zhao might have been more willing to yield on such policy issues without fear of losing power. The logic of "struggle politics" (*douzheng zhengzhi*) was quite apparent in such instances, and as such conflicts accumulated, compromise became even less possible. Zhao's ouster, like that of Hu

Yaobang, was the result of the implicit understanding of the game of politics.

This overview of elite conflict in the reform period suggests a basic continuity in the conduct of elite politics as the view of politics as a struggle to win or lose all colored the actions of both conservatives and reformers. Conservatives articulated a systematic critique of reform, faulting it on economic, organizational, and ideological grounds. As reform deepened, inevitably encountering the problems of partial reforms, conservatives tended to blame the reform project itself, not just the methods by which it was conducted. For their part, reformers pushed ahead, paying scant heed to the concerns of conservatives. The tensions between the two wings of the party exploded into full view as social pressures built up in the late 1980s. Following the purge of Zhao Ziyang in June 1989, the conservative critique of reform became quite explicit and was clearly directed at Zhao's patron, Deng Xiaoping.[46] Soon Deng was being treated, as Mao once claimed he had been, as a dead ancestor at his own funeral. At one point, Deng is reported to have fumed, "*People's Daily* wants to comprehensively criticize Deng Xiaoping."[47] Indeed, it was not until the Fourteenth Party Congress in October 1992—following Deng's dramatic trip to Shenzhen in January of that year and a series of sharp political maneuvers that spring—that one could say that Deng had regained the inner-party influence that he had enjoyed in the years prior to Tiananmen.[48]

Nevertheless, despite the evident continuity in the rules of the game of elite politics, it is possible to discern reform's impact on the conduct of elite politics. Although the struggle to win all was evident in the tensions between conservatives and reformers and was particularly conspicuous in the battle between General Secretary Zhao Ziyang and Premier Li Peng, it did not, in the final analysis, extend to the highest level of the regime. Whatever the tensions between Deng Xiaoping and Chen Yun, and there is no doubt that they were great, even the political crisis of June 1989 did not trigger a decisive showdown between them. This was in part because Chen (as he had in the Maoist period) respected party norms regarding inner-party policy differences (in particular, not challenging Deng openly once Deng had made a decision) and in part because Chen had no ambition to be the number one leader. However, it also appears that the turn away from mobilizing ideology, the reaffirmation of inner-party norms, and the focus on economic modernization that defined the reform period all contributed to a sense of limitation on elite struggle. As serious as the political crisis of the spring of 1989 was, the scope of conflict was constrained. At the highest level, Deng and Chen continued to co-exist with each other (even as they continued to disagree on policy), while at lower levels the anticipated purge was not as wide or as deep as anticipated.

The eighteen years since the inauguration of reform have entailed both the destruction (or at least the redefinition) of institutions as well as the construction of new institutions. Thus, on the one hand, the span of control of the State Planning Commission and the Propaganda Department were curtailed, while, on the other hand, new or reinstated norms, such as those governing retirement and the regular convening of party meetings, have developed. Although institutions such as the Organization Department of the party appear to have been strengthened by attention to bureaucratic rules, many other institutions have become deeply involved in the economy, leading to corruption and the societalization of the state bureaucracy, that is, an intermingling of state and society in ways that seriously corrode the autonomy of the state.

The coexistence of these conflicting trends with traditional assumptions about the rules of the game of politics have given the reform process an uneven, "jerky" quality. The critical question is whether the changed environment, consisting of the growth of institutionalization, and the elevation of a younger, better-educated, and more technocratic leadership, might finally be affecting the conduct of politics within the highest echelons of the party. The answer is not yet clear, but perhaps we can gain some insight from the literature on democratic transitions.

Chinese Politics in Transition?

The era of reform has been one of intense contradiction, where new norms and institutions stand in tension with long-standing norms and traditions, where indications of state building coexist with signs of disintegration. The CCP is attempting to carry out the dual task of transforming itself from a Leninist party to an authoritarian party while presiding over the transition from a planned economy to a market economy. This is an enormously difficult economic *cum* political task—as the fate of other Communist states suggests.[49] Yet the costs of not accomplishing it, given the implicit rules of the political game and the revolutionary *leitmotif* of twentieth-century Chinese politics, would be very high indeed.[50] Ding Xueliang, a knowledgeable observer of contemporary China, has gone so far as to say that "if an anarchic situation appears in China, the violence that Chinese will inflict on each other will far exceed the barbarism inflicted by the Japanese army when it invaded in the 1930s."[51]

Divining the future of China is risky indeed, but some guidance can be garnered from the literature on political transitions. One conclusion of this literature is that the window of opportunity for successful democratic transitions is relatively small and the likelihood of a hardline crackdown, reversal, or unconsolidated democracy is correspondingly great.[52] In general, the combination of a strong state and a strong civil society appears to provide the best backdrop for a successful transition.[53] Another important factor is the development of a legal framework and the creation of a "usable bureaucracy," both of which might be said to be components of a strong state.[54] Thus, in thinking about China's development, we should direct our attention to such issues as state capacity and social organization.

Viewed from this perspective, China's transition appears delicate at best. There are indeed indications that China's state capacity is increasing. The institution of a retirement system, the recruitment of younger and better-educated cadres, and the procedures that China's central state has put in place to monitor local cadres all point to a rationalization of China's bureaucratic structure. Moreover, as Hong Yung Lee points out, the increasing complexity of the tasks undertaken by the bureaucracy and the recruitment of cadres with diverse backgrounds are likely to increase the importance of bureaucratic technocrats and diminish the role of personalistic ties.[55]

At the same time, however, there are trends that suggest that

China's state remains far from the Weberian ideal and may in fact be weakening. In his study of the ideological realm, X. L. Ding chronicled the emergence of counterelites as the center's control over ideology declined.[56] Similarly, Minxin Pei has argued that "reform in the communist systems tends to generate and accelerate the decay of the key institutions it seeks to preserve and revitalize."[57] Walder has argued that this decay occurs because economic reform, in and of itself, changes the structure of incentives and makes lower-level agents of the state less willing to comply with the demands of administrative superiors. Indeed, he argues that reform sets off a "chain of consequences" that often leads "to the point where Communist party rule can no longer be sustained."[58]

The economic decentralization carried out in the course of reform diminished the economic capacity of the central government. The share of total state revenues as a percentage of GDP fell from 35 percent in 1978 to 11.3 percent in 1995, before increasing slightly to 11.4 percent in 1996.[59] Despite the sharp increase in central revenues as a percentage of all government revenues (from 22 percent in 1993 to 55.7 percent in 1994), the central government's bargaining power vis-à-vis the localities seems not to have increased for the simple reason that central tax collection efforts appear to remain in the hands of local tax collectors. As Naughton concludes, "[l]ocal governments are much more effective at getting their taxes actually collected than is the central government."[60] While such figures may well exaggerate the degree of decentralization, as Yasheng Huang has argued, they nonetheless indicate the difficulty China has in constructing a "usable bureaucracy."[61]

The biggest change, however, is not the shift of fiscal and financial resources from the central state to local governments but rather from the state as a whole (both central and local) to individuals and, to a lesser extent, enterprises. As Cheng Xiaonong, former head of the Comprehensive Section of the Economic Reform Institute, points out, the percentage of financial resources in the hands of the state, enterprises, and individuals, respectively, changed from 31.6, 18.9, and 49.5 in 1978 to 14.5, 23.8, and 61.7 in 1990. In other words, at the same time that financial resources controlled by the state (both central and local) declined by 17.1 percentage points, those held by individuals increased by 12.2 percentage points. This trend, Cheng argues, reflects the state's continual effort to "buy" political compliance by increasing the incomes of individuals. This need to secure political obedience reflects a "softening" of the state that may undermine effective governance in the future.[62]

Potentially the most important weakness in China's central state capacity derives from the entrepreneurial activities of the central government itself. Government bureaucracies facing budgetary shortfalls have gone into business on their own, sometimes spinning off profitable subsidiaries. Even the State Planning Commission, the bulwark of the old planned economy, set up six major investment corporations that have the dual functions of guiding investment in their respective sectors and making profits for themselves. This bureaucratic entrepreneurship has extended to state organs not normally associated with economic activities, such as the Ministry of State Security and the People's Liberation Army. At least in the case of the military, such entrepreneurship has set off deep concerns about professionalism and the ability of the PLA to conduct itself as a modern military.[63] What such bureaucratic involvement in the economy suggests is an institutionalization of corruption, making even the organs of the central state itself less responsive to central direction. It also suggests the emergence of a combination of "soft state" and entrenched interests feeding off one another to the detriment of both effective bureaucracy and civil society.[64] Even though Jiang in 1998 ordered the military to divest itself of its business enterprises, the process will take a long time, if it happens at all.

Societies that make successful transitions also tend to have well-developed, if not necessarily consistently implemented, legal structures. The existence of legal frameworks can provide a limited but important form of leverage as dissidents try to hold regimes to the standards that they themselves have articulated. Legal frameworks can also provide guidance through the uncertain passage that frequently exists between the fall of the existing order and the establishment of a new order.[65] Although China has made much progress in the articulation of a legal structure since 1978, it has a long way to go. Traditional China, with its understanding of law as a means to control society rather than to regulate public-private relations, provided little basis for the growth of modern legal norms and an autonomous legal profession.[66] In the PRC, prior to the Cultural Revolution, Soviet-based views of law as bureaucratic regularity vied with Maoist antibureaucratic and antilegal prescriptions. The overwhelming victory of the latter in the Cultural Revolution meant that there was little legal framework as China emerged from that national nightmare. After nearly two decades of trying to create a legal system almost *de novo,* Chinese law is still largely conceived of as a "tool of state administration."[67] Efforts to elevate law and the legal profession have run aground on deeply embedded concepts of state-society relations (which are generally hostile to the emergence of autonomous entities that might voice the interests of particular groups)[68] as well as such factors as local protectionism and the view that courts are simply one, co-equal part of China's bureaucratic apparatus.[69] Even Minxin Pei, who takes an optimistic view of legal progress in China, admits that the enforcement record for the more than 600 laws passed by the National People's Congress (NPC) remains "abysmal."[70]

Turning to the society side of the equation, it is apparent that Chinese society today remains very much dominated by the state, so much so that many specialists are reluctant to apply the term "civil society" to China at all. Although the state has retreated from society over the course of reform, creating a "zone of indifference" around individuals, the social space created by the retreat of the state appears to have been filled primarily by organic organizations—such as clan organizations or corporatist interest associations—rather than by independent associations of private individuals. Indeed, the process of economic decentralization that has taken place over the course of reform has had the effect of strengthening the role of local government to the detriment of autonomous society.[71] The most important finding of several studies of state-society relations is the degree to which state and society are intermingled and the degree to which nominally autonomous groups are in fact dominated by the state.[72] The *danwei* (unit) system remains the central organizing feature of Chinese life, and the *danwei* continue to conflate state and society as those concepts are generally understood in the West.[73] Although it can be argued that there has been substantial progress from the period of the Cultural Revolution, in which there was no civil society, however defined, to the present, the overwhelming fact is that in today's China social groups pursue their interests through the state rather than against the state.

In short, the corrosion of the state bureaucracy (even as there is bureaucratization) has been mirrored by a very weak civil society. What has *not* emerged is a strong, bureaucratic (in the Weberian sense) state dealing with autonomous social organizations along the lines of what Peter Evans has called "embedded autonomy."[74] States may not have to maintain the hands-off approach to society favored by neoliberal interpretations, but blurring the lines between state and society to the degree China has is not conducive either to the formation of a strong state or a strong society, and hence, very likely, not conducive to democratic transition, at least in the short run.

Another factor that must be taken into account when thinking about the state-society relationship in contemporary China is the obvious decline of Marxism-Leninism as a legitimating device. As ideology was transformed from the central fulcrum of the system to a mere border that was not to be transgressed (the "four cardinal principles"), there was an inevitable tendency for reform to diverge increasingly from the previously accepted understanding of "socialism." The cynicism and raw use of power that filled the vacuum left by the collapse of the Maoist ideological system not only left the liberal intelligentsia alienated from the regime but also caused conservative thinkers to rebel against the lack of a moral vision. The popular neoconservative writer Wang Shan wrote in his 1994 bestseller, *Looking at China through a Third Eye:*

> As soon as the traditional ideology of Mao Zedong's idealism begins to be broken, then the government's defense line must retreat step by step. Local governments continuously extend their hands asking for new "policies" and the central government has no choice but to compromise in the face of [the need to] solve new problems. China's economic structural reform was really created this way. Now, when we look back, what is left of Mao's inheritance? How

much is left? Deng Xiaoping has repeatedly said that the four cardinal principles must be upheld, but how much has really been upheld?[75]

On the one hand, the decline of ideology and legitimacy deprive the Leninist party of a powerful tool for eliciting compliance; on the other hand, the resulting failure of social norms makes the creation of new, impersonal norms around which bureaucratic structures could be built difficult.[76]

One reaction to the decline in Marxism-Leninism and the resulting ideological confusion has been the rise of nationalism.[77] Nationalism has always been a concomitant part of the Communist revolution (and the Nationalist revolution before that); it helped fuel those revolutions and bolstered their ideological claims. What is different about the current wave of nationalistic feeling is its occurrence outside of, indeed as a replacement for, the formal ideological structure of Marxism-Leninism-Mao Zedong Thought. National power is being touted as a value in and of itself.

It should be noted that nationalism in China is rising not just because the influence of Marxism-Leninism-Mao Zedong Thought is declining, but also because of China's growing confidence in its own economic strength and development and because of the widespread perception that the twenty-first century will be a Pacific century.[78]

To the extent that the growth of nationalism reflects a decline in ideology and a secularization of politics it should be welcomed as a normal and even healthy part of state building (what Oksenberg calls "confident nationalism"),[79] one that can give the state a *raison d'être* and bolster central government authority vis-à-vis lower levels. If, however, nationalism becomes a significant component of elite political competition, it will work against emerging pressures to "normalize" politics. Moreover, nationalism easily turns toward organic metaphors, which are deeply embedded in Chinese culture in any case, and, as Adam Przeworski notes, "organicist views of the nation are incompatible with the toleration of partial interests" necessary for democratic transitions.[80]

What is perhaps most troubling about the current rise of nationalist feeling is its resonance with the recent past. As Li Zehou has argued, one of the preeminent themes of twentieth-century China has been the struggle between "enlightenment" and "salvation." The New Culture and May Fourth movements were efforts to reconceive and, in some ways, to remake Chinese culture in order to better respond to the pressures (and opportunities) represented by "Mr. Science" and "Mr. Democracy." This effort to remake Chinese culture "drop by drop," as Hu Shi put it, was interrupted then, and many times since, by the demand to save the nation.[81] The demand for salvation, fueled by the rise of modern nationalism, repeatedly overwhelmed the enlightenment project and became an integral part of China's revolutionary history and "struggle" politics. If nationalism again becomes central to elite politics, it will be difficult for Chinese politics to say "farewell to revolution."

Conclusion

The reform process has witnessed conflicting political impulses as the concept of politics as a struggle to win all has coexisted with the reassertion of old party norms and the generation of new, more legal rational norms. With the death of Deng, there will be an opportunity to assess which of these conflicting principles will dominate.

Although both state implosion and hard-line authoritarian rule are possible, there is reason to be cautiously optimistic about the future. The winner-take-all tradition of Chinese politics suggests that sooner or later one person will emerge as the preeminent leader. Jiang Zemin seems to have taken a significant step in this direction at the Fifteenth Party Congress in September 1997. But whether Jiang or someone else ultimately emerges triumphant from this process, that person will not have the personal authority of Deng Xiaoping, much less of Mao Zedong. Once the post-Deng power struggle is settled, the leader is thus likely to have to rely more heavily on formal authority and institution building, both to secure his authority vis-à-vis his Politburo colleagues and to increase the state's authority vis-à-vis society. These processes will entail a process of legitimization, institutionalization, and legalization.

Indeed, the very effort to secure authority in the post-Deng era seems to require a greater reliance on the invocation of norms and the building of institutions. For instance, Jiang Zemin's successful ouster of Beijing mayor Chen Xitong in 1995, which certainly involved a struggle for power, was nevertheless conducted in terms of a campaign against corruption. In other words, even if the purpose of campaigns such as that against corruption is not primarily to strengthen party norms, they may in fact have that effect. Similarly, the retirement of NPC head Qiao Shi at the Fifteenth Party Congress, which contained elements of a power struggle, was accomplished by invoking party rules governing retirement, a norm that Jiang himself may have to adhere to at the next party congress.

Furthermore, the decentralization of the economy, which many see as undermining the authority of the central state and leading to institutional decay, could lead to the institutionalization of more stable authority relations. The readjustment of the incentive structure associated with the devolution of authority and the development of the local economy has been absolutely vital to economic reform, marketization of the economy, and the development of the economy overall. Even strong advocates of decentralization and democracy admit, however, that the process has gone too far and threatens the stability of the state.[82] Two measures appear essential to stabilizing central-local relations, and both would contribute to institutionalization and state building. The first is to turn the blueprint of a national tax system, adopted in the 1994 tax reform, into a reality. This would build a level playing field both in types of ownership and in geographical location and thereby regularize central-local relations. Second, the center should grant the localities greater participation in decisionmaking in exchange for their yielding greater fiscal control to Beijing.[83]

Some years ago, Tang Tsou wrote, "The Chinese have never succeeded in finding a set of arrangements in which the formal institutions are firmly established and in which informal relationships are supplements to the formal institutions, enabling the latter to function effectively and efficiently instead of overwhelming them and turning them into empty symbols."[84] They have not done so largely because of the nature of elite politics as a game to win all. Today, generational succession, the promotion of younger and better-educated cadres, the institution of a more professional bureaucracy, the decentralization of the economy, and other factors make it conceivable that China will finally address this historical problem. Whether or not China can do so depends largely on whether the political conflict can be contained in ways that do not trigger the logic of the game to win all. If so, the processes of institutionalization will have a better chance to take hold, eventually facilitating a transition toward a more benevolent understanding of politics. The present, however, is a moment of great fluidity. As Li Zehou and Liu Zaifu put it in their recent work, "China is again in the midst of a new social transformation. China at the present time is full of hope and also full of danger: it could really rise up from here, but it could also decline [*chen lun*]."[85]

4 | Party-Military Relations

Economic reform has done far more than simply enrich China. Accompanied by extensive and systematic military reforms, defense modernization programs have laid the groundwork for what could well become Asia's most powerful defense establishment. By providing China with the potential for continued growth and technological enhancement, economic reform could give Beijing's armed forces the armaments and equipment to make them a world-class military force. The opening to the outside world that accompanied China's reforms made the People's Liberation Army leadership increasingly aware of their armed forces' obsolescence. As they traveled across the globe, and especially as they viewed weapons, equipment, and facilities on visits to the military bases of advanced industrial states, the leadership became increasingly aware of both its aged equipment and its inability to conduct military operations requiring advanced technology. This appreciation dramatically increased during the Persian Gulf War's display of high-technology warfare in 1991.

Thus it is perhaps no surprise that with the growth of China's economy and exposure to the West, the slogan of mid-nineteenth-century reformers has come back into fashion: *fu guo qiang bing* (a wealthy country, a strong army). China's "self-strengtheners" of the nineteenth century understood that a country's military power is based upon its economic strength and technological capabilities. For China's present military leaders, the success of economic reform now grants them the opportunity to achieve what Chinese elites have sought since the humiliating diplomatic and military defeats of the nineteenth century—armed forces powerful enough both to prevent China's domination by hostile foreign powers and to be recognized as a major world power.

This opportunity looms as two decisive factors coincide to critically influence the relationship between China's civil and military leadership. First, with the death of Deng Xiaoping and the retirement of China's two most senior serving officers, Generals Liu Huaqing and Zhang Zhen, from the Central Military Commission at the Fifteenth Party Congress in the fall of 1997, the era of revolutionaries in uniform has come to an end. Second, Deng Xiaoping's reforms initiated at the Third Plenum of the Eleventh Party Congress in December 1978 refocused the PLA on modernization programs that had been undermined by Mao Zedong in the late 1950s and subordinated to his domestic political objectives in the 1960s and 1970s. The coincidence of these two factors will directly affect the state of civil-military relations in China as it enters the twenty-first century.

Generational change among military and civil elites has specific implications for China's leadership style. First, China's postrevolutionary civilian and military leaders lack the previous generation's common heritage of fighting as comrades-in-arms in the wars against the Guomindang and Japan. Their relationship with each other will no longer be mediated, as it was in the past, by the mutual experience and prestige of serving as political-military leaders in the wars that transformed China and created a Marxist-Leninist state. As a consequence, with the passing of Deng Xiaoping there is no party leader with the stature to personally direct China's armed forces. Only Mao Zedong and Deng Xiaoping held such prestige within the armed forces that they could assume what was in fact personal command of the PLA. Therefore, while both civilian and military elites will remain party members, their organizational affiliation will more distinctly distinguish and separate them than was the case for previous generational elites. Second, the PLA's corporate interests will increasingly come to dominate the military leadership's perception of its role in China's polity as modernizing the armed forces and preparing for the twenty-first century's uncertain security environment become their primary concern.

These factors, though central in determining the PLA's future relationship with the Chinese Communist Party and China's politics, are accompanied by two less easily evaluated elements. First is the consequence of an initial reluctance within the PLA leadership to threaten and then apply lethal force to quell the massive demonstrations that gripped Beijing in the spring of 1989. The CCP's civil leadership saw this early hesitation as wavering military support for the party, and subsequently directed an intensive political campaign designed to ensure PLA loyalty in any future domestic disorder. A second element is the consequence of the PLA's extensive excursion into commercial enterprises. Although it is difficult to measure the effects of these two considerations, initial PLA reluctance to comply with the party's order at Tiananmen continues to cast a dark shadow over party-military relations, and the corrupting effect of extensive military involvement in the economy severely undermines the PLA's image in society, paralleling the erosion of public confidence in both the party and the state apparatus. Neither element contributes to a smooth transition in party-military relations.

Party-Military Relations in China

Civil-military relations as a generic term does not fit the PLA's relationship with the Chinese Communist Party.[1] In a Marxist-Leninist political system, the Communist Party dominates both the state (government) and the society. The military institution comes under the direct control of the party as do all other societal institutions. Although the party is the source of political authority, it is not "civilian" in the sense that this concept is used in paradigms of civil-military relations based on the European experience. The party dominates both the state and the military. The party's relationship with the military is also not one of symbiosis. A symbiotic relationship exists when two *dissimilar* organisms unite in a mutually beneficial relationship. The CCP is neither military nor civilian, but the supreme political institution within China. It is the CCP Central Military Commission (CMC), staffed by China's senior serving officers and subordinate to the Politburo and currently chaired by the party general secretary, that determines policy for the military as did its predecessors during the civil war with the GMD and the war with Japan. The Politburo determines the relationship of the armed forces to the state, which is itself subordinate to the party. Thus the party-army parallels the party-state as one of the principal avenues of CCP control over the Chinese polity. Furthermore, all officers are party members and their primary loyalty should be to the party, not to the military as an institution. The military in China is thus an extension of the party. Civil-military relations in Marxist-Leninist systems are therefore best described as party-military relations.

The Role of Corporate Identity and the Military Ethic

The corporate self-identity of an officer corps is defined as the sense of unity officers have with members of the military profession in general, but specifically with their own officer corps. A military ethic consists of the values, norms, and symbols that relate the military as an institution to the society and its government and that determine the relationship among members of the military hierarchy.[2] Although the technical and theoretical expertise of an officer corps is universal, its military ethic reflects the history and culture of the particular society it serves. Consequently, although the functional requirements of an officer corps will be universal, stemming from a common dedication to the technical and theoretical expertise required to be an effective officer—the crux of an officer corps' corporate identity—its military ethic will reflect the particular context of the culture and history of a given society and the place of the military in that milieu.

The revolution and the war with Japan were the crucible of party-military relations in China and the genesis of the PLA's traditional military ethic. The Red Army of Workers and Peasants was established as a revolutionary army in 1927, some six years after the CCP's founding, and its senior commanders and commissars were simultaneously the leaders of the Chinese Communist Party. Zhu De, Mao

Zedong, Zhou Enlai, Deng Xiaoping, and the other members of the party elite were concurrently leaders of the army. The military doctrine of the Red Army was itself an amalgam of military and political principles and given the title "People's War."[3] When the Chinese People's Liberation Army, as successor to the Red Army of Workers and Peasants, triumphantly entered Beijing in 1949, its military leaders as senior party members in uniform, saw their role in the new People's Republic as far more encompassing than simply that of national defense. They were the fathers of a revolution as much concerned with the goals of the party for the new state and society as they were with the future of the army. They were political as well as military leaders. Similarly, leading PLA cadres doffed their uniforms and assumed civil duties as the PLA's field armies swept over China and brought the country under CCP control.

Changing the Officer Corps' Corporate Identity

The Chinese officer corps' military ethic remains primarily based on the PLA's heritage as a party-army. Traditional components of the PLA's military ethic continue as the armed forces assist communities during times of local disasters and help farmers during the agricultural cycle. Similarly, military units continue to run their farms, but primarily to lower the cost and increase the quality of food in their dining halls. Much of what the PLA does for local communities would be classified as disaster relief and civic action in Western armed forces. For PLA forces, however, these activities still connect them to the years when they were a revolutionary army. Even though the traditional ethic of the PLA defines the armed forces as a revolutionary army and "liberators" of "the people," this ethic blended with a new emphasis on national defense and technical and theoretical military expertise in the 1950s when the PLA started to become a modern military under the tutelage of the Soviet Union's defense establishment. The officer corps directing this modernization program began to develop a corporate identity built around the skills required for command, staff, and support roles in a technologically advanced military. Mao Zedong, however, was suspicious that this revised corporate identity was eroding the PLA's traditional and highly politicized military ethic. Mao's misgivings, combined with the Sino-Soviet breach and his commitment to building a revolutionary society, ended the first stage of this transformation in 1960.[4] PLA involvement in the politics and conduct of the Cultural Revolution from the years 1966 to 1976 pushed systematic military reform further until Deng Xiaoping initiated the second stage of reform and modernization in 1979. Thus, in the two decades prior to 1979, the Chinese armed forces did not form a military ethic fitting a modern military. In essence, the PLA was in limbo as a partially modernized defense force, with a corporate identity and military ethic that had yet to bridge the gap between a highly politicized revolutionary army and modernized armed forces.

The decade of reform prior to the June 1989 bloody suppression of the Tiananmen demonstrations did, however, create major changes in the PLA and its corporate identity. Indices of change can be seen in the essays and articles in *Liberation Army Daily* (*Jiefangjun bao*—the official organ of the PLA General Political Department) and the journals published by the PLA National Defense University (NDU—established in late 1985) and the PLA Academy of Military Sciences (AMS). In the decade prior to the Tiananmen crisis, their focus increasingly stressed the role of the armed forces in national security and defense. Furthermore, they emphasized the need to study the military doctrine, strategy, and concepts of operations developed by the armed forces of advanced industrial societies. As part of this process, the NDU and the AMS were both declared *kaifang* (open to the world) and began extensive and regular contact with the armed forces and professional military education centers of the West, especially the United States. By the late 1980s the content of Chinese military journals and discussions with the students, faculty, and researchers at professional military education centers across China, and with officers studying national security issues at universities in Europe and the United States, gave the clear impression that the PLA's fundamental purpose was to transform itself into a modern armed force with its officer corps primarily focused on becoming militarily competent and technically proficient. Moreover, despite continued political criteria overseen by the PLA's General Political Department, promotions and appointments to higher command and staff positions were based in large part upon what Western military establishments would define as "professional" criteria, including attendance at the required professional military education centers prior to promotion and assignment to higher-level duties. In the early 1980s General Xiao Ke, vice minister of defense and the architect of the new system of professional military education, referred to the education of the officer corps as the PLA's "capital construction."[5]

By the spring of 1989, a major part of the Chinese officer corps had developed a sense of corporateness based upon a new identity stemming from its focus on military modernization and its role in China's national security, a role defined by the late 1980s as defense against external enemies. With Deng Xiaoping as the embodiment of political and military authority directing military reform and modernization goals, the officer corps had every reason to believe it was loyally pursuing the party's goals.

The Post-Tiananmen Political Attack on the PLA

PLA responsibility for the lethal suppression of the Tiananmen protestors was the direct result of the failure of the People's Armed Police (PAP) to control the massive demonstrations in and around Tiananmen Square in the spring of 1989. Internal security had been the PAP's responsibility since its founding in 1983. Despite PAP's six years of experience, its ineffectiveness in 1989 was due to a lack of riot control training and appropriate equipment. PLA units brought into Beijing to restore order were equally unprepared for the task. As the *Liberation Army Daily* reported in December 1989, their weapons and equipment were "designed for military operations and were strongly lethal. They lacked anti-riot capabilities and non-lethal and defensive weapons. They also lacked the technical means for communications and information processing under special conditions."[6] Not only were these troops unprepared and improperly equipped for what had become a political crisis, but "some people were unavoidably wounded by mistake (including people knocked down by vehicles, wounded by crowds of people, and hit by stray bullets)."[7] Until they used deadly force, China's armed forces were as ineffectual as the PAP when faced with massive resistance from the demonstrators. General Chi Haotian, then PLA chief of staff and later defense minister, referred to these factors as inhibiting PLA capabilities to control the protests without the use of deadly force in his March 1990 interview with *U.S. News & World Report.*[8]

In the aftermath of the Tiananmen crackdown, however, the officer corps came under methodical criticism and was subjected to a political campaign directed by the PLA General Political Department (GPD).[9] The essence of this criticism was that although the PLA had met the party's political criterion by crushing Beijing's "counterrevolutionary rebellion," the armed forces' continued loyalty to the party could not be assumed without systematic and intense efforts to rebuild the PLA's political commissar system and a deliberate program of political education within the officer corps. This effort to repoliticize the armed forces began in the summer of 1989, accelerated in the late fall and winter while paralleling the disintegration of Marxist-Leninist regimes in Eastern Europe, and became even more intense following the involvement of the Romanian armed forces in the December collapse of the Ceauşescu regime.

The root cause of the political leadership's apprehension was the reluctance of some senior officers to support the declaration of martial law and carry out their orders to use lethal force against the demonstrators.[10] Of even greater concern, many members of the High Command who had retired to the Central Advisory Commission of the Central Committee in 1987 and 1988 were reported to have written a letter questioning the declaration of martial law. Among them were former defense minister Zhang Aiping; former vice-minister of defense Xiao Ke; former chief of staff Yang Dezhi; former commander of the navy Ye Fei; and Song Shilun, a former president of the PLA Academy of Military Sciences. The letter they allegedly sent to the Beijing Martial Law Command on May 17, two days before martial law was announced, contained a section that reflected more the traditional ethic of the PLA than the new values:[11]

The People's Army belongs to the people, it cannot stand in opposition to the people, much less oppress the people, and it absolutely

cannot open fire on the people or create a blood-shedding incident. In order to further worsening of the situation, troops should
not enter the city.[12]

China's most senior officers had invoked the PLA's traditional
military ethic to oppose the declaration of martial law and the
potential use of lethal force against Chinese citizens—"the people."

China's military leaders were not isolated in their aversion to
martial law. Deng Xiaoping's June 9, 1989, speech to senior commanders of the martial law forces demonstrates the severe disagreement among both civil and military senior party leaders over the
decision to declare martial law and ultimately use lethal force. Deng
declared:

> This storm was bound to happen sooner or later. As determined by
> the international and domestic climate, it was bound to happen
> and was independent of man's will. It has turned out in our favor,
> for we still have a large group of veterans who have experienced
> many storms and have a thorough understanding of things. They
> were on the side of taking resolute action to counter the turmoil.
> Although some comrades may not understand this now, they will
> understand *eventually* and will support the decision of the Central
> Committee.[13]

That Deng would point to "some comrades" as only understanding
the decision "eventually" is an indication of the breach over these
decisions. Although Deng goes on to express great confidence in the
PLA, asserting that it "passed muster" in a "severe political test,"[14] the
campaign to repoliticize the army that began later that summer
showed no such confidence.

Whereas Deng stated that those who disagreed with his decisions
in May and June would eventually accept them as necessary, the PLA
General Political Department at the behest of the Central Military
Commission was clearly apprehensive about the future loyalty of the
PLA. Although the military leadership had accepted their orders,
albeit reluctantly, to suppress the demonstrations because they saw
the stability of China threatened by the extreme disorder in Beijing
and other major cities, party authorities reinforced the principle of

"the party's absolute leadership over the army" to ensure that the armed forces would support the party in any future internal crisis. Former party general secretary Zhao Ziyang, purged as a consequence of the Tiananmen demonstrations, was blamed for the military's political deficiencies. The *Liberation Army Daily* in August denounced Zhao's "bourgeois liberalization" as undermining political and ideological work in the party and the PLA. The extent to which this work had been eroded was seen as "distressing."[15]

Press accounts in early 1990 provide some indication of this erosion. The Japanese press reported that some 1,500 officers and soldiers were punished for refusing to use deadly force.[16] The *Far Eastern Economic Review* reported that 3,500 officers were under investigation for suspected involvement in the pro-democracy movement or for violation of their orders in the spring of 1989. Further, General Yang Baibing, then director of the PLA's General Political Department and secretary general of the Central Military Commission, stated in November 1989 that twenty officers at the division level or above and thirty-six officers at the regimental and battalion level were under investigation.[17] The possibility that this number of officers were either involved in the pro-democracy movement or refused to carry out orders, when combined with the opposition of senior retired officers to martial law, would unquestionably raise doubts about the willingness of the PLA to follow party orders and use lethal force in any future crisis.

Because PLA mobilization and martial law had been brought about by the failure of the then 600,000 strong People's Armed Police to respond effectively to the Tiananmen demonstrations, its leadership was replaced and programs were initiated to improve the PAP's riot control capabilities.[18] There is no evidence that China's leaders saw the PAP as a counterbalance to a potentially disloyal PLA. Rather, improving PAP performance in its primary responsibility would minimize the probability that regular PLA units would have to be called upon to perform an internal security function. Nonetheless, the intensity of the party's political campaign to repoliticize the PLA reflected the leadership's deep fear that the support of the armed forces could not be easily and confidently assumed should PLA mobilization be required in a future domestic crisis.

An enlarged meeting of the CMC held on November 10–12, 1989, following the Fifth Plenum of the Thirteenth Central Committee, called for an intensification of the political campaign within the armed forces. At a November 1989 All-Army Political Work Conference, General Yang Baibing defined the problems that had to be addressed. First, the "counterrevolutionary riots in Beijing" raised questions about the efficacy of the PLA's political work. Second, changes in the international and domestic environment required a fresh look at the dangers presented by the "peaceful evolution strategy promoted by international hostile forces." Third, "bourgeois liberalization" presented a continuing danger to the political purity of the armed forces. Yang said these factors led to the leadership's concern that:

> In the future we cannot avoid running into new political storms. Given the neglect and relaxation of political construction and no effort in solving the problem of being forever up to standard politically, it is very difficult to guarantee Army units responding to the party's commands at crucial moments. Then a historical mistake on our part is likely.[19]

General Yang stated that while preparation for war was very important, "guaranteeing the rifles being grasped by politically reliable people are matters of top importance that must be taken note of at all times. In no way can we treat them lightly."[20]

In his January 1990 essay in the party journal *Qiushi* (Seeking Truth), General Chi Haotian, then PLA chief of staff and a career political commissar, expanded on General Yang's analysis.[21] Opening up the army in the process of reform had introduced the problem of "bourgeois liberalization" into the PLA, and had "seriously challenged" the principle of the party's absolute leadership of the army. "Bourgeois liberalization," Chi Haotian affirmed, sought to politically neutralize the PLA and separate it from the party while "a tiny number of people blindly copy bourgeois military theories of the West."[22] General Chi said this predicament was especially noticeable among the younger officers who had been recently appointed to leadership posts, had no personal experience with the early years of the army, and were not deeply imbued with the principles of the party-army relationship. He noted that such doubts had initially arisen following the adoption of the 1982 State Constitution, which had established a Central Military Commission under the State Council paralleling the party CMC, for some then argued that the state, not the party should lead the army. The 1982 State Constitution's creation of a State Central Military Commission may have presented a minor difficulty, but the continuing authority of the party over the PLA would have been obvious to anyone directly involved in the Chinese political system.[23] That the new constitution was used to raise the issue of who "should" control the armed forces is without question,[24] but anyone doing so would be fully aware of the consequences of the argument.[25] The post-Tiananmen party leadership's heightened concern was not related to a debate over constitutional issues, but stemmed from the crumbling of Marxist-Leninist regimes in Eastern Europe.

In the winter of 1989–90 the collapse of Eastern Europe's Communist regimes and the failure of their armed forces to sustain party rule exacerbated Beijing's apprehension over the political reliability of its own armed forces. In a clear reference to the situation in Eastern Europe, General Chi observed:

> An important characteristic of the present international climate is that monopoly bourgeoisie of the West makes use of the temporary difficulties of socialist countries and the opportunity of their implementation of the policy of reform and opening up, to try and turn socialist countries into bourgeois republics and the appendages of Western powers.[26]

The failure of Eastern Europe's armed forces to uphold their Marxist-Leninist regimes, and particularly the Romanian military's participation in the overthrow of Ceauşescu, was conclusively seen as an empirical verification of the Chinese leadership's apprehension.

Recounting a December 1989 interview with party general secretary Jiang Zemin and Politburo member Li Ruihuan, the Hong Kong newspaper *Wen wei pao* reported Jiang as saying that "the situation in Eastern Europe can only arouse our concern." Jiang, however, stressed the differences between East European communism and China's experience. Whereas Eastern Europe was "liberated by the Soviet Red Army," the PLA had liberated China through a revolutionary war. Jiang emphasized the loyalty of the PLA, saying that it is "armed with Marxism-Leninism-Mao Zedong Thought, has strict discipline, and is under the absolute leadership of the party."[27] The confidence Jiang expressed in his interview was not reflected in the continuing campaign to repoliticize the PLA officer corps.

Following the winter of 1989–90, the *Liberation Army Daily* focused on the efforts of "international antagonistic forces and a small handful of people at home" who were still advocating a politically neutral PLA and seeking to separate the armed forces from the party and place them under the exclusive control of the State Council.[28] Similarly, younger officers were criticized for not understanding that the "absolute" leadership of the party was a basic principle, and that failing to find "a solution to this issue of understanding will lead to a weak discernment of the various erroneous concepts of bourgeois liberalization that sow discord between the Army and the party."[29] Defense against "peaceful evolution," the *Liberation Army Daily* insisted, required the meticulous selection, promotion, and training of cadres (officers). Those selected must have "both ability and political integrity and ensure that the guns are in the hands of those who are politically reliable."[30] Ensuring that the PLA will be "invincible" against the subversion of "peaceful evolution" and "will always be politically reliable and up to standard will be a major question which needs to be urgently solved through ideological and political education."[31] The collapse of East European Communist regimes had undoubtedly added to the party leadership's apprehension over PLA loyalty.

The effort to repoliticize the armed forces developed specific foci, indicating that elements of military reform over the previous decade were receiving singular reevaluation. The PLA's military ethic received special attention. It is noteworthy that criticism leveled at the armed forces was specifically directed at concepts of military professionalism that originate in the West. The post-Tiananmen political campaign was particularly critical of officers who allegedly accepted core values integral to Western models of civil-military relations. The General Political Department charged that "hostile forces at home and abroad are targeting our Army as a major target of infiltration in a vain attempt to change the nature of our Army,"[32] declaring that some "diehards" argue the CCP should not play any role in the armed forces and that the PLA should be separated from the party.[33] These efforts were seen as attempts to turn the armed forces into a neutral "bourgeois" military institution modeled on armed forces in the West.[34]

In the party leadership's post-Tiananmen perception, the decade of military reform, focused on rebuilding the officer corps with younger, better-educated men and women, improving the PLA's military effectiveness, and preoccupied with the defense and national security roles of the PLA, had engendered in the officer corps a sense of corporateness and a military ethic based more on military responsibilities than on duty to the party. Nevertheless, even as the *Liberation Army Daily* decried the pernicious influence of Western concepts of civil-military relations on the PLA, it stressed that even in the West, when "ordinary means" could not resolve a domestic crisis, the armed forces are called upon to restore order.[35] The General Political Department implicitly criticized the PLA by noting that even Western armies, adhering to the principle of political neutrality in internal political disputes, accept their responsibility to put down internal disorder.

The PLA's Military Ethic: Genesis of a Political Dilemma

Blaming erosion of the PLA's political reliability on the West, "peaceful evolution," and "bourgeois liberalization" was, in reality, transparent criticism of a central aspect of military reform—the opening up to the outside world pursued by the armed forces since 1979. It is doubtful, however, that "peaceful evolution" had so eroded the PLA's loyalty to the party that the Western norm of military neutrality had led to its initial hesitation during the Tiananmen crisis. In the spring of 1989, a divided party leadership faced a crisis as massive political protests in Beijing spread across China. As senior party members and soldiers, members of the PLA's revolutionary elite had questioned the wisdom of placing Beijing under martial law. Even though there was little outright disobedience, there had also been resistance to the use of lethal force among officers commanding the martial law forces. With China suffering from intense internal political pressure, and with Eastern Europe's example before them, in the winter of 1989–90 the civilian party leadership was fearful that without the PLA they could not sustain their own political regime. There was undoubtedly suspicion that exposure to Western norms of civil-military relations had contributed to resistance to martial law and the use of lethal force, but the root cause of the problem was that disagreement within the highest levels of the party over how to respond to a domestic crisis had created a clash between two core norms of the PLA's military ethic. With the civil party leadership divided over the potential consequences of resorting to martial law, loyalty to the party had clashed with the PLA's obligations as a "people's army."

The GPD's political campaign, however, was not directed primarily at the most senior levels of the PLA High Command, both active and retired, who were the source of the military uncertainty over the wisdom of resorting to martial law. Rather, the campaign was directed at younger officers bonded together by their common experience of modernizing the PLA in the 1980s. A decade of military reform and modernization within the Chinese armed forces had created a large number of officers who saw their highest duty as improving PLA military effectiveness, not instilling political reliability. Furthermore, officers in command and staff positions for professional military education, training, planning logistics, combat support, communications, and weapons and equipment acquisition not only had to reform a large and complex defense establishment, but also had to improve the quality of the services they rendered. Those who excelled in these duties would be promoted; officers who did not or could not because of age or poor education were retired in the million-man force reduction implemented over the years 1985–1987.

Consequently, officers dedicated to the new values, who had moved into senior command and staff positions based upon their military competence, developed a new sense of corporateness. In essence, their experience and commitment to building a new PLA created a cohesion among them that differed from that found among senior officers bonded primarily by the common experience in People's War and revolution. This new source of cohesion led to a corporate identity and military ethic distinct, but not disconnected from, the party ties that are supposed to form the officer corps' primary loyalty. For conservative party leaders, if members of the PLA's revolutionary generation had opposed a crucial party decision related to sustaining China's internal stability when Deng Xiaoping was China's "paramount leader" and de facto leader of the CCP, then their successors could be expected to be even more "unreliable." The collapse of Soviet Marxism-Leninism and the attempted military coup in Moscow in the summer of 1991 followed by the disintegration of the USSR only reinforced the more conservative leaders' efforts to ensure the PLA's loyalty to their authority.[36] To ensure this loyalty, the core of the PLA's traditional military ethic had to be enforced: absolute, unquestioning obedience to the party.

The Fourteenth Party Congress and After: Sanctioning a Revised Military Ethic

Jiang Zemin, like Zhao Ziyang and Hu Yaobang before him, had neither military experience nor personal status in the PLA when Deng Xiaoping selected him to replace Zhao as party general secretary in 1989.[37] Unlike Hu and Zhao, however, Jiang Zemin was also appointed chairman of the Central Military Commission, and in that position he systematically sought to establish personal standing with military leaders, both active and retired. Jiang balanced his pursuit of status within the military leadership with support of the political rectification campaign being conducted by General Yang Baibing. This balancing act came to an end with the Fourteenth Party Congress held in October 1992. Although the details remain murky, it appears that Yang Baibing combined his rectification campaign with a quest for personal power in the PLA, and did so with the support of his elder half-brother Yang Shangkun, the CMC's first vice chairman. The PLA leadership and retired elders were opposed to what they saw as the "Yang family's private army" and the deleterious consequences for the PLA's combat readiness brought about by the political campaign to rectify the armed forces' political failings. Evidently with Deng's support, the Fourteenth Party Congress marked significant changes within the Central Military Commission that removed the Yangs from power and boosted military representation in the highest levels of the party.

The elderly Yang Shangkun's retirement from his post as senior vice chairman was not unexpected, but the removal of his younger half-brother Yang Baibing from his appointments as CMC secretary general and director of the PLA General Political Department came as a surprise to all observers. Their removal and other reshuffles within the PLA hierarchy were seen within China as removing the influence of the "Yang family's private army" from the military system.[38] Removal of the Yangs was but part of a series of personnel changes that resulted in increased PLA presence in the Politburo and the Central Committee. General Liu Huaqing replaced Yang Shangkun as senior vice chairman of the CMC, and was appointed one of the seven members of the Politburo Standing Committee; he was the first serving officer since 1985 to receive this appointment. Yang Baibing's appointment to the Politburo, but not its standing committee, was viewed as a face-saving device without political substance. The new Central Committee saw PLA membership increased from 19 to 23 percent (six generals, thirty-seven lieutenant generals, and one major general). The lowest representation had been in 1985, when the PLA constituted 16.2 percent of the full membership.

Appointments to the CMC were also significant. General Zhang Zhen, president of the National Defense University and a highly respected officer from the Long March generation, joined General Liu Huaqing as one of the two vice chairmen serving party general secretary Jiang Zemin in his capacity as CMC chairman. The appointment of Zhang Zhen to join Liu Huaqing meant that two of China's most revered soldiers were now the PLA's senior serving officers. There were two critical aspects of these appointments. First, Deng Xiaoping had confidence that they were loyal to him and the party, and that this loyalty would extend to Jiang Zemin. Second, Liu Huaqing had long been associated with the technological modernization of the PLA, while Zhang Zhen, in his role as NDU president, essentially supervised the education of the PLA's new senior officer corps—the emerging elite of the armed forces. Thus loyalty to the party and Deng Xiaoping was balanced by the commitment of Liu Huaqing and Zhang Zhen to the PLA's modernization.

Jiang Zemin emerged from these major adjustments in PLA leadership as the first party leader since Hua Guofeng to hold concurrently the posts of party general secretary, state president, and, as CMC chairman, commander-in-chief of the armed forces. In this last role he moved swiftly to promote younger officers to full general status. Six were promoted in spring 1993, the first such promotions since military ranks were restored in the fall of 1988. A year later, nineteen more officers were elevated from lieutenant general to general. These promotions brought the number of active-duty full generals to twenty-nine, with twenty-five elevated to the highest military rank by Jiang Zemin. When military rank was restored in 1988, only seventeen officers received the rank of full general. Jiang Zemin now enhanced his position within the armed forces by establishing a coterie of senior officers whose career success was due in large part to his personal influence.

A Revised Military Ethic Sanctioned?

As Jiang Zemin increased the number of general officers, he turned the PLA's focus away from political rectification to military effectiveness and readiness. As the *Liberation Army Daily* declared in March 1993:

> Central Military Commission leading comrades have repeatedly stressed that army building should focus on modernization and that military training is [the] regular central task for the armed forces. We should conscientiously implement Central Military Commission leading comrades' instructions, carry out ideological and political work in the course of military training to have a perfect mastery of military skills, to ensure the armed forces combat effectiveness, and to promote Army modernization.[39]

Jiang Zemin reiterated the same theme in his speech at the ceremony where he promoted the nineteen new generals.[40] He emphasized that "a strong army and strong national defense always provide powerful support for reform, opening up, modernization, as well as a reliable guarantee for consolidating state power, promoting social stability and economic development."[41] Jiang set the following promotion criteria: "In building up leadership bodies, we should earnestly groom and select prominent young cadres who are both professionally competent and politically reliable."[42]

Refocusing the military on modernization and military effectiveness and basing promotion on professional skills and political reliability were deliberate decisions demonstrating a distinct break with Yang Baibing's almost sole emphasis on political reliability as the preeminent criterion for promotion. The CMC continued to insist that the armed forces pay "absolute obedience to the party" and maintain internal stability, but their central tasks were defined in specific order as "guarding the motherland's security and unity, and maintaining social stability and unity."[43] The ordering of these responsibilities with the emphasis on a "strong army and strong national defense" was precisely what the PLA leadership sought. Jiang Zemin had recognized the PLA's need for a revised military ethic, and his policies supported the military modernization objectives desired by the military leadership—the PLA's corporate interests. Similarly, Beijing responded positively to the Clinton Administration's quest to reopen military-to-military contact with the PLA in the fall of 1993, thereby indicating that the officer corps was now immune to the wiles of U.S. "peaceful evolution" strategy. With Liu Huaqing and Zhang Zhen as the CMC's senior military members, the officer corps was assured that its priorities would be sustained.

Although PLA priorities were supported beginning in the early 1990s, it is equally evident that emphasis on "party building" in the military continues. Two core issues are involved. First, there lingers the question of PLA reliability in the event of major internal instability. Second, widespread corruption stemming from PLA commercial enterprises remains a major problem for the leadership. The Fourth Plenary session of the Fourteenth Party Congress, meeting in the fall of 1994, initiated a new campaign to reinforce the authority of PLA party committees, placing great emphasis on "grass roots" or company-level organizations.[44] Party branches were instructed to "play close attention to all fields of their endeavor, which mainly center around education and military training,"[45] thereby maintaining the PLA leadership's preferred focus. That said, the campaign was equally adamant that while officers should be promoted on the basis of "ability and political integrity,"[46] selection of those to be promoted "is a strategic task in our bid to guarantee the party's absolute leadership over the Army and promote the modernization building of the Army."[47] The intent of this statement can be seen in the assertion that party organizations and members are to "rally closely around the party Central Committee and the Central Military Commission with Comrade Jiang Zemin as the core."[48] The question was less the party's authority and far more the issue of Jiang Zemin's status within the PLA leadership. Certainly, with almost all of the full generals promoted under his auspices, his frequent visits to military facilities, and his courting of the military elders, Jiang Zemin, with the support of Liu Huaqing and Zhang Zhen, was trying very hard to establish his personal authority within the military. As David Shambaugh has suggested, Jiang could very well be seeking to exchange his support of military modernization and professionalism for PLA loyalty to himself.[49]

Corruption within the armed forces stemming from the PLA's operation of commercial enterprises was the second concern.[50] Corruption gradually became a major issue following the mid-1980s decision encouraging military units to engage in commercial operations to make up for shortfalls in defense budgets that were not keeping up with inflation. Even though inflation began to fall in the early 1990s, double-digit percentage increases in defense allocations that began in 1989 became the norm. PLA commercial enterprises continued to expand, nonetheless, and corruption became an increasingly salient issue.[51] The control if not the elimination of corrupt practices in PLA business operations was sought by improving the General Logistics Department's supervision of military enterprises and by the military leadership's emphasis on the PLA's "fine tradition" of self-sacrifice and hard living. In a 1993 *Liberation Army Daily* article,[52] Liu Huaqing and Zhang Zhen frankly acknowledged that China's market economy had introduced temptations that were eroding military discipline and allowing the infiltration of "decadent capitalist ideas and lifestyles." They also recognized that younger officers had not fully absorbed the PLA's "fine traditions" from the past. Liu and Zhang warned that history is replete with examples of periods of peace when both civil officials and military officers "became pleasure seekers, lost their combat readiness, and were eventually defeated in peace, as well as by themselves."[53] China's two most senior and respected officers were explicitly fearful that corruption stemming from involvement in commerce was eroding the PLA's military ethic and potentially undermining combat effectiveness. There are insufficient data to draw any firm conclusions about the damage done to combat effectiveness, but the problem clearly persists and corruption only detracts from the PLA's image, already blemished by its use of lethal force at Tiananmen. Despite the military leadership's efforts, reports of corrupt practices in the military continue unabated.[54]

Party-Military Relations: The Consequences of Reform and Generational Change

With the death of Deng Xiaoping and the retirement of Generals Liu Huaqing and Zhang Zhen, the era of revolutionaries in uniform has come to an end.[55] Nonetheless, these officers and their retired associates remain national figures. This elite's personal stature in the military and the party and their extensive *guanxi* network give them influence despite their retirement from active service. Below this level are the officers who now command the armed forces. They originate from two basic groups: officers who won their spurs in the Korean War and were the driving force of military modernization in the 1950s, and others who achieved flag rank following the military reforms that began in 1979.[56] These officers tend to see the armed forces, but especially the officer corps, as an institution unified by its responsibility for national defense and by its own corporate interests. This officer corps directs and manages an increasingly complex military organization that must prepare the PLA for defense and deterrent roles in an uncertain, potentially threatening international system. The stature and influence of these officers are based upon their institutional position and competence. They are bound together by their common experience in rebuilding the PLA and associations formed within the revitalized professional military education system, especially the National Defense University.

Civil party leaders succeeding Deng Xiaoping have neither the personal stature nor the military background that so fundamentally influenced party-military relations in the past. Moreover, the authority of the new civil party elite is based upon their institutional position, not their personal status. They have no strong personal network binding them to the emerging military elite. Jiang Zemin, despite his efforts to establish a foundation of personal loyalty within the armed forces, currently falls into this category. His strength is based upon his patron, Deng Xiaoping, and the support he received from Liu Huaqing and Zhang Zhen in the Central Military Commission. With Deng's death and the retirement of Liu and Zhang, Jiang Zemin will have to rely primarily upon his organizational positions and whatever personal network he has developed since 1989, when he assumed the positions of party leader and CMC chairman. By the same token, the current military elite lacks both the personal stature and the long-standing connections with the civil party elite held by their predecessors. This lack of party standing is indicated by the results of the Fifteenth Party Congress in 1997. No military representative was appointed to the Politburo Standing Committee following General Liu Huaqing's retirement, and PLA representation on the CCP Central Committee was reduced from 23 percent to 19 percent.

Military and civilian party elites are thus more separate than at any time since 1927. As China enters the twenty-first century, the PLA will become ever more focused on its corporate interests, especially defense modernization. The civil party apparatus will become more focused on managing and directing the increasingly complex society and political system that has accompanied China's reforms. Although civil and military party elites will remain congruent in their overriding concern with the economic modernization and technological enhancement required to transform China into a great power, their respective foci will cause them to concentrate on different facets of their common goal. In short, their differing foci will confirm and sustain their separation.

With the officer corps concentrating on military reform, modernization, training, and combat readiness, and with promotion based on professional as much as on political criteria, sustained defense budget increases combined with the acquisition of advanced military technologies and weapon systems now promise significantly improved military effectiveness over the next decade or two. Thus the PLA's corporate interests are being fulfilled, even if not at the pace many officers would desire. Nonetheless, PLA vacillation during the internal crisis of 1989 continues to cast a shadow over party-military relations. Political campaigns since the Fourteenth Party Congress reflect uncertainty over the PLA's loyalty, if not to the party then to Jiang Zemin. Although there has been dramatic change in PLA leadership over the past twenty years of reform and the era of revolutionaries in uniform has ended, the transition to a sharper division between the military and the civil party apparatus is not without its own hazards.

A Praetorian PLA?

Although PLA participation and influence will vary according to the issue, following CCP practice of six decades, military officers as senior party members remain directly involved in the policy process.[57] In the event of another fratricidal party crisis like the one that occurred in 1989, could the unifying corporate identity of the PLA lead to a determination of the outcome by the military institution? For the current civil party leadership, the lesson of Tiananmen is that in a future crisis the PLA could determine who governs the party. Because the military elite wavered in its support for the civil party leadership in the spring of 1989, the current leadership senses potential peril. Members of the military leadership as party members share the CCP's concern that it should not suffer the same fate as Marxist-Leninist parties in Eastern Europe and the former Soviet Union, and they are committed to restoring China to greatness. Should leadership incompetence or indecision result in economic failure, thereby undermining political stability and the restoration of China's greatness, the PLA could well take a unified position on a particular leader or leaders they believed had greater competence. PLA leaders with their unifying corporate identity and military ethic could define themselves as the true "guardians"[58] of the party and custodians of China's recovery from the humiliations of the nineteenth and early part of the twentieth centuries.[59] In the face of a sharply divided civil party leadership, a united PLA could decide "who governs." There are therefore a number of specific conditions under which the PLA could act in a praetorian manner.

Frail and unstable political systems propagate praetorian militaries. What is unclear, however, is the degree to which the Chinese political system is fragile and unstable, and the extent to which the potential for a unified, monolithic PLA is undermined by its corrupting involvement in commercial enterprises. Factionalism within the PLA elite may also limit the military's ability to act as a unified institution.[60] At the apex of China's political system, moreover, personal influence and informal processes still count for more in the outcome of a political struggle than institutions and formal processes. The extent to which this will change as party leaders, both civil and military, are sustained more by their institutional position and competence than by their personal prestige is as yet unknown. The trajectory of party-military relations even in the near-term future is so clouded by unknowns that it is not possible to chart any certain future course. It is nonetheless paradoxical that the politicized military ethic of the Chinese armed forces, so long a source of confidence for the CCP, is now a potential cocoon of praetorianism.

5 | The National People's Congress

In one of the most significant changes in the Chinese political system during the Deng Xiaoping era, China's legislature, the National People's Congress (NPC), began behaving in ways very unlike what Western scholars have come to expect from legislatures in Leninist political systems. Following the model of the former USSR's Supreme Soviet, Leninist legislatures have traditionally been "rubber-stamp" institutions. Their function was to provide the party with a veneer of legal-democratic legitimacy by incorporating large numbers of both nonparty and party luminaries and turning party decrees into state laws. But Leninist legislatures historically spared the party the rigorous debate and compromise politics of genuine democracy by dutifully ratifying laws and motions decided upon elsewhere in meetings of party and government officials. Typically, Leninist legislatures did not seriously debate important issues; nor did they disagree with, amend, delay, or turn back proposals that had already received approval from the party leadership. The NPC's pro forma unanimous votes of approval became so common and predictable that the Chinese people derisively referred to the NPC as a "hand-raising machine."

The NPC has moved far from this model since 1978, and the term "rubber stamp" has now become an indefensible exaggeration of the NPC's pliability. There is now regular animated debate over important policy issues, and the top party leadership's proposals and performance often face serious criticism. NPC staffers now regularly influence the contents of major policy issues. And although draft legislation still receives prior vetting by the party Politburo and State Council, it now rarely passes the NPC without substantial review, delay, or revision. The NPC's once ubiquitous unanimous votes are now rare indeed.

All of this legislative activism has sparked vigorous debate among China scholars regarding how much has really changed and what this change may portend for China's future. Skeptics of legislative change stress what has *not* changed about the NPC: its leaders are still Communist Party members; the NPC has not become a unified institutional rival of the party; and the most vital, life-or-death issues of the Communist Party–state are still decided either in party decision-making bodies or informally among senior party leaders, but not within the NPC. The indisputable evidence of this last point came at the height of the 1989 crisis, when roughly a third of the NPC's top leaders signed a petition calling on the NPC Standing Committee to meet and reconsider the State Council's martial law order. Such a meeting might have produced a "constitutional" resolution to the crisis, and would have represented a huge leap toward "rule by law" in China. But this bid fell far short of the mark when the petition received no discernible public support from any top CCP leaders, not even those who had built up the NPC in recent years, such as Standing Committee Chairman Wan Li or former chairman Peng Zhen.

Distinguishing Policy Influence from Liberalization

We can get a better perspective on what *has* changed in the NPC during the Deng Xiaoping era if we distinguish between two separate but ultimately related aspects of any legislature's development. One aspect—the one almost exclusively focused upon by most skeptics of the NPC's changes—is the liberalization of the legislature and the broader political system. The second aspect, almost entirely ignored by most analysts, is the institutionalization of the NPC's policy influence. Distinguishing these two dimensions of legislative development not only permits us a clearer view of what has and has not changed in the NPC since 1978; at the end of this chapter we will look at ways in which this distinction can help us discern the path the NPC may take toward even greater influence in the post–Deng Xiaoping era.

Institutionalized influence is the legislature's established capacity for sustained, significant influence in making policy and governing society. It includes influence over the policy and legislative agendas, involving both recognition of key political problems and influence over the range of acceptable policy solutions to be considered. Policy influence is also measured by the propensity for major issues and policy solutions to be debated within the legislature, and to be enacted in the form of laws or motions promulgated by the legislature, as opposed to policies just promulgated by the party or the cabinet. It also includes legislative influence over the content of possible solutions and the timing of their adoption. Finally, institutionalized legislative influence includes effective involvement in or at least oversight over the implementation of laws and policies, and oversight of government behavior.

Legislative liberalization or democratization also assumes a good deal of institutionalized legislative influence over governance. Its additional dimensions include ever-broader and more equitable popular consultativeness, accessibility, representativeness, participation, and relatively effective accountability to an ever-widening share of the population. Kevin O'Brien's definition of legislative "liberalization" in China captures both the dimension of "institutionalized influence" and the other dimensions of liberalization:

> Liberal reformers, at various times, have sought to limit central power and to transform the legislature into an institution with an established role in policy-making. They have envisioned outside control over leaders and regular influence over policy: they have aimed to build a legislature that has the ability to veto misguided policies and the power to remove incompetent or corrupt leaders. They have sought to strengthen the nation by diffusing power. When permitted to do so, liberalizers have urged leaders to be more responsive, have championed electoral reform and elite ac-

countability; they have supported close legislator-constituent ties and active representation of individual, partial, and national interests. Despite repeated setbacks, several generations of liberal-minded reformers have periodically reintroduced the idea of popularizing autocratic rule and allowing limited political competition. Though never strong in numbers, advocates of liberalization have galvanized the nation with bold proposals and have explored the outer bounds of permissible debate.[1]

In almost any country, the acid test of legislative liberalization is the regime's willingness to permit direct, fair, competitive, multicandidate elections. In the earliest days after the 1978 Third Plenum, the party leadership adopted a new electoral system for people's congresses that initiated controlled direct election of deputies to the county-level people's congresses, but not the provincial or the national congresses. The very limited choice of candidates froze popular choice and "accountability" over the legislature at a very low level.[2] The system from the very beginning, therefore, foreclosed serious progress toward liberal legislative development for the remainder of the Deng era. As a consequence, NPC development during the past seventeen years has been channeled overwhelmingly toward institutionalizing the NPC's influence in policymaking and, to a lesser extent, oversight. Though gradual and quiet, this progress has been fairly impressive, and most of this chapter will focus on this growing influence. Moreover, the increased autonomy of the party-member leaders of the NPC, subject to increasingly fuzzy notions of "party discipline," has greatly loosened the party's centralized control over lawmaking. This "loosening," in turn, has opened a window for NPC and NPC Standing Committee deputies to become far more assertive and to increasingly reconsider whom they "represent" in Chinese society. Equally important, there is also more access to the NPC by groups such as the women's federation, unions, ethnic minorities, intellectuals, peasants, and so on, but thus far this access has been very informal and usually organized in a highly patrimonial or corporatist way. Thus, while this increased "access" may have made the system more consultative, it is still a far cry from genuine popular "accountability" over the legislature. Despite these shortcomings, however, the NPC's focus on institutionalizing influence rather than liberalization—that is, becoming "influential" before becoming "democratic"—may have significant advantages for the NPC's long-term transition toward a more liberal legislature.

Deng's Vague Role

Deng Xiaoping's speech to the 1978 Third Plenum, which symbolically launched the reform era, revealed key ambiguities in his thinking about legal development and the role of the NPC. He called for greater rule by laws, developed through broader consultation, which were to be far more stable than the late chairman's whims. Deng even provided an agenda, listing several priority pieces of legislation to be drafted.[3] He also called for strengthening "socialist democracy." But Deng's speech said nothing about expanding the role of the National People's Congress in lawmaking. The NPC was only alluded to separately and briefly in the plenum communiqué, which explicitly endorsed greater independence for such legal institutions as judicial and procuratorial offices but remained mute about greater legislative power for the NPC.[4] Deng's failure to link these two initiatives—greater rule by law and stronger, more democratic people's congresses—betrayed his own uncertainty about the degree to which the NPC should be involved in policy issues and the degree to which increased social consultation through the people's congresses would be connected to stable policymaking through lawmaking. How much legislative involvement and how much open debate, criticism, and detailed revision of major policy initiatives was Deng prepared to accept from the *nomenklatura*-approved NPC leaders and delegates? When and how should this influence be institutionalized into the policymaking process? Deng's fifteen years of published speeches between 1978 and 1993 give no guidance on these important issues of the party-state's constitution beyond his three vaguely worded anti-liberal principles that party leadership must be maintained, that the people's congress system is "China's basic political system," and that China will never follow the U.S.-style system of a tripartite division of powers.

Except for ruling out liberalization, Deng's apparent lack of direct personal attention to the NPC left its growing policy role to be determined by other forces. These included the system's changing legislative needs, the competing political views and desires of the powerful party leaders who have led the NPC since 1979, the erosion of detailed central party leadership with regard to lawmaking, and the NPC's growing bureaucratic-organizational capacity to involve itself in policymaking.

Institutionalizing Policy Influence

The state of the Chinese legal system in 1978 in part dictated the sequence and pace of the NPC's development of its policymaking capacity. In the wake of the Cultural Revolution's legal nihilism, China had neither a body of laws nor a legal drafting apparatus in the central party offices, the State Council, or the NPC worthy of the name. The political and policy needs of domestic stabilization and China's external opening required rapid enactment of symbolically important laws such as the Criminal Code and the Sino-Foreign Joint Venture Law. Party and government organs at all levels throughout the country had to be rebuilt before much serious thought could be given to the role of the people's congresses in overseeing them. Consequently, the resurrection of legal drafting work would have to precede the slower, and in many ways more difficult, work of rebuilding and reshaping effective legislative oversight, legal implementation, and enforcement mechanisms at lower levels of the system.

Views of Party Leaders in the NPC

Beginning at least as early as 1982, Politburo member Peng Zhen, who had served as NPC secretary general during the 1950s, emerged as the party's strongest voice for greater NPC assertiveness and autonomy under fairly general party leadership. This view would be embraced and elaborated upon by both of his successors as NPC standing committee chairman, Wan Li and Qiao Shi.[5] Peng's post-1978 speeches on strengthening the NPC Standing Committee elaborated upon his statements and actions as an NPC leader in the mid-1950s.[6] Thus it is impossible to determine to what extent his later views on party-NPC relations reflected a long-term ideological view on party-state organization, and to what extent they reflected his political ambitions to strengthen his power base after 1979. Pitman Potter argues in his analysis of Peng's legal thought that Peng's accession to the NPC Standing Committee chairmanship coincided with his recognition that he was not going to be named to the Politburo Standing Committee at the 1982 Twelfth Party Congress, and that Deng was not going to permit him to rise higher in the party.[7] Like so many of the other senior party leaders rehabilitated and added to the NPC Standing Committee after 1978, Peng realized that his leading position within the party apparatus would be brief and transitional, and the NPC would hereafter be the principal platform and organizational conduit for his still considerable personal influence.[8]

Potter's analysis also reveals that by the mid-1980s Peng's views on the relationship between the party organization and the people's congresses had begun to evolve. In an increasingly elliptical style, Peng always affirmed party leadership with regard to lawmaking, but time and again appended modifications to that formula which suggested that "leadership" should be broad and general. The NPC was by no means bound to ratify every legislative suggestion of the party and State Council quickly, uncritically, and without amendment. He argued that party policies enshrined in legislative drafts represented the party's "suggestions" (zhuzhang), which only achieved the status of law after NPC review. Echoing Deng Xiaoping, he also advocated a diminished role for party organs in day-to-day administration and economic management, but surpassed Deng in explicitly advocating a more assertive role for people's congresses in dispute resolution and in representing the views of the masses to local governments.[9] By 1986, at the height of the bitter struggle between the State Council and the NPC Standing Committee to pass the Bankruptcy Law, Peng noted that in the past, some people had accused the NPC of being a "rubber stamp." "Now," Peng joked, "there are some who *wish* the NPC were *more* of a rubber stamp. That's fine. That's their affair."[10]

Peng's successors as NPC Standing Committee chairman, Wan Li and Qiao Shi, in turn embraced the views that the NPC deserved greater power and that an assertive NPC was essential to the survival of the regime. Wan Li initially came to this view as part of his broader vision, voiced during the brief 1986 debate on "political structural reform," which urged that China's political system provide greater protection for loyal policy specialists and officials who criticized current policy.[11] The 1989 demonstrations and subsequent suppression strengthened Wan's views on the need for rapid political reform. Although Wan Li failed at the critical moment in the crisis to join those NPC officials who called on the NPC Standing Committee to play a role in resolving the crisis, Wan emerged afterward convinced that further policy mistakes and catastrophes could be avoided if the party used the NPC as an institutionalized device for listening to the complaints of the people. On the eve of the March 1990 NPC session, Wan Li and Jiang Zemin engaged in a public disagreement on the NPC's role under party leadership. In separate addresses before the session, Jiang stressed the need for delegates to obey party directives; Wan Li reemphasized his point that the party could learn from a vocal NPC.[12]

During his tenure as Standing Committee chairman, Qiao Shi echoed this view. By the mid-1990s Qiao sounded very much like Peng Zhen and Wan Li in his assertions that party policies acquire a special legitimacy when the NPC approves them as laws, and that the NPC should have greater power to discuss and debate major party policies.[13] Qiao also reportedly called for gradual but significant political reform that would give the NPC Standing Committee greater power to supervise government offices, oversee legislative implementation, review and amend the state budget, and impeach state officials who do not faithfully implement state laws.[14]

Evolving leadership attitudes toward lawmaking have also shaped the NPC's growth and helped define its policy role vis-à-vis the party center and the State Council. Throughout his post-Mao NPC tenure, Peng Zhen and most NPC leaders were vocal adherents of the theory of "experience-based lawmaking" (jingyan lifa), according to which law should be used as an instrument to codify and stabilize party policies once they had been proved correct through experience and experimental implementation, usually in more flexible forms such as party circulars and State Council temporary regulations. Laws would follow reform, not precede it, and not lead it. Premature efforts to enshrine party and government reform policies in law, in the view of Peng, Chen Pixian, and many other NPC leaders, ran the risk of undermining the authoritativeness, stability, and continuity that gave law its special importance as a policy vehicle. Not surprisingly, adherents of experience-based lawmaking, such as Peng Zhen, have usually discussed it with reference to China's most rapidly changing area of policy: economic reform.[15]

Despite Peng's desire to increase the NPC's power, experience-based lawmaking in some ways restricted the NPC's potential influence over lawmaking because it meant the NPC would generally enter the drafting process rather late in the game. The NPC would review, critique, and weigh the long-term wisdom of a policy that had already undergone several rounds of internal review and local-level experimentation under the guidance of party central offices, State Council ministries, and a number of local-government testing sites. The NPC thus would become an "agenda-taker" rather than one of the "agenda-setters." Nevertheless, Peng Zhen and his fellow NPC leaders have often used the "experience-based lawmaking" theory as a device to set the NPC apart from and, they have suggested, above the other party and state organs involved in policy. By arguing that law is a vehicle for confirming party policies proved correct by practice, NPC leaders have effectively set themselves up as arbiters of the "correctness" of party policy experiments—a judgment that the NPC has repeatedly withheld from important policy decisions until the State Council has modified, ameliorated, watered down, or even dropped them. Although the experience-based approach is far more than a pretext for legislative obstructionism, it has given NPC legislative activity a "conservative" procedural cast that many actors have found politically useful. It provided both those social groups injured by reform, such as the official trade unions, and the NPC leadership, which during the 1980s was dominated by "conservative reformers" suspicious of markets and liberalism, with a forum and a justification for resisting these reforms without appearing openly disloyal to the party leadership.

With the departures of Peng Zhen and NPC vice chairman Chen

Pixian in 1988, the NPC leadership implicitly moved beyond experience-based lawmaking and took a more active role in setting and pushing the legislative agenda, especially in the economic law sector traditionally dominated by the State Council. In part, this reflected an impatience among NPC staff and scholarly advisors who were critical of the "experience-based" approach to lawmaking.[16] In part, this may also be due to a reversal of leadership orientations in 1988, as the more cautious and statist Li Peng assumed the premiership from Zhao Ziyang, while Peng Zhen yielded the NPC Standing Committee chairmanship to Wan Li, a pioneer of economic reform. After the Tiananmen suppression, Wan Li and his secretary general, Peng Chong, felt the NPC's principal mission was to rapidly draft the legal infrastructure to support market-based reforms. Their speeches betrayed increasing irritation with the State Council and its ministries' reluctance to produce this economic legislation.[17]

While the party leaders who have guided the NPC's work during the Deng era have thus been men of widely differing ideological orientation, each has come to see an open, assertive NPC and a powerful Standing Committee as positive forces for political reform and the life of the CCP. The NPC leaders after 1988 have also eased away from the theory of experience-based lawmaking and have tried to transform the NPC into more of a legislative agenda-setter and reform activist.

Changing Patterns of "Party Leadership" over the NPC and Lawmaking

The NPC leaders in the post-Mao era have also developed the NPC's bureaucratic organization so that it could step into the gap created by the CCP central organs' declining control over lawmaking, and begin to rival the State Council for leadership over the legislative agenda. NPC leaders were helped in this endeavor by the CCP's post-1978 shift toward increased policymaking through lawmaking and the simultaneous erosion of centralized party control over lawmaking. In contrast to the last decade of Mao's life (1966–1976), when the destruction of regular party and state policymaking organs and intense, often violent political struggle over centralized decision-making power in the top leaders ended all lawmaking, by the mid-1980s the post-Mao movement away from this concentration of authority had blurred the boundaries between party "policymaking" and state "lawmaking."[18] "Lawmaking" became an integral part of much "policymaking," and the substance of an increasing number of important "policies" was thrashed out and emerged through the process of drafting them as "law." While Deng was still functioning, it appeared that an "issue-area" division of labor was gradually emerging, whereby certain policy issues tended to be drafted as documents of the party Central Committee (agriculture, ideology, and military affairs, for example), while other issues were typically addressed in State Council and ministerial regulations (most notably urban/industrial, economic and financial administration); and only a small subset were drafted as laws promulgated by the NPC or its Standing Committee. But even this very rough division of labor appears to have broken down since the late 1980s. The party leaders overseeing the NPC have found ways to interject that body into an ever-widening array of high-profile and controversial policy issues such as the Three Gorges Project, the regulation of public demonstrations, bankruptcy, administrative authority in special economic zones, agricultural contracts and fees, state industrial enterprise management, intellectual property rights, education, state secrets, banking and financial markets, the environment, and administrative litigation law. Indeed, when we consider that in May 1989 approximately one third of the nearly 150 members of the NPC Standing Committee reportedly signed one of the three famous petitions calling on the Standing Committee to meet and review the State Council's martial law decision, it is interesting to contemplate just how close the NPC came to becoming significantly involved in a decision affecting the very life of the party-state.[19]

Since 1978 central party leadership with regard to lawmaking has become far less organized and detailed than in the past, and this has provided the NPC and other state lawmaking organs with opportunities to assert themselves. To a great degree, this change stems from the organizational evolution of the policymaking process. Chinese legislative officials have pointed out that at least since the mid-1980s, the party's top leadership has rarely been able to communicate its desires on legislative matters to the NPC with sufficient unity and clarity to prevent the NPC from becoming a powerful new adjunct arena of political struggle.[20] Neither the Central Political-Legal Leading Group nor any other single Central Committee organ any longer functions as a central legislative coordinator.[21] In February 1991, apparently after an unsuccessful effort by Jiang Zemin and others to reassert tighter control over the NPC, the CCP issued Central Committee Document *(Zhongfa)* Number 8 (1991), which for the first time in a party document codified the already rather loose arrangements for party leadership over NPC lawmaking work that had evolved unofficially during the previous five or six years.[22] Party leadership was to be limited to establishing the overall policy line and direction, and having the Politburo "review and confirm" draft laws before they were sent for final discussion and approval by the NPC. But while a few clauses of a draft law might be discussed in these meetings, the "great majority" of these clauses would not require the party center's discussion. Central Document Number 8 even suggested that certain categories of less "important" laws might not need Politburo review and approval. The document also strengthened the NPC vis-à-vis the State Council bureaucracy by requiring ministries to report major political laws they were drafting to the NPC leadership in advance, and by putting NPC leaders in charge of working out any problems in such legislation with the party Politburo or Secretariat. The issuance of the document, a year and a half after Tiananmen and at a time of particularly intense high-level "leftist" counterattack against political and economic reform, suggests that there is fairly strong support among the top leadership for looser party control over the NPC.[23] *Zhongfa* Number 8 (1991) also established a powerful precedent that would make future reassertion of tighter central control much more difficult.

The erosion in party leadership over the NPC is not only organizational; it is also encouraged by several new social and ideological realities that have emerged during the Deng era. *Nomenklatura* controls over NPC and NPC Standing Committee delegates now yield far less control over delegate behavior than in the past.[24] Although the top leadership convenes meetings of all party-member deputies before all NPC and NPC Standing Committee meetings to ensure that the votes and the tone of the meetings are all in accordance with leadership desires, the norms of obedience to party discipline have eroded greatly. Even at NPC meetings, such as those in 1989, 1990, and 1993, before which party leaders have reportedly insisted upon a high level of party unity, large numbers of delegates have felt increasingly free simply to ignore or defy these orders.[25] *Nomenklatura* controls have been further undercut by unofficial post-Mao delegate selection norms, which allocate almost all Standing Committee seats to noteworthy bureaucratic, organizational, and sectoral interests. These delegates' "normal" pursuit of organizational interests on relatively noncontroversial legislative matters has further undermined delegate discipline. More important, in an era when even committed Leninists have reconsidered many cherished fundamentals, as the 1989 case of Hu Jiwei and the other party members who led the effort to convene the Standing Committee to review the martial law decree dramatically demonstrate, *nomenklatura* vetting of NPC delegates has provided no guarantee that these officials would not become radicalized during their tenure as deputies and Standing Committee members. Despite the purge of Hu Jiwei, incidents in which NPC deputies have been severely disciplined for ignoring party directives have been rare—a fact that virtually guarantees an increased lack of discipline in the future.

Improved Delegate Quality and the "Retirement" of Party Elders to the Standing Committee

In nondemocratic systems that lack an established rule of law, legislatures tend to gain real institutionalized policy influence only when they become a useful "tool" or "vehicle" of other actors who are already powerful in the system. Before the early 1980s, the NPC could be ignored in large part because it was not a useful vehicle for any such powerful actors. During the Mao period, NPC and Standing Committee deputies could largely be divided up into two categories: honorary deputies, such as model workers, peasants, soldiers, artists, ethnic minorities, democratic party or nonparty social luminaries, and high-ranking party and state officials whose real work was in other national and local administrative positions. The former usually lacked the intellectual abilities (often including bare literacy), political connections, policy knowledge, and sheer courage necessary to employ their NPC memberships toward any significant policy-related goal. The latter possessed most of these policy-related gifts in abundance, but they also had much more powerful institutional avenues through which to express them. Like a muscle left unexercised, the NPC could hardly be expected to grow strong.

The former problem, officially labeled "low delegate quality," has long been a subject of debate among NPC reformers.[26] While there has been little disagreement on the need to improve the assertiveness and lawmaking skills of the average delegate, the implications of that improvement have evoked strongly worded debate. Some have sought to raise delegate quality simply to strengthen the NPC bureaucratically in policymaking. Others have called for delegate recruitment standards that would encourage intellectual elites to dominate the organization at the expense of worker and peasant deputies.[27] Regardless of the motivation, O'Brien and Li's data reveal dramatic improvements since 1980 in the educational levels and professional-technical skills of the deputies elected to both the local and the national people's congresses—a trend that could strengthen these organizations' capacities for institutionalizing more powerful policy roles.[28]

Deng Xiaoping "solved" the second problem, perhaps inadvertently, in the early 1980s, when he and his more youthful, technocratic allies arranged for many elder party and state officials to be nominally "retired" from top leadership positions to the NPC Standing Committee (as well as to the CCP's Central Advisory Commission). Among the several dozen Long March–generation veterans transferred to the NPC were at least seven ex-Politburo members and dozens of former central department heads and State Council ministers and vice ministers. These restless ex-revolutionaries possessed impressive *guanxi* ties, organizational resources, and policy expertise, which they used to strengthen the NPC.

Whether or not Deng Xiaoping had intended for the seniors' transfer to provide the momentum for the NPC's rapid organizational development and assertiveness in matters of policy, during the 1980s and 1990s these senior leaders increasingly began to see the NPC as the principal organizational conduit for their already impressive individual influence. They transformed the NPC Standing Committee into an organization "searching" for someplace to assert itself in the policymaking system.[29] Peng Zhen, the consummate organization builder, immediately recognized the elders' bureaucratic value, and noted in a major speech in 1986 that over half of the 155 members of the Sixth NPC Standing Committee had held ranks equal to vice minister, provincial deputy party secretary, or above.[30] He lavished praised on the feisty retirees for their unwillingness to be intimidated by others in the leadership, their *guanxi* ties, and their willingness to involve themselves in policy work. From a policy standpoint, moreover, many of the elders had been what Harry Harding has called either "restorationists" or "conservative reformers," dismissed from party and state posts to make way for younger technocrats or "radical reformers." Several of them, including Wang Renzhong, Chen Muhua, Ni Zhifu, Zhang Ruiying, Geng Biao, Wei Guoqing, and others, seemed to take genuine delight when they could cast themselves in the role of protectors of the working classes against the alleged predations of radical market-oriented reforms.

Organizational and Bureaucratic Development

The history of legislatures in other developing countries makes clear that before a legislature can enjoy sustained, genuine policymaking influence, it must develop a strong subcommittee system and legislative bureaucracy.[31] This has been no less true of the NPC. The NPC's rapid bureaucratic development during the Deng era can be broken down into roughly three stages: (1) 1979 to 1982, (2) 1983 to 1987–88, and (3) from 1988 to the present. Not until 1982–83, when the new Sixth NPC established six special committees and a number of permanent staff offices, did the NPC begin to assemble the bureaucratic and subcommittee resources necessary for sustained involvement across an array of laws and through all stages of the legislative process. Until that time, the NPC had only a small General Office staff and a Legislative Affairs Committee made up of seventy very recently rehabilitated elders, whose ambition and energy could hardly make up for a lack of bureaucratic resources and youthful staffers. Peng Zhen and the NPC leadership only had the resources for drafting a few, selected, major laws such as the Sino-Foreign Joint Venture Law, the Criminal Code, and the Economic Contracts Law. In addition, rank-and-file NPC delegates at this time only sporadically involved themselves in policy issues, and their involvement was more often tied to leadership infighting than to detailed policy positions. Normally, only a relative handful of deputies dared voice even the most general opinions on major policy issues, such as the overall state of the economy or the weakness of the education system. Overall during this period, the NPC engaged in little more than a cursory review and discussion of major pieces of draft legislation that had already been drawn up and hammered out elsewhere in the system, usually among the ministries of the State Council.[32]

In 1982 the NPC's institutional assets and capacity for involvement in lawmaking began to grow rapidly. The 1982 State Constitution gave the NPC Standing Committee the right to pass many laws, a right previously reserved entirely to the full NPC. Under the new NPC Organic law, the Standing Committee could establish a variety of subordinate work offices and subcommittees. As a result, both the NPC General Office and the Legislative Affairs Committee rapidly expanded their staffs over the next several years, adding large research organs, libraries, and specialist offices on criminal, economic, administrative, and civil law that attracted many of the most talented new graduates from China's recently revived law schools. The NPC's total staff nearly quadrupled from about two hundred in 1981 to almost eight hundred by 1987. Several sources report that the NPC budget increased greatly as well, although no figures are available to measure or confirm this. The six special committees endowed the Standing Committee with the expertise and connections of former high-ranking officials and policy specialists from the departments concerned with their respective issues. The leadership of Peng Zhen and NPC secretary general Peng Chong in 1987–88 undertook a major reorganization that strengthened and unified the NPC's internal bureaucratic leadership. The Secretary General's Office (*mishuchu*) was given control over the General Office and Legislative Affairs Committee staffs, which had often battled over turf. Party leading groups within the NPC were also streamlined so that they no longer overlapped; their membership coincided precisely with the party membership of the policy-setting Committee Chairmen's Group.

The result was a major increase in NPC policy influence. Chinese legislative experts report that by the mid- to late 1980s, NPC Standing Committee officials and staff were able to participate in or take charge of the drafting groups for many more laws than had been the case in the early 1980s. The NPC also expanded its influence on the legislative agenda, especially the annual and five-year legislative plans that up to this point had been dominated almost exclusively by the State Council. In 1991–92 Wan Li and Peng Chong led the NPC and the State Council in formulating a two-year legislative plan to accelerate drafting work on several pieces of legislation, mostly market-oriented economic reform legislation that had been sidetracked in the wake of Tiananmen. Never before had NPC leaders been able to bring such blunt pressure to bear on the State Council's policy agenda. The NPC was also freer to determine which draft laws it would get to review. NPC personnel began serious involvement in drafting work on a given law at earlier stages in the process and expanded its influence over other key processes, such as the interorganizational review, researching "experimental" locations, and "soliciting opinions" of concerned departments, mass groups, localities, and basic-level units. The State Council and its ministries were still the initial drafters of the bulk of the legislation reviewed by the NPC, but the NPC was an increasingly able and assertive rival in drafting work.

Detailed case studies of major laws drafted during the late 1980s and early 1990s demonstrate that the NPC was gaining policy influence vis-à-vis both the party center and the State Council, and its involvement in the process often had a significant impact on the content of important legislation. The easing of bureaucratic secrecy since 1979 now makes it possible to compare multiple drafts of a single law as it undergoes consideration and debate at each stage of the lawmaking process. This permits an assessment of how much the law's contents have been changed at each stage. These case studies provide many examples of important revisions forced by the NPC:

- In the wake of the 1989 crackdown, the Ministry of Public Security (MPS) attempted to rush a highly restrictive law on public demonstrations through the NPC. On the law's first try at passage, the Standing Committee attacked the draft and reportedly voted it down, returning it to the MPS for extensive revision. Although the final draft was indeed restrictive, NPC subcommittee members, including a former minister of justice, delayed its passage until the MPS revised it to reaffirm some limited citizen rights to demonstrate.
- Over eight months in 1986, the Standing Committee thrice debated and amended the highly controversial Enterprise Bankruptcy Law. The draft law was strongly supported by Zhao Ziyang's State Council, and had been repeatedly approved in principle by the Politburo. Standing Committee delegates nevertheless attacked the law, reportedly voting it down once, and forced several amendments that greatly narrowed the number of enterprises to which the law would apply, made it applicable only for "trial use" rather than nationwide, and made its implementation conditional on the prior passage of the even more controversial State Industrial Enterprise Law.
- Between 1985 and 1988 the State Industrial Enterprise Law was also in turn repeatedly delayed and amended by the full NPC and the Standing Committee. Although the Politburo publicly endorsed the draft in January 1988, the NPC in April revised the core features of the draft, weakening the powers it would grant to state factory managers and reasserting the powers of official unions and factory CCP committees.[33]

There is also evidence that the NPC's new influence is becoming institutionalized and resistant to the type of organizational rollback it suffered twice during the Maoist years. The most telling evidence of institutionalization came after 1989, when the legislature's organizational development was not reversed during the antireformist crackdown after Tiananmen, despite the fact that many Standing

Committee members had opposed Li Peng's martial law decree. Total NPC staff increased from 802 to 870 between 1987 and 1990, and then ballooned to 1,896 when the Central Committee General Office transferred back to NPC control the 1,026-member staff of the Great Hall of the People, which it had taken from the legislature during the Cultural Revolution.

By the late 1980s NPC officials could look back on several years of the fastest organizational growth in the body's history and a rapidly expanding capacity for legislative influence. At the same time, NPC leaders were becoming increasingly concerned that they lacked the power of oversight necessary to ensure effective implementation of the legislation that the NPC passed, or to extend meaningful legislative influence over the State Council. Throughout Peng Zhen's tenure as Legislative Affairs Committee and Standing Committee chairman, oversight seems to have been a willful blind spot. In the same 1986 speeches in which he praised the Standing Committee elders, Peng mildly scolded them for devoting too much time to overseeing the administrative affairs of State Council departments, especially those departments from which they had just retired. He seemed to fear that oversight work would sap the legislators' time and focus on lawmaking. He also chided them for clogging up their younger successors' work in the ministries, asking rhetorically, "If the NPC Standing Committee delegates constantly supervise this ministry or that ministry . . . what will the *Ministers* have to do?"[34]

By the end of his tenure in April 1988, however, Peng had apparently rethought the matter and concluded that the oversight power needed to be strengthened. Several of Peng's NPC colleagues and successors, most notably Secretary General Peng Chong, were already convinced of the need. By spring 1989 NPC leaders were engaged in "self-criticism" for their neglect of oversight and implementation. They asserted that "having no laws to refer to" was no longer as great a problem as "having laws that were not enforced." During the tenures of Wan Li and Qiao Shi, strengthening oversight over State Council departments and implementation became the watchword.

The NPC's pursuit of this goal, however, posed enormous institutional dilemmas. As recent scholarship on China has shown, the power of central party and government organs to enforce effective implementation at lower levels is probably the fastest-deteriorating aspect of the entire party-state system.[35] It is not enough for the NPC to expand its power vis-à-vis the State Council and the party center; it must also help these central organs build new avenues and methods to reassert their power at the local levels, or the NPC must develop its own independent channels to ensure effective enforcement of NPC-passed laws. Strengthening courts and procurators who are relatively dedicated to rule by law may be part of the long-term answer, but to focus on courts and procurators shifts the NPC's organizational dilemma down a geographical level. For the courts to strengthen their commitment to the rule of law would require weakening the party political-legal system's control over the courts. But the political-legal system at present may be one of the few sets of institutions that still retains the power and effectiveness to ensure the implementation of court decisions. Effective expansion of the NPC's implementation and oversight capacity will be extremely difficult. Major progress may have to await fundamental reforms in the organizational capacity and political orientation of several other institutions in the political system.

Obstructing Liberalization Prospects: Formal versus Informal Dimensions

Significantly, from the standpoint of making the people's congress more accountable to citizens, one of the Deng era's earliest decisions on China's political structure—the 1979 electoral reforms for the national and local people's congresses—has also proved to be one of its most enduring.[36] Only people's congresses at and below the level of the county (and some cities subordinate to provinces) are chosen by direct popular elections. Although these elections in principle involve secret ballots and approximately twice as many candidates as positions, and citizen groups at this level are permitted to nominate candidates to local electoral committees, local party-dominated committees still retain a great deal of control over determining which candidates' names actually appear on the ballot. This decision process is still quite secretive, though it is supposed to be reached through consultation with voters.

Delegates to the provincial and national people's congresses are still indirectly chosen by delegates from the next lower level of the people's congress. After the candidates for these levels are chosen, the process of discussing candidates tends to spotlight those who have been nominated by the party and by officially sanctioned mass organizations. This process consigns other candidates nominated from the floor or by delegate groups to relative anonymity. Central officials still intervene strongly in candidate selection, assigning delegate quotas based on party membership, gender, ethnicity, and membership in certain mass organizations. Top-ranking central leaders are also assigned as supplemental members of various provincial delegations, frequently to provinces in which they grew up or formerly served.

The higher one looks in the system, the narrower the degree of "choice" in people's congress elections. Not only is the "selectorate" for provincial and national congresses controlled, but the percentage by which the number of candidates typically exceeds the number of positions decreases as one moves upward from the provincial level to the NPC, its Standing Committee, and its chairman and vice chairmen. Only in 1988 and 1993 did elections for the Standing Committee involve "excess" candidates, and in both elections, the number of candidates only exceeded the number of seats by a mere handful. NPC deputies have never been given any choice in the selection of their chairman and vice chairmen.

Although Western scholars still know relatively little about why Deng and his colleagues undertook electoral reform in 1979, the system they devised was apparently calculated to balance at least two pairs of potentially contradictory goals:

- The leaders wanted to revive the party's deeply wounded legitimacy by granting citizens greater electoral participation and a slightly enhanced choice of candidates. But they also wanted to continue to guarantee unquestioned party leadership over both national and local legislatures and governments.

- Deng and his reformist allies sought to develop a mechanism for mobilizing and channeling popular power to help them overcome their *(presumably)* less popular rivals who had risen to power during the Cultural Revolution. Yet they insisted on simultaneously shackling and eliminating the uncontrolled, often violent, mass "big democracy" of the Cultural Revolution.[37]

At the time of its adoption, the new electoral system attracted a good deal of controversy. Several scholars were highly critical of the fact that the new law did not permit direct election of people's congress deputies above the county level. Their calls for immediate direct election of people's congresses at all levels, however, were quickly rejected. Since 1979 some high-level leaders have occasionally suggested that direct election should ultimately be extended to higher-level people's congresses, but action on any such reform has been consigned to the indefinite future. The several revisions to the Election Law since 1979 have done more to confirm and stabilize the current system than to open it up. For example, these revisions have placed greater limitations on campaigning, thus putting candidates who are not supported by local party leaders at a further disadvantage. Indirect elections and restricted candidate choice above the county level deprive citizens of even the most pro forma direct constitutional means for removing deputies or officials who are incompetent or corrupt. It is difficult to imagine any significant progress toward increased accountability until and unless the CCP reopens discussion on direct election to the provincial and national people's congresses. But given the undermining of other Leninist states by even modestly competitive legislative electoral reforms, such reforms are unlikely in the immediate future.

The foreclosure of formal electoral reform, however, has not prevented modest progress toward other aspects of liberal legislative reform. These include the increased assertiveness of NPC deputies in their dealings with the central party and government leadership and expanding avenues of informal popular access to NPC and Standing Committee deputies. Unlike major changes in accountability, which will probably require fundamental formal restructuring of the current system, these improvements in assertiveness and access can occur informally. Over time, they may significantly increase the system's openness and consultativeness at two levels. Near the top of the system, increasing delegate assertiveness has already caused top party and state organs to consult more with NPC deputies and Standing Committee members on a widening variety of issues, and concede to more NPC views. Further down in the system, at least a certain percentage of NPC deputies and Standing Committee members are evolving new views about just who it is they "represent" in the Chinese political system, what "representation" means, and how it affects their relationship to the party center and the broader society. The impact of these changes must still be kept in perspective, but it is clear that these increases in assertiveness and accessibility have already made the NPC a much less passive, compliant organ for ratifying party decisions as law and explaining them to the masses.

The most powerful and reliable evidence of increased delegate assertiveness over the past two decades is the increase in dissenting votes by NPC delegates on draft laws, motions, budget reports, and personnel appointments. Recently available data on NPC and NPC Standing Committee voting show a steady increase in the willingness of delegates to vote "no" or abstain since about 1986.[38] To be sure, "no" votes and abstentions may have any number of political meanings, some implying more fundamental change in the system than others. These votes might reflect an effort to embarrass an opponent in a factional or bureaucratic struggle, or a delegate's effort to prove that he or she is not a "rubber stamp," or they might be seen by NPC officials as a relatively low-cost way to demonstrate that "socialist democracy" is not a sham. Still, since virtually every draft law, nomination, or major motion which is voted upon by the NPC or its Standing Committee must first be approved "in principle" by the party Politburo, the willingness of large numbers of legislators to vote down a draft law or motion is perhaps the single most dramatic indicator of the legislature's increased assertiveness and autonomy. When the NPC actually votes down a Politburo-approved draft law or motion, or nearly half of the delegates cast dissenting votes, it becomes increasingly difficult to assert that the party continues to maintain a tightly unified control over the legislature.

NPC voting data reveal a number of new phenomena. First of all, the once automatic practice of passing laws unanimously is now quite rare. Second, it is no longer the case that all laws pass. At least twice since 1986, the NPC Standing Committee has actually voted down and returned for extensive revision draft laws submitted by the State Council, which also bore the Politburo's approval "in principle."[39] Third, these two cases were not isolated revolts of an otherwise quiescent congress. Large dissenting vote totals are becoming relatively common. Of the full NPC's twenty-three known votes on personnel appointment and other motions in the 1990s, six of them—over 25 percent—received dissenting vote totals of over one fifth. Of its twelve known votes on draft laws since 1989, dissenting vote totals exceeded 10 percent on seven occasions, 20 percent on five occasions, and reached an embarrassing 32 percent–41 percent on three occasions. As these dates suggest, this "normalization of moderate dissent" within the legislature continued even in the antiliberal climate after Tiananmen. The data also provide evidence of a great increase in delegate assertiveness. The State Council and other top leaders involved in the legislative process have had little choice but to adapt, making changes in legislative drafts to meet the objections of the NPC deputies and leadership.

Some NPC members' changing views of themselves as representatives are opening up new avenues of access between the broader society and themselves. The former "top-down" consciousness of these delegates is shifting toward a "bottom-up" delegate consciousness that is leading them to consult with a variety of groups and interests in society, and to represent these groups in seeking special favors or remedies from the bureaucracy or in drafting and amending legislation to advance these groups' interests. Kevin O'Brien's interviews with people's congress deputies and officials at various levels provide the most impressive evidence of changing delegate attitudes toward their roles as representatives. O'Brien found that increasing numbers of deputies have abandoned their recommended role as central "agents" who explain the top leadership's policies to lower levels and the masses. Instead, he found that many behaved more as "remonstrators" to higher levels by representing their self-defined constituencies. These deputies often serve as middlemen by voicing popular complaints to government offices and trying to negotiate mutually acceptable solutions.[40]

NPC and Standing Committee delegates' efforts to represent the interests of various mid- and lower-level constituencies in revising draft legislation is another emerging form of representation. NPC deputies who are attached to the official All-China Federation of Trade Unions (ACFTU), for example, have been particularly frank about their willingness to confront, criticize, and amend draft laws that they feel harm the interest of state workers and their unions, even when these reforms enjoyed the open endorsement of the party center. It was in this context that ACFTU-member NPC delegates and others bitterly, and in many ways successfully, attacked the Bankruptcy Law and the managerial powers in the State Industrial Enterprise Law. Despite their expressed support for "party leadership" over the NPC, they were developing a "bottom-up" view of their proper role as deputies which saw their union members, and not the party center, as their true "constituency."

In more liberal legislatures, these new forms of representation constitute important aspects of the legislators' "lawmaking" and "constituency service" functions. So far, however, there is not enough evidence to say just how prevalent these trends have become and what percentage of delegates function as "representatives" who are accessible to broader social constituencies.

Moreover, these new forms of delegate accessibility and representation are still highly informal. They fall far short of laying a base for future, more liberal reform. Some of these delegate-constituent relationships still smack strongly of particularism; others smack of patrimonialism and/or corporatism. O'Brien's respondents focused not so much on lawmaking as on winning particular favors and special remedies for their constituents. Such particular solutions to constituent problems do not necessarily contribute to the growth of a "rule of law" and institutionalization that can further liberal legislative reforms. In fact, they may undermine them to the extent they turn legislators toward special favors and bribery. It would be an ironic but a plausible outcome of strengthening Chinese legislative institutions if legislators finally became powerful enough to be "worth bribing." NPC officials who "represented" members of the official trade unions did so at least in part because they chose to see these people as their constituents—but also in part because the party leadership has granted a certain number of NPC and Standing Committee seats to trade union delegates. The center still has a good deal of control over the avenues of access. Social constituents, such as rank-and-file ACFTU members, still lack institutionalized formal control over even the few NPC deputies who see themselves as "representing" them. Thus increased social access to the NPC is still not much stronger than the various delegates' informal commitment to forge those social links and is too informal to begin to contribute to genuine popular accountability.

Possibilities for Post-Deng Legislative Reform

Early in the Deng era, the party leadership structured the people's congress and electoral system in a way that largely froze out any prospects for substantial liberal legislative reform, particularly in placing greater obstacles to popular accountability as one went higher up in the congress system. As a result the NPC has focused on institutionalizing its influence over lawmaking, in which it has become a very significant player. What impact will the NPC's development pattern during the Deng era have on legislative development, particularly its prospects for further liberal reforms, now that Deng has passed from the scene? Deng's vision of the NPC's development, to the limited extent we can know it from his writings, held the NPC to a modestly influential policy role. It granted the NPC no more than a "consultative" voice to the CCP-appointed leaders of the key organizational, social, and ethno-regional groups that the party wants to court. This may be as powerful a role as Deng would ever have felt comfortable with.

In considering the NPC's future in the post-Deng era, we can envision a possible scenario in which the top leadership is relatively effective in establishing its power within the NPC (as Jiang Zemin certainly appeared to be when he eased out rivals such as Qiao Shi

at the 1997 Fifteenth Party Congress) and attempts to use this power
to suppress the NPC's new openness and influence. To what extent
have the changes in the NPC become institutionalized and difficult
to reverse? The analysis here suggests they would be difficult to roll
back, because they are rooted in several traditionally powerful forces
in the Chinese system: the organizational interests of a cohort of
powerful party leaders, backed by a growing policy bureaucracy, and
emerging elite norms supporting moderately strong internal debate.
All of this suggests that if Jiang directly tried to re-silence the NPC,
he would not only be undermining his popular legitimacy by attacking the most prominent party-approved institution of "socialist democracy," but would also be creating a number of serious enemies
among his own party elite.

The NPC's current role may also change in the post-Deng era
if some contenders in a future power struggle feel tempted to
strengthen the NPC as a means of establishing their own populist
credentials at the expense of Jiang Zemin (or some subsequent
successor). Some NPC advisors, speaking before Deng's death, believed that proposals for direct, multicandidate elections for the
provincial congresses, and later for the NPC itself, were likely to
circulate among the top leadership within no more than two to three
years after Deng's passing. At this writing, some Western scholars
report that such proposals are already circulating in Chinese intellectual circles.[41]

The NPC's institutionalized influence with little liberalization during the Deng era may lead in the post-Deng NPC, or a successor
legislature, to liberalization via an "elite path." That path would
extend legislative influence gradually to a variety of key leadership
factions, bureaucratic interests, and leading representatives of the
social, ethnic, or regional interests that form the traditional support
base of the ancien régime. Only cautiously would it extend influence
to other interests that the regime wished to court, or which it felt it
could no longer safely exclude. This is the path to development that
a large number of Western and Central European legislatures took,
and even parallels the gradual expansion of suffrage and legislative
development in the United States.[42] The greatest obstacle on this
path is that various groups, and not just the Communist Party, may

try to freeze or limit the growth of legislative access. O'Brien and Li's research reveals that there is chillingly strong support among a number of intellectual reformers for an elitist "democratic" vision of the legislature. In an effort to strengthen its institutional influence, they advise the NPC to focus on recruiting delegates of "high quality"—that is, intellectuals. These delegates would be permitted to engage in far freer and more open policy debate than is currently possible. But O'Brien and Li also quote advocates of this view as supporting efforts to keep the number of peasant and worker delegates to a minimum.

Nonetheless, there are also powerful reasons for believing that the NPC's long-term development may benefit from having started to become influential before it becomes "open" or "democratic." Jeffery Hahn, a scholar of legislative development in the Soviet Union and Russia, has argued that the rancor and stalemate which preceded Boris Yeltsin's violent abolition of the Russian Parliament resulted from the rapid mobilization of small parties and social interests into the historically weak Parliament, which made it impossible for the parliamentary leadership and Yeltsin to reach workable consensus policies concerning reform.[43] Hahn's argument echoes Samuel Huntington's famous formula that when social mobilization exceeds political institutionalization, disorder and praetorianism may result.

Even though such arguments may disturb those of us with democratic biases because they betray far greater trust in the political elite than they do in the "unruly" masses, from the long-term standpoint of institutionalizing the legislature and effecting its stable liberalization, the path of "influence" before democracy may still be preferable—not because we should have little faith in civil society and the masses, but rather because we have so little faith in the current leaders. For some time to come, any genuine progress toward stable liberal legislative reform in China will require the assent of those leaders who currently hold executive and coercive power. In the years after Deng's death, when the CCP and the PLA are likely to confront dramatic issues of liberalization and social order, the most imminent threat to China's legislative development is likely to come from leaders who threaten to use their executive and coercive power, à la Yeltsin, to close down the NPC if they feel threatened by it. The current holders of executive and coercive power are likely to be far less apprehensive of a legislature which is at first led by "loyal" members of the ancien régime (in this case, the party elders), then institutionalizes its policymaking influence, and expands access and accountability to broader social groups later and gradually. If this proves to be the stable path to a liberal legislative transition in China, then those who succeed to power in the future will, ironically, owe at least a small debt to Peng Zhen, Wan Li, Qiao Shi, and the NPC's party elders for the increasingly influential, if illiberal, legislature that they built.

LIANJIANG LI
KEVIN J. O'BRIEN

6 | The Struggle over Village Elections

The decade leading up to Deng Xiaoping's death produced few headlines announcing breakthroughs in political reform. Now, a host of outside observers, including the U.S. President, Vice President, and Speaker of the House, have been quoted praising China's village elections. Is the long drought over? Has meaningful political reform begun—not in Beijing, but in China's one million villages?

There are indeed signs that democratic reform is taking root in the countryside. For one, efforts have been made to increase the popular accountability of grass-roots leaders. In 1987 the Organic Law of Villagers' Committees established villagers' committees as mass organizations of self-government through which villagers manage their own affairs, educate themselves, and meet their own needs. These committees are composed of three to seven members, each of whom serves for three years. Committee members are chosen in popular elections, in which all adult, registered villagers have the right to vote and stand for office. Under the law, elected cadres have prescribed powers and limited but real autonomy from township officials directly above them. Township leaders are no longer, for example, permitted to order village cadres about; instead, they can only guide (zhidao) them in their work. Since the Organic Law came into effect in 1988, self-government has been rolled out in several waves. By the late 1990s, in parts of the countryside, villagers had participated in as many as four elections.[1]

These reforms have received much attention outside China. The Carter Center, the International Republican Institute, and various embassies have sent observers to monitor village elections. At the same time, the Ford Foundation, the United Nations Development Program, the Carter Center, and the Asia Foundation have worked with Chinese authorities to standardize election procedures and to train local election officials.

Western scholars, for their part, have examined both the rationale behind the Organic Law and the law's implementation. Kevin O'Brien has described village self-government as an effort to exchange limited democratic rights for popular compliance with state policies.[2] Daniel Kelliher has suggested that elections are designed to improve the quality of village leadership and are regarded, even by their proponents, as a way to implicate villagers in the execution of unpopular policies.[3] Survey research by Melanie Manion has shown that well-run, competitive elections can improve congruence between cadres and villagers.[4]

Meanwhile, a number of conjectures about the relationship between economic development and the spread of self-government have been put forward—often based on research in different regions. Susan Lawrence has suggested that poor, agricultural villages may be the pacesetters in village democracy; O'Brien has argued that autonomy is easiest to promote in villages that are not among the poorest and, in fact, have prospering collective enterprises; Amy Epstein has hypothesized that free elections are most likely to occur in middle-income, developing villages; and Jean Oi has found some evidence that as income increases, participation in villagers' assemblies and the competitiveness of elections generally decrease.[5]

Why would an authoritarian regime promote grass-roots democratic reform? Where has opposition to village self-government appeared and how, if at all, has it been overcome? What effects do elections have on village governance? Using interviews, leadership speeches, and archival sources, this chapter examines the struggle over village elections. It starts by explaining how and why several party elders championed the Organic Law in the face of widespread opposition. Then it outlines why some local leaders, from the province down to the village, have doubts about village elections. Next, it shows that in many places ordinary villagers have played an unusually active part in implementing the law, including engaging in open conflict with rural officials who deprive them of their rights. It concludes by discussing the impact that free and fair elections can have on rural governance.

Peng Zhen's Vision (and Bo Yibo's Timely Support)

It is well known that the Organic Law was hotly debated in the National People's Congress and was literally pushed through by Peng Zhen, then chairman of the NPC Standing Committee.[6] But why Peng was so committed to villagers' autonomy remains to be explored. Excerpts from several of his speeches suggest that Peng's sponsorship of the law sprang from his understanding of how to construct "socialist democracy." According to Peng, inasmuch as China has almost no tradition of self-rule, democratic habits must be cultivated among both party leaders and ordinary citizens. Realizing socialist democracy thus has two dimensions. For the leadership, regard for democracy is to be nurtured by strengthening people's congresses; for the masses, democratic ways of thinking are to be inculcated by self-governance. The heart of "democratic training" in the countryside is the promotion of villagers' autonomy (cunmin zizhi). By electing their own leaders and participating in grass-roots decisionmaking, 900 million Chinese villagers will learn how to manage village affairs. After rural residents have become skilled at running their own villages, Peng has said, they may move on to govern townships and counties.[7]

Behind Peng's desire to boost the nation's democratic consciousness lay a concern that worsening relations between cadres and farmers might cripple the party's ability to rule. Peng expressed this fear most clearly when the Organic Law met with unexpectedly strong opposition at the 1987 NPC. Though few legislators questioned the law's overall rationale, many said that Chinese villagers were not ready for self-government and that elections would make it more difficult for township officials to enforce state policies; some NPC deputies even predicted that the law would lead to an immediate breakdown of political control.[8] Peng agreed that villagers' autonomy might "make rural cadres' life a little harder" (that is, it might complicate policy implementation in the short run), but he also insisted that self-government would not produce chaos because "the masses accept what is reasonable." In response to the argument that villagers' autonomy was premature, Peng countered that grass-roots democracy was in fact urgently needed. He lamented how relations between cadres and villagers had deteriorated since the 1950s, noting that some rural leaders had become "local emperors" (tu huangdi)—cadres who flattered officials at higher levels but "used excessive force against villagers and even illegally jailed them." If such trends were not checked, he warned, villagers would "sooner or later attack our rural cadres with their shoulder poles." To prevent a further decline in cadre-mass relations, according to Peng, top-down supervision was not enough: "Who supervises rural cadres? Can we supervise them? No, not even if we had 48 hours a day." The only solution, Peng concluded, was to promote village self-government, so that China's rural masses themselves could select and oversee village cadres.[9]

A belief that grass-roots elections would reduce the risk of rural unrest is even more apparent in party elder Bo Yibo's defense of village self-rule. One year after the Organic Law went into effect, it again became a center of controversy as political reforms stalled following the suppression of the 1989 protest movement. Opponents of villagers' autonomy demanded that the law be scrapped, arguing that it was an example of the "bourgeois liberalization" condoned by fallen party general secretary Zhao Ziyang. Some critics even credited the law to Zhao, who in fact had no great sympathy for grass-roots democracy.[10]

To resolve the debate, a high-level team was dispatched to study how village-level political organizations were functioning. A subsequent report prepared by the Ministry of Civil Affairs (MoCA) made an especially strong case for village democracy. With unusual frankness, ministry participants in the investigation wrote: "The evidence indicates that the political situation in the countryside is extremely serious. It is entirely possible that an even greater crisis may be triggered if erroneous policies regarding the construction of basic-level rural government are adopted." In their view, to deter instability, the relationship among the party, government, and China's rural population needed to be modified. The leadership had already attempted to resuscitate basic-level political organizations using various methods, and elections had proved to be the best way to improve relations between cadres and villagers.[11]

But the MoCA report only fueled the controversy further. As late as early 1990, supporters of tighter party control and other skeptics who worried about instability remained unconvinced that villagers would vote for cadres who enforced unpopular state policies. As the debate dragged on, efforts to implement the law nationwide were suspended.[12]

Then Bo Yibo came to the rescue. Bo's staff obtained a copy of the ministry's report, and after Bo read it he declared it "brilliant."[13] As a party elder and one of Deng Xiaoping's closest allies, Bo's backing for villagers' autonomy was decisive. Shortly after Bo threw his support behind the reforms, Song Ping, then a member of the Standing Committee of the Politburo, put the controversy over the Organic Law to an end. At a National Conference on the Construction of Village-Level Organizations in August 1990, Song instructed that the law should be implemented rather than debated. The summary report of the conference accordingly affirmed that the law should be enforced throughout the nation.[14] Four months later, the Central Committee issued the conference report as CCP Document Number 19 (1990). With these endorsements in hand, the MoCA resumed its efforts to implement village self-government and directed provincial governments to set up "demonstration villages."

Bo Yibo's support for grass-roots democratization was no accident. After communes were abolished in the mid-1980s, relations between cadres and villagers had worsened in many places, largely because villagers became more knowledgeable about their exploitation and less dependent on village cadres. Like Peng Zhen, Bo was deeply concerned with rural political decay, and he agreed with Mao when Mao said that people's democracy was the surest way to maintain the party's popular base.[15] In his 1991 memoirs, Bo recalled Mao's 1945 conversation with the historian Huang Yanpei, in which Mao argued that the party could escape the historical cycle of rapid rise followed by quick decline by letting the people oversee the government. Then Bo added: "More than forty years have passed. . . . Today we cannot say we have completely escaped this 'cycle'; . . . The task remains undone; the whole party must work hard!"[16] Considering how tense relations between cadres and villagers had become by the late 1980s, it is not surprising that advocates of village self-government found a sympathizer in Bo Yibo.

It should be noted, however, that the text of the Organic Law does not make it obvious that grass-roots elections are the linchpin of the villagers' autonomy program. In fact, the law only mentions elections twice and it places self-management on a par with self-education and self-service. This is most likely due to Peng Zhen's failure to disclose his reasoning when the MoCA began drafting the law in 1984. Until the law drew fire at the 1987 NPC, Peng's commentary on the law usually centered on how villagers' autonomy would improve public order by curbing gambling, preventing theft, and reforming idlers, and how it would enhance self-service by enabling cadres to extract the sums required for paving roads, building schools, and maintaining irrigation systems.[17] Only when NPC deputies (many of whom were local officials themselves) insisted that self-rule would interfere with policy implementation and lead to rural unrest did Peng shift to arguing that village elections were precisely what was needed to reinvigorate grass-roots governance and to ward off political instability.[18]

Implementing Village Elections: Local Opposition

Since the Organic Law, as passed in 1987, is brief and vaguely worded, even Ministry of Civil Affairs officials were at first unsure how to enforce it. The first director of the ministry's Rural Division of the Bureau of Basic-Level Governance Construction, which is responsible for implementing the law, admitted that it took two years for the MoCA to realize that the core of villagers' autonomy was electing village cadres.[19] Because of this uncertainty, the ministry's first circular (February 26, 1988) on the law did not even mention elections. Not until the end of 1989 did Lian Yin, deputy minister of civil affairs, announce that village elections were the crux of implementation. And it was only on September 26, 1990, that the ministry decreed that village elections must be held.[20]

From the start, self-government met with local opposition. Even before the law was placed in the ministry's hands, while it was awaiting final approval by the Standing Committee of the NPC, several provinces established village administrative offices *(cun gong suo)*.[21] These offices were de facto arms of the state staffed by township appointees; they were subordinate to townships much as brigades had been to communes. Zhao Ziyang had praised their formation in Guangxi, but the MoCA attempted to brake their spread by arguing that this experiment should be limited to that province. In practice, however, Yunnan, Guangdong, and Hainan ignored the ministry's edict and set up village administrative offices as well.[22]

Provincial misgivings were also made clear by the sluggish rate at which provincial people's congresses enacted legislation concerning the Organic Law. Of the twenty-four provincial implementation regulations promulgated to date, only two were approved in 1988, the year the law came into effect. Notably, Guangdong, Beijing, and Shanghai remain among six provincial-level governments that have failed to pass enforcement guidelines.[23] And even in provinces where implementing statutes exist, top provincial officials have often communicated their lack of enthusiasm for village self-governance by failing to say a single word in support of the law.

Opposition to grass-roots elections appears to be most intense in the lower reaches of the state hierarchy. It is here that concerns about policy implementation and potential instability are most immediate. County resistance to village self-rule, for example, is visibly stronger than that of provinces. Before the Central Committee endorsed the Organic Law in 1990, some county leaders warned that any official who dared to implement it would be subject to disciplinary action.[24] Even when provincial leaders, such as deputy governors responsible for rural work, have actively promoted villagers' autonomy, county party chiefs and government heads have often flouted the law. Particularly in locations where the "cadre responsibility system" *(ganbu gangwei mubiao guanli zerenzhi)* has been introduced, many county leaders go to extraordinary lengths to enforce "hard targets," such as birth control and tax collection, but ignore "soft targets" such as village elections. These officials sometimes transmit provincial election regulations to townships, but then fail to monitor their enforcement.[25]

When county leaders show little interest in villagers' autonomy, townships often do not convene elections. A 1989 survey in Shandong, for instance, revealed that over 60 percent of township leaders disapproved of village self-government.[26] In Hebei, a township official bluntly told a Xinhua reporter that "presently, villagers don't know how to govern themselves, and we won't allow them to govern themselves!"[27] Even when county officials instruct township leaders to enforce the law, they often hold elections only if they believe the incumbents will win. They may also feign compliance with the law or impose onerous restrictions on nominees proposed by ordinary citizens. They frequently, for instance, monopolize nominations, ban unapproved candidates, or conduct snap elections, in the hopes of catching challengers unprepared.[28]

The aversion township cadres feel to village elections is not, as some Chinese observers claim, entirely a product of their "low democratic consciousness."[29] It arises partly because township leaders rely on village cadres to carry out unpopular policies and they fear that elections may cost them their most dependable agents. In the words of a township party secretary in Hebei, "I already have difficulty leading (lingdao) village cadres, I guarantee that guiding (zhidao) them will not work."[30] Why? Township governments have dozens of ongoing responsibilities, including arduous, time-consuming jobs such as enforcing birth control, procuring grain, and collecting taxes and fees. They are also assigned many extraordinary tasks such as conducting the "strike-hard," anticrime campaign. Township leaders often complain that they are overburdened and must count on village cadres to be their "legs."[31] In one large Hebei township, where few villages had paved roads and several did not have a single telephone, the township had only twenty-four staff members; with "one thousand strings above threading one needle below," the township party secretary felt that unless all village cadres were firmly on his side, he could not meet the county's expectations.[32]

Almost all township officials are initially skeptical that free elections will produce dutiful village leaders.[33] Decollectivization and the end of class labeling have weakened the ability of village cadres to elicit compliance from reluctant villagers. Under the commune system, village leaders "could use a chicken feather to issue an order. Now, even when they have a real order, some villagers ignore it as if it were a chicken feather."[34] At the same time, township leaders have few rewards to offer their most conscientious "underlings"; they generally cannot, for example, make them state officials (that is, promote them out of the village) or increase their salary much. Townships thus find it necessary to wink at grasping or corrupt behavior by cooperative "local emperors" who are willing to do their bidding.[35] Insofar as the township's most dutiful agents are often allowed to be predatory and are despised by many of the villagers they rule, township officials resist exposing them to elections they would certainly lose.[36]

Some local bosses, who are sure they have popular support, have little to fear from self-rule.[37] But few village cadres brave elections eagerly. Instead, they often grumble that they alone confront the masses at the ballot box: village self-government subjects them to risks that cadres above them do not face. In the words of one cadre in Shandong: "Elections at higher levels are all scams, why should village elections be taken any more seriously?"[38] When they suspect they will be voted out of office, village cadres may go so far as to bribe township officials to subvert the Organic Law. They may, for instance, coax township leaders to cancel or fix an election by offering gifts, hosting banquets, or purposefully losing at Mahjong.[39]

Popular Demands for Village Elections

That village elections have not been thwarted by local opposition, according to one MoCA official, is partly a consequence of actions taken by ordinary villagers.[40] Rural residents have been quick to recognize that grass-roots elections give them a way to dislodge corrupt, partial, and incompetent cadres. A villager in Hebei said when he first heard about elections: "We didn't know there was a law that permits us to speak up and take charge. Had we known, we would have long ago voted out cadres who do nothing but wine and dine."[41] Given that township party and government officials are usually willing to tolerate very unpopular village leaders as long as they meet their hard targets, clashes between villagers and township leaders over elections often occur.

In some cases, when township officials fail to organize an election, villagers may refuse to cooperate with revenue collection, grain procurement, or family planning. In a Hebei village, for instance, several township appointees were corrupt and managed the community's collective enterprises poorly. A group of villagers protested by withholding their taxes and fees. Although local police were dispatched to pressure the recalcitrant villagers to pay up, they were unable to collect the outstanding sums. The township then reshuffled the village leadership twice, but both "operations miscarried" because the resulting blend of new and old appointees failed to investigate the complaints of financial irregularities. After nine rounds of consultation, the township party secretary conceded that the village had lost faith in whomever he appointed. As a last resort, he called an election, which produced a wholly new leadership that had credibility with the local population and was able to extract revenues and promote economic development. From the township's vantage point, the "worst plan had turned into the best plan."[42]

Besides turning their backs on appointed cadres, villagers often confront township leaders who fail to comply with the Organic Law. In one poor Hebei village, for instance, a group of farmers lodged a series of complaints requesting the dismissal of several inept cadres. After the township rejected their appeals, the villagers stationed rotating groups of petitioners in the township to pursue their complaints. One day, one of the villagers came across a copy of the Organic Law lying on a desk in a township office. Immediately realizing its import, he showed it to his fellow petitioners. After they studied the law, they resolved to "lodge complaints against the township government for violating the Organic Law by not holding democratic elections." The complainants then came up with a scheme to ensure that their pressure would not be ignored. They divided themselves into three "teams," two of which went to the township government and the county civil affairs bureau, while a third, composed of village party members, traveled to the county organization department. Facing the indignation of villagers demanding enforcement of a law that had been casually ignored, the township government promptly agreed to convene an election. In the subsequent balloting, the villager who had originally discovered the Organic Law was elected as the villagers' committee director.[43] In a similar case, when township officials in Shanxi publicized the Organic Law but refused to carry out an election, farmers from two villages occupied a township office and would not end their "sit-in" until officials agreed to conduct free elections in which unpopular cadres could be voted out.[44]

To enhance their bargaining position, resourceful villagers often seek support from higher-level officials in the expectation that they will take village self-government seriously.[45] When defying township leaders who fix elections, villagers often lodge complaints at the county or even higher levels. In one case, after a township in Liaoning forbade unapproved candidates from running for office and did not allow secret balloting, over a dozen villagers traveled at their own expense to the county town, then the provincial capital, and finally Beijing to lodge complaints. They knew the Organic Law by heart and recited it when petitioning officials for a new election.[46] In 1996 a group of villagers from Yixian county, Hebei, went all the way to the MoCA to protest unfair elections. The widely watched television program *Focus/Interview* broadcast three reports on their complaint and its origins. Finally, at the instruction of the MoCA, civil affairs officials from Hebei and Baoding city were sent to organize new elections. Soon after this collective complaint became public knowledge, the director of the Hebei Bureau of Basic-Level Government Construction, who had not been keen on village self-rule, was transferred to another position. And Hebei's party chief then made grass-roots elections a key element of his "fish-water project" (*yu shui gongcheng*)—an effort to improve cadre-mass relations so that leaders and ordinary people were no longer separate like "oil and water" or antagonistic like "fire and water."[47]

As these examples reveal, the implementation of village self-government has generally been somewhat sluggish. The Organic Law has encountered much opposition, especially at the township level.

Unless the incumbents are likely to be returned to office or village government has collapsed, township leaders are strongly inclined to prevent or to sabotage elections. Consequently, villagers almost invariably need to apply pressure and locate elite allies in order to realize their electoral rights.[48]

How many of China's one million villages have conducted free and fair elections? Estimates vary widely. Ministry officials claim that "at least one round of relatively democratic elections have been carried out in about 80 percent of China's villages," the U.S. State Department estimates that the correct figure is one quarter to one third, and the editor of a Chinese magazine that focuses on township affairs puts the number at "no more than 10 percent."[49]

The Impact of Village Elections

Grass-roots elections have been welcomed by many villagers and tolerated by a growing number of local leaders. It is true that in some places "local bullies" *(eba)* have bought elections or coerced villagers to vote for them, while electoral competition has also, at times, intensified lineage conflict, particularly in the southern provinces of Jiangxi, Hunan, Zhejiang, and Guizhou.[50] Nevertheless, village self-government has often made cadres more accountable to villagers. Where elections are the norm, village cadres live in a different world than officials above them. One villagers' committee director explained: "We village cadres depend on the 'ground line' *(dixian)* [that is, villagers' votes], those at higher levels depend on the 'antenna' *(tianxian)* [that is, appointment by higher levels]. If we wish to be cadres, we must win the masses' support. Unless the masses raise their hands, we can't be cadres."[51]

At the same time, village elections have not noticeably reduced the responsiveness of village cadres to lawful instructions received from township leaders. To the surprise of many township officials, village cadres who identify with villagers are generally scrupulous about carrying out township-assigned tasks. Closer relations with villagers, in other words, can actually smooth policy implementation. In order to ensure that election committees, which are ordinarily chaired by a representative of the township or by the village party secretary, do not disqualify them, nominees as a rule announce that they will execute all state policies. To win popular support, challengers may pledge fairer policy implementation, but few pander to villagers by vowing to defy all demands from above. Moreover, after they are elected, village cadres often take the lead in complying with state policies, especially family planning.[52] Insofar as they can then induce most villagers to follow suit, village leaders are in a strong position to apply pressure on the few remaining hold-outs. They may, for example, threaten to single out recalcitrants for public humiliation. In Shandong's Zhaoyuan county, elected cadres assign up to ten "stars" to every household. This system has reportedly been remarkably effective in stigmatizing villagers who violate state policies or village rules, such as allowing livestock to graze their neighbors' crops. Young women, for instance, have refused to marry into households that receive eight stars or fewer.[53]

Elections can also produce material benefits for a community.[54] When putting together a platform, candidates invariably promise to "do good things for fellow villagers." Opening village accounts to public inspection and developing the collective economy are two common pledges. Other platform promises include impartially allocating land for house building and paying more attention to schools, roads, and the provision of running water. Often elected cadres are able to deliver on their pledges. They are, for example, well placed to enlist mass support for public projects. In two remote villages in Fujian, newly elected cadres, who said villagers now respected their authority, raised funds and mobilized labor to complete a 15-kilometer road that had been started and abandoned on three occasions under township supervision.[55] In a Hebei village, appointed cadres had been unable to repair a run-down school because villagers suspected that their "donations" would end up in the cadres' pockets. After free elections, however, the new leadership was able to collect nearly 40,000 yuan, with which they promptly rebuilt the school.[56]

In addition to improving ties between cadres and villagers, grassroots elections have also helped restructure relations between villagers' committees and village party branches. This relationship was not addressed in the original Organic Law, and all indications are that it will not be clarified in the revised law that in mid-1998 awaited approval.[57] In some locations, nevertheless, elected cadres openly try to undermine the village party secretary.[58] In a Hebei village, for example, as soon as a nonparty member was elected director of the villagers' representative assembly (VRA), he made the following announcement over the village loudspeaker: "I was elected by the whole village, the party secretary was elected solely by party members. From now on, I am the number one leader in the village. You should come to see me when you have problems."[59] According to an MoCA official, "contradictions" of this sort are increasingly common; in fact, "challenging the party secretary is one of the first things many villagers' committee directors do."[60]

Where a party branch enjoys little support, villagers in some areas have disputed its right to nominate individuals to run in villagers' committee elections.[61] Recently, in response to popular demands, a "double-ballot system" (liangpiao zhi) was introduced in selected locations. In one Shanxi county, all villagers can now participate in candidate screening; party members who do not win over half the votes are then barred from standing for membership in the party branch.[62] The Central Organization Department has recommended that all provinces experiment with this remarkable and largely unreported reform.[63]

While there are only scattered signs that grass-roots democratic reform, as Peng Zhen envisioned, will soon expand from villages to townships, elections are certainly affecting the relationship between village cadres and township officials. Elected cadres may be willing to meet township quotas, but they are also more willing, in the name of their constituents' lawful interests, to confront township officials who concoct unauthorized "local policies" (tu zhengce). An elected cadre in Hebei, for instance, proudly said that he would resist township meddling in the management of a village orchard because "this is the masses' business and it falls within the scope of villagers' autonomy."[64] Elected cadres are also becoming more courageous in standing up to grasping township officials. In one township, granary cadres offered villagers below-market prices and demanded that the agricultural tax be paid in cash rather than beans. A group of angry farmers went to the home of the director of the villagers' representative assembly and brought this to his attention. The VRA head immediately went to the township, where he persuaded the township party secretary to halt the granary's effort to inflate its own profits. His actions, according to one of the members of the VRA, would have been inconceivable if the VRA director had been appointed by the township.[65]

Conclusion

Grass-roots political reform makes it possible for villagers to hold officials accountable in exchange for their compliance with state policies. But this exchange, even in the best of circumstances, is not self-implementing. Enforcement of the Organic Law often involves a struggle between villagers who demand improved accountability and township leaders who, initially at least, refuse to cede their authority to appoint village cadres.

Because villagers must often fight for their rights, they tend to be realistic about what can be gained from basic-level elections. On the one hand, they exploit any opportunity to rid themselves of unfair, corrupt, or self-serving village cadres. On the other hand, they typically do not vote for candidates who run "against the state." Although some villagers, for instance, have threatened to vote out village leaders who enforce family planning, most reports suggest that cadres do not lose elections if they are fair and honest when allocating birth control quotas.[66] Villagers seem to be similarly practical about local fees. In a Shandong village, a candidate for villagers' committee director promised to resist all new impositions, saying: "If I am elected committee director, you don't have to pay any fees. If any township official dares to ask me for fees, I'll beat him up." He was not elected.[67]

Though implementing village elections remains a challenge, the reforms are picking up momentum. Both Li Peng's Government Work Report at the 1997 NPC and Jiang Zemin's report to the Fifteenth Party Congress reaffirmed Beijing's commitment to "grass-roots mass autonomy."[68] Provincial people's congresses, for their part, continue to enact legislation detailing election procedures. In Fujian, a provincial pacesetter, primaries became mandatory in 1997 and elections for *all* villagers' committee positions were, for the first time, slated to be competitive.[69]

At the same time, popular demands to hold free and fair elections continue to grow. Under pressure from villagers, more and more county leaders have urged township leaders to hold multicandidate, village elections.[70] Some township officials have also recognized that failing to permit free elections often produces a flood of complaints and may risk collective action.[71] Some township cadres have even come to appreciate the benefits that village elections offer to officials such as themselves. Although the Organic Law still is a trial law, MoCA officials are confident that "the spread of free village elections, just like the household responsibility system, has become an irreversible trend."[72] It is not yet clear if they are right.

TIANJIAN SHI

7 | Mass Political Behavior in Beijing

"Perhaps the most widespread generalization linking political systems to other aspects of society has been that
democracy is related to the state of economic development."[1] Economic development has important social consequences, some of which have a significant impact on
a nation's political life. Studies of modernization, for example, have demonstrated that economic development
sharply increases the general level of political participation in many societies.[2] Among the reasons offered for
this empirical connection, a common idea is that the
process of economic development leads to clusters of social changes that drastically alter the class, organizational,
and social structure of a nation and that these are associated with new forms of political participation.

Social mobilization theory identifies three areas of social and political life known to vary with the level of economic development. First, economic development
changes the function of government. As a nation develops, its government becomes responsible for more regulation and redistribution. Individuals' relationships with
the nation-state become critical.[3] As the welfare of the
people is affected by government decisions, they realize
the relevance of public authority to their needs and try to
influence its decisions.[4] Second, economic development
changes the social structure. As a nation develops, the

social stratification of the population is altered.[5] Levels of political participation are found to increase with increases in crucial socio-economic resources. Finally, economic development changes individuals' psychological orientation.[6] By dramatically changing the relationship between citizens and the state and increasing socioeconomic resources for individuals, economic development may transform people's orientation toward politics.[7] As members of the population become more aware of the impact of politics on their lives, more concerned about politics, and more politically effective, they are more likely to engage in political activities.[8]

Following the death of Mao in 1976, the Chinese government embarked on a series of reforms to transform a highly centralized socialist economy into a market-oriented one. The new policies facilitated rapid economic development as well as revolutionary changes in many aspects of China's social life. Per capita income and median level of education increased. With the gradual retreat of the government from economic life, its ability to control society declined.[9] Although independent associational interest groups are still not allowed, the regime's existing organizations used to control people at the grass-roots level, such as trade unions and women's associations, have begun to represent their members in bargaining with the authorities.[10]

How do the changes brought about by economic reforms influence political behavior? What are the prospects for a democratic transition in China? Some scholars argue that economic development and the move to the market in China, as elsewhere, will eventually bring dramatic changes and lead to a full-fledged democracy.[11] Others believe that China's party-state sociopolitical establishment and authoritarian political culture will twist the relationship between economic development and political change.[12] At the heart of the debate is whether political leaders, institutions, and culture in China can cripple the relationship between economic development and democratization.[13]

If democracy is interpreted as rule by the people, then understanding changes in people's participatory behavior is crucial in charting the impact of economic development on the political process in China. Using survey data gathered at two points in time in

Beijing, this chapter examines the impact of economic development on resources and participation. The analysis is developed in four steps: First, it identifies changes in the social context, social structure, and individuals' psychological orientation brought about by economic development between 1988 and 1996. Second it investigates whether the level and intensity of participation changed from 1988 to 1996. Third, the structure of social contextual, sociostructural, and individual orientation correlates of participation are compared at two points in time to examine the changes in their impact on individual participation. Finally, with the aid of multivariate analysis, the chapter examines the impact of the changes in social context, social structure, and individuals' psychological orientation on these variables with regard to people's political behavior when the effects of other variables are controlled.

Data

The data used here come from two surveys of the urban population in Beijing. The first survey was conducted from December 1988 to January 1989. Although some of the reform measures had already been introduced at the time of the first survey, they had yet to bring significant changes to urban China.[14]

The second survey was conducted in July 1996. By this time, dramatic changes in the function of the government, in the social structure, and in individuals' psychological orientation had occurred. Per capita income and the median level of education had increased substantially. The structural changes brought about by economic development also began to alter residents' orientation toward politics.[15]

After June 4, 1989, the regime tightened control over the population and became more willing to suppress unauthorized expression. Because this tightened surveillance influenced people's political behavior, the differences revealed in the analysis may seem spurious. This would be true, however, only if we were to find that the level of participation in Beijing declined over the eight-year period. If, on the contrary, we find participation there increasing despite the regime's becoming more repressive, our confidence in these findings can only be strengthened.

The two surveys were not designed as a panel study, and therefore the populations sampled were not identical.[16] Can we compare these two populations to study the impact of economic development on political behavior? The answer to this question is positive, for both theoretical and technical reasons. Theoretically, both population replacement and individual changes are assumed to play equally important roles in the process of modernization.[17] Technically, certain statistical procedures can be employed to disentangle the impact of population replacement from the impact of individual change on political behavior. A difference of eight years warrants a middle-range interpretation of the observed changes in behavior. Although the findings regarding changes in the marginal distribution of individuals' political attitudes and political participation in Beijing do not necessarily apply to the rest of China, the change in the relationship between resources and participation can be generalized to the whole society.

Changes in Social Context, Social Structure, and Psychological Orientation over Eight Years

The economic reforms from 1988 to 1996 brought dramatic changes to people's lives. The average yearly salary for urban residents in Beijing increased from 1,066 yuan in 1988 to 1,638 yuan in 1996.[18] Per capita living space changed from 7.17 to 8.87 square meters, which represents a net increase of 23.7 percent.[19] When the general standard of living increased, the middle stratum of the population expanded, as predicted by modernization theory. Figure 7.1 shows the change in meat consumption for families at different income levels. The yearly meat consumption of lower-income Beijing families increased from 29.28 kilograms in 1988 to 35.49 kilograms in 1996.[20] More important, the shape of the curve becomes flatter, which indicates that the differences in the meat consumption level between higher- and lower-income families were reduced. The decrease in the gap is due to dramatic increases in meat consumption by lower-income families.[21]

Figure 7.2 examines the ownership of durable consumer products and reveals the same pattern of change. By 1996, higher-income families in Beijing had more than one color television and refrigerator. At the same time, though, nearly all poor families had at least one of each of these items. The shape of the population had changed over the eight-year period.

The literature on modernization predicts that an expansion of government activities will bring previously apathetic people into contact with the authorities. To determine the impact of economic reform on the social context, we asked respondents to report whether government activities at various levels had an impact on their lives. The answers presented in Table 7.1 suggest two major changes.

More people in the 1996 survey reported that local government was relevant to their lives than in the 1988 survey. Ten percent more people in 1996 think neighborhood committees have some impact on their lives, and 18 percent more people believe that the activities

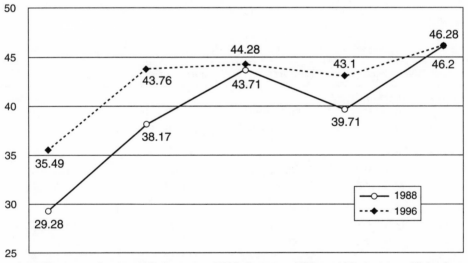

Figure 7.1 Meat consumption for families of different income levels in 1988 and 1996 (in kilograms) (*Beijing tongji nianjian, 1989, 1997*)

of the municipal government have some influence over their lives as compared with 1988. The percentage of people who think municipal government has a great effect on their lives nearly doubled between the two surveys.

The impact of the central government on people's lives declined, however. One of the most important goals of market reforms in urban China was to lessen the central government's involvement in economic activities. Many functions of the central government, such as planning production and providing social welfare and education, are now the responsibility of local government or nongovernmental organizations. Economic development in China, contrary to the process in other developing societies, has shifted many functions of the central government to local levels. The changes brought about by the economic reforms have made people feel that the *direct* impact of the central government on their lives has declined. They have yet to realize the indirect effects of government activity.

Our inquiry into the impact of economic development on social structure will focus on education and media participation.[22] Table 7.2 presents the mean scale scores of educational achievement for

Table 7.1 Government impact on people's lives

	No effect (*N*)	Some effect (*N*)	Great effect (*N*)	Don't know (*N*)
Neighborhood committee				
1988	60.1 (455)	29.5 (223)	7.9 (60)	2.5 (19)
1996	52.2 (469)	39.0 (349)	6.6 (59)	1.9 (17)
City government				
1988	63.4 (480)	22.6 (171)	7.5 (57)	6.5 (49)
1996	40.8 (365)	40.8 (365)	13.2 (118)	5.1 (46)
Central government				
1988	33.2 (251)	26.7 (202)	33.9 (257)	6.2 (47)
1996	43.0 (384)	33.7 (301)	18.7 (167)	4.7 (42)

Source: Beijing surveys, 1988 and 1996.

Note: Missing data are excluded from calculations. All differences are statistically significant at least at the .001 level.

the population in Beijing and their access to newspapers, television, and the "grapevine," that is, information from unofficial channels.

The educational level in Beijing increased between the two surveys. The population as a whole gained nearly one year of formal schooling over the eight-year period. Associated with increases in educational achievement was an increase in media participation. Not only did the frequency of newspaper reading and television watching increase, but more people read newspapers and watched television to acquire information on politics and governmental affairs in 1996.

In a previous analysis of political behavior, I found that information from unofficial channels is an important political resource in China. When the government was the sole provider of resources associated with people's daily life, an awareness of loopholes in government policies governing resource distribution enabled political actors to "borrow normative power" from government policy to defeat local bureaucrats, asking them to faithfully implement

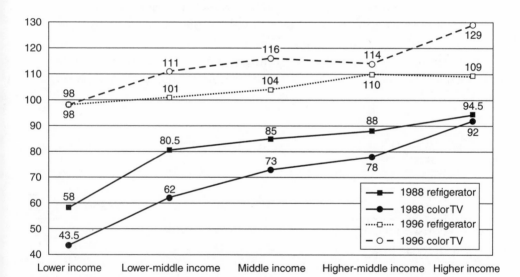

Figure 7.2 Ownership of durable consumer products (units per hundred households) *(Beijing tongji nianjian, 1989, 1997)*

the existing policies of the government.[23] To relieve local bureaucrats from pressure from below, the government deliberately kept most of its policies semi-secret. Political activists in China understood this dynamic and sought information through unofficial channels.

When the government's function changed from directly providing resources to regulating economic life, authorities in China could no longer keep their decisions hidden. Rules and regulations had to be made public for people to follow. An analysis of the survey data indicates that by 1996, fewer people had an incentive to seek information from unofficial channels.

Economic development may also affect political attitudes.[24] Two attitudes are thought to have a significant impact on people's political behavior: political interests and political efficacy. In both surveys, we asked respondents to report if they were interested in politics and governmental affairs. We also asked them to identify national political figures. Figure 7.3 reports the percentage of respondents who were interested in politics and governmental affairs, and those who could correctly identify the premier of the government, president of the country, chairman of the National People's Congress, and general secretary of the Chinese Communist Party. The surveys found that more people in 1996 were interested in politics than in 1988. While 76.5 percent of respondents reported that they were inter-

Table 7.2 Mean scale scores on media access, grapevine access, and formal education

	1988		1996	
	Mean (N)	S.d.	Mean (N)	S.d.
Years of formal school education	9.12 (744)	4.16	9.97 (882)	4.28
Reading newspapers	2.84 (754)	1.45	3.06 (891)	1.32
Watching TV	3.44 (744)	0.92	3.65 (891)	0.80
Grapevine access	0.89 (751)	1.19	0.65 (890)	1.00

Source: Beijing surveys, 1988 and 1996.

Note: Missing data are excluded from calculations. All differences are statistically significant at the .001 level.

ested in politics in 1988, 81.3 percent reported they were interested in 1996. More people in 1996 gave correct answers than in 1988.

Political efficacy has two dimensions. Internal efficacy refers to beliefs about one's own competence to understand and participate in politics. External efficacy refers to beliefs about the responsiveness of governmental authorities and institutions to citizen demands.[25] Changes in external efficacy are primarily determined by government behavior. Internal efficacy is more likely to vary with socioeconomic resources related to the process of economic development. Internal efficacy was measured in the survey by a set of three questions that asked respondents to evaluate their own ability to understand political issues facing the country, the city, and the *jiedao* (neighborhood) they were living in.

External efficacy was measured by two questions asking respondents to evaluate the responsiveness of the government. The questions were added together to build internal and external efficacy scales. As illustrated in Table 7.3, the mean score of people's confi-

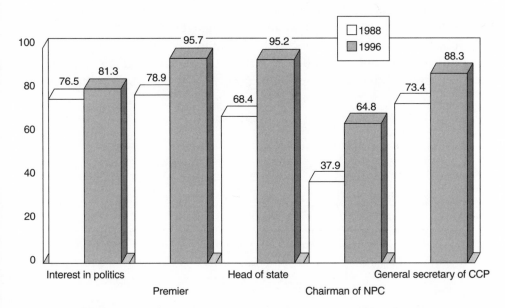

Figure 7.3 Changes in political interest and knowledge (in percent) (Beijing surveys, 1988 and 1996)

dence in their ability to understand local and national politics increased from 3.77 to 5.0, and the mean score for their beliefs about the responsiveness of the government increased from 1.76 to 1.91 over the eight-year period.

The analysis thus far reveals that changes in many areas of social and political life have occurred in Beijing. Economic development changed not only the structure of the population but also the relationship between individuals and the state. Even in a Leninist state that has penetrated deeply into society, economic development still brings hitherto apathetic groups into contact with government and makes people more confident in their ability to understand politics and to deal with the authorities effectively.[26] What about political behavior? Do changes in social context, social structure, and psychological orientation change individuals' participatory behavior in Beijing?

Stability and Change in Participation in Beijing

Changes in the structure of participation may be analyzed by comparing the frequency of respondents' engagement in different political activities in 1988 and in 1996. Table 7.4 displays the proportion of respondents who reported being engaged in various participatory acts at each point in time. As predicted by social mobilization theory, the general level of participation for residents of Beijing increased over the eight-year period.

Table 7.3 Mean scale scores on internal and external efficacy for 1988 and 1996

Mean	1988 (N)	1996 (N)
Internal efficacy	3.77 (741)	5.00 (829)
External efficacy	1.76 (757)	1.91* (894)

Source: Beijing surveys, 1988 and 1996.

Note: Missing data are excluded from calculations. All differences are statistically significant at least at the .001 level, except the one with an asterisk, which is significant at the .05 level.

Table 7.4 Percentage engaging in different acts of political participation

Type of political act	A 1988	B 1996	B – A
Complained through the trade unions	18.9	24.4	5.5**
Complained through deputies to the people's congresses	8.6	14.1	5.5**
Complained through the bureaucratic hierarchy	43.0	47.5	4.5
Persuaded others to go to campaign meetings for deputies	8.9	13.0	4.1**
Reported to complaint bureaus	4.0	8.1	4.1**
Gave gifts in exchange for help	4.6	8.0	3.4**
Brought cases to court	1.2	4.5	3.3***
Persuaded others how to vote in deputy elections	4.7	8.0	3.3**
Persuaded others to boycott unfair deputy elections	3.7	6.8	3.1**
Contacted leaders of the work unit	51.2	54.2	3.0
Wrote letters to government officials	12.5	15.3	2.8
Complained through political organizations	15.0	17.7	2.7
Strikes	0.9	2.6	1.7*
Wrote letters to the editors of newspapers	6.8	8.3	1.5
Guanxi or connections	15.5	16.6	1.1
Participated in demonstrations	0.4	1.4	1.0*
Persuaded others to boycott unfair elections in work units	4.6	2.9	−1.7
Persuaded others how to vote in elections at the work unit	5.7	3.5	−2.2
Persuaded others to go to campaign meetings at the work unit	7.7	5.4	−2.3*
Slowed down on the job	12.6	9.3	−3.3*
Whipped up public opinion in work units against leaders	5.1	1.7	−3.4***
Organized a group of people to fight against leaders	7.6	3.0	−4.6***
Reported voting for deputies to local people's congresses in 1988	81.0	71.5	−9.5***
Reported voting for leaders in the work unit	34.8	16.1	−18.7***

Source: Beijing Surveys, 1988 (*N* = 757) and 1996 (*N* = 894).
* = significant at .05 level; ** = significant at .01 level; *** = significant at .001 level.

A closer look at the changes in the marginal distribution of the two samples reveals that engagement in political acts within one's work unit has either remained stable or actually declined. For example, there was no statistically significant change in contacting one's leaders. At the same time, participation in acts challenging the authority of individual officials, such as slowing down on the job, organizing a group of people to resist, or whipping up public opinion against leaders in one's work unit, decreased substantially.

Concurrently, participation in political acts requiring participants to go beyond their work unit increased. More people reported that they had gone to trade unions, people's congress delegates, higher governmental organizations, and complaint bureaus to express their opinions. Participation through strikes and demonstrations also doubled in 1996 as compared with 1988. The percentage differences revealed here may seem minor, but if we translate the figure into the difference in the number of individuals who have engaged in those political acts between the two time points, the significance of the changes revealed in the table becomes more evident. For example, the table shows that 0.9 and 2.6 percent of the respondents reported that they engaged in strikes in 1988 and 1996 respectively, reflecting a difference of 1.7 percent. The change tells us that roughly 138,788 more people in 1996 reported engaging in strikes as compared with 1988.[27] Given the fact that the regime became more repressive after June 4, 1989, the increase in strikes is surprising. It tells us that the authorities failed to prevent people from getting involved in these highly forbidden activities even though the regime increased its efforts to suppress unauthorized political expression.

A more diverse picture emerges concerning electoral participation. On the one hand, voter turnout in elections for deputies to people's congresses declined substantially: nearly 10 percent fewer respondents in our 1996 survey reported having voted in elections for deputies to people's congresses than those in the 1988 survey.[28] On the other hand, the percentage of people who reported having engaged in campaign activities nearly doubled. More people in the 1996 survey also reported that they tried to persuade others to boycott unfair elections. If voters believed that elections did not provide them with an opportunity to express their opinions, few of them would try to persuade others how to vote. Similarly, it is only when people expect elections to be fair and believe that those elections may bring them certain benefits, that they will bother protesting against "unfair elections." The finding that there are substantial increases in individuals' engagement in both campaign activities and election boycotts suggests that people took elections more seriously at the time of the second survey than at the time of the first.

Finally, we find a substantial decline in people's participation in electoral activities associated with work unit elections. Less than half of the respondents reported having voted for *danwei* leaders in 1996 as compared with 1988. Engagement in campaign activities during *danwei* elections also declined proportionally. Because elections are structured political acts, engagement in them depends not only on the motivation of individuals but also on the availability of institutions.[29] Unlike elections for deputies to people's congresses, which are regulated by the constitution, elections at the level of the work unit are set by local officials. If they do not want such elections, there is no rule forcing them to hold them.[30] Because the data presented here do not reflect whether such elections were available, the decline in political activities associated with *danwei* elections revealed in the table may be due to the fact that fewer such elections were held, rather than a decline in people's desire to vote.

Examination of the data reveals that while 42.1 percent of the respondents reported that their *danwei* held elections for leaders in the 1988 survey, only 19.6 percent claimed that they had an opportunity to vote for their *danwei* leaders in 1996. Table 7.5 examines the proportion of people who had the opportunity to vote and actually voted in their work unit elections, as well as their engagement in other activities associated with such elections. The analysis confirms our expectation that the reason behind the decline in people's participation in electoral politics associated with *danwei* elections should be attributed to the fact that fewer work units in Beijing held such elections from 1993 to 1996, rather than to a decline in people's interest in participating in such elections. If we limit our inquiry to those who had the opportunity to choose their leaders through elections, we find that (1) the turnout rate remains roughly the same, and (2) people's engagement in campaign activities associated with *danwei* elections actually increased substantially in 1996. Citizens in Beijing are no longer satisfied to limit their participation in *danwei* elections simply to voting on election day. More of them choose to engage in various political acts to help the candidates they like get elected.

Political acts differ in how they relate the individual to his or her government. The differences among the modes of political activity are important, because the processes by which individuals come to be political activists differ from one mode of political activity to another; the consequences of alternative modes of political activities differ as well.[31]

Next is a comparison of the differences in mean scores of participatory scales based on different modes of political participation developed from the 1988 data.[32] The scales presented in Table 7.6 are composed of simple additions of respondents' involvement in various acts belonging to each participatory mode. Since electoral participation is a structured political act and fewer elections were available at the time of the second survey, they were omitted from the analysis in order to avoid a compatibility problem. Table 7.6 ex-

Table 7.5 Percentage of people who voted in their work unit elections for leaders and/or engaged in different forms of electoral politics

	1988	(*N*)	1996	(*N*)
Voted in election for work unit leaders	84.3	(263)	84.6	(143)
Participated in campaign meetings	56.1	(179)	55.0	(94)
Mobilized others to participate in campaign meetings	18.2	(58)	28.1	(48)*
Mobilized others to boycott unfair elections	11.0	(35)	15.1	(26)

Source: Beijing surveys, 1988 and 1996.
Note: Missing data are excluded from calculations.
* = significant at .05 level.

amines the changes in the mean scores for five participatory modes from the cross-sectional surveys at the two different times.[33] They are

1. Appeals: Including complaints through the bureaucratic hierarchy, political organizations, trade unions, and through deputies to local people's congresses.[34]
2. Adversarial activities: Including letters to newspaper editors and to government officials at higher levels, and registering complaints with complaint bureaus.[35]
3. Cronyism: Including the use of connections, or the sending of gifts to bureaucrats in exchange for help.[36]
4. Resistance: Including slow-downs on the job, whipping up public opinion, and organizing groups to fight against leaders.[37]
5. Protest: Including strikes, demonstrations, and suing bureaucrats in court.

The table shows that increasing numbers of people became involved in appeals and adversarial activities between 1988 and 1996. With regard to political activities challenging the elite, the picture is more diverse. As illustrated in Table 7.6, participation in resis-

Table 7.6 Mean scores of five participatory modes in Beijing

Mean score	1988	1996
Appeals	0.87	1.04**
Adversarial activities	0.25	0.32*
Cronyism	0.22	0.34***
Resistance	0.28	0.16***
Protest	0.05	0.19***
N	757	894

Source: Beijing surveys, 1988 and 1996.
* = significant at .05 level; ** = significant at .01 level; *** = significant at .001 level.

tance—a group of acts challenging the authority of individual officials at the grass-roots level—declined. At the same time, people's engagement in protests significantly increased. The increase in adversarial activities and protests and the decline of resistance suggest that targets of participation in Beijing have begun to move from influencing the decisions of individual officials at the grass-roots level to influencing decisions made by the government.

The Predictors of Political Participation

What are the linkages between contextual, structural, and psychological variables and political participation? Do these variables play the same role at two different times? Table 7.7 examines the structure of correlates between resources and participation to see whether there is any major change in the relationship between Time 1 (1988) and Time 2 (1996).

With regard to changes in the structure of correlations between 1988 and 1996, the increase in the importance of governmental activities in mobilizing people to make appeals is striking. Compared with the situation in 1988, the effect of the perceived impact of local government activities on appeals nearly doubled in 1996. With an increasing number of people aware of the fact that the activities of city government and their neighborhood committees affect their lives, it is not surprising to find an increase in the explanatory power of perceived impacts of government at those two levels. Consequently, the probability that people will make appeals and get involved in adversarial activities has increased. A more important finding is that the impact of the perceived impacts of central government activities on appeals and adversarial activities also increased substantially. As seen in the data presented in Table 7.1, though fewer people in Beijing in 1996 claimed that central government outputs had an influence over their lives, the predictive power of the variable increased. This comparison shows that the decisions of the central government played a more important role in mobilizing political actors in Beijing to engage in political activities in 1996 than in 1988.

Although the impact of media access on participation in conven-

Table 7.7 Bivariate correlations between mean scale scores and five participatory modes

	Appeals	Adversarial activities	Cronyism	Resistance	Protest
Impact of neighborhood committees					
1988	.096***	.048	.070*	−.002	.067*
1996	.151***	.073**	.028	−.005	.049
Impact of city government					
1988	.079**	.129***	.064*	.073**	.011
1996	.176***	.126***	.048	.036	.034
Impact of central government					
1988	.112***	.114***	.112***	.034	.037
1996	.191***	.161***	−.009	.047	.061
Reading newspapers					
1988	.167***	.088**	.032	.065*	−.004
1996	.184***	.119***	.096***	.099***	.021
Watching TV					
1988	.090**	.048	.004	.033	−.018
1996	.094***	.026	.023	.004	−.025
Grapevine access					
1988	.167***	.179***	.175***	.123***	.097***
1996	.124***	.122***	.137***	.101***	.025
Years of formal schooling					
1988	.187***	.105***	.102***	.116***	.027
1996	.234***	.187***	.170***	.114***	.062
Interest in politics					
1988	.093**	.089**	.012	−.027	.012
1996	.165***	.062*	−.034	.009	−.012
Political knowledge					
1988	.073**	.035	.011	−.009	−.029
1996	.175***	.107***	.092***	.057*	.057
Internal efficacy					
1988	.277***	.130***	.121***	.113***	.016
1996	.251***	.138***	.110***	.064*	.058
External efficacy					
1988	.073**	−.005	−.078**	−.038	−.061*
1996	.095***	.053	−.059*	−.065*	−.051

Source: Beijing surveys, 1988 and 1996.
* = significant at .05 level; ** = significant at .01 level; *** = significant at .001 level.

tional political activity remained stable, newspaper reading in 1996 had a statistically significant effect on the probability that people would get involved in resistance and cronyism to articulate their interests. The finding shows that the propaganda machine used by the regime to socialize people to conform to the party line can no longer prevent people from getting involved in semi-legal elite-challenging political acts. Instead, people are now mobilized to use channels previously kept closed by the regime to articulate their interests.

Education continues to play a significant role in mobilizing people to make appeals. Its correlation with adversarial activities nearly doubled between 1988 and 1996. Adversarial activities include a cluster of risky political acts. Engaging in them usually leads to ruthless retaliation by local bureaucrats. The tightening of government control after June 4, 1989, has made it easier for bureaucrats to punish those who dare challenge their authority through political acts. Despite the changes in the external environment faced by the people in Beijing, these who are more educated have become more willing to use such political acts to express their opinions.

Changes also occurred in the impact of psychological resources on certain modes of political participation. The analysis shows that while political interests became more closely correlated with conventional participatory modes, the correlation between feelings of efficacy and participation remains stable. Given the fact that people's sense of efficacy has increased, the findings indicate that participation in 1996 may be less contingent on psychological factors and more likely a response to outside stimuli, that is, the behavior of the government. The bivariate analysis shows that changes in governmental function, education, and psychological orientation played an increasingly important role in mobilizing people in Beijing to participate in politics.

The Causal Links between Macroeconomic Processes and the Changes in Citizen Participation in Beijing

What is the respective impact of each cluster of variables on political behavior? The objective is to find which changes in these three clusters of predictors—contextual, structural, psychological—caused changes in people's participatory behavior in the eight-year period. This task requires us to investigate the impact of each variable on the probability that people will participate and their respective interaction with time. Since the general linear model (GLM) allows us simultaneously to control covariates and covariate interaction of other variables to examine the effects of individual variables as well as interaction between variables, it fits our purpose here.[38]

The data from the two surveys were merged to create a new data set. A dummy variable representing the time of the survey was added to the data set. If there is no interaction between the dummy variable and other predictors, we will be able to conclude that the reasons for the changes in people's political behavior between 1988 and 1996 have nothing to do with changes in the contextual, structural, and psychological variables used in the model. On the contrary, if we find interaction effects between the dummy variable and certain independent variables in the model, we should be able to conclude that changes in people's participatory behavior between 1988 and 1996 can be attributed to the change in that particular variable.

Table 7.8 presents the selected results of the GLM analysis for appeals and adversarial activities.[39] The upper part of the table shows the overall influences of the contextual, structural, or psychological variables on people's participatory activities. The lower part of the table explores whether there was any change in the impact of these variables on people's behavior between 1988 and 1996. Since the purpose of the analysis is to find not the best predictor for each participatory mode, but which cluster of changes brought about by economic development makes people become more politically active, the same variables to predict individuals' engagement in different political activities were used. Although such a decision prevents one from finding the best fit in models predicting political involvement in each participatory mode, the analysis allows examination of the central theme here.

Take appeals as an example. The figures in the upper part of the table reveal the perceived impact of government, information from unofficial channels, and education; internal efficacy and external

Table 7.8 General linear model (GLM) estimates of the changing
impact of contextual, socioeconomic, and psychological
variables on appeals and adversarial activities for the whole
population

GLM estimates	Appeals	Adversarial activities
Intercept	−0.32	−0.25**
Intercept (88)	0.70**	0.25*
Intercept (96)	0.00	0.00
Impact of government	0.16***	0.05***
Education	0.05***	0.03***
Hearing via grapevine	0.38***	0.20***
Reading newspapers	0.00	−0.01
Political interest	0.06	0.00
Internal efficacy	0.14***	0.02*
External efficacy	0.09***	0.03
Impact of government (88)	−0.11**	−0.01
Impact of government (96)	0.00	0.00
Education (88)	−0.02	−0.02**
Education (96)	0.00	0.00
Hearing via grapevine (88)	−0.10	−0.02
Hearing via grapevine (96)	0.00	0.00
Reading newspapers (88)	0.05	0.02
Reading newspapers (96)	0.00	0.00
Political interest (88)	−0.14	−0.02*
Political interest (96)	0.00	0.00
Internal efficacy (88)	0.00	−0.01
Internal efficacy (96)	0.00	0.00
External efficacy (88)	−0.05	−0.04
External efficacy (96)	0.00	0.00
R^2	0.12	0.06
N	1,533	1,535

* = significant at .1 level; ** = significant at .05 level; *** = significant at .01 level.

efficacy increase the probability that people will make appeals. They are important resources in mobilizing participation in politics. Contrary to our expectations, political interest does not have an independent effect on the likelihood for people to make appeals. Now we know that the correlation between political interest and appeals in Table 7.7 was a spurious one—since political interest is closely associated with one's educational level, the reason that the variable is associated with appeals is that those who are interested in politics have higher levels of education.

The data in the lower part of the table examine the respective impact of these variables on the probability that people will make appeals in different years. The analysis tried to find out whether there was any significant change in the variables' respective impact on the probability that people will make appeals when the impacts of other variables were controlled. There was a significant increase in the effect of the perceived impact of government on the probability that people will make appeals. Over the eight-year period, governmental activities played an increasingly important role in mobilizing people to deal with the authorities through political acts belonging to appeals, even after the impact of other variables was controlled for. This finding is important because it shows that even in China, one of the few remaining repressive Leninist states, changes in the political context have mobilized people to participate more actively.

The impact of education on participation in adversarial activities also increased, even though engaging in them usually led to direct confrontation between participants and political leaders and ruthless retaliation.[40] Unlike the contextual variables, increases in resources at the individual level mobilized people to engage in those more difficult and riskier political acts. The impact of psychological resources on the likelihood that people will get involved in these participatory modes remained unchanged over the eight-year period.

The analysis thus far demonstrates that the contextual and structural variables have an increasingly larger impact on people's participatory behavior. Yet we do not know if the reasons behind these changes are population replacement between 1988 and 1996 or variation of various resources at the individual level. For example, the growing importance of the perceived impact of government might be due to the fact that people who were aware of such impact entered the population and people who were unaware of such impact left the population rather than being due to any actual change in the effects of governmental activities on people's lives. One way to deal with this problem is to delete from the data set people who entered the population between 1988 and 1996 and people who were seventy-five years and older, assuming they departed from the population by the time of the second survey, and rerun the model. This kind of data manipulation allows a certain degree of control for the problem of population replacement.

If the pattern of the relationship revealed in the previous equation appears in the new one, then the changes revealed in the previous model cannot be attributed to population replacement over the past eight years. Economic development not only increased the contact between individuals and the state but also made certain resources at the individual level, especially education, more important in motivating people to participate in politics. The results of the analysis presented in Table 7.9 confirm such expectations. The changes in the effects of both contextual and structural variables on political behavior revealed in the earlier model manifest themselves in the new model. The changes in the impact of education on adversarial activities becomes even stronger, which indicates that education plays an increasingly important role in mobilizing people to participate.

Conclusion

Economic development over the eight-year period between 1988 and 1996 has led to several social changes in Beijing. Although the rich may have become even richer, the standard of living of the poor by 1996 caught up with or even exceeded that of the uppermiddle-income families of eight years earlier. During the same period, the general level of education for the population increased. Even though China remains a Leninist state and during these years the regime increased its efforts to suppress unauthorized political ex-

Table 7.9 General linear model (GLM) estimates of the changing impact of contextual, socioeconomic, and psychological variables on appeals and adversarial activities, excluding people entered into or departed from the population from 1988 to 1996

GLM estimates	Appeals	Adversarial activities
Intercept	−0.38	−0.27**
Intercept (88)	0.78**	0.25*
Intercept (96)	0.00	0.00
Impact of government	0.18***	0.06***
Education	0.04***	0.03***
Hearing via grapevine	0.38***	0.23***
Reading newspapers	0.02	−0.02
Political interest	0.09	0.03
Internal efficacy	0.12***	0.02
External efficacy	0.08**	0.02
Impact of government (88)	−0.13***	−0.01
Impact of government (96)	0.00	0.00
Education (88)	−0.01	−0.02*
Education (96)	0.00	0.00
Hearing via grapevine (88)	−0.12	−0.05
Hearing via grapevine (96)	0.00	0.00
Reading newspapers (88)	0.03	0.02
Reading newspapers (96)	0.00	0.00
Political interest (88)	−0.16	−0.04
Political interest (96)	0.00	0.00
Internal efficacy (88)	0.02	0.00
Internal efficacy (96)	0.00	0.00
External efficacy (88)	−0.05	0.04
External efficacy (96)	0.00	0.00
R^2	0.12	0.07
N	1,473	1,475

* = significant at .1 level; ** = significant at .05 level; *** = significant at .01 level.

pression, people in Beijing still became more concerned with politics and governmental affairs. Furthermore, their confidence in their own ability to understand and to participate in politics increased.

During the same period, both the frequency and the intensity of Beijing residents' political activism increased. In 1996, they were more willing to go beyond their work units to express their opinions and to confront government officials directly. The analysis also reveals another important trend in China's political development: political activists moved from parochial participation, such as contacting *danwei* leaders and resistence within work units,[41] to acts with a broader scope of consequences and requiring more participation in public life. Both adversarial activities and protest increased substantially between 1988 and 1996.[42] Although still quite different from political activities in other societies, the way interests in China are organized and the resources required for people to participate in politics have begun to change. At the same time, the relationship between resources and participation have also changed. Among clusters of change brought about by economic development, two factors emerge as increasingly important in influencing the level and intensity of political participation. One is government activity and the other is education.

The design of these two surveys allows us to compare individuals' political behavior when attitudes of the regime toward unauthorized political expression change in order to examine institutional effects on people's participation. The findings suggest that structural change plays a more important role than institutions on political development in a society. The behavior of a regime may delay or twist the pattern of development, but the analysis here shows that it is beyond the ability of a regime either to prevent people from more actively participating in politics or to limit people's political acts to certain confined channels. When people realize that they need to use certain channels, including those prohibited by the regime, to resolve problems facing them, they will engage in these political acts to express their opinions.

Although "democracy is never a one-way ladder that countries climb as their economy and social structures develop,"[43] this analysis shows that as the economy and social structures have developed, Beijing residents in China have become more politically sophisticated and more assertive in the articulation of their interests. As the regime's ability to control society gradually erodes, people are more assertive in articulating their interests.[44] The change in the balance of power between state and society may lead some leaders to think of introducing different forms of governance. In their study of democratic transition in Latin America, Guillermo O'Donnell and Philippe Schmitter found the political calculation of autocrats to be the most critical factor in the transition from authoritarianism.[45] In Beijing, with more and more people becoming politicized and getting involved in various political acts to express their opinions, the regime feels increasingly heavier pressure from below. Such pressure will not lead communist leaders to give up their political power, but it may stimulate reformers within the government to propose a new way to rule. Indeed, pressure from peasants made the Chinese government introduce competitive elections in rural areas.[46] Although the changes among Beijing's residents and elsewhere may not bring democracy to China in the near future and hard-liners may continue to suppress political expression, economic development has at least planted some latent seeds of democracy in Chinese soil.

III | Fragmenting Society

8 | The Changing Role of Workers

It is one of the great ironies of our age that something close to a proletarian revolution helped spell the doom not of capitalism, as Marx had predicted, but of state socialism. A national uprising of workers in Poland in 1979–80 marked the beginning of the end of Polish social-ism, though Soviet threats and martial law postponed the day of reckoning for another nine years. Although some-thing close to a revolutionary upsurge of the working class occurred only in Poland, in other East European states and even in the Soviet Union the alienation of workers helped spell the doom of state socialism in 1989–1991.[1]

A further irony is that the important role of the working class in the downfall of socialism in Eastern Europe might be explained in terms more or less consistent with Marx's original analysis. Although the engine of capitalist accu-mulation was not at work in these cases, in other respects conditions Marx saw as conducive to the formation of a uniform and hostile proletarian class consciousness arose. Similar conditions and results did not occur in capitalist states. While advanced capitalist states saw the share of workers in the labor force decline with the growth of the service sector, in East European socialist states the nu-merical dominance of the workers changed little. In the latter societies the priorities of planners led to a prolifera-tion of giant plants, often with associated housing complexes and other facilities. Average plant sizes much larger than in capitalist states, along with their associated residential and service complexes, were conducive to heightened worker solidarity. In the early years of these regimes, the rapid expansion of industry and wholesale recruitment from among the peasantry combined with pervasive political controls and terror acted in the other direction, inhibiting worker class consciousness. By the 1980s, however, the dominance of lifelong and even second- or (in the case of the USSR) third-generation proletarians helped to enhance worker solidarity.[2] The constant emphasis in regime propaganda on the special nature and mission of the working class likely reinforced these tendencies. Furthermore, after the 1960s the stagnating living standards of workers and the growing awareness of the special privileges of managers, experts, and intellectuals plus weakened regime coerciveness and control over communications helped turn worker solidarity from a force in support of the state into a growing threat. An increasing sense of being exploited, even if not by capitalists, helped to lay the groundwork for Solidarity and subsequent worker rumblings against other East European socialist states.[3]

China's leaders were acutely aware of and very worried about these portents of a proletarian counterrevolution emanating from Eastern Europe.[4] They feared similar infections spreading to Chinese workers. Consequently, modest worker efforts to establish independent trade unions during the spring 1989 demonstrations were met with an especially hostile response. However, complex changes were under way in the nature of the Chinese economy after 1978, and these changes have accelerated in the 1990s. Have these changes made it more or less likely that China's workers will follow on the heels of their East European brethren and help undermine the regime in the PRC?

China's Workers in the Era of Mao Zedong

To evaluate the changing role of workers during the reform period, it is necessary to review briefly the nature of China's working class in the Mao era, particularly during the Cultural Revolution. The development of the post-1949 economy, initially modeled after the

Soviet Union, produced a significantly enlarged Chinese proletariat. From approximately 9 million workers of all types (roughly 3 million industrial workers and 6 million handicraft workers) in 1949, there was a growth to 29 million workers in state industry alone by the beginning of the reform period. Workers in state enterprises were the largest proletarian category, but in the early 1980s China also numbered about 15 million employed in urban collective factories, 19 million employed in rural collective industry, and about 4 million urban and 9 million rural temporary workers (mostly employed by urban state factories).[5]

As these figures reveal, an important legacy of the Mao era was the promotion of rural industrialization—a growing proliferation of small-scale factories employing village personnel. Only in the most loose sense of the term, however, can those employed in rural factories at the time be considered "workers." Official policy kept the proportion of village labor power employed in rural factories below 5 percent, and in most cases those so employed received not wages, but work points channeled through their home production teams. Production teams in turn attempted to set the compensation of those members employed in rural factories so that it did not much exceed the average work-point levels of field laborers. Any fringe benefits (such as collective medical insurance) came from the team and not from the factory. In some locales rotating employment schemes along with periodic leaves to participate in harvest activity were instituted to ensure that those working in rural factories did not become too divorced from agricultural labor.[6] As a result of such policies, those employed in rural factories in the late-Mao era remained more cultivators than proletarians.[7]

China's workers in the Mao era, properly speaking, were overwhelmingly concentrated in the cities. In the late 1970s two other sectors that were to become important in the post-Mao era—private firms and foreign-owned/joint venture enterprises—were virtually nonexistent.[8] In addition, toward the end of the Mao era, the conditions of work and the treatment of workers in urban collective enterprises increasingly approached those found in state enterprises.[9] As a result of this convergence, a certain uniformity in the lot of Chinese workers had developed prior to the reforms.[10]

Industrial organization and worker life in China during this period bore many similarities to their counterparts in the Soviet Union and Eastern Europe, but with some key differences as well. In China as in other socialist states, the emphasis on material production and on large industrial complexes with attached housing and other facilities produced a proletariat relatively more numerous than in capitalist states at the same level of development and unusually concentrated spatially.[11] As in Eastern Europe, work units directly distributed a range of goods and services to their employees, and those employed in the largest and most important firms were particularly privileged. Workers in general enjoyed a high security of employment, a fairly broad range of fringe benefits, and wage levels that often surpassed those of lower white-collar workers and professionals, another contrast with the situation in comparable capitalist states. The security of employment and favored treatment of state firm workers constituted the "iron rice bowl" that subsequently became a major target of attack by reformers. Chinese workers also shared with their brethren in Eastern Europe the propaganda image of being the leading class, though they had little ability to protest or resist abuse. China's party-controlled trade unions followed the same supine, "transmission belt" model as in other Leninist systems.

Despite these similarities, in a number of respects the lot of Chinese workers differed greatly from that of their brethren in Eastern Europe. In contrast to the continued recruitment of new workers from the countryside in labor-short East European socialist states, in labor-rich China after the 1950s it was extraordinarily difficult to move from farmer to worker status. Even the limited exception of temporary workers hired from the countryside by urban factories proves the point: they received few of the benefits of "regular" workers and continued to rely on their home production teams for grain rations. Chinese industrial firms also came closer to providing permanent employment, without the high labor turnover rates found in the Soviet Union and elsewhere. The opposite side of the coin is that China, unlike other socialist states, had no real labor market; individuals could not readily change jobs even when faced with intolerable conditions or treatment.[12] These features produced the common phrase "work unit ownership system *(danwei suoyouzhi),*" to characterize the serflike bond between employee and enterprise.

Mao's mobilization of hostility toward experts, intellectuals, managers, and even party officials also had no clear counterpart in Eastern Europe. This policy may have led Chinese workers to take more seriously than their colleagues in other socialist states the claim that they were the leading class. At the same time Chinese workers experienced some distinctive disabilities that they shared with other urbanites. The virtual freezing of most wages after 1957 and the elimination of bonuses, piece rates, and other material incentive systems during the Cultural Revolution decade meant that unlike other socialist proletarians, Chinese workers continued to toil for years with set monthly wage rates regardless of their efforts or aspirations. This rejection of material incentives was the antithesis of the industrial regime developed in the Soviet Union in the 1930s and subsequently imposed on Eastern Europe.

In addition, the Chinese *danwei* system is also more highly accentuated than in the Soviet Union or the East European satellites. The absence of market distribution of most basic goods and services made Chinese workers more dependent upon their work units than was the case in Eastern Europe. Furthermore, the political control systems and monitoring of the private life of employees were more pervasive in China than elsewhere, making personal autonomy and privacy virtually impossible.[13] These features contributed to greater dependency of workers upon their firms and their superiors, with little opportunity to exercise "voice" or "exit" options.[14] Toward the end of the Mao era this social encapsulation by the *danwei* increasingly spanned generations, as the *dingti* system allowed workers to retire early and have a son or daughter given a job in the same enterprise. No such system of formal employment transmission to children existed in Eastern Europe. The authorities in China did not use this dependency on the *danwei* to foster strong loyalties to the enterprise and its activities, as often occurs in Japanese companies or even in some industrial firms in the West. Rather, workers were expected to reserve their loyalties for more distant, transcending sources—the Chinese Communist Party and Mao Zedong.[15]

How did these social structural features of worker life in the late-Mao era affect worker solidarity and the potential for protest? Although there are some well-documented instances of strikes and other industrial protest activity (notably in 1957 and 1975), in general Andrew Walder's conclusion that the post-1949 changes produced the "unmaking" of China's working class is valid.[16] As mentioned, certain elements in the post-1949 changes had the potential to foster proletarian self-consciousness and activism, particularly the concentration of workers in large firms with attached residential complexes, the virtual elimination of recruitment of industrial labor from the countryside after the 1950s, the public stress on the vanguard role of the working class, and the failure of post-1957 economic gains to show up in worker paychecks. These features, however, were outweighed by forces working to forestall the development of proletarian class consciousness: the substantial horizontal social barriers between workers employed in different enterprises, the relative advantages that workers enjoyed compared with other social groups, the extreme dependency and arbitrariness in the relations between workers and their supervisors, and the tightness of official controls on information and communications. Consequently, there was little sign at the time that Mao died that workers would constitute any significant political challenge to the regime.

The Strategy and Timing of Reform-Era Changes

A large number of changes have fundamentally altered the nature of China's working class since 1978. These changes are of two types: changes that altered the nature of working-class organization and experiences within traditional state and collective industrial firms, and changes that produced new (or revived from the presocialist era) segments of the working class outside of these sectors. By the 1990s it became increasingly difficult to generalize about the nature of both sets of changes, because the very nature of the reforms heightened local governmental and firm autonomy. This autonomy increasingly generated variation within each type of enterprise in the ways in which workers were hired, paid, organized, promoted, demoted, and fired. Despite this complexity, I will delineate trends in the lot of workers first in the "new" quasi-capitalist firms, and then in the traditional urban state and collective enterprises.

China's Quasi-Capitalist Industrial Firms

Perhaps the most dynamic sector of the Chinese economy since 1978 has been township and village enterprises (TVEs). Employment in rural firms has increased from about 19 million at the onset of the reform period, as noted above, to around 120–125 million in the mid-1990s. The latter figure, however, includes all types of rural nonagricultural firms, and not just rural industry. Rural industrial enterprises employed about 73 million in 1993, and of this total probably about 80 percent, or roughly 58 million, were production workers.[17] Strictly speaking, TVEs are not a single organizational type, but an internally differentiated category based upon the administrative levels that own or supervise them (townships and villages) and upon not being state enterprises (although some have close subcontracting and other relations with state firms). Within this broad category exists a combination of collective enterprises, private firms, and even foreign-owned or joint venture firms (the last particularly in areas such as the Pearl River Delta of Guangdong). The proportion of different kinds of ownership within the TVE category is a matter of considerable debate. At the extremes, there are those who argue that the great majority of TVEs are collectively owned entities of villages and townships that are subject to control and even entrepreneurial guidance from local cadres.[18] At the other extreme are those who argue that a high proportion of the supposedly collectively owned TVEs are actually privately owned firms which have adopted the collective label as a political cover and aid to obtaining bank loans and other resources.[19] The fact that some ostensibly collectively owned village enterprises have contracted out management rights to private individuals or groups or have received investment from private or foreign sources further muddies the water.[20]

What is clear is that the life of a worker in a TVE is very different from that of the cultivators who worked in village-run enterprises during the Mao era. No longer are there efforts to cap the growth of nonagricultural employment. In fact quite the opposite is the case. Village leaders strive to establish and expand local enterprises as rapidly as possible, even if this means hiring outside labor for either factories or fields.[21] Work points and production teams ended with decollectivization, and those employed in TVEs generally receive cash wages, often in the form of piece rates. In many cases they receive nothing else in the form of fringe benefits, housing, or subsidies. Although some firms reportedly reduce operations or close temporarily to allow employees to help with the harvest, generally TVE workers are clearly proletarians rather than cultivators.

Available accounts depict working conditions in TVEs as ranging from paternalistic to dreadful. In instances of genuine collective firms supervised by village officials and employing local residents exclusively, the complexities of local social and political alliances may limit the firm management from treating workers arbitrarily and abusively.[22] In firms involving private ownership and management, especially those employing labor from outside the village, conditions are often much harsher. The Labor Law of the PRC was passed in 1994 and took effect in 1995. It contains provisions specifying maximum hours of work per week, maximum overtime that can be demanded, minimum pay, overtime pay, and many other particulars.[23] After considerable debate during the drafting stage, it was decided that the provisions of the law dealing with working conditions should apply to all enterprises, including those employing former cultivators holding agricultural household registrations. Available evidence, however, indicates that in TVEs the provisions of the law are widely ignored. Very low pay levels and working days of twelve hours or longer, seven days a week, are common, as is mandatory overtime with no increase in pay. In the context of no labor protection, poor working conditions with minimal safety equipment lead to high accident rates. Workers who because of injury are unable to perform their jobs are replaced, and reductions in wages and firings for arbitrary reasons are also common.[24] In most such firms there is not even the minimal protection of worker interests provided by a trade union organization or party branch; instead managers have free rein to exploit their workers as they see fit in order to maximize firm profits.

It has been suggested that one reason that TVEs have been so much more competitive than China's state enterprises is because of this ability thoroughly to exploit workers, thereby keeping wage and benefit expenses to minimal levels which state firms cannot match.[25] Abysmal working conditions periodically provoke protests against particularly blatant forms of mistreatment of TVE workers. Two key factors, however, undermine the power of TVE workers to demand improvements in their working conditions: the heavy stress local authorities place on attracting new investment and making local TVEs profitable and the fact that a reserve army of the unemployed exists—other villagers. Most rural cultivators would prefer Dickensian industrial working conditions to a life of agricultural toil.[26]

Another major form of new (or revived) industrial employment involves urban private enterprise. Originally much urban private employment occurred in very small operations, typically only involving self-employed individuals *(getihu)*. By the mid-1980s, however, a variety of these small operations expanded and some individuals employed by state firms began to take leave or quit to "go into the sea" *(xiahai)* of private enterpreneurship. These trends led to a growing number of mid-sized or even large private firms *(siying qiye)*. By the end of the 1980s official regulations had legitimated these private firms and overridden the former limits of only 7–8 employees. According to official figures, in 1992 there were 8.4 million employed in urban private enterprise (up from 320,000 in 1979).[27] However, this figure appears to be a serious underestimate. Because urban as well as rural private firms often register as collective firms in order to obtain political cover and favorable access to resources and because migrants from rural areas employed by such firms are often omitted from official statistics, the true size of employment in China's private urban economy in 1992 was much larger. The true figure has been estimated at somewhere in the range from 36 million to 60 million.[28]

Less clear is what proportion of these totals comprises industrial workers. The bulk of urban private enterprise activity is concentrated in commerce and the services; a minority is involved in manufacturing. Yet, even if manufacturing accounts for only a small part of the total, workers in urban private firms would still constitute an important portion of China's contemporary working class.

The nature of the treatment of workers in private urban manufacturing firms is difficult to assess because of substantial variation. Early in the reform period private employment offered fairly low pay and status, but over time both have risen so that by the 1990s wage levels of those employed privately surpass those of people still working in state and collective firms.[29] Some larger and successful private firms have begun to provide a range of fringe benefits for their workers comparable to those received in the state sector, although few private firms are yet able to provide housing.[30] Although the state encourages urban private firms to employ primarily urban residents, it appears that this policy is ignored. Surveys reveal that 70–75 percent of those employed in urban private firms are rural migrants.[31] The treatment of workers in these firms varies widely in response to factors such as the market position of the firm, the proportion of migrant workers employed, and the presence or absence of subcontracting arrangements with state firms.[32] Despite substantial variation, it appears that the treatment of urban workers is considerably better than in rural TVEs and sometimes better than in state firms.

The other major type of "new" industrial employment is the various versions of foreign-owned and joint venture firms. This sector is still relatively small in employment terms. According to official statistics, in 1992 there were 2.8 million people employed in foreign-owned and joint venture firms.[33] The major distinction within this category is not between firms established by foreign investors versus those formed by a partnership with an existing firm (usually a state enterprise). Instead the most important distinction is between those firms established with Western capital versus Asian capital. Broadly speaking, workers in foreign-owned and joint venture firms established with Western capital treat their workers somewhat better than do their counterparts in state and collective firms. Firms established with capital from Hong Kong, Taiwan, or South Korea, on the other hand, treat their workers much more poorly, and perhaps even more poorly than workers in TVEs.[34]

Available accounts indicate that Western firms which invest in China tend to bring with them substantial parts of the institutional culture of industry in their own society, including the institutions regulating the treatment of workers. In the case of joint ventures,

Western managers are also eager to comply with state labor regulations in order not to provide pretexts for disputes with their workers or their Chinese venture partners. The result is that pay levels are generally higher than in comparable state firms, fringe benefits are comparable or better, and the treatment of workers is formalized in ways that limit management arbitrariness. At the same time the roles played by the party and trade union are often more restricted than in state enterprises, and other features of the institutional culture of state firms are diluted.[35] Workers in such firms as a result have a somewhat more meritocratic and formally specified set of procedures for promotion. Consequently, jobs in such firms are generally the "plums" that workers in all the other types of industrial enterprises covet. One might argue that the reasons that Western firms invest in China (for example, to gain access to the Chinese market, to save on labor costs compared with the West) do not require that managers exploit their workers too ruthlessly in order to be successful.

In contrast, the smaller and more labor-intensive firms established in China with capital from Hong Kong, Taiwan, and South Korea have a similar level of, or surpass, the abuses described for the TVEs. The capitalists involved come from societies in which managers face few limits from organized trade unions or the state on how they treat their workers. Moreover, they are trying to save on labor costs that are much lower than those in Western societies. Accounts of conditions in these firms portray harsh and extended work regimens, arbitrary dismissals, abusive treatment, high accident rates, and other problems. Management often enforces complex manuals full of rules and detailed fines governing every aspect of worker behavior, including styles of dress, timing of toilet breaks, and procedures for asking leave for medical or family emergencies.[36] The official and trade union presses in China carry regular reports of these abuses, indicating that some segments of China's political establishment would like to change the situation and provide better conditions for workers in this sector. To date, however, the countervailing concern to attract increased foreign investment (as well as to serve political objectives in regard to Hong Kong, Taiwan, and South Korea) has outweighed any attempts at amelioration.

As one example of this imbalance, an official campaign launched in 1993 to complete the establishment of trade union organizations in foreign firms (only 20 percent of which were said to have union organizations at the time) led to such hasty efforts to fulfill targets on paper that the great majority of trade union organizations created were controlled completely by firm managements. As a result, even the official trade unions' minimal level of concern for worker welfare did not occur.[37]

The various types of nonstate, noncollective industrial forms that have mushroomed as a result of the economic reforms reveal considerable diversity within and across types of firm. At one extreme are firms in which workers are generally treated substantially worse than their counterparts in state factories; at the other extreme are enterprises in which workers are substantially better off than their counterparts in both state and other private firms.

Reforming State and Collective Firms

There are a variety of approaches to reforming the industrial leviathans of prereform socialist states. One strategy is to view such behemoths as hopeless and to try to either sell them off to private or foreign owners or close them, while nourishing newly emerging private enterprises and entrepreneurs. Broadly speaking, this approach has been adopted in many of the former East European satellite states. A second strategy is to keep state firms operating mainly for political reasons—to avoid the potential unrest unleashed by sending much of the working class into the unemployment lines. Under this strategy there is little new hiring by state firms, which are allowed to wither as their workers retire or leave to find jobs in the new and more dynamic sectors of the economy. Oversimplifying once again, this second approach characterized the initial experience of Russia and some other parts of the former Soviet Union.[38] A third and more optimistic approach is to preserve socialist firms and even allow them to expand while they are increasingly forced to compete with the quasi-capitalist sectors of the economy. Stated in these terms, it becomes obvious that China has mainly followed the third approach. Employment in state and urban collective firms has continued to expand, although not as rapidly as employment in nonstate firms.[39]

It is useful to consider three stages—1978–1984, 1984–1992, and from 1992 to the present—in the reform of state and collective firms. The first period, from 1978 to 1984, emphasized eliminating Cultural Revolution practices from industrial enterprises; the second stage, 1984–1992, required state and collective firms increasingly to operate in a marketized external environment, while only experimentally doing much to alter their internal work practices; and the third stage, since 1992, brought the beginnings of major changes in the internal labor practices of such firms.[40]

During the period from 1978 to 1984, the effort to repudiate the Cultural Revolution legacy in state and collective firms initially focused on remuneration issues. The ban on material incentives was repudiated, and various bonus and piece-rate schemes, many of them revivals of pre-1966 practices, were implemented. The post-1957 wage freeze was also rescinded, and large-scale promotions and wage increases were carried out. Perhaps with an eye to events in Eastern Europe, China's leaders, recognizing the potential political dangers of consumer frustrations, began a series of major efforts to ease urban shortages of housing, food, and consumer goods. As these measures proved substantially successful, it was possible by the latter part of the 1980s to reduce dramatically the scope of urban rationing.

Although there was much discussion of the need to eliminate the "iron rice bowl" for workers and employees, with a few exceptions, reforms to actually destroy the system of guarantees for urbanites (including urban workers) were not carried out. While the *dingti* practice of a retiring parent passing on employment to a son or daughter was formally terminated in 1983, severe pressure on firms to solve the employment problems of family members of valued employees caused many enterprises to continue being enmeshed in complex webs of kinship.[41] Although experiments with new remuneration systems designed to reduce the pay portion that was fixed and increase the portion that depended upon performance were carried out, these were not generally adopted. Indeed, in this period it was common for bonus payments to be given out indiscriminately and fairly equally, rather than in any strict relationship to firm or worker performance. The clamoring of all employed to share in long-delayed pay increases prevented most managements from being discriminating with bonus funds. The continuation of the "soft budget constraints" within which state and even many collective firms operated meant that enterprises were able to obtain funds to continue and were not penalized for such wasteful practices. Similarly, the need to increase managerial autonomy to hire and fire workers and to institutionalize procedures for firm bankruptcy was much discussed, but again not much changed outside of a few experimental firms. The contentiousness these proposed changes evoked within the political elite and strong opposition to them from workers made it uncertain whether such fundamental reforms could ever be enacted in state firms.[42]

The launching of a more systematic attempt to reform the urban economy occurred in 1984. As indicated earlier, the major emphasis in these post-1984 reforms was to subject firms, rather than individual workers, to a more fully marketized environment. Existing firms were given increased autonomy to operate outside of the state allocation system. Some state firms even experimented with contracting management rights out to private entrepreneurs, who could enrich themselves if they increased firm profitability. Firms that were successful in finding new markets and in acquiring the resources to increase production to meet new market demands were able to retain portions of their profits for spending internally, in part on their own employees. Perhaps even more important, managerial compensation and particularly bonuses came to depend increasingly on firm profits. Some firms were able to enter into joint ventures with foreign firms. Successful operation of such a venture again yielded funds that could be expended internally. Nevertheless, the budget constraints within which existing state firms operated were still fairly flabby. Bank loans to cover losses remained relatively easy to obtain. Since most inefficient firms continued in business, the much-delayed but finally passed Bankruptcy Law (1987) had little initial impact.

The mode of implementation of a new system of employment in state and collective firms based upon limited term contracts, launched in 1986, made it appear that the iron rice bowl of China's workers would not be smashed but, rather, would be allowed to live to a ripe old age and die. Only newly hired workers were subjected to a full range of insecurities and incentives, while existing workers were able to retain their full set of guarantees and benefits. If this practice continued, it would take decades for retirement to eliminate the old-style, privileged state workers. In fact, it initially appeared that the new contract system might become a formality. If all new hires were based on fixed, 3–5 year contracts, but at the end of the initial contract virtually all were reemployed, regardless of firm and employee performance, then the iron rice bowl would suffer only a minor dent.

In their internal operations most state firms continued to see their obligations to their workers more in terms of providing employment and welfare than in strictly performance-based terms.[43] It appears that a good portion of the increased funds designed for improving the lot of workers were expended on housing and on collective goods (health care, recreational facilities, and so on), rather than on individualized incentive payments. Although there are increasing accounts during this period of employees of state firms being laid off, managers continued to be reluctant to fire workers outright. Those laid off were generally provided with partial wage payments for substantial periods of time or reemployed in "labor service companies" or other subsidiaries created by the parent firm. Furthermore, the overall pattern, as noted earlier, was for such firms to continue to add employees, rather than to reduce their payrolls. As a result of these conflicting trends, state and collective firms for the most part adapted to new market demands without making substantial progress in attacking the iron rice bowl system of job benefits and security enjoyed by most urban workers.

The relaxation of political controls over the thinking and private lives of workers combined with the emphasis on the *danwei*'s paternalistic obligation to relieve the long-standing material frustrations of their workers enhanced worker ability to obtain better treatment regardless of firm performance.[44] One study of a sample of 514 state firms attributes an increase in the share of bonuses in compensation from 20 percent in 1986 to 27 percent in 1992 largely to increased worker bargaining power.[45]

Before 1992 the employment generated by private and foreign

capital in China's urban economy was still relatively modest, with state and collective enterprises remaining predominant.[46] A schizophrenic situation developed in which market exchanges increasingly predominated in the urban consumer economy and even in the cultural realm, but the proportion of urban individuals who operated in a substantially reformed and marketized labor environment remained fairly small. The impact of the reforms had been more thorough outside of the cities; workers in TVEs could not even rely on a "clay rice bowl."

This rural-urban contrast produced a curious reversal of the usual pattern of attitude differences between social groups in a developing society. Urban people, and particularly those employed in urban factories, tend to have more "modern" attitudes than do rural people in every other country studied. They have stronger feelings of personal efficacy, more faith in the ability to get ahead through personal effort, more openness to new experiences, more faith in the ability of science to solve problems, and so forth. A 1990 survey in rural and urban areas of Tianjin, in contrast, found rural residents, and particularly those employed in rural industrial enterprises, to have the most modern attitudes in these terms. Urbanites, and those employed in state factories in particular, were significantly less modern. They were much more likely than their rural counterparts to be fatalistic, to feel they had little ability to get ahead through their own efforts, and to be distrustful of new experiences.[47] The findings of this survey suggest that most urbanites, including urban workers, had not had the institutional structures in which they worked altered by the reforms of the 1980s, except at the margins.[48]

Furthermore, a series of surveys conducted in a variety of Chinese cities in the late 1980s indicated that urbanites in general and workers in particular turned increasingly hostile toward the reform process at the end of that decade. In these surveys the percentage of respondents who said the reforms were going too fast rose from 27 percent in May 1987 to 65 percent in May 1989; the percentage who said the pace of reforms was just right dropped from 49 percent to just 18 percent.[49] It would appear that even though the iron rice bowl remained largely intact for most urban workers in the period leading up to 1989, the widely publicized experiments in retracting existing guarantees combined with rising inflation made workers, in particular, increasingly hostile toward the whole reform process. Insofar as workers were sympathetic toward the student demonstraters in 1989, that support was based more on the perception that the reforms were going too far than on the idea that they should be pushed further.[50] Even the indications of modest worker unrest visible in 1989 convinced many observers that official fear of proletarian anger would continue to be a fundamental obstacle to reforms designed to smash the "iron rice bowl" of state worker privileges.

The third period of reform of state and collective firms, launched in 1992, has yet to run its course. Although the onset of this phase is often connected with Deng Xiaoping's "Southern Tour" early in that year, some of the measures taken were already under way before China's leading reformer gave the green light for new initiatives.[51] Major efforts to finally smash the iron rice bowl have been launched. The success of these efforts has been the subject of considerable debate among outside observers. In line with earlier predictions, some analysts claim that the reform of state enterprises during 1993–94 was effectively stalled because of intense local resistance.[52] Others, including longtime skeptics, are increasingly persuaded that the "urban public goods regime" enjoyed by state enterprise workers in the past has finally begun to be dismantled.[53] The Fifteenth Congress of the Chinese Communist Party in 1997 provided a new impetus for overall reform of state enterprises. The Asian financial crisis that erupted later in the same year increased the competitive pressures on state enterprises still further.

The dismantling of the structural elements of the system of state sector job security and benefits accelerated toward the close of the century. Although earlier it was stated that the phasing in of limited-term labor contracts would take a generation or more, the basic assumption behind that scenario—the prediction that state employees who started work prior to the mid-1980s would retain their permanent status—may no longer be valid. Although by December 1994 only 26 percent of state unit workers and employees and 20 percent of collective unit personnel were governed by the contract system, one Chinese source claimed that by May 1996 the figure of contract workers had risen to 80 percent, with completion of the transition to 100 percent limited-term labor contracts projected for the end of the year.[54] Another Chinese source, however, presented figures indicating that at the end of June 1996 the figure for urban contract workers had only risen to 36 percent.[55] In the face of such statistical confusion, the extent and pace of the effort to convert permanent workers to contract worker status is somewhat unclear.

In the last few years new official policies have also been adopted to give managements in state industrial firms broad autonomy to hire and fire workers without relying on approvals from labor offices or supervising agencies.[56] At the same time, the ability of individuals to obtain, quit, and change jobs on their own initiative has increased. The system of state assignment to jobs of college graduates has been reduced to a marginal status (largely for those unable to find jobs on their own). Moreover, the refusal of a state employer to grant permission for a job change has become increasingly ineffective.[57] Reports have begun to appear of state firms offering higher pay and improved benefits in order to retain valued personnel.[58] Preliminary studies indicate that these changes have finally begun to weaken the labor immobility long characteristic of Chinese firms. Younger members of the labor force are getting accustomed to the idea that one's first job is not likely to be one's last.[59]

As increasing numbers of urban residents either start their careers in private or foreign employment or switch out of state and collective firms into these sectors, the rosters of state and collective factories are being filled increasingly by migrants from China's countryside.[60] In contrast to the Mao era, when the small number of temporary workers from rural areas employed in state industrial firms mostly performed separate and relatively dirty or menial jobs (in construction, hauling, and so on), by the 1990s increasing numbers of rural migrants were working alongside urban co-workers at lathes and looms. This growing trend is attributed to the increasing difficulties some kinds of state factories (for example, in textiles) have in recruiting urban employees, with dirty and low status jobs disfavored.[61] In some cities and industrial sectors (and especially in textiles) rural migrants constitute more than 50 percent of current workers, although overall in 1995 such migrants were still only 5 percent of the work force in state enterprises.[62]

A 1991 State Council decision proclaimed that such rural contract workers were to receive treatment on a par with urban workers.[63] Since in actual practice, however, rural migrant workers receive
lower wages and fringe benefits than their urban-origin colleagues,
it is conceivable that under the profit-conscious pressures of reforms, some firms may lay off urbanites and replace them with
cheaper workers from the countryside. One variant of this practice
involves an urban state enterprise's reducing its operations and laying off personnel while subcontracting production to a TVE. Sym-
bolizing such practices, a 1993 *People's Daily* article proclaimed that
state firms had "fallen in love with" peasant labor.[64] It seems clear
that the pace of layoffs has increased in state firms in the 1990s.
Thomas Rawski has estimated that as of 1994, 17–28 percent of
the workers and staff in state-owned enterprises in Shanghai,
Chongqing, and Shenyang had effectively been dismissed—laid off
with only partial, subsistence pay, no bonuses, and reduced benefits.[65] As a result of such trends, a modest downturn in urban industrial employment was reported in 1996, although it remains to be
seen whether this reversal of pattern is temporary or long term.[66]

The reforms are also transforming the wage systems and fringe
benefit provisions under which state and collective sector workers
operate. Enterprise management has been given substantial autonomy to experiment with and implement new wage systems. While
substantial variation across firms and over time makes generaliza-
tions difficult, the old fixed monthly wage plus bonus systems that
dominated in the past are either gone or rapidly becoming less
common. One substitute is some version of a piece-rate system,
sometimes implemented with constantly revised (that is, increased)
quotas to spur higher individual productivity. A more common system is a complex and quasi–"scientific management" point scheme
for determining wages and bonus payments, with the evaluation of
the points monopolized by management.[67] Still another recent variant is termed "concealed wages" *(mohu gongzi),* which involves individualized determination of pay levels by management, with the
worker forbidden to reveal his or her payment to colleagues. Supposedly this system stimulates productivity more than the old, transparent system in which each worker knew what everyone else

was earning, but it also arouses considerable anger and distrust in workers.[68]

The new round of reforms is also modifying the distribution of bonuses, subsidies, and benefits. It is generally estimated that by the mid-1990s the value of subsidies, benefits, and bonuses received by personnel in state firms had risen to about equal what they receive in wages. Since these items have tended to be distributed in an egalitarian fashion, changing the wage system alone would have only a weak incentive effect. Another important consideration in these reforms is a recognition that the financial burden on work units of providing so many benefits and subsidies to employees and also to retirees is a major contributing element to the fact that so many (40 percent or more) state firms continue to report financial losses. These concerns have led to attempts to reduce the benefits to which workers (and other urban personnel) are entitled, to require partial and increasing payment for some benefits (such as for medical treatment and housing), and to make remaining subsidies and bonuses subject to performance-based rather than egalitarian distribution.[69]

In addition to the carrots, there are also sticks—systems of fines and pay deductions have been implemented regarding a whole range of worker behavior, including matters ranging far and wide beyond production output and quality. In some reported cases issues such as attendance at political meetings, cleanliness of a worker's locker, and compliance with rules about what can be carried in lunch bags are counted in determining compensation.[70] In some instances supervisors receive quotas for the number of fines they are supposed to levy each month. In addition, they get to keep a percentage of the fines collected or have their diligence in levying fines counted in their own bonus calculation.[71] Occasionally a worker can end up owing the factory at the end of the month. Consequently, some analysts conclude that the reformed incentive systems are not designed solely or even primarily to stimulate productivity, but to redress the balance of power between management and workers. Where these reforms have been thoroughly implemented, they seem to have had their desired effect in making workers feel that their actions are subject to tight and arbitrary management control.[72]

Although uncertainties remain about how thoroughly the new

stage of reforms of state enterprises has been and will be implemented, it seems clear that the iron rice bowl has been significantly weakened, even if it has not been totally smashed. Despite the evident unpopularity of these reforms within factories, workers face new uncertainties and competitiveness regarding job security, compensation levels, and access to fringe benefits.[73]

With these changes as well as the exodus of some state workers to foreign and private firms and their replacement by rural migrant workers, the sharp distinctions in the treatment of workers by type of firm are being reduced. A degree of convergence is visible as the privileges of state firm workers are whittled away.[74] Full convergence, however, is still in the distant future, if it ever occurs. The lot of workers in most state factories and foreign and joint venture firms built with Western capital remains much better than in the other types of firms.

Worker Discontent and Its Potential Implications

A combination of liberalized policies, foreign investment, and spectacular growth rates has produced a significant expansion of China's working class since 1978. As noted earlier, this expansion has occurred across state, collective, TVE, and foreign-funded sectors, particularly in the latter categories. It is notable that by about 1992 industrial employment in rural Chinese firms achieved rough parity with industrial employment in state and urban collective firms, with further rapid increases expected to make rural proletarians more numerous than urban ones.[75]

Although the way workers are treated varies across and within types of firm, the average worker is substantially less privileged and more insecure than in the Mao era. The relative decline in the status of China's workers is the result of two processes. The most important is the explosive growth of new (or revived) types of factories in which workers are compensated and treated quite poorly, in comparison with their counterparts in state factories. In some cases the arbitrariness and exploitation experienced seem the equal of the worst industrial regimes reported in other countries and time periods. The second process, which made little headway until the 1990s, involves the erosion of the privileged treatment of workers in state firms. In part this erosion is a consequence of the first process, as state firms have had to adapt to competition from private and foreign-funded firms and from TVEs. Although workers have shared with others in the general increase in incomes since 1978, overall the evidence reviewed here confirms the common judgment that they are among the major "losers" as a result of the reforms. Any pretense that the workers are the leading class has largely disappeared from public discourse in China.

China's workers have not accepted their fall from grace since 1978 quietly. Available sources indicate that many types of industrial conflict are on the rise. Individual complaints, group petitions, slowdowns, strikes (illegal since 1982), acts of sabotage and physical violence against managerial personnel—all are reported to be increasing at a rapid pace in China in recent years.[76] The state has responded by developing labor dispute mediation committees, passing a new Labor Law in 1994, and advocating the implementation of collective bargaining.[77] As noted earlier, however, state laws and regulations designed to protect workers are often ignored or violated, particularly in TVEs and private and foreign-funded firms. Such measures, therefore, do not counteract the growing feeling by many workers that they have no effective institutional channels through which to express discontent or complain about unfair treatment. As the post-1992 reforms spread more broadly within state industrial enterprises, the potential for industrial conflict can only increase.

Should this growing contentiousness be taken as an indication that China's workers may at some future point pose a serious political challenge for the regime? Does the combination of declining worker status and increasing convergence of conditions across enterprise types mean that China may yet have a Solidarity movement in its future? Although it is hard to be definitive in responding to such speculative questions, there are several reasons to doubt such a scenario.

The most obvious point is that major changes that many observers had predicted could not be carried out (in particular, the smashing of the iron rice bowl in state factories) are in fact being pushed through. Despite the rising number of industrial conflicts, these new reforms for the most part seem to be occurring with little fanfare and without effective resistance. Reports on firms that have implemented these reforms describe widespread unhappiness but general compliance.[78] In those nonstate firms in which the conditions are worst, the availability of an "exit" option and the presence of a reserve army of the unemployed help to keep acts of protest at unfair treatment from escalating into general mobilization against the firm, not to mention the state. From this perspective, the rising tide of industrial conflicts might be interpreted not as signs of a future political challenge, but as another indication that China is becoming a "normal" country. After decades in which worker protests were viewed as illegitimate and suppressed, to tolerate such protests and search for ways to deal with them may be a healthy trend.

Further reasons to doubt the politically destabilizing nature of worker dissatisfaction come from a consideration of the structural features of China's contemporary proletariat. Even if there is eventual convergence in the lot of workers in all types of enterprises, at the moment a cardinal feature of China's enlarged proletariat is its diversity. It now includes about as many rural as urban members; increasingly even its urban worksites include a portion of rural migrants; there is a growing portion of newly recruited workers and substantial turnover; small-scale firms have proliferated faster than large firms; the wage and benefit systems employed vary a great deal from firm to firm; and the management faced by workers is of widely different types, many not closely identified with the Chinese state. Conditions of Chinese workers now vary widely, from enviable and still privileged to abysmal.

The implications of this increased internal complexity of the Chinese proletariat can be debated. Elizabeth Perry has argued that the internal differences within the working class should be seen as a source of conflict rather than stability. With industrial relations practices in flux since 1978, resentment by members of one group against unfair treatment compared to the members of another group provokes persistent worker protests against management.[79] Despite the accuracy of this analysis, these conflicts still appear manageable rather than explosive. Resentments of contract workers against permanent workers, of rural migrants against urban-origin co-workers, of workers drawn from one locality against those from a different place, and even of groups of workers against their management do not readily translate into shared worker anger against the state.[80] Despite the deplorable conditions in which large portions of China's workers currently operate, the reform era changes have if anything decreased the likelihood that they will mobilize to effectively challenge the system.

If, however, we adopt as our standard of comparison not Poland but the former Soviet Union or other East European socialist states, then we reach a different conclusion. Although the likelihood of mass mobilization of workers against the state appears low in China, we see there the same kinds of rising worker discontent visible prior to the collapse of East European regimes in 1989–1991. China's political leaders no longer can take comfort in their ability to turn to the workers for support in facing a crisis.[81] Instead, they must worry about whether they can maintain control over their increasingly unhappy and fractious proletariat. Furthermore, if China's elites once again fragment into conflicting factions, it is not unlikely that more conservative leaders will denounce exploitation of workers and attempt to recruit proletarian support for their cause. If that happens workers may yet play a central role in determining China's political future, with the outcome uncertain.

THOMAS P. BERNSTEIN

9 | Farmer Discontent and Regime Responses

To what extent have the political relations between China's regime and the country's social groups undergone change in the reform era? In particular, have China's rulers become more responsive to the interests of social groups than was the case under Mao? Are there new, public channels through which social groups can voice grievances, demands, and interests and bring them to the attention of officials and policymakers? If there are such new channels, can conclusions be drawn about their effectiveness in influencing policy?

This chapter examines the extent to which the interests of farmers, China's largest social group, can now be publicly articulated. Farmer interests with regard to the state can be inferred from their economic situation as well as from the extensive discussions in the Chinese media.[1] China's farmers are concerned with policies that affect the prices of industrial inputs in relation to the agricultural commodities that they sell, with state support for rural development, and with taxes. Informal and arbitrarily levied taxes and assessments are of great importance to farmers, as is the accountability of local officials and, more generally, the stability of regime policies, particularly with regard to the maintenance of household farming.

Farmer or agrarian interests are articulated both at the

grass roots and at higher or elite levels of the political hierarchy by "advocates," a term used because of the absence of organized and autonomous interest groups. Advocates for farmers and agricultural interests come from among the rural deputies to the National People's Congress. Their outspokenness is a manifestation of the more active role played by the NPC in reform China (see Chapter 5). Advocates also come from among the members of the agrarian research community of State Council and Central Committee institutes as well as from the academies and universities; from officials in ministries such as Agriculture; and from among editors and journalists in the specialized and general media.

Elite advocates are not independent actors but members of party and state agencies and their affiliates, reflective of the absence of interest groups outside the boundaries of the party-state. Public advocacy can be seen as a visible part of bureaucratic and elite politics, often expressive of and tied to the policies pushed by particular leaders.[2] This connection makes it difficult to assess the impact of public advocacy on policy outcomes, and only loose inferences can be drawn about its role in the policy process. It is worth noting that even in open, pluralist systems, "political outcomes are decided by a multiplicity of factors . . . and political scientists of an earlier era erred in attributing to organized interests a virtually exclusive role in policy determination."[3]

A variety of motives seems to impel members of the elite to play advocacy roles. One is concern for the public good, for example, the political and economic consequences of neglecting agricultural interests. Another is bureaucratic or local interests, an example being buck-passing. This occurs when local officials plead with the center to allocate money to agriculture that they themselves are unwilling to provide because of the low profitability of farming.

This chapter draws heavily on advocacy published in the Chinese media. Sometimes advocacy is blunt and outspoken, as when a NPC deputy labeled the practice of paying farmers in IOUs rather than cash for their sales to the state as "a kind of peasant exploitation."[4] Sometimes it is passionate, as in headlines such as these, run by *Nongmin Ribao* (NMRB), the national farmers' paper: "Don't harm the peasants' interests yet again" or "Reporting on the voice of the peasants is an obligation we should fulfill to the utmost."[5] Sometimes it is more restrained, as in research journals such as *Nongye Jingji Wenti* (Problems of the Agricultural Economy).

At the grass roots, villagers express grievances and demands through the nascent legal system and through elections, which at the village level allows more choice (see Chapter 6). Farmers appeal to officials at administrative levels above the village, and send enormous numbers of letters to central agencies. In 1988 NMRB reportedly received more than a thousand letters a day, mostly complaints against "village tyrants."[6] Villagers use these means to engage in "policy-based resistance." They protest and lodge complaints by invoking rules, regulations, and central policies against local officials who violate them.[7]

In the post-Mao era three periods of regime receptiveness or responsiveness to farmer interests can be distinguished. Responsiveness was high during the initial stage of reform, 1978–1983, when the regime allocated new resources to the agricultural sector and came to support the historic abolition of the commune system. During the second period, roughly from 1984 to 1990, regime responsiveness to agrarian interests was low, despite evidence of accumulating problems in agriculture and despite remarkably intense advocacy.

In contrast, regime attention to agriculture increased significantly in the 1990s, as seen in the increased pressure on local officials to fund agriculture, the extension of family land contracts, and the passage of a "Law on Agriculture." During this phase, advocacy also was intense. But the primary cause for increased responsivness was probably the regime's fear of potential or real instability, as manifested by the widespread rural riots of 1992–93.

Social Interests in the Mao and Deng Eras

During the Mao period, the scope for group interests was systemically limited by the goal of building a new society in accord with an ideological and developmental vision which overrode partial interests. In extreme phases of mobilization, rulers paid little or no attention to group interests, even if information on negative popular reactions reached them. The goal of attaining breakthroughs was so important to key leaders that they deliberately suppressed, ignored, or downplayed evidence of popular suffering. Mao repeatedly and forcefully silenced those who spoke out on behalf of the peasants. In 1953 he lashed out at Liang Shuming, the well-known non-Communist rural reformer; in 1955, at Deng Zihui, the head of the Central Committee's Rural Work Department, and most notably, in 1959, at Peng Dehuai, the Politburo member and minister of defense, who criticized the "petty-bourgeois fanaticism" of the Great Leap Forward and the damage that it had done. In this case, the records of the Lushan meetings strikingly show how Mao disregarded information on the real state of affairs in the countryside so as not to dampen the mass enthusiasm that he believed to be widespread.[8]

During the consolidation periods that followed intense campaigns of mobilization, the real interests of social groups became more salient to the leaders because of the mounting costs of ignoring them. Leaders responded to evidence of the peasants' "declining enthusiasm for production" or, as in the case of the Leap, to evidence of mass famine and instability. During such phases, there was more scope for bringing into play Mao Zedong's own concept of balancing interests by means of the "correct" management of contradictions among the people, which implied recognition of the legitimacy of partial interests even within the context of the primacy of the interests of the whole. But invariably new mobilization efforts followed and group interests were once more pushed into the background.

During the post-Mao reform period, the goal of building a socialist and communist society largely lost its salience. The pressure to override group interests for the collective good has declined, and the regime instead relies on material incentives. Moreover, declining political control capacities increase pressure on the regime to pay attention to the interests of strategically important groups. A case in point is the regime's sensitivity to the destabilizing effects of unemployment that results from the restructuring of inefficient state enterprises.

Regime willingness to make concessions to societal interests varies with the issue at stake. China's rulers do not hesitate to repress dissidents or the Tibetan and Muslim minorities who aspire to greater autonomy if not independence. In the countryside, the regime's coercive family planning policy has been a prime example of its continued determination to override societal preferences. Tyrene White observes, "Mobilization [for family planning] has remained an integral, active part of the post-revolutionary Chinese political process."[9] To be sure, reform-induced opportunities for evasion and declining state capacity have compelled the regime to compromise on the one-child family policy, but it continues to make major, often ruthless, efforts to enforce birth quotas.[10]

The Deng regime also learned from the catastrophic record of the Mao period that policy discussions and advice are needed in making decisions. Policy communities are formed and specialists are asked to evaluate various policies on the agenda. The press is able to carry franker and more detailed news as well as discussions of policy options, making possible public advocacy. This tolerance is not unlimited: the NMRB, for example, after the suppression of the 1989 Tiananmen demonstrations, was criticized for one-sidedly overemphasizing peasant interests and ordered to play its appointed role as the party's "mouthpiece" (houshe).[11]

The end of major political campaigns, class struggle, and class labeling has made possible greater outspokenness in the villages. The reform regime's own efforts to inform households of their rights and to spread basic knowledge of laws and regulations reinforce willingness to speak out, as does exposure to local and national media. The increase in mobility opportunities, including long-term migration to the urban sector, contributes to the loosening of political control in the countryside. Most important, the structural changes of the rural reforms themselves raise the awareness of villagers of whether or not their rights are being violated. As members of production teams, peasants knew little about commune finances except for the year-end value of their residual work points. Now farm households know where their incomes come from and whether or not officials squeeze them.

Party leadership, so vital to Mao's campaigns, is supposed to continue in the reform period. However, the new central task of party secretaries—to lead their villagers to prosperity utilizing the market—differs both in principle and in method from their previous task of promoting collectivist and egalitarian projects. In a significant subset of villages, party leadership is paralyzed or weak. In another subset, in contrast, development does take place under the authoritarian, paternalistic, benevolent, or despotic leadership of local party secretaries, who have taken on entrepreneurial roles but maintain high levels of control over the population. This is the case in many of the developed, wealthy, "corporate" villages in the coastal provinces, where nonagricultural enterprise, especially collectively owned town and village enterprises, grow at spectacular rates. There, ordinary people benefit enormously in material terms, provided they comply with the directives and rules of the local boss and accept their own subordinate status. In this subset of villages, there may be as little room for input from the masses as there was under Mao.[12]

A significant change in public discourse is that now, frequent references are made to the "legitimate rights and interests" of social groups, peasants, women, or migrants. It is recognized that policies may adversely affect short-term or immediate interests. The official response should not only consist of political education but also of measures to take care "of the interests of all concerned wherever and whenever possible."[13] At the Thirteenth Party Congress in 1987, General Secretary Zhao Ziyang also recognized the need for new channels through which differing interests could be "transmitted to the leading bodies."[14] This idea was not repudiated even after Zhao's purge during Tiananmen: "interest bodies and groups with relative independence" can exist, provided they put the general interest first.[15]

At the same time, official discourse often denies the existence of conflicts of interest. When local officials implement their own policies rather than those of the center, it is not because the interests of center and locality are in conflict, but because local officials lack a full understanding of the nature and spirit of central policy. More generally, the pluralist model of competition among independent interest groups continues to be explicitly rejected. Instead, when the establishment of interest-oriented organizations is permitted, they are called upon to cooperate with and accept party leadership. This seems similar to authoritarian corporatism, as practiced in the past in Latin America, and indeed, some PRC scholars now make explicit use of the term.[16]

Whether the Leninist transmission-belt system is being replaced by an authoritarian corporate one is not yet clear. The distinction between the two hinges on the extent of bargaining that occurs between an interest group and the regime. Under authoritarian corporatism, the state confers a monopoly on an organization to represent a given interest, bargaining with it for material benefits in exchange for the group's political quiescence. In contrast, the primary task of transmission-belt organizations is to mobilize their members for the attainment of party goals.[17] An example of informal bargaining in China by organizations representing large social groups was reported in 1988 by the deputy director of the State Administration on Commodity Prices:

> At every meeting, departments in charge of production will demand price increases for their products. In a meeting attended by a dozen departments, the Commodity Prices Administration will have only "one ally," that is, the National Federation of Trade Unions, which represents the workers and staff and is strongly opposed to price increases.[18]

This statement indirectly highlights the discriminatory status of China's farmers. Had they been represented at these meetings, the Price Administration might have had a second ally in holding back industrial price increases. But unlike workers, women, young people, or overseas Chinese, farmers do not have their own national mass organization. Without even a transmission-belt organization, farmers are not able to take advantage of the informal processes that may be leading in a corporatist direction. On numerous occasions advocates have called for the establishment of a national farmers' association in order to strengthen the voice of farmers in policymaking. This demand arises in part because China's political system continues to privilege the urban sector and is permeated with urban biases against rural people.[19]

Phase One: Peasant and Regime Interests in the Transition to Household Contracting, 1978–1983

During the initial reform period, the regime went to unusual lengths to accommodate peasant interests. In late 1978 it sharply raised base and above-quota procurement prices, and it moved rapidly to restore the private sector. Most remarkable, policymakers moved from outright rejection at the watershed Third Plenum to at first highly restricted and ultimately full acceptance of the household responsibility system (HRS), that is, of family contract farming, despite its earlier harsh repudiation as capitalist by Mao Zedong in 1962.

Some scholars attribute this historic turn to "peasant power," arguing that peasants seized the initiative to do away with collective farming, surreptitiously at first and increasingly openly later, essentially confronting the regime with a fait accompli.[20] Chinese post-hoc accounts agree. They claim that household contracting was an invention of the peasants, that the center "respected the pioneering spirit of the masses," and that peasants broke through obstacles erected by cadres and officials.[21] This thesis suggests that peasants' capacity to push their interests to the point of restoration of family farming was a cause of China's reforms rather than a consequence. Other scholars, however, put much more weight on changes in the political system, such as Deng's encouragement of experimentation, and on the role of local officials in enabling HRS to take hold.[22]

In analyzing the efficacy of demands from below versus regime initiatives from above, regional differences play a major role. Dali Yang has shown that in those areas that had suffered acutely from the famine of the Great Leap Forward, demand for HRS was extremely strong. Memories of the role that family farming had played in the recovery from the Leap were still vivid; rural society retained an "alternative agenda" to that of promoting collectivism.[23] Early in the reform period, in the fall of 1978, in drought-stricken Anhui villages—a province devastated by famine in 1959–1961—desperate peasants openly voiced demands to their own party secretaries and to outside officials for permission to practice family contracting, which in quite a few cases was given even while HRS was officially illegal.[24] However strong the demand from below, as long as HRS was prohibited, satisfying peasant demand required connivance and cover-ups by sympathetic local and higher-level cadres.[25]

This complicity was made possible by elite awareness of the political dangers of the crisis in agriculture bequeathed by Mao. In 1978 Li Xiannian warned that without accommodating peasant interests, party power could not be consolidated. Chen Yun conjured up the specter of village party secretaries leading hungry peasants to beg in the cities. Wan Li, then party secretary of Anhui province, and an early champion of HRS, reportedly voiced fears of rebellions and of large-scale migration by impoverished peasants.[26] Perceptions of threat helped HRS to gain a foothold.

National policy gradually opened the door to the sanctioned adoption of HRS in a process that began extremely cautiously at the Fourth Plenum in September 1979, which permitted "a few" isolated and extremely poor households to convert.[27] In the next two years, restrictions were progressively loosened. During this period, HRS spread far more rapidly than did the loosening of official prohibitions, a point that supports the thesis that strong peasant demand played a major role in decollectivization. Nevertheless, official yielding to peasant initiatives was facilitated by central documents, speeches, and editorials. On the one hand, these kept insisting that HRS only be allowed in the poorest one third of villages, but not in the middling and more prosperous two thirds of villages. On the other hand, they increasingly emphasized the criteria of suitability of HRS to local conditions and the importance of mass demand, legitimating conversion to HRS outside of the one-third limit.[28] For instance, in late 1981, Zhao Ziyang reportedly changed his mind about the one-third limit after talking with villagers.[29] The process was one in which peasants were increasingly empowered to exercise a right to choose.

Peasant demand was by no means the only factor prompting the reform leaders to agree to HRS. First, political conflict played an important role in propelling HRS forward, since reformers came to use HRS adoption as a club with which to beat leftists. Indeed, by 1982, adoption of HRS became a matter of compliance with the current political line and was pushed through regardless of local preferences.[30] Second, elite proponents of HRS secured the support of policymakers by presenting the reform as compatible with socialism, especially since land remained in the hands of the collectives. Restoration of private ownership in land, especially to former owners *(tudi hui laojia)*, was strongly repudiated; peasants were only allowed to pursue their interests in the contracting of collective lands.[31] Third, HRS was made more acceptable because output of grain and cotton continued to be planned and subject to state procurement, a point of great importance to leaders such as Chen Yun, who insisted that peasants could not be permitted to adopt practices that "happen to be . . . in their interest" but were in conflict with the state plan.[32]

A fourth factor was elite learning. Reform leaders became convinced of the efficacy of household contracting as a generally applicable method for raising output, productivity, incomes, and diversification, thereby laying the foundation for all-round rural development. Initially, HRS was seen only as a temporary relief measure; gradually, it came to be seen as a more long-term solution. In this learning process, positive investigation reports, a form of advocacy, played a significant role. The reports focused not so much on peasant demand as on the efficacy of HRS in increasing output. For instance, in two important reports published by Wu Xiang, a senior central-level rural researcher, in *Renmin Ribao* (People's Daily) in April and November 1980, Wu claimed to have found that the advantages of HRS far outweighed its disadvantages, which included greater difficulty in mobilizing peasants for collective projects. Wu claimed that the disadvantages were temporary and could be overcome.[33]

Among the positive investigation reports, those submitted by the Research Group on Problems of China's Agricultural Development require special mention.[34] Its members were urban young people from elite backgrounds who had spent years in the countryside in the wake of the Cultural Revolution. Shocked by rural backwardness, they set up discussion groups on rural development after their return to Beijing, merging into the Research Group in 1980. Using high-level contacts, members investigated villages, especially those in which HRS had gotten an early start. Their reports strongly emphasized the usefulness of HRS in stimulating the growth of output and incomes. The former leader of the group, Chen Yizi, claims that these reports exerted significant influence on top leaders.[35]

In agrarian advocacy during the reform period as a whole, the Research Group most closely resembled a Western-style interest group, since it formally functioned outside the agencies of party and government. Consequently, the group was reportedly attacked by party conservatives as a "third road force aiming to seize the party's leadership." A national Agricultural Work Conference held in October 1981, however, conferred approval on the group's existence and a year later, its members were incorporated into the central party–State Council rural research agencies, ending the group's anomalous quasi-independent existence.[36]

A fifth and perhaps most important reason was that leaders came to believe that HRS would save the state money. As early as May 1980, *People's Daily* editorialized about the savings to the state from no longer having to ship costly relief grain to poor villages that now practiced HRS.[37] Gradually leaders came to believe that rising rural incomes would enable the peasants themselves to bear more of the investment burden in agriculture, a thesis increasingly prominent in official comment.[38] At the Third Plenum in late 1978, the leaders had agreed to boost state agricultural investment from its current level of 11 percent of capital construction funds to 18 percent. This commitment was not kept. Instead, state agricultural investments were cut not only during periods of budgetary stringency such as that of 1979–1981, but over the long term. By 1986 state capital construction funds slated for agriculture dropped to 3 percent, the lowest level since 1953. The official calculus that the new wealth of peasant households would significantly substitute for state investment in agriculture turned out to be erroneous, since peasants invested mainly in housing and in more profitable nonagricultural enterprise.[39] In sum, decollectivization cannot be explained simply by invoking peasant demand.

Phase Two: Strong Advocacy but Low Response, 1984–1990

If peasant influence was unusually strong during the transition, it declined in the years that followed.[40] While rural industrial and commercial enterprise grew during this period at astonishingly rapid rates, especially in the coastal regions, the agrarian sector was beset by a series of problems. Grain output stagnated until 1989, staying below the peak level attained in 1984. Agricultural investment from all sources lagged, leading to stagnation or even decline in indicators such as area covered by irrigation. Because industrial profits and taxes became the primary source of local prosperity, officials "emphasized industry and neglected agriculture" (zhonggong qingnong). Agriculture was a drain on local resources. Thus the proportion of all local state spending devoted to agriculture reportedly decreased from about 6.0 percent in the 1981–1985 period to 0.8 percent in 1994.[41] Instead, local officials diverted state funds slated for agriculture to more profitable uses or they engaged in buck-passing: "Nearly every province has asked for more money from the central government to pump into agriculture, but none has been too willing to invest its own funds."[42] The low comparative advantage of agriculture led to a "large-scale outflow of agricultural funds."[43] Once villages had become rich from industrialization, however, they were in a position to subsidize agriculture, including the incomes of households still dependent on farming. Higher-level policy demanded that "industry support agriculture" (yigong bu nong), and there are impressive cases from highly developed areas where agriculture throve because of subsidies.[44]

Nevertheless, rural per capita incomes, which had more than doubled between 1978 and 1984, largely stagnated in real terms during the remainder of the 1980s. This stagnation, however, concealed striking disparities between those whose earnings came largely from nonagricultural sources and those whose income depended largely on farming. Rural incomes in the coastal provinces, where TVEs were concentrated, grew much more rapidly than in the central and western provinces, resulting in rising rural territorial inequalities.[45] Increasingly, farmers complained that it didn't pay to farm.

Stagnation in agriculture was also caused by the state's lowering of procurement prices for quota grain and cotton in 1985. This step was taken to reduce the state's heavy burden of subsidizing urban consumers, which had arisen because the regime did not dare to pass on to urban consumers the additional costs from the procurement price increases granted from 1978 on.[46] In the late 1980s prices paid to farmers for selling to the state were increased, but they continued to lag behind the free market price for grain and the inflation-fueled rise in industrial input prices. When the government tied the supply of low-priced inputs such as diesel oil and chemical fertilizer to sales of grain to the state in order to raise incentives, local officials found it easy to make money by selling the inputs on the free market, putting farmers at a further disadvantage. The corruption of local officials extended to the diversion of state procurement funds to profitable investment, usually in TVEs. This was a major cause of the large-scale issuance of IOUs *(baitiao)* to farm households from 1988 on, a practice bitterly resented by the peasants.[47] Moreover, farm incomes were adversely affected by unpredictably variable fees, fines, and apportionments—the *san luan*—that were exacted by local and higher-level authorities and that also greatly angered villagers. Since villages and townships without TVEs had no sources of funding other than farm households, these fiscal burdens took a disproportionate toll in agriculture-dependent villages.[48] Enforcing these policies and practices required extensive coercion of farmers.[49]

Farmers' advocates exposed these conditions. The editors of NMRB claim credit for having been the first to publicize the IOU problem in 1988.[50] The paper carried numerous, often vividly written articles depicting farmer anger. Once it printed a farmer's complaint about how local cadres implemented a central directive ordering them to explain to peasants why the state couldn't raise procurement prices:

> Guess how the xiang-cun cadres did this work? They posted a notice on the village committee door, which read: "Households failing to fulfill the grain quota will not be allowed to send their child to school, will not be given a planned birth quota, and will have their contracted land taken back."

When farmers complained that these threats couldn't have come from party central, cadres "outrageously" replied: "Aren't policies set by men?"[51] An NPC deputy from Hubei who complained about payment of farmers in IOUs said that "peasants have no money to consult a doctor, go to school, or even to buy salt."[52]

The Beijing journal *Liaowang* depicted peasants as being in a "rebellious state of mind" *(zaofan xinli)* in the winter of 1986–87 in reaction to the "extreme measures" taken by local authorities to compel fulfillment of state sales quotas. The same term was used in 1990 in a Ministry of Agriculture report on the impact of farmers' financial burdens.[53] Reports of violence and riots appeared.[54] One researcher wrote of numerous cases of "forced purchase" *(qianggou)* of chemical fertilizer by angry peasants.[55]

Advocates demanded policy remedies. NMRB editors wrote in March 1989 that state-peasant relations were no longer "so harmonious and had even become distorted." They conceptualized state-farmer relations in terms of bargaining, noting that "when peasants contribute more to the state, the state [should] give more warmth to the peasants."[56] Advocates in the NPC urged greater government efforts to close the price scissors between industrial and agricultural commodities, end the IOU crisis, and increase state investment in agriculture.

Advocates attributed the neglect of agriculture to excessive optimism at the top. In 1988, Chen Xiwen, a prominent agricultural researcher, complained that after the bumper harvest of 1984, when "some policymakers became over-optimistic," they lowered procurement prices, damaging incentives and causing drops in grain output.[57] Indeed, the unprecedented harvest of 1984 seemed to signal to top leaders that the grain problem had been solved, and that attention should focus on rural industrialization as a solution to the deep-seated rural problems of underemployment. Deng Xiaoping was mesmerized by the "unexpected" growth of TVEs.[58] Wan Li, the agricultural reform leader, thought that county party secretaries should no longer function merely as "agricultural secretaries" or "grain secretaries" but should concentrate on industrial and commercial development.[59]

Chen Yun was an exception to the optimism. In 1985 and later as well, he warned against neglect of agriculture. Quoting from a report that said that "peasants engaged in industry and business earn more than those who grow crops," Chen said that there could be "no economic stability without agricultural development," for "without grain there will be chaos" *(wuliang ziluan).*[60]

Despite Chen's warnings and evidence of instability in the countryside, top leaders treated agricultural problems in terms of business as usual. They issued bland assurances that agriculture was indeed the foundation of the economy and therefore always at the top of their agenda.[61] In 1993, when widespread rural rioting was in progress, Wan Li, then the outgoing chairman of the NPC Standing Committee, claimed that only now had he obtained "first-hand knowledge about the problems facing agriculture." Wan Li evidently hadn't paid attention to what rural deputies had been saying about these problems since 1988, when he became chairman of the NPC.[62]

Farmer advocates, particularly rural NPC deputies, criticized the verbal attention that in reality meant actual neglect of agriculture, nicknaming it "slogan" or "conference" agriculture (*kouhao* or *huiyi nongye*). In 1988 deputies criticized Premier Li Peng's Government Work Report for offering "insufficiently concrete" remedies for the agricultural sector.[63] "Some comrades—and particularly some leading cadres—relegate very real, very concrete, and even very critical work in agriculture to the sidelines."[64] A year later, complaints were voiced that "our leading cadres are not familiar with the peasants' situation and have serious bureaucratic tendencies."[65]

In order to compel governmental attention to agriculture, NPC advocates called for a law on agriculture. Without a law, agrarian interests had to rely on policies that were easily changed and subject to the "sudden whims" (*xinxue laichao*) of leaders. Besides, "few" leaders "listen to the appeals of peasants" for government assistance. A law would genuinely establish the status of agriculture as "the foundation," and impose legally binding governmental obligations with regard to investment and financial burdens, thereby ending "slogan agriculture." Moreover, it would restrain departments and local governments that diverted funds targeted for agrarian purposes and give farmers the right to sue in court against violations of the law. Demand for such a law was heard first at the 1989 session of the NPC and each year thereafter until 1993. At each session, groups of deputies ranging from 30 to 70 members submitted a motion on this subject. These were referred to the NPC Finance Committee, which in 1991 reported favorably to the Standing Committee. State Council "departments concerned" thereupon started to work on a draft in April 1991, consulting "nearly a hundred" legal and economic specialists in central and provincial units. In 1992 the minister of agriculture publicly expressed support for the law. But when the NPC met in 1993, a draft had still not been submitted, a delay that "is really very difficult to understand," according to an official from Ningxia province. Numerous voices at the spring 1993 NPC and Chinese People's Political Consultative Conference called for passage. The chairs of three provincial people's congress standing committees—Anhui, Jiangsu, and Shandong—told NMRB that "peasants were thirsting for the 'basic law.'" Finally, the PRC Agricultural Law was adopted by the NPC Standing Committee in July 1993, at a time when the attention of China's leaders was focused on the countryside, probably because a wave of rural disturbances prompted regime action.[66]

Phase Three: Rising Regime Receptivity to Agricultural Interests in the 1990s

In late April 1989, when the Tiananmen demonstrations were gaining momentum, Deng Xiaoping assured Li Peng and Yang Shangkun that there "is no problem with the peasants."[67] Indeed, the demonstrations seemed to confirm the proposition that the urban sector was *the* source of instability in China. Nevertheless, Deng's confidence in the stability of rural China disregarded evidence of mounting discontent in the countryside. Had rural people joined the 1989 protests and had urban protestors been willing to link up with them, the Tiananmen crisis would have been far more severe. This point was made by the party secretary and governor of Shaanxi province in June 1989:

> At this crucial moment, peasants have been siding with the party and the government. By doing a good job in the three summer tasks, they demonstrate their faith in the party and the government and their opposition to the upheaval, thereby contributing in

a special way to the stabilization of the situation and setting the people's minds at rest. The party and the government are indebted to you.[68]

In 1991, however, Deng Xiaoping reportedly reversed his 1989 view, saying that China's stability hinged on whether or not the lives of peasants improved.[69] And again, sometime in 1992, Deng warned that "should problems arise in the economy in the 1990s, they would most likely arise in agriculture."[70] In 1992 and 1993, hundreds of protests, demonstrations and riots erupted, mainly in heavily agriculture-dependent districts where villagers had become increasingly enraged by the financial burdens imposed on them by the local and higher-level bureaucracies and by the failure of state procurement agencies to pay farmers in cash. The most publicized case was that of Renshou county, Sichuan, where villagers rioted in January and again in June 1993 in protest against assessments for road construction.[71]

The riots shocked central leaders. Vice Premier Tian Jiyun, who had major responsibilities in the agricultural system, reportedly told Tianjin NPC deputies at the 1993 session: "If there are problems in the villages, no one in the present regime can hold on to power," and the consequences would be "unimaginable."[72] Wan Li charged that peasants had been driven to revolt by official exploitation. He noted that when a visitor asked peasants what they needed, the response was "we need nothing but Chen Sheng and Wu Guang," leaders of China's first great peasant rebellion during the Qin dynasty.[73]

The rural disorders galvanized the regime. In late 1992 General Secretary Jiang Zemin issued an urgent call to action, explaining that "problems in the rural areas have provoked the peasants' discontent and anger."[74] The most acute problems were tackled energetically in 1993. Resources were mobilized to redeem farmers' IOUs, and an intense campaign was launched to eliminate "unreasonable" burdens. Beijing canceled 37 fees charged by administrative agencies and 43 "target-setting" programs such as "building educationally advanced counties," the expenses of which were apportioned among villagers.[75] The enactment of the Law on Agricul-

ture in the summer of 1993 was clearly a response to the disturbances. It gave farmers the "right to refuse" or to reject *(you quan
jujue)* payment of improperly authorized fees, fines, apportionments,
and compulsory fund-raising. The term "right to refuse" was used
four times in the text.[76] The law also prohibited the withholding or
diversion of procurement or investment funds. "Serious" violators
could be subjected to administrative punishments and could also be
subjected to criminal investigation. Violators could be sued when
they caused losses or damages. The regime, however, failed to eliminate the burden problem, which "rebounded" *(fantan)* and continued to arouse intense anger in the rural areas.

In addition to taking action on the IOU and burden issues, central leaders promulgated two policies designed to protect farmer
interests. One firmed up the regime's commitment to the household responsibility system; the other recognized the special developmental needs of agriculture. First, with regard to HRS, land contracts were extended to fifteen years in 1984, but fear that HRS
would not last was widespread among farmers in the 1980s and the
early 1990s.[77] The regime sought to allay these anxieties by repeatedly pledging that the policy would "not change for a long time"
(changqi bu bian). This ambiguous formulation indicated an unwillingness to make a binding commitment to HRS, largely due to
strongly held Marxist beliefs that family farming is not compatible
with modernity and the application of industrial methods to agriculture. When grain output stagnated for four years beginning in 1985,
seemingly showing that HRS no longer produced results, proposals
were made for one or another form of recollectivization or for
placing land in the hands of fewer but efficient farmers in order to
attain economies of scale.

Throughout the 1980s and 1990s, advocates strongly opposed attempts to impose change from above.[78] Some researchers argued
that the rural productive forces were still suitable for family management, suggesting that this would change in the future to the detriment of HRS. Others rejected the Marxist premise that agriculture
is similar to industry in requiring large-scale operations. Citing Western studies on the economics of farming, they maintained that fam-

ily farming could be efficient even at the most advanced levels of modernization.[79]

Proposals to recollectivize gained strength during the conservative upsurge in the wake of the Tiananmen upheaval.[80] Rumors about the impending restoration of the "big collective" circulated widely in villages, prompting anxious letters to the authorities and cases of sale of livestock and destruction of property.[81] NPC deputies reported on these fears.[82] NMRB argued that the peasants had earned "indelible" merit by abstaining from the Tiananmen upheaval. Since this stability demonstrated the success of the rural reforms, the regime had an obligation to maintain them.[83] If the farms were recollectivized, advocates conjured up the specter of instability:

> It is quite evident that if movements were launched to collectivize the farmers' means of production . . . the result would inevitably lead to a severe deterioration [*yanzhong e'hua*] in the relations between the peasantry and the party and government. Severe damage to the rural means of production would result.[84]

As reform currents regained ascendancy from 1992 on and pressure from the countryside rose, the leaders made up their minds to maintain HRS. In 1994 regulations were issued to extend most land contracts to thirty years. The leaders, however, did not abandon their interest in larger-scale farming. They adopted a carefully worded but flexible formula in which, under certain conditions, farmers could, "on the basis of fully respecting" their will, be guided to farm "on an optimum scale."[85] The regime yielded to farmer interests, but by no means completely, and there are continued signs of farmer insecurity and consequent unwillingness to make long-term investments in land.[86]

Central policymakers recognized that agriculture had become the "weakest link" in the national economy, requiring state protection (*guojia baohu*), without which it could "easily land in a disadvantaged position" in the market economy. They recognized that growth in agricultural output without growth in farmer incomes could not be sustained. They concluded that agriculture should no longer be exploited on behalf of urban and industrial growth but required more state investment. They called for an end to "slogan agriculture."[87] Specifically, the Law on Agriculture required the state to adopt measures for the maintenance of "rational price parity" between industrial and agricultural commodities, to set protective prices and establish risk funds for grain and other key agricultural commodities. Further, it stipulated that the "state shall gradually increase the level of overall agricultural investment and the amount appropriated each year should exceed the growth in revenue."

These commitments reflected long-standing themes in the agrarian research and policy communities. In late 1991, the editors of *Nongye Jingji Wenti* (Agricultural Economic Issues) wrote about the "severe erosion" of the interests of grain growers, arguing that the stage of "primitive accumulation" of capital for industry had passed: "No longer can we continue to allow a fragile agricultural sector to be the source of industrial accumulation."[88] Researchers also had called for protecting agriculture from the market, since "all governments adopt policies to protect, subsidize, and support agriculture."[89]

Adopting new policies was one thing; implementing them was another. After the enactment of the Law on Agriculture, an enforcement group was set up under the NPC Standing Committee, with members from the Ministry of Agriculture, the State Planning Commission, and other agencies. Inspection in three provinces in 1994 showed that there were serious problems with insufficient investment, price rises for inputs, and continued imposition of heavy financial burdens on farmers.[90] In 1995 and 1996, central leaders severely berated local authorities that devote

> thousands of words to talking about agriculture while devoting tremendous efforts to developing industry. . . . Consequently, input in agriculture has declined, farmland irrigation works have become antiquated . . . acreage under cultivation has dwindled with each passing year, while peasants' financial burdens have increased with each passing day and prices of agricultural means of production have risen steadily.[91]

Consequently, in the mid-1990s, procurement prices were raised substantially in an effort to offset the impact of inflation. State investment in agriculture also increased by a record 27.5 percent in 1996. Initial steps were taken to establish risk funds.[92]

However, with regard to the issue that provoked the most intense rural anger, arbitrary exactions, the regime proved incapable of acting in the interests of villagers. In May 1996, three years after the adoption of the law and the campaign against financial burdens, the Central Committee and State Council issued another harshly worded edict against burdens, which had provoked "extremely intense" *(shifen qianglie)* reactions from the masses.[93] In the autumn of 1996, new outbreaks of rural protest against arbitrary financial exactions erupted on a substantial scale in Jiangxi, Hunan, and other provinces.[94] Once again, central leaders exhorted the localities to abide by the rules and reduce burdens on farmers, issuing another major edict late in the year.[95] Replacing the burdens with a fair system of taxation is a major task that has yet to be adequately addressed, but in the meantime, the regime has clearly lacked the capacity systematically to protect farmers from local bureaucratic predation by enforcing its regulations.

If directives from above have only a limited effect on issues as vital to rural stability as the burdens, could the central authorities achieve better results by encouraging pressure from below? The central authorities unwittingly did this by disseminating central regulations to the villages. This enabled villagers to compare central regulations with local rules or practices, implicitly empowering them to engage in "policy-based resistance" by confronting local officials in the name of central or provincial rules.[96] This happened in the Renshou riots of 1993 and again in tax riots in Hunan province in 1996.[97]

If farmers had institutions through which to protect their "legitimate rights and interests," they might not have to take to the streets. As noted earlier, legal institutions are spreading in rural China while liberalized village elections give residents more choice in the selection of their leaders. Thus far, however, there is little evidence that elected village leaders have enabled farmers to protect their interests with respect to burdens when these are levied by higher-level authorities.[98]

Elite advocates have long suggested still another approach to enable farmers to defend their interests in an organized way, namely, establishment of a national farmers' association at all levels of the hierarchy.[99] Such an association would seek to "safeguard" farmer interests by "consulting and coordinating" with government agencies.[100] As a central researcher put it, without their own organization, farmers are always in a "passive position," unable to conduct an "equal dialogue" with those outside agriculture.[101] If organized at all levels of the administrative hierarchy, a national farmers' association could conceivably exert horizontal pressure to secure proper implementation of central directives.

In 1989 a motion to set up a farmers' association was submitted by thirty-one NPC deputies. In 1990, the "departments concerned" of the State Council were reported to be studying the subject.[102] Proposals have continued to be published since then, but no action has been taken. That it has been possible to discuss the issue at all in an era when liberalizing political reforms have been kept off the official agenda is testimony to awareness within the Chinese regime that more needs to be done to protect agrarian interests. By the same token, failure to act is testimony to the leaders' fear of the potential consequences of giving farmers an organized national voice.

Conclusion

Extensive public advocacy exists on behalf of farmers' interests. Although a specific link between advocacy and policy has not been established, it seems reasonable to conclude that advocates do play a role in the policy process. They lack the clout to compel attention, however, even when they communicate reports of local discontent. Top leaders seem to act mainly when they see unmistakable evidence of substantial societal instability and when they see a large threat to their developmental goals. When they do act, they experience great difficulties with implementation of remedial measures.

At the same time, advocacy of the interests of farmers has become a part of an ongoing public discourse on interests. This represents a substantial change from the Mao era. Whether this interest-oriented discourse becomes fully institutionalized remains to be seen.

One of the insights of the literature on democratization is that authoritarian rulers may choose democratization when the costs to them of not doing so become too high. Adapted to the Chinese case, this could mean that in order to attain their goals, Chinese leaders may at some point come to recognize that permitting the establishment of organized farmers' interest groups could be in their own interest. If this came to pass, it is highly likely that many of the advocates would rapidly join in providing leadership for such organizations.

DOROTHY J. SOLINGER

10 | China's Floating Population

The persistent penetration of market forces into once-socialist China since the early eighties, as a replacement for the domination of the state plan in dictating economic activity—and the attendant shift toward relatively freer and freer flows of the factors of production—has brought in its wake a set of new juxtapositions: first, the collapse of old oppositions and the obliteration of once-rigid boundaries; and second, a collision between elemental institutions. The juxtapositions are regional, sectoral, and occupational. In each case, categories that had been forced to be separate since the Communists reorganized Chinese society in the fifties have been (as they always had been before 1949)[1] thrust into contact, while social categories that had been clearly drawn have become blurred, as brand-new collectivities, such as the "floating population," have come into being, producing a major social change.

At the same time, the economic institution of the market has challenged the hitherto seemingly unshakable political institution of urban citizenship, determined for decades by the city *hukou* (household registration). With its weakening, a repositioning of the state, and of the extent of its authority, is taking place. This potentially major political consequence is especially apparent in the confrontation between the agents (and agencies) of the state, on the one hand, and the urban-dwelling, unlicensed migrant laborers, the "floating population," on the other.

To understand the nature and magnitude of these rearrangements and this confrontation, I begin by presenting key features of the prereform period. I then spell out the nature of the changes—in policy and in practice—of the last dozen years or so, as the floaters have participated in, been affected by, and contributed to them. Next I show how the relationship of the transients both to markets and to the state has gradually mutated over time.

I conclude that the outcome for the foreseeable future is a hollowing out of the state and a narrowing down of its authority in regard to the migrants, as it cast them outside its embrace despite permitting them to move into its municipal sanctum. The emergence of parallel, largely nonintersecting realms of dailiness within the city—sojourners in one realm and the state, its officers, and its beneficiaries in another, even as they share the same space—has already begun to unfold.[2]

Boundaries and Oppositions: The Prereform Period

Once the state had conquered the capitalist class and confiscated its property and resources by the mid-1950s, state officials possessed the wherewithal to direct the allocation of productive factors, canceling the operation of market forces for the most part. Soon after that victory, the regime was able to sequester the various segments of the populace into one of two sorts of locations, either a city or a spot in the countryside, and conferred a corresponding label, a kind of graded citizenship, upon the residents of each. By late 1955, everyone in China had either an urban or a rural *hukou*.[3]

At various junctures in the first Communist decade, vigilant associations—neighborhood committees and workplaces *(danwei)* in urban areas, communes in the countryside—nailed these assignments into place, making any hopes of their members' departure from their homeplaces nearly futile. The famine of the late 1950s—which brought home to the leadership the absolute priority of keeping tight control over grain supplies, especially for urbanites—climaxed and clinched the division of the populace into two huge groups, indelibly delineating people's places within either "urban" or "rural" areas of the map.[4] Thus, by the early sixties, people were definitively pinned into position, as the walls around the city thickened and hardened;[5] "peasant" and "urbanite" became unbridgeable classifications. Regardless of the actual content of their labor, only those in cities could be called "workers"; all those in the rural areas, whatever their real line of occupation, were stamped "peasants."

During the fifties as the capabilities for planning were collected into bureaucrats' hands, the leadership established what one scholar has labeled a "circular resource allocation system."[6] This system worked in terms of oppositions, as it masterfully redistributed the profits of the more productive coastal areas, especially Shanghai, to the more backward but resource-rich provinces of the interior, and from the places where light industry had higher returns to the locales where heavy industry was stronger, supplying the coast with raw materials in return. This combining of contradictory parts was a highly interdependent, integrated arrangement that guided the movement of materials, funds, and personnel by administrative fiat for the purposes of the state.

Even the migration of ordinary people had to fit into this plan and be sanctioned by its executioners. Indeed, formal, officially recognized geographical mobility, in the sense of changing one's address, in the sixties and seventies generally occurred only administratively, in accord with the aims of the state. And east and west China, or "coastal" and "hinterland/interior" China, though interlocked into a synchronized mechanism, became dichotomous and wholly distinct.

By means of these various segregations, seemingly fixed in stone until the eve of the initiation of economic reform, the state thus succeeded within less than a decade in fashioning a series of starkly structured oppositions that helped make the nation it ruled generally manageable and marketless. Consequently the state was able to anchor its legitimacy in its own ability (without the aid of a market) to provision or subsidize the residents of the urban sector. It also rested its authority (with the exception of the period at the height of the Cultural Revolution) in its capacity to control (or relatively rapidly bring under control) the behavior of urbanites, while barring uninvited outsiders from trespassing. The state's clout in the cities in the prereform period was firm, ultimately uncontested, and simplistic.

The Reform Era: The Collapse of Opposition and the Obliteration of Boundaries

The Policies

With the opening of markets after 1978 the segregations began to break down, as some rural residents made their way into town.[7] But it took until April 1983, with rural reform attained nationwide, for central politicians to begin to relent on the policy on migration. The State Council's "Regulations concerning Cooperative Endeavors of City and Town Laborers" was the first to permit rural residents to move into market towns, albeit without shedding their rural registrations. Once there, unlike the towns' "proper residents," they would have to rely not on the state's grain rations but on food they had brought in themselves.[8]

A more lenient ruling appeared at the end of the next year. At this point, the state offered peasants a chance to obtain a new kind of nonagricultural registration. According to this 1984 circular, this opportunity came as a result of "urgent demand" from the growing numbers of peasants who by that time were "streaming into the market towns." Like all the later decisions of the regime on this topic, this one was probably more a recognition of a fait accompli than it was a license for a sudden change in peasants' behavior.

This decision, a "State Council Notification on the Question of Peasants Entering Towns and Settling" of October 1984, however, had its limitations. It was specifically aimed at those who could raise their own funds, take care of their own grain, and find a place of abode in the market towns. It was also narrowly targeted at those who had the ability to run a business or who had served in rural enterprises. And it specifically excluded peasants from moving into county seats.[9]

In July 1985 a new document, the "Provisional Regulations on the Management of Population Living Temporarily in the Cities," represented an effort by the Ministry of Public Security to ensure its control over the floating population and to increase its data on it. Perhaps this measure's greatest significance lay in its implicit recognition that the coming of peasants to towns was now a fact of life, and thereby tacitly legitimized the indefinite presence of peasants in cities of all sizes. It created a category of peasants whose work would keep them in town for more than three months and gave them their own special certificate, labeled the "card for residents living with others" (jizhu zheng).[10]

In 1986 it became legal to sell grain at negotiated prices to peasants at work in the cities; this did much to facilitate longer stays.[11] Thus, by the middle of the decade, the state had acquiesced in the right of those from rural areas to make at least a temporary home in the cities. It took no responsibility, however, for their material or physical well-being. Another big change was the citizen identification card, which the government introduced in the mid-1980s in addition to—and to strengthen—its control over household registration;[12] it became mandatory for everyone over sixteen years of age on September 15, 1989.[13]

In 1988 the State Council and the Ministry of Labor put still another stamp of approval on the outflow from the countryside, this time with a recommendation that provinces with impoverished populations "export" their labor.[14] As with the earlier reform announcements, this one too was probably the legitimization of practices already under way. Though spurred along by the market in advance of action by the state, the official permission surely gave further impetus to the practice.

In 1989 and again in 1991, the State Council issued rulings on the management of temporary labor in state enterprises,[15] which, in contrast to similar measures of the 1950s, allowed managers to sign contracts directly with the worker him- or herself, and only afterward report this to the local labor department for approval. Certainly the authorization to hire peasants one by one (instead of in groups from communes) enhanced the likelihood that these rural workers would leave home, once again something that had already been occurring on a sizable scale by that time. In less than a decade, from 1978 to 1987, more than 10 million rural residents obtained urban jobs following legal procedures.[16] The numbers who did so without reporting their employment is unquestionably far higher.[17]

The direction of policy evolution was obviously toward greater liberalization over the first decade after reforms began. This process was also one in which the leadership simply accepted developments that were the product of other decisions, paired with its inability to brake the effects of market forces which those decisions had set into motion. It spelled a shrinking and, it appears, a progressively overwhelmed state. Yet despite the increasingly lenient policies, state leaders retained their urge to monitor and regulate the migration and, by keeping peasants as temporary residents, to ensure that this mobility would be cheap and fiscally advantageous. Thus, in the design of those determining their status, the peasants in the cities were to be maintained as floaters, as impermanent outsiders for whom the state was not responsible, in order to serve the state's own fiscal and modernization needs.[18]

The By-product of Other Policies

Certainly the state's explicit sanction for sojourning propelled many peasants to desert the soil. But their migrations were also a by-product of practically all of the other policies that made up the general program of economic reform—the termination of the communes in the countryside, the pro-coastal developmental strategy, profit-consciousness in urban firms, and the creation of urban labor markets. All of these moves upset the totality of the state's power over what now were newly and suddenly grossly expanded urban populations: over the course of a decade, the average proportion of peasants in the largest cities shot up from 12.6 percent in 1984 to 22.5 percent in 1987 and to 25.4 percent in 1994.[19] As their numbers multiplied, "floaters" chipped away at the oppositions, segregations, and heretofore inexorable perimeters keeping peasants as a group apart.

Each of these related economic reform policies had at least one of two effects, both of which were crucial for enticing peasants to live and work in urban areas. First of all, several of these measures provided channels for obtaining the necessities of daily existence outside the state's monopoly: by legitimizing markets for necessities, the various reforms made feasible the livelihood of farmers in the cities, even if that had not been their initial intention.[20] Second, these policies engendered an urgent hunger for low-paid and flexible labor that the peasants were particularly well placed to provide.

New financial arrangements after 1980 allowed local governments to retain a portion of the revenues from tax receipts;[21] and enterprises were allowed more leeway, including the right to keep some of their own profits, along with less supervision over their hiring practices. These various incentives propelled a feverish construction drive that cried out for extra labor.[22] Judith Banister calculated that between 1978 and 1988 nonagricultural employment increased at more than 6 percent a year.[23] Capital construction alone rose in Beijing, Tianjin, and Shanghai 2.3-fold, but the urban-based labor forces in those cities went up from 16.65 million to only 18.2 million, a growth of just 9 percent between 1981 and 1988. Outside workers would have had to make up the difference.[24]

It was not just that jobs increased in the cities; other factors were also at work. After 1978, the Ministry of Labor relaxed the former recruitment system, whereby young people were forced to wait for job assignments from their local labor bureaus.[25] With the reforms inviting foreign investors into the country, city youth found new employment opportunities on their own in classy occupations such as tourism and foreign trade and therefore rejected careers in the traditional trades, such as textiles, machinery, and building materials.[26] As one source decried, "City people would rather do nothing than this" (referring to such arduous jobs as drilling waterways or repairing roads and bridges).[27] This attitude, of course, created openings for the peasant workers.

The termination in 1979 of the Cultural Revolution–era policy of sending city youth to the countryside meant that rusticated young people started returning home. That summer, the economic advisor Xue Muqiao proposed permitting young people to set up their own privately funded and operated enterprises to remove from the shoulders of the state the strain of creating jobs for them all.[28] The party Central Committee's assent to urban outside-the-plan employment in the summer of 1980 laid a foundation for private enterprise that peasants soon built upon as well.

Contributing to this same outcome was a sharp reversal in official attitudes toward commerce. Produce marketing and the service sector in general in the cities were decimated after twenty-five years of denigration and banning.[29] But once legitimacy was lent the realm of circulation and competition after 1978,[30] for the first time in decades big cities had a chance to satisfy their gaping demands for fresh food as well as for services of all sorts.

Once having launched the floaters on their move, the state's investment decisions did much to influence the direction of their flow. In large part, the phenomenon of floating has involved a transfer of excess rural labor from the more backward provinces of the interior eastward to the coast. This surge derived directly from state policies of 1980 and later that privileged the coastal areas, where the potential for rapid wealth generation seemed greatest. This was accomplished by offering preferential treatment to foreign (especially compatriot Hong Kong and Taiwanese) financiers in that region alone.[31]

All these switches in programs that came with the post-Mao leadership's validation of markets as the engine of growth had payoffs for peasants whose labor could now bring much better returns off the farm.[32] Their cumulative effect was to intermingle categories that had been pried apart and kept isolated under the prior, prereform regime. Now urban and previously rural folk freely walked the same streets, ate food from the same markets, and shared the same city facilities and structures; people (still) called "peasants" labored on urban construction projects and toiled in municipal plants. Though income differences, even among the peasantry itself, showed wide and growing gaps between regions as of the mid-1990s,[33] at least now there was a chance for an inlander with the means to travel and adequate information to journey eastward voluntarily, enter the coast, and work there.

What we see, then, with the unfettering of market forces, and in the consequent creation of the floating population in the cities, is a melding of the contradictions and an evisceration of the borderlines among opposed categories that had helped to undergird the domination of the Maoist regime.

Institutional Collision

The economic reforms did more than destruct long-standing divisions. They also caused a collision between two forms of institutions. That is, the new economic institution of the market that let farmers, entirely on their own, flee from the fields, clashed with the old statist, political institution of urban citizenship (privileges, prerogatives, and public goods[34] just for those born in the city to city-born parents), as structured for decades by the *hukou*. The migrants are poised at the intersection of these two institutions, just where they collide: in bringing ruralites to the urban areas, markets undermined the former exclusivity of urban residence. So without any political pressuring, but just by subsisting in the city, peasants shattered urban citizenhood as it had been understood in China for nearly half a century. A significant transformation took place over time both in the relationship of migrants to urban labor markets and in their stance with respect to the state.

Migrants and Labor Markets

At the start of the reform period, peasants' principal entrée into the city was via contracts between their rural units and urban state enterprises.[35] Sometimes this meant their serving as supplemental or seasonal labor in state factories; other times it entailed digging on subcontracted building projects. As the impetus for "modernization" swelled, by the middle of the eighties, rural builders and excavaters hired by state construction firms nationally had already amounted to nearly a third of the permanent construction work force.[36]

Rural migrant laborers continued to take on contracted work in state industrial firms in the cities in increasing, if difficult to document, numbers as time went on. An official report noted that 12.8 million of 107.4 million total workers, or 11.9 percent of the payroll, were holding temporary jobs in state industries as of the start of

1993.[37] Regional variation complicated the picture, but one 1994 study of peasants working in cities in Henan found that a full 30 percent of them were employed in state-owned firms in that province.[38] The types of work sites in urban settings and the avenues for arriving at them quickly expanded beyond state channels. Well before the end of the eighties a wide array of urban opportunities for performing odd jobs had appeared, wholly separate from any form of official employment. These included marketing and services; cottage-style garment processing; manufacturing in foreign and other nonstate factories; nursemaiding in private homes (baomu); and begging and scrap collecting.

Landing a spot in most of these trades usually involved no contracts or ties with the state at all. Instead, most peasants acquired their positions either through their personal connections (by far the more common method)[39] or else at anonymous "spontaneous" labor exchanges held in the open in city streets and squares. It wasn't long before even construction labor for a state-owned firm might be arranged through a series of deals whereby work teams successively further and further away from any licit transaction obtained "subcontracts" by bribing.[40] Once country folk were commonly encountered in the cities, a myriad of labor markets developed and supplemented, even overwhelmed, the official one and its cadres in placing peasants in work posts.

The Range of Occupational Options outside the State

The numbers of former farmers supplying eatables, small consumer goods, and petty services on city sidewalks grew rapidly. As just one sign of this, by early 1993, an official source reported that of all the workers at the 140,000-odd stalls and booths operated by Beijing City's self-employed individuals, more than 70 percent were nonlocals.[41] More than 90 percent of them had relied on informal modes, such as getting help from relatives or friends or coming to the gate of the employer, in seeking their jobs.[42] Others, especially those from the South and the coast, traveled on their own to northerly regions where crafts and services were scarce, and either set up their stands, solicited jobs as they strolled through the streets, or appeared at "spontaneous" labor markets, offering their artifacts or their knack at repair. Yet others settled down in strange locations, organizing themselves into native-place clusters.

In the carpentry trade, which flourished in the mid-1980s, incessant streams of tradespeople had outpaced demand by the late 1980s.[43] As a result, many people from Zhejiang who had earlier landed in Lanzhou, for instance, moved on to Ningxia and Inner Mongolia.[44] The case suggests the vitality of this particular labor market. Cobblers, who mostly came from Zhejiang and congregated together, operated under yet another sort of labor regime. In Tianjin, allegedly 10,000 of them were making their homes in rented rooms around the north train station in the early 1990s.[45]

A different kind of life and workstyle belonged to the sweatshop stitchers from the south, sojourning away from home. Large concentrations populated Beijing and Tianjin, where they lived and worked in "Zhejiang tailor villages," which began to take form by 1983.[46] They grew so rapidly that by 1987 over one third of the legally licensed proprietors in the Beijing garment industry were ruralites, mainly from Jiangsu, Zhejiang and Anhui, while as many as 90 percent of the employees were peasants from Zhejiang.[47] By the late 1980s these outsider tailors had begun to take over the trade.[48]

In their urban "villages" (as in Beijing's Fengtai district's Dahongmen township), a coordinated division of labor prevailed, perfected by the late 1980s, totally disconnected from state commercial channels.[49] Wenzhou natives obtained their cloth from their Zhejiang villages, and then produced, retailed, wholesaled, and transported the products exclusively through networks of fellow townspeople.[50] Simple partnerships, graduating into large-scale mutually interdependent partnerships, undergirded the businesses.[51] Not just hiring but even credit relationships were sometimes based upon blood and geographical ties.[52]

Recruitment of peasant temporary labor into the nonstate and foreign sector also involved personal ties, sometimes accompanied by bureaucratism. According to a journalistic account from Guangzhou, "In enterprises in the Pearl River Delta, processing firms[53] and town and village enterprises hire mostly from Guangdong, Guangxi,

Hunan, and Sichuan, and they mainly go through friends and relatives in doing so."[54]

Two Chinese journalists offer a graphic account of rural hiring by one of these nonstate firms:

> Last year, the director of the labor bureau in Guizhou's Bijie county went to Dongguan twice to try to arrange for the export of his county's surplus labor . . . Bijie is in the mountains, cursed with little land and many people. . . . Its labor surplus is monumental. . . . In 1987, Guangdong and Guizhou agreed that Guangdong would accept surplus labor from Guizhou in the form of "using labor recruitment to support poverty." . . . When the news spread that Dongguan would be hiring . . . many household heads, facing fierce competition, sent gifts. The county labor bureau, as if recruiting formal labor, let individuals apply, so the household head or a town or village presented certificates, and then the girls went through examinations and formal procedures. But when the recruiter made his selection . . . the urban girls' cultural level was higher . . . plus *they mostly had connections and a patron,* so Bijie had to favor them. So the majority chosen were the urban girls. [Emphasis added.][55]

In the case of the nursemaid *(baomu)* trade, we find two channels of recruitment outside the official one, each with its own rules and practices. The first one formed from the informal interactions of maids who were already employed. Since most in a particular city came from the same home area, casual associations grew up naturally among them. In a number of cities, *baomu* associations had taken shape by the early 1990s, organized as loose networks based on hometown origin, which spread information on wage levels and job opportunities.[56]

The other channel—also outside the state—was structured by the spontaneous labor markets that became common in Chinese cities in the reform period. Although quite risky, and unlikely to yield positions that afforded decent treatment, this channel offered jobs where earnings might be the highest.[57] But it was in these markets that women could be preyed upon by "illegal elements," be raped, robbed, abducted, cheated, or, at a minimum, be forced into unsavory employment situations.[58]

Finally, journalistic writers have portrayed beggar bands and "garbage kingdoms" as much more tightly regulated (but certainly not by the state) than one encountering individual vagabonds on the street might imagine. Their accounts refer to turf, gang warfare among competing regionally based bands (and between local and outsider beggars) and chieftains who live in glory. Their bosses lord it over frequently shifting and rank-ordered underlings, who must placate them with booty; scavengers from outside the band are forced to ingratiate themselves with gifts.[59]

A survey of the city's beggars in 1994, undertaken by an independent pollster in Beijing working with Horizon Market Research, revealed that nearly a third were members of such tightly organized cartels.[60] But not all the beggars and trash collectors were cozily knitted into cliques; there were also many who were isolated, passing their days at the constant mercy of marauding official functionaries.[61]

This description of various lines of work uncovers a rich and vibrant realm of markets that floaters themselves fashioned, once freed from the commune and the contracts with state units that commune cadres once had arranged for them. Thus, not only did migrant laborers from the countryside quickly embrace means of finding work in the city once this possibility was presented to them; they also devised markets fully separated from the state's surveillance and managed them completely by their own dictates. Their mastery of this process is just one sign of the growing incapacity of the state to encompass—or even to regulate—the activities of its entire urban populace.

Migrants and the State: New Forms of "Citizenship"

In one definition, offered by Bryan S. Turner, citizenship has two critical components: it is possessed by those who have authoritatively been determined (a) to belong to the community, and (b) to have rights to a share in the public distribution of its goods.[62] Put otherwise, the concept of citizenship is about the rights and privileges of "members," who are, most fundamentally, simply those legally living within specifically designated borders.[63] According to this characterization, because floaters from the countryside who have taken up residence in cities lack the urban *hukou*, they are certainly not citizens there, and are by no means treated as such.

This deprivation is evident when we consider the official ineligibility of peasant migrants for any medical, housing, educational, welfare, or services of any sort in the cities up through the first half of the 1990s. This stark picture was only softened if a migrant was willing—and able—to make payments of variable amounts, the sum depending on the city in question and the level of assistance or service desired, or if he or she curried favor and cultivated connections with cadres in charge of dispensing these benefits. The contrast with the treatment of "proper" city dwellers who had urban household registration was especially sharp given the continuing minimal cost of these benefits for them. Despite a decade and a half of economic reforms, these rights for the most part remained practically equivalent to entitlements for urbanites.

In the face of the state's denial to them of these services, the transients' solutions and substitutions harked back to the miserable lives of China's urban underclass, also ignored by the state, in the first half of the twentieth century.[64]

Housing

The relevant rulings were particularly strict in the case of housing: only short-term, registered sojourning with relatives or in hotels, rentals arranged by contracted agreements with landlords, or work-unit-provided beds were legal. Regulations forbade outsiders not just from building or buying houses (unless one was an overseas Chinese), but even from occupying land.[65] But the severity of these regulations lessened as transgressions against them increased with time. By the end of 1993, some outsiders were "buying or building houses in Beijing and acquiring properties in the hopes of settling down and striking root in the city."[66]

This was true in the famous "Zhejiang village" in Fengtai district of Beijing, temporary home of 100,000 outsiders as of late 1995 (about half of them from Zhejiang),[67] where peasants bought old, broken-down dwellings for use as combined living and working quarters. In 1992 the local authorities (illegally, since they lacked higher-level consent) in this region actually permitted wealthier, share-pooling residents to construct some forty buildings in large courtyards in Zhejiang village and even signed leases with them.[68] In Guangzhou and Shenzhen as well the practice of throwing up structures and shantytowns had taken root in the early 1990s, but an observer categorized this behavior as "illicit."[69]

Besides the bar against building, peasants could not even rent the massive proportion of floorspace owned by either urban governments or work units.[70] But these rules too began to change by 1991.[71] So even if Chinese stipulations on the books, left over from the time of the planned economy and the walled-up privileged city, were most inhospitable, the creeping progression of market relations, with which the migrants joined forces, tended to obliterate their impact.

Alongside this informal rewriting of laws, sojourning peasants also opened up a range of novel housing options offered by Chinese cities in the reform era (usually not following legal procedures), most of them linked to the sprouting of new kinds of urban jobs. By the end of 1995, in Shanghai, a survey of 4,714 employed persons found that almost half were renting accommodations, one quarter were in dormitories, and one fifth in shelters on worksites.[72] As in pre-1949 days, for many work routine and rest shared the same paltry space.[73]

There were others, however, who were less fortunate. These were the jobless people, whose work did not afford some form of shelter or who lacked the money to rent a room or a bed. By the mid-nineties, their numbers had multiplied in the cities. They holed up in hidden back streets, in tunnels, under trucks and buses in parking lots, in the waiting areas of railway stations, and under bridges. For instance, Cheng Li reports on shacks of just 300 square meters in Beijing holding more than 500 people, or offering just one toilet for over 6,000 people.[74] When sheltered at all, this marginal, undomiciled group made do with the crudest of adaptations of scrap metal, cardboard, and wood.[75] But one way or another, alternatives to the state's designs had been devised.

Health Care

Since state funding for public health facilities, medications, and personnel was pegged to a planned level based on the official urban populace per city, it appeared to local bureaucrats to be out of the question to arrange for health care for unattached newcomers from the outside. Even as responsible authorities decried the implications for the settled population of ignoring the epidemics and contagious diseases carried in by the migrants, they were too strapped for resources to do anything much about it.[76]

Consequently, migrants had to find other options. Into the early 1990s, chances for at least some modicum of health care were by far the best if a floater was able to land a position in a successful state-owned firm. Such individuals could qualify for basic attention, at any rate, even if the level of care varied with local regulations, the financial standing of the firm, and management decisions.[77]

Those ensconced in a thriving migrant enclave where entrepreneurial ventures had been undertaken became members not just of residential, but also of collective occupational communities, sharing many traits with what are termed "ethnic enclaves" elsewhere.[78] Those who lived in the urban Zhejiang village in Beijing, for instance, had created their own clinics and hospitals by the mid-1990s, where treatment was provided by fellow Zhejiangese, all holding medical licenses from home.[79] Rumor held that most without collectivities of any kind (whether public or private) were forced to try their luck with untrained traveling "doctors" who floated among migrant communities and treated maladies, such as venereal disease, believed to be common to this segment of humanity.[80]

Education

Reinhard Bendix targeted "the right and duty to receive an elementary education" as "perhaps the most universally approximated implementation of national citizenship," since it is a benefit over which the government itself has authority and it is an obligation that all parents with children in a certain age group are required by law to fulfil.[81] Indeed, China's Law on Compulsory Education stipulates that all children aged seven to fifteen must enroll and receive education for nine years. For these reasons, the quite uneven availability of basic schooling—more often absent than present—for the floating folk from the country underlines their lack of valid membership in the official urban community. In Beijing, for instance, where 100 percent of native five- to twelve-year-old children were enrolled in school in 1995, only 40 percent of migrant ones were.[82]

Despite the press of market relations, educational funding, like that for health care, was allocated officially at the local level just for licensed city residents up through the mid-1990s, leaving behind—at least legally[83]—the two to three million school-age children of the floating population (as of mid-1995).[84] As late as 1996, there was no national policy or any regulation on educating the offspring of the floating population. A few local governments had set up unstable, unaccredited makeshift schools, whose quality varied greatly—hardly a case, even, of "separate but equal"—but the central government had provided no funding for the migrants.[85] In the words of a cadre in the Beijing Municipal Bureau of Education:

> Beijing is very short on money for education. Looking after the present 1.5 million middle and primary school students in the city already strains resources, and there are 300,000 school-age children among the migrant population. Middle and primary schools in the city have already taken in more than 30,000 migrant children. Though the parents of some have paid, the amount of money paid is far from enough to educate these students . . . formerly these [children] were the responsibility of the receiving area, but nowadays Beijing can't possibly solve the education problems of 300,000 migrant children.[86]

Since the offspring of the floating population had domiciles that were registered in the countryside, city officials had no sense of legal obligation to teach them in the cities. Therefore, because they were without a local residency permit, migrant children found that schooling was legally unavailable for them up through the mid-1990s.[87]

Furthermore, even the urban immigrants who lived in clusters were technically forbidden to establish their own schools beyond the level of day care centers and kindergartens through 1996.[88] But in two districts of Guangzhou migrants cobbled together some forty "shack schools"—though they were soon ordered shut down by the local authorities.[89] In defiance of local regulations, in 1992 the newly established large courtyards in Zhejiang village set up educational facilities of their own.[90] A nursery was run by junior high school graduates in the village and staffed by hometown teachers, despite the fact that it was not even permitted to register.[91]

Services

Transients huddled in the midst of the city, or taken care of by work units or landlords, could partake of at least some of the basic amenities of city life—water, sewerage, transportation, electricity—though certainly not in comfortable quantities. But those on the outskirts, as in Zhejiang village, depended entirely on their own resources. As such inhabitants built up a life of their own, their need for outside assistance steadily decreased.[92] Instead of waiting vainly for the Beijing authorities to service them, migrant enterpreneurs in the village had established fairly complex undertakings by 1993: daily buses to and from the home counties, rudimentary toilets, and long-distance phone lines. And in the large courtyards constructed in 1992, even water, electrical, sewerage, postal, educational, and recreational facilities appeared.[93]

"Villages"

The foregoing survey of services demonstrates that by the early 1990s, in a corner of Beijing as well as in scattered sites elsewhere, well-organized sojourning peasants with skills and means had substituted communities of their own for the ones from which they were barred. The very existence of what were called co-provincial "villages" openly challenged the state's wonted capacity to overwhelm—indeed, to prohibit—the formation of groups outside its aegis.

Here in the midst of the once tightly regimented urban areas, places where officialdom had for decades prided itself on its ability to contain and suppress incipient nonstate organizations, burgeoned an array of what amounted to nascent, ascriptive, and corporate associations. Unlike its stance toward the other folk who populate the cities, the state did not—indeed could not—fit floating and often very transient migrants into the neighborhood associations that customarily had structured and kept up a steady oversight over the "proper" urban residents' domestic existences. Nor were the itinerants, for the most part, members of the workplace *danwei* that directed daily behavior at the office or the plant.[94] Thus, not only were no city services supplied to their areas of congregation; neither were there any official associations there that could absorb and direct their energies or see to their social needs.

Although the agencies of the state periodically tried to obliterate these settlements, they never did so successfully.[95] There was thus a great paradox that characterized floaters living in collectivities. They were at once constrained by the state's registration system, excluded from its privileges, and neglected by its service network. Yet at the same time, they were freed, if to a limited but growing extent, by congregating altogether outside the pale of the state's organizations of administration and often beyond its watch. They were also empowered by their own growing numbers and their autonomous success in markets they themselves had made.

Because they were barred by the state's *hukou* prohibition from acquiring city citizenship and its trappings, including the right or the means to press their needs legally on urban and higher-level governments, those with the wherewithal to do so were forced to form alternate societies, nearly totally unconnected with the mainstream. As one researcher explained, "The population [in Zhejiang village] has no sense of belonging to Beijing society."[96] Eighty-three percent of the respondents of a sample of 290 had not established any relations whatever with Beijing people as of 1992. Treated as foreigners, and seeing themselves that way too, some even felt they would benefit from setting up an ambassadorial organ to protect their interests.[97]

Conclusion: The Impact of the Market Economy

In the transitional era, as the Chinese state was forsaking its socialist pattern, by the very act of sanctioning markets, its leadership was also involuntarily relinquishing its ability to mold society into rigid, contradictory categories. The result in this case was that markets, with their own modes of developing productive forces, worked to erase state-imposed oppositions among regions, sectors, and occupations. Markets also became available to outsiders venturing into settlements previously strictly delimited against them. Consequently, peasant sojourners collided against and proceeded to knock down the intangible but once solid barricades around the cities that state fiat had erected against them.

By activating markets, the state was also forced to abandon its monopoly position as the only source of the trappings of urban citizenship, defined in terms of membership and a right to a share in a community's jointly allocated goods.[98] The upshot was the emergence of a multi-tiered social structure, at least insofar as citizenship was concerned: one tier of urban residents, more or less embedded in the state, the extent of whose take from the state might be diminishing, but who still could generally count on a basic entitlement; another tier of floaters from the fields who were somehow bonded to the state, whether through contracts or personal connections, who were second-class members; a third tier of sojourners who became part of well-articulated communities of their own, and who derived their services and their unauthorized badge of belonging just from that enclave; and finally a range of stragglers bereft of any form of citizenship whatsoever.

What is most important for our purposes here is the solution devised by this third group, the most emblematic of whom were the urban "villagers" who inhabited Zhejiang village. They were rewriting the rules of city life.[99] In their daily lives these "villagers" were forging an interim, alternative, nonauthoritative, ersatz form of urbanhood for themselves, one that was materially (for most) poorer than that of state-paid temporary workers, but better than that of vagabonds.

As this new sort of nonstate "citizenship" replaces that granted by the state, at least for these tens of thousands of people, it could also be said to be confronting the state, in demonstrating by its very existence the diminishing scope of the state's authoritative command over the lives of city dwellers. In time, this confrontation must be the seed from which some brand-new style of citizenship—and citizens—are born, some so-far unseen sort of city community in post-1949 China.

DAVID S. G. GOODMAN

11 | The New Middle Class

Economic reform has created new social categories of wealth and power that have been identified by many commentators as China's "new middle classes." This identification implicitly—and sometimes explicitly—emphasizes the homogenizing impact of economic modernization on social change and political development, particularly the potential for the emergence of capitalism and democracy.[1] It is far from clear, however, that the structures and processes of change currently under way in the People's Republic of China are identical to those that occurred earlier in the European environments which engendered the concepts and vocabulary of modernization and middle-class revolution. Modernization may well result in synthesis rather than a complete Europeanization, and in any case it seems likely that the East Asian experience—in Japan, Taiwan, and South Korea in particular—is more instructive for understanding China's later development and the emergence of its new middle classes. In particular, there has been little evidence of the political space and subsequent potential for conflict between the state and the middle classes that was a major source of the drive to democratization in the European experience. On the contrary, the emergence of China's new middle classes indicates a lack of social pluralism more reminiscent of Meiji Japan or the late transforming authoritarian societies of

Korea and Taiwan.[2] The party-state has remained the central social as well as political influence in the formation of China's middle classes during the reform era, as it had been earlier during and after the first phases of modernization.

The Formation of Middle Classes

In general terms, the identification of emerging middle classes suggests individual wealth, new markets, and more open societies, especially the potential for democracy. However, there is no necessary connection between increasing wealth and democratic values. The middle classes are historically complex phenomena, including not only the owners of capital—who are often the most high profile sector—but also the managers, bureaucrats, and professionals who service and support capitalist enterprise and the modernizing state. Even within these broad categories there are clear distinctions to be recognized: most notably large- and medium-scale capitalists have different perspectives on social and political change than the owners of family-based or smaller-scale enterprises.[3]

In China the era of economic reform has indeed brought the creation of considerable individual wealth and the emergence of greater social and political diversity, as has generally been the case with modernization. The relatively sustained and rapid growth of China's economy during the 1980s and 1990s—an annual average rate of approximately 10 per cent of GNP[4]—has created new categories of those who either own or control substantial wealth and thereby have the ability to affect significantly the lives of others. Society and politics have become more complex as the Chinese Communist Party's exercise of authority in society, the economy, and politics has been replaced by multiple hierarchies of wealth and status. Even the political system has become more diversified. Although the authority of the Chinese Communist Party has remained inviolate, political power and influence have become more localized, not only at the provincial level but also at the county level and below.[5]

Economic reform has also brought substantially increased real disposable income for certain social groups as well as patterns of expenditure—on housing, clothing, entertainment, private education for children, restaurants, and travel—all of which are suggestive of contemporary middle-class behavior elsewhere.[6] In 1997 a monthly income of 5,000 to 6,000 RMB[7]—the annual GNP per capita was 5,634 RMB[8]—was regarded as "well-off" in the more developed, coastal areas of South and East China, whereas further inland a monthly income of between 3,500 and 4,500 RMB was regarded as a more usual indicator of a "comfortable" lifestyle. Suggestive as these phenomena are of middle-class behavior, there is every reason to believe that their cultural and political consequences—and the attendant increased consumerism—may not be identical to standard accounts of modernization, not least because of China's changing economic structures.

The new middle classes who have emerged in China during the 1980s and 1990s do not fall easily into the usual categories. The capital-owning entrepreneurs who have emerged in the reform era are much fewer in number than the attendant publicity would seem to suggest, and more likely to be found in small-scale enterprises. While the new breed of owner-operators are a defining characteristic of reform economics, most, and particularly most of the larger-scale and most successful, are hard to equate with the independent bourgeoisie of the European experience. In particular, the medium- and large-scale owner-operators are rarely if ever independent of the party-state.

Small-scale private entrepreneurs who grow and want to continue their expansion usually do so through close cooperation—often legally confused as well as complex—with local government.[9] In most cases this is institutional interaction rather than just an associational relationship. Local government in its various guises often has a substantial share of the equity in any sizable local enterprise, as well as receiving management fees and related payments. Although these enterprises are rarely run (as would once have been the case) as agencies or departments of local government, the latter's involvement extends well beyond macroeconomic guidance.

Owner-operators are a new socioeconomic feature of the reform era, but the same is not generally true of managers, bureaucrats or professionals. China's reform era is a later-stage restructuring rather than an initial modernization, and these categories of the middle classes had already been generated by the development of the Chinese state in the 1950s and (to a lesser extent) 1960s. China's economic growth was not insignificant from 1952 to 1978—an average of 6 percent per annum of GNP—despite fluctuations, some of which, such as the worst excesses of the Great Leap Forward, were severe. As a result, well before 1978 China had already achieved some of the milestones usually associated with the process of modernization: the creation of a modernizing state system and bureaucracy; a higher percentage of GNP derived from industrial rather than agricultural production; and the growth of a substantial service sector of the economy.

For China by the late 1970s the major economic problems were not simply those associated with low levels of growth or a desire to achieve first-stage modernization, but the inefficiencies and deficiencies of a Soviet-style system. For both political and economic reasons, a wholesale economic restructuring was required to redistribute resources into more productive channels with greater potential for long-term sustained economic growth—notably a transfer from heavy to consumer industrial production—and ultimately the creation of a consumer society.[10] The distinction between modernization and economic restructuring is important to understanding the genesis, location, and aspirations of the new middle classes of the 1990s. The new middle classes are inherently more entrepreneurial than the modernizing middle classes of state bureaucrats, managers of state enterprises and technocrats who already existed in China before 1978. They have been the individuals most willing or able to take advantage of the changed policies of the reform era—whether they are owner-operators, managers of state sector enterprises or bureaucrats in government agencies faced with the imperative to commercialize their activities, or service providers (probably a more accurate description than "professionals" at this stage of development) for the new range of activities required to support commercialization of the economy.

One consequence is that there is probably a greater potential for conflict between competing middle classes—the modernizing forces of the 1950s, on the one hand, and of the reform era, on the other—than there is between the institutions of the state and any supposed politically excluded emerging middle classes. However, even that potential for polarization is far from clear. Entrepreneurial managers and bureaucrats have emerged from within the structures of the former system of state socialism, and represent the vanguard of transformation rather than new, distinct, socioeconomic categories. For the most part these entrepreneurial managers and bureaucrats not only maintain their links with the party-state, but much of their successful, entrepreneurial activity is based precisely on exploiting those links.[11]

In short, the party-state remains central to China's economic development and its emerging new middle classes. This is clearly in sharp contrast to the rise of the middle classes in the European experience, where their independence and distance from the state was a key feature of social change with distinct consequences for the emergence of liberal-democracy. The centrality of the party-state also underlies the importance of access to influence, which wealth does of course often bring, as a definer of China's new middle classes rather than immediately realizable wealth. All of the new middle classes certainly have privileged lifestyles, and their relative individual wealth is an important feature of their position in society. However, there are vast income differentials within the new middle classes—managers (and those bureaucrats who are part of the new middle classes) in particular often receive technically relatively low salaries, even when bonuses and additional emoluments are included—and control of and access to resources are clearly more important than ownership.

Shanxi in Reform

The information on China's new middle classes presented here is drawn from a survey of social change in Shanxi province, North China, undertaken during 1996 and 1997. Examples are taken from that survey to illustrate the various categories highlighted in this analysis. Shanxi is not usually regarded as one of China's most modernized or fastest-growing provincial economies, and so perhaps might not be considered the most promising of fields for the study of the new social categories generated by the reform era. Certainly it could not be regarded by any standard as a "rich" province—fifty of its hundred counties have standards of living below the poverty line.[12] Its most usual associations, even for people within the PRC, are with the front-line base areas and revolutionary history of the CCP during the Sino-Japanese War and, later, with peasant radicalism, not least because of Dazhai—the model production brigade of the Mao-dominated era of China's politics—which is located in eastern Shanxi. However, after the three large municipalities of Shanghai, Beijing and Tianjin, and the similarly heavy industrialized northeastern province of Liaoning, Shanxi is one of the most industrialized parts of China—as measured by the percentage of provincial GDP generated by the industrial sector—and has been so since the 1920s. Although it is only in the mid-1990s that the province has started to achieve sustained above-average rates of growth, its less spectacular economic profile provides an additional reason for its choice as the subject of examination of the sociopolitical impact of reform: many of China's provinces have more in common with Shanxi than with the relatively wealthy Zhejiang, Jiangsu, Guangdong, Shanghai, and Beijing.[13]

The origins of Shanxi's industrialization are to be found in its natural resources and the policies of the province's Republican era warlord, Yan Xishan. Shanxi is a resource-rich province by any definition. It has China's biggest coalfield and produces about one quarter of national coal production, two thirds of national coke output, and a substantial proportion of the electricity generation for North China.[14] During the 1920s and 1930s, Yan Xishan, a committed modernizer—indeed he was much feted contemporaneously as the "model modern provincial governor" despite being morally conservative—established a heavy industrial sector and developed the province's economic and transport infrastructure.[15] Particularly in the early 1930s when he was under threat from Chiang Kai-shek, Yan Xishan developed a command economy explicitly modeled on the experience of the USSR.[16] Though it is currently unfashionable in the province to recognize Shanxi's debt to Yan Xishan, over fifty of the enterprises he established before the Sino-Japanese War were still operational in the 1990s, including the Taiyuan Iron and Steel

Company, and the Coal Mining Administrations in Datong, Taiyuan, and Yangquan.

In the reform era, although coal still dominates the economy— approximately 20 percent of provincial GDP is derived from coal extraction and processing, and a further 10–13 percent from coal-related industry[17]—it has become more diversified. In heavy industry Shanxi has concentrated on new products and materials with advanced technology, high added value and strong market demand. This has meant increased production of specialized steels and aluminum, heavy-duty trucks, fertilizers and refined chemicals, concrete, glass and ceramics, and newly developed construction materials, as well as energy production and its associated industries. The diversification of the economy, however, has been most apparent in the town and village enterprises that have concentrated on the development of a processing and a consumer goods industry, particularly in coal-derived and coal industry–supporting activities, foodstuffs, and textiles. By 1996 this sector accounted for about 35 percent of provincial GDP.[18]

In 1996 Shanxi had a population of 31.09 million, or 2.5 percent of the national population. However, its GDP was only 130.7 million RMB, or 1.9 percent of the national total. Its GDP per capita in 1996 was 4,220 RMB, 74.9 percent of the national average. During the late 1980s, the provincial economy, though continuing to develop, was still falling behind the national rates of growth. Shanxi only started to catch up with national economic performance again in 1995 and 1996, when growth in the provincial economy outstripped China as a whole. In 1995 China's GDP increased by 9.0 percent, compared with a provincial increase of 11.1 percent; in 1996 the national increase was 9.7 percent, while Shanxi's GDP rose by 11.1 percent again.

Shanxi has a smaller agricultural sector than most provinces and a greater concentration in heavy industry and mining. It also has an above-average urban population and a remarkably low level of urban unemployment. Even allowing for statistical problems in the reporting of such figures, it is clear that Shanxi has the lowest level of urban unemployment of any province or equivalent administrative unit other than Beijing by a wide margin. Given Shanxi's heavy industrial involvement, it is not surprising to find that 36.5 percent of the gross value of industrial output (GVIO) was produced by the state sector in 1996, compared with a national average of 28.5 percent. Thirty-seven percent of Shanxi's GVIO was generated by the province's collective sector, compared with a national average of 39.4 percent; and a little surprisingly, 23.4 percent of GVIO came from the province's individual sector, as opposed to a national figure of 15.5 percent. However, only 3.1 percent of GVIO in 1996 was derived from the foreign-funded sector of the economy, compared with a national average of 16.7 percent. This lack of foreign economic involvement is currently a distinctive feature of the provincial economy. Foreign trade is only 7.4 percent of provincial GDP compared with the national figure of 35.1 percent. In 1996 total realized foreign capital in Shanxi only accounted for 1.3 percent of the provincial GDP: nationally it was 18.9 percent.[19]

Owner-Operators

The most highly publicized of the new middle classes are the owner-operators: initially private entrepreneurs who have developed their own businesses. Originally regarded by the CCP as rather small-scale entrepreneurs who could be mobilized to meet the demands for flexibility and other demands not easily met by the planned economy, these owner-operators have become a key feature of the reform era and one that exceeded those limitations. The retail sector of the economy rapidly came to be dominated by owner-operators, and as the state withdrew from direct economic management of enterprises and market reforms were introduced, owner-operators developed larger enterprises in a wider range of activities. At the same time, whereas many of the first owner-operators were individuals with what had previously been regarded as unsatisfactory political backgrounds, and thus had other channels of advance blocked to them, economic expansion and the changed political environment of the 1990s meant that owner-operators were drawn from a wider range of society.[20]

One reason for the high profile of owner-operators is their conspicuous wealth. In a society where in the recent past any consumption was regarded as ostentation and where with few exceptions private entrepreneurship was discouraged, its relatively sudden reemergence is likely to be equated, at least in the popular mind, with untold wealth. It is quite clear, however, that far from all owner-operators have businesses that can become large in scale or are themselves wealthy. The vast majority of owner-operators are business people on a very small scale indeed. For example, they are street traders, hairdressers, shop owners, or run local repair shops and small eateries, and often earn less than they did before striking out on their own. One often-stated reason for becoming or staying an owner-operator is the (sometimes) noneconomic choice of preferring to work for oneself. At the same time, there are newly created "captains of industry" on a large scale, even in Shanxi: Liang Wenhai, general manager of the Shanxi Huanhai Group Company in Yuci and China's "Boiler King" is one;[21] the even more famous Li Anmin, president of the Antai International Enterprise Group Company of Jiexu—and private railway train owner—is another.[22]

Shanxi also has middle-sized industrialists such as Hu Jianping, the chairman of the Shanxi Zhenzhong Coal and Coke Company, of Zhongyang county in the Liuliang Mountains. The company is technically registered as a township and village enterprise but as Hu himself points out, it is really a private enterprise—40 percent owned by his Taiwanese joint venture partner and 60 percent by himself.[23] Hu Jianping is a native of Zhongyang county born in 1963, and his father is not only a CCP member and veteran of the Korean War, but also a former leader of the local militia. The junior Hu set off on his own in 1985 as a truck driver, and once he had saved enough opened a restaurant and established his own transport company. By 1989 he had personal assets of approximately 300,000 RMB and at that stage was invited to become manager of the village enterprise in his native village.

Hu Jianping's personal investment in the village enterprise, plus a matching grant from the provincial Poverty Relief Fund, enabled the new enterprise eventually to obtain bank loans of 600,000 RMB. The original enterprise was a coking plant based on the village coal mine; the company has grown to include an additional three factories that exploit the local bauxite resources as well as coal. The company now owns the local mine as well as a research institute and restaurant in Taiyuan. The company has major business partners in Taiwan, Japan, and Australia, with exports since 1994 going to Brazil, Turkey, the United Kingdom, Spain, the Netherlands, and Japan. Hu is wealthy by any standard: he has built his own house; his six-year-old son attends a private school costing 20,000 RMB a year; and his wife has started her own business running local petrol stations. Not originally a member of the CCP, he was invited to join in 1992 and subsequently became the secretary of the village branch.

Managers

As already indicated, not all China's managers and bureaucrats are part of the new entrepreneurial middle classes. In general terms it is possible to identify three subgroups within this section of the new middle classes: state capitalists, social capitalists, and suburban executives. These categories of the new middle classes are each differentiated not only by their successful response to reform imperatives, but also by their control rather than their ownership of capital and resources. The term "state capitalists" refers to those with managerial responsibility for state sector enterprises who, under the stimuli of market reforms, have restructured the assests they control with considerable success. "Social capitalists" are those with similar managerial responsibility for enterprises described as "social-owned" or "all-people's" organizations. These include enterprises and activities established and developed by educational institutions, neighborhood associations, and various kinds of sociopolitical organizations, of which perhaps the most obvious are trade unions. The suburban executives are those with managerial responsibility for the rapid and entrepreneurial development of suburban villages, which in many ways have seen the greatest change in the urban political economy.

State Capitalists

Aggregate data for the changes in China's political economy mask equally fundamental changes taking place, if somewhat more slowly, within the state sector. State sector enterprises in 1996 produced only 28.5 percent of GVIO compared with 76 percent in 1980, and a large number—estimates range from a quarter to a third—are regarded as technically bankrupt.[24] At the same time a substantial number of state sector enterprises have successfully restructured their activities, or used their resources to establish new enterprises— sometimes under the ownership and direction of the original parent company. Throughout the state sector, and even in nationally pres- tigious heavy industrial concerns, some managers have transformed themselves into a form of state capitalist by decentralizing their corporations, establishing conglomerates, developing new enter- prises based on previous workshops or sections of state sector enter- prises, and generally utilizing state sector assets in a more economi- cally efficient way.

For these members of China's new middle classes, immediately realizable personal wealth, though it may exist, is less important than the influence they wield and their control of economic wealth. The new breed of state capitalist, like the earlier prereform managers in the state sector, are ultimately responsible for considerable invest- ments of state capital and the employment of large numbers of people. Moreover, they are likely to have considerable hidden per- sonal income. Since the economy is in the middle of its transition from plan to market, they are able to gain access to the benefits of both. In particular, their housing, health insurance, retirement and welfare provisions (including education for their children) is likely to be at no charge or heavily subsidized. Moreover, almost all will be on performance-loaded contracts or receive bonuses and additional emoluments for their endeavors.

Wang Mengfei is the sophisticated president and general manager of the Shanxi Nanfeng Chemical Industry Group Company, a large- scale state enterprise.[25] This company was founded in 1996 as a joint stock enterprise based on the former Yuncheng Salt Chemical Company and the historically famous Yuncheng Salt Lake. As Wang Mengfei himself pointed out, there can be few enterprises in China that can trace their industrial activities back to the Han dynasty and few enterprise managers whose responsibilities include a temple visited by thirty emperors. The Group Company has attracted invest- ment from Xi'an, Tianjin, and Zhejiang, and its twelve separate enterprises and total work force of more than 10,000 produces substantial proportions of the national output of inorganic salts, fertilizers, and daily-use chemicals, such as detergents, with predicted 1997 sales of 1.4 billion RMB.

Wang Mengfei was born locally in 1944 into a peasant family. In 1969 he graduated from the China University of Science and Technology, and was assigned to the Yuncheng Salt Industry Bureau, becoming director of the bureau in 1988 and general manager of the Group Company on its establishment. Wang has traveled widely, including to the United States, Canada, Australia, South Korea, and New Zealand. All three of his children are university educated, with his eldest son working in the Nanfeng Chemical Industry Group headquarters, a daughter who is a cadre in the Yuncheng legal system, and another child pursuing a research degree in Beijing. In this case Wang's access to power and influence over others is matched by his total income (salary and bonuses), which is in excess of 10,000 RMB a month.

Social Capitalists

In exactly the same ways that managers of state sector enterprises have been encouraged to respond to reform policies and to restructure their activities, managers of social-owned enterprises have been able to establish or develop various activities, and in the process to gain status and to some extent personal wealth as entrepreneurial managers. Social-owned enterprises are usually to be found in the collective sector of the economy and owe much to the ideological imperatives of the prereform era, where almost every social organization—notably schools and neighborhood committees—were encouraged to establish small enterprises for political as much as for economic reasons.[26] By no means all of the current social-owned enterprises have grown out of prereform institutions, but there can be little doubt that the encouragement to such collectivism before 1978 has created a climate for their later establishment and development, particularly where neighborhood economic activities are concerned. The new middle class managers of social-owned enterprises are those who have either restructured existing operations or who have created new businesses based on some form of such social capital.

Zhao Guifa was born in Zhaojiabao, Qingxu county, Taiyuan, in 1940. He was originally the Zhaojiabao accountant and secretary of the CCP committee, having joined the CCP in 1973. In the mid-1970s he encouraged the residents of Zhaojiabao to establish a radiator factory, and since then he has led the enterprise as it has grown into the multiproduct Enterprise Group Zhaojiabao General Company.[27] The original factory was established in 1975 by eighty residents of Zhaojiabao who collectively invested their own 30,000 RMB. Zhao Guifa developed the idea after bringing in an industrial development advisor through a friend, who recommended that Zhaojiabao could produce radiators given that it had access to large amounts of both pig iron and coke, both of which were needed for their production. Individuals own 49 percent of the company and Zhao Guifa is chairman of the board, to whom the managers of each of three subordinate companies report. Directors and managers earned 3,000 RMB per month in 1996.

The company still produces radiators (10 million in 1995, though most are now somewhat more technologically advanced than the original products), but has now established two additional subsidiary companies—one for advanced technology development and the other a service company. Altogether it has twenty-seven workshops and factories, including those that produce aluminum products, threaded steel, laser glass, plastics, and smelted magnesium, all of which were originally developed because of their role in the production of radiators. The company's service company owns and operates a hotel, dance halls, a cinema, a theater, schools, a training center, shops, and a department store. In 1995 the whole group re-invested 100 million RMB of its own money in its own activities, and its GVIO was half a billion RMB.

Suburban Executives

The development of township and village enterprises has been only slightly less publicized than the private sector within the PRC since 1978.[28] The overwhelming majority of this rural industrial development, however, has actually been a function of urban development, located in the suburbs and rural districts of administratively higher-order cities and urban areas. The explanation for this phenomenon may be found in the PRC's policy on urban and rural designations born out of a 1950s desire to control urbanization. The boundaries between rural and urban areas were set at that time, as were different regulatory regimes for housing, work, and economic management. Suburban villages had always benefited from the availability of both technical inputs to their production and urban markets for their output. They were consequently well-placed to take advantage of decollectivization and other aspects of economic reform that were first implemented only in rural areas. This comparative advantage was further increased when economic reforms were extended to urban areas after October 1984, and economic activity began to grow exponentially. In many cases with economic growth the physical difference between rural and urban areas became no more than a white line down the middle of a road, but there have been significant differences in land usage and the regulation of economic management on either side of the road.

The economic wealth of these suburban villages is not personal but is wielded collectively on behalf of villages and townships by executives who are another part of the new middle classes. Although the personal wealth of these new suburban executives is not negligible—they almost all have substantial salaries, together with bonuses or contract earnings—their importance is also derived from the economic wealth they control. Village enterprises often expand and develop subsidiaries in a largely unregulated way. In any one village the enterprises come together to act as a conglomerate owned nominally by the village. There remain few national standards for management practices or economic activities, though there have been some attempts in various locations to establish uniformity at the city level.

There is a close relationship between these new suburban executives and the new conglomerates they preside over, on the one hand, and the previous collectivized economy, on the other. The former agricultural machinery repair workshops have been transformed into light industrial enterprises; village construction departments have moved into property development, and particularly the hotel and hospitality industries; local marketing and supply cooperatives have taken advantage of market reforms and become more specialized as well as economically efficient. For the most part those who were the village-level cadres and administrators of the former activities have become the managers and executives of the new enterprises.

Zhang Zhengwu is just one such suburban executive, in Xiaqian village, in the suburbs of Yangquan, where he is the village head, CCP branch secretary, and general manager of the Qianheng Industrial Head Company.[29] Zhang was born in 1953 and is a native of Xiaqian. A middle-school graduate, he joined the CCP in 1974. In the 1980s he realized that Xiaqian could develop rapidly by involving itself in zircon-oxide processing and other process industries, with large numbers of its inhabitants abandoning their former agricultural occupations. As village head he led and master-minded its transformation. The village is now completely urbanized: the villagers no longer grow their own food and their productive activities are all organized through the Qianheng Industrial Head Company. Its main industrial activities are linked to the coal industry of Yangquan, either supplying its needs or using its by-products for production. Qianheng has a refractory plant, a zinc-oxide plant, and a bauxite processing plant, and it also produces aluminum in a number of forms, zinc-oxide related materials, and coal-based chemicals.

Service Providers

Far from being counted among the new middle classes, those who were the professionals created by the modernizing state before the reform era—teachers, researchers, medical and nursing professionals, welfare workers, and even to some extent administrators in those sections of the party-state less privileged or sidelined by reform—have come to regard themselves in a new category of poverty. State-supported activities in general have seen their budgets cut and their numbers of employees reduced. At the same time, though salaries and wages have increased they have on the whole not kept pace with inflation, let alone economic growth: most would be fortunate to earn 500–800 RMB per month.

Yet there are new professions and occupations that have been created with the economic restructuring of the reform era. These include, most obviously, financial managers, business administrators, and perhaps most dramatically, lawyers. Wang Jijun is one of Shanxi's most celebrated lawyers, as well as dean of the Faculty of Law at Shanxi University.[30] Born in 1956, he has made his reputation through providing legal advice to government departments and units—for example, CAAC, the Departments of Commerce and Roads of the Shanxi Provincial Government—and through taking on several spectacular "civil rights" cases in defense of "ordinary people." These civil rights cases include that of a Yuncheng cadre unjustly accused of corruption in 1992;[31] and that of a Taiyuan cadre accused in 1993 of negligence when a bridge collapsed in Yingze Park under the weight of the large number of people who had come to watch the Lantern Festival.[32] Wang's father was a former cadre in the Eighth Route Army of the Sino-Japanese War who later became a cadre in the Shanxi public security system, a career Wang Jijun followed during the mid-1970s when he became a "model policeman."[33] It was this recognition that enabled Wang to attend university during the late 1970s as a "worker-peasant-soldier" student, and then later to become part of the first cohort of legal trainees who eventually graduated in 1980.

Even more than the professional occupations, there is a general need for service providers to overcome the deficiencies of the weak and developing financial, legal, and technological transfer infrastructures. The need for credit facilities, access to resources and new technologies, the provision of ready investment, and the facilitation of all these aspects of entrepreneurialism has created considerable space for middlemen and brokers. Individuals with relatively liquid funds of their own or with access to such funds through the companies they manage have been much in demand as potential investors.

One of the problems in considering such activities is that they exist on the boundaries of the permissible and the questionable, though not all such behavior can be described as illegal. The legal framework is frequently unclear or ambiguous. There is a general imperative for unused or under-utilized resources to be used efficiently and productively. Yet it is equally as certain that specific aspects of the current economic system can be and are exploited for all they are worth, as for example when individuals contract for the provision of service. Particularly when officials of the party-state become entrepreneurial both within and outside public service, there is not only cause for concern but also the possibility of misjudging their behavior as either criminal or unacceptable when it may be neither.[34]

The most obvious examples of the middleman role are found in the share-trading houses that have been established in the wake of the fast-growing open exchanges of Shanghai and Shenzhen, and the wide range of proto-merchant banks that have mushroomed. Taiyuan and Datong—like other cities in China—have fairly large trading houses in their central business districts that generate interest in capital markets generally as well as stocks and shares. These trading houses reproduce share listings and other indicators in the local press and in their own premises. Although it is usual to find much street activity surrounding such trading houses, as in the money markets the serious business takes place well off the streets and out of public sight. Merchant bank–type activity is less visible and less publicized but is important in encouraging capital growth and economic development. This is largely the role of institutions such as the Taiyuan Trust Stock Exchange[35] or the Shanxi Rongtong Credit Cooperative. In general, the less obvious work of such service providers is to be found in the private deals that often depend not only on personal ties but also frequently on access to the party-state system.

The Shanxi Rongtong Credit Cooperative was established in 1994 with an initial investment of 1 million RMB provided by a number of social enterprises which now own stock in the Credit Cooperative through the Taiyuan Urban Cooperative Bank. By 1996 it had deposits of over 700 million RMB and a healthy annual profit, largely generated through real estate projects, including the development of bankrupt state sector enterprises. Wang Hualun is the president of the Shanxi Rongtong Credit Cooperative and certainly has the right credentials for the job.[36] Born in 1955 in Yangquan, his father was a pre–Cultural Revolution mayor of both Yangquan and Datong. He himself joined the CCP in 1974; his elder brother is a cadre of the Provincial Legal Commission; and his younger brother is a cadre in the Provincial Planning Commission. He served in the PLA during the early 1970s, the Taiyuan Public Security Bureau during the late 1970s and early 1980s, and the Provincial Veteran Cadres Association in the 1980s. The Credit Cooperative is even housed in a building that belongs to the Shanxi CCP Provincial Committee.

Identifying the New Middle Classes

On the whole, the picture that emerges of the new middle classes in Shanxi is consistent with their portrayal elsewhere in China, allowing for differences in provincial political economies related to stages of development as well as to physical and social environments.[37] Shanxi's levels of industrialization and particularly its coal-centered heavy industrial development necessarily mean that its economy has a larger state sector with more central government involvement than many provinces. In consequence, its new middle classes are perhaps more likely to be oriented toward the party-state: a feature of sociopolitical life in Shanxi reinforced by the CCP's deep social roots developed during the Sino-Japanese War.

Despite the greater social and political diversity that has emerged with economic growth during the reform era, the different categories of the new middle classes remain remarkably homogeneous in social, cultural, and political terms. These middle class identities are by no means identical, however, to those contained in the standard accounts of modernization based on the earlier European experience, or automatically reflective of universal trends. Where there are similarities these are more to be found in the comparison with other parts of East Asia. China's new middle classes are the product of the economic restructuring of a state socialist system which has much in common—through the operation of conglomerate capital—with the varieties of the transforming developmental state in East Asia, notably at different stages of the experience of Japan, South Korea, and Taiwan.[38] In particular, Shanxi's new middle classes of the reform era have most definitely emerged from within, and remain to a large extent part of the local "establishment"; and they espouse values consistent with their origins in local society and culture as well as from elsewhere.

Socially, the new middle classes are characterized by their intense parochialism: the overwhelming majority are natives of the locality in which they work, and their careers provide evidence of remarkably limited social mobility, either upward or across country. Identification with native place is a strong characteristic of the new middle classes. It is not just that they are overwhelmingly natives of Shanxi, but rather that most still live and work in (and are committed to the development of) their family's hometown. Their parochialism is reinforced by marriage: very few indeed do not have a spouse from the same village or neighborhood, and in almost every case if those spouses work then they are also to be found in the same company or unit.[39] When any of the new middle classes are any kind of "outsider," they are usually from another province entirely, but as with some of the former technocrats of the party-state system, having been assigned to Shanxi on graduation (and some time ago), have made their homes in the province.

Culturally, the new middle classes are important because of their influence as trendsetters. It is a function that many of the new middle classes accept with an apparently high degree of self-consciousness. They are flamboyant in small ways in their newfound identities and develop public obsessions or hobbies that cover a wide range of unusual activities—for example, they drive expensive or unusual cars, establish soccer teams, take snuff they import (at a high price) from Thailand, or collect postage stamps and souvenirs of the Cultural Revolution. Their behavior and activities set standards that others aspire to follow, especially in their patterns of consumption. Some of these trends would appear to be universal features of economic growth, with increased expenditure on housing, clothing, cars, and education for their children. Almost all the new middle classes own their own houses or apartments, and most of these are well above the average size and value. Clothing is not only fashion conscious, but bought from new-style clothing boutiques.

Cars, and particularly the most obvious luxury cars, also have an immediate appeal—though in most cases they are technically bought by the enterprise rather than by the individual. In Shanxi during 1996 and 1997 the upper-range BMW was the car of choice, together with a car registration plate bearing a "lucky" number (usually 8 or 9, or a combination of the two) that will have been bought at exhorbitant price at auction, and that sometimes may change hands at a cost as high as that of the car itself. Private education has grown rapidly in Shanxi with increased real disposable income, and a network of nonstate schools has been established, many of which have been established by public educational institutions and all of which maintain close links with the public sector.

At the same time, some of the new middle-class fashions seem more specific to the time and place. China's new middle classes have generally adopted the cell phone and digital technology as their hallmarks. The education that the children of the new middle classes receive in their private schools is distinctly modern, but it also includes emphasis on the Confucian tradition and Chinese folk culture. Most of Shanxi's new middle classes even in the urban areas seem to have larger rather than smaller families. Very few have only one child; it is not uncommon to find families with three or four children, often where the earlier children are girls and the last child is a boy. It is almost equally as rare to find members of the new middle classes who are not heavy smokers of the most expensive imported luxury cigarettes.

Entertainment in general is also a function of increased real disposable income. As elsewhere in China the more expensive and exotic restaurants have become not only the haunts of the new middle classes but also often their meeting places. In addition, in Shanxi in general and in Taiyuan in particular, there are a well above average number of karaoke bars—more than 1,000 in 1995, roughly ten to twelve times as many per capita as in Beijing.[40] Christianity of various kinds has also become something of a fashion for the new middle classes. In addition to expanded congregations, funds have been provided for the construction of new churches.[41]

Politically, the new middle classes, far from being alienated from the party-state or seeking their own political voice, appear to be operating in close proximity and through close cooperation. As long as the CCP maintains its commitment to economic growth there are few if any grounds for structural conflict between the new middle classes and the party-state. Almost all categories of the new middle classes—large- and medium-sized owner-operators, the state capitalists, the social capitalists, the suburban executives, and most service providers—depend heavily on the party-state. Social and political systems are becoming more open, particularly at the local level. This trend, however, is being led by the community of interest that encompasses the party-state and the new middle classes, from the top down rather than through the exploitation of any hypothetical political space between them.

12 | The Rise of Private Business Interests

One of the most dramatic aspects of economic reform in China has been the growth of the private economy. Once made up of a small number of marginalized petty commodity operators, the private sector is now a dynamic and growing sector of the economy that attracts public sector workers, managers, party members, and even college graduates with the promise of personal wealth and apparent independence. The popular image of the successful private "boss" *(laoban)* complete with cell phone *(dageda)*, private car, and a villa *(bieshu)* in the suburbs provides an attractive alternative lifestyle for many. This image is in glaring contrast with the communist model, Lei Feng, the self-sacrificing young PLA soldier who ceaselessly devoted himself to the public good, and it marks a significant shift in society from public life to private interests.

While Western societies move periodically from a preoccupation with public-minded pursuits to the zealous pursuit of private gain and back again, the turn from public to private is helped along by the view that self-interested behavior is not just legitimate but even contributes to the public good.[1] In China, however, such "shifting involvements" from public to private are more problematic. Until recently the CCP denied the legitimacy of private interests altogether, insisting that individual citizens reject private interests and dedicate themselves wholly to the public good as defined by party ideology. Thus the process of economic reform, with the accompanying rise of private business, calls into question previously accepted meanings of public and private and the boundary between them. It also necessarily entails a reconsideration of what it means to be a member of the political community. An analysis of the changing role of private business and public debate surrounding it reveals the changing balance of power between, and the complex interpenetration of, public and private in China today.

Expanding the Public and Denying the Private

The Chinese Communist Party understanding of the relationship between public and private both draws on and contrasts with Chinese traditions. The CCP, like the Confucian state, came to power claiming a monopoly on truth and sought to identify itself with the public good and to deny the legitimacy of private interests *(si)* that were associated with selfishness.[2] Unlike earlier formulations, however, the CCP introduced class analysis into its interpretation of the good society. Indeed, Marxism-Leninism gave a new ideological authority to the party's claim to be the sole arbiter of the public interest, which was now equated with socialism. As the vanguard of the proletariat, the party, like the traditional Confucian scholar-officials, was the guardian of the public good and merged with the state to rule in the interest of the proletariat and their class allies, who together constituted "the people" *(renmin)*.

While the Confucian state subordinated private interests to the public good, there was an expansive private realm of family, kinship, business, and religion that acted as a buffer and intermediary between the state and the individual.[3] In contrast, Chinese communism sought to establish a direct link between the party-state and the individual citizen, eliminating all intermediary societal organizations not directly under party control. Indeed, the CCP under Mao sought to get rid of private interests altogether, beginning with private business interests. Marxism-Leninism saw private business as inimical to the public good and criminalized most forms of private production and exchange. The party controlled virtually all industry and commerce by the late 1950s. A marginal petty commodity economy remained, but it had low status and was legally tenuous and politically risky. During unremitting mass mobilizations and political campaigns, even these operations were denounced and closed down.

Mao developed a critique not just of capitalism, private property, and inequality, but of material interest itself. Prosperity had become an obstacle to, rather than a goal of, communism.[4] Despite the denial of private interests among the people, the party recognized that the people did have needs. The party-state defined and sought to provide for the basic needs of its citizens through its system of bureaucratic redistribution and work units. Choice of housing, education, purchase of scarce consumer goods, decisions about marriage, divorce, and whether to have children, once considered private matters, were all subject to the approval of unit officials and thus became the domain of public concern.[5]

In spite of the expansion of the state-dominated public realm and the official denial of private concerns, private interests were in fact pursued. A wide repertoire of strategies for the pursuit of household needs and individual interests developed, including cultivation of personalistic ties with officials, trading of ration tickets, moonlighting, smuggling, and so on. Even as these strategies penetrated the party-state and became a central feature of socialism in China, the official interpretation of public and private was maintained. The result, as Lowell Dittmer argues, was not so much the elimination of the private by the public as a fundamental rift between them, with the public increasingly dominated by empty ideological rhetoric and ritualistic action while the private consisted in the promotion and discussion of particularistic interests through the back doors and in the back alleys of the system.[6]

Relegitimizing Private Interests

With the initiation of economic reform, Deng sought to mend the rift between public and private by endorsing the pursuit of private interests and by tying the realization of the public good to the attainment of material prosperity and national power rather than the attainment of an abstract revolutionary vision. In December

1978, at the Third Plenum of the Eleventh Party Congress which officially marks the beginning of reform, Deng rejected the Maoist cult of poverty and encouraged individuals to work hard for personal material interests.[7] Now it was possible to do good in China by doing well for oneself and family. Deng called on the people to "seek truth from facts." Those who got rich first proved that the party's new reform policies were working. Deng and his colleagues introduced economic reform in China in order to reinvigorate the economy and to bolster the party's legitimacy, which was now to be tested against improving standards of living. A central principle in this effort was to reduce dependence on the state-run economy and to encourage private initiative. At the outset of reform in 1978, its purpose was not to embrace private business. Nevertheless, as reformers became concerned with unemployment and the provision of consumer goods and services in the late 1970s and early 1980s, they initiated policies that legalized private production and commerce.[8] Individual enterprises *(getihu)*, small operations with less than eight employees, were officially sanctioned in a series of policy statements and regulations. The individual economy now was seen as a "necessary supplement to the socialist economy that would continue to exist for a long time."[9] Individual entrepreneurs, who were still seen by many as the money-grubbing remnants of capitalism, were now "to be regarded as part of the working people and as such they will not be politically discriminated against as in the past. In other words their work will be respected by society and their legitimate business activities protected."[10]

Although regulations on the individual economy issued in 1981 allowed for no more than eight employees, a significant number of individual and household firms had already gone well beyond this limit. There were also large numbers of "fake collectives" *(jia jiti)* or "red hat" *(hongmao)* enterprises that, though privately funded and managed, were registered as collectives. In his report to the Thirteenth Party Congress, Zhao Ziyang, well known for his support of the private sector, recognized and confirmed the existence of these private enterprises that went beyond the limits set by the state.[11] In 1988 the Seventh National People's Congress drafted a constitutional amendment giving private enterprises with more than eight employees legal status for the first time since the 1950s. Such enterprises were officially called *siying* or "privately run" enterprises. Article 11 now states that *siying* enterprises are permitted to exist and develop within the limits decreed by the law as a supplement to the publicly owned economy and that the state protects the legal rights and interests of private enterprises and exercises supervision and control over them.[12] Several months after this amendment in June 1988, the State Council promulgated the first national regulations on *siying* enterprises. These regulations state that investors in *siying* businesses enjoy property ownership and inheritance rights.[13] The reforms provide for limited entrepreneurial rights and create at least a theoretical limit on the powers of the state. That these rights are regularly violated is made clear by the number of articles and letters appearing in journals and newspapers in the 1990s complaining that the rights and interests of private entrepreneurs are not getting legal protection.[14] The fact that such complaints appear in print, however, is evidence that private entrepreneurs and their supporters in universities and the press have come to think in terms of rights that should be protected.

As the legitimacy of private business was affirmed, the numbers increased and the characteristics of the business owners changed. In the 1970s and early 1980s those who engaged in private business were typically without other options, such as older people with little or no education, the "socially idle," and individuals who had been released from prison or labor reform camp. Reflecting the low status of this sector, relatively few youth were registered, typically making up less than 5 percent of the total. In Shanghai, for example, in 1980 80 percent of those registered were over fifty years old.[15] By the 1990s private business owners had become a diverse group, including former cadres and workers from state units. According to a national survey of private entrepreneurs in 1995, 45 percent were between thirty-five and forty-five years old, the Red Guard generation. Nearly 30 percent were high school graduates and 5 percent had graduated from a university.[16] Although the vast majority of private businesses are still very small petty traders, hairdressers and shopkeepers, private business is growing in scale and significance. Almost 10 percent of *siying* firms surveyed in 1995 had over five million yuan in registered capital and over 19 percent had more than one hundred workers.[17] Some private business owners barely make enough to get by from month to month; other private owners are quite wealthy. In 1990, for example, when average urban workers in state enterprises made an average 2,500 yuan annually, 11 percent of *getihu* made less than 1,000 yuan while just over 9 percent of *siying* business owners made over 80,000 yuan annually.[18] According to recent reports, between 2 and 5 percent of all *siying* owners have incomes in excess of 10 million yuan.[19]

The private sector has grown rapidly in the 1990s. By 1995 there were over 25,280,000 individual and 650,000 *siying* enterprises registered with the state, and the "nonpublic economy" officially accounted for 14.6 percent of the GDP. The State Statistical Bureau reported in 1996 that more than one in twelve Chinese workers was employed by a private company. Private business created 14 million new jobs in towns and cities in the early 1990s, amounting to 40 percent of all new jobs in urban areas.[20] Moreover, in a growing number of localities, especially along the eastern and southeastern coast, the private sector has taken on a major role in the local economy and society. In Zhejiang province, the *geti/siying* enterprises officially accounted for approximately 20 percent of the gross provincial product in 1994. Wenzhou is well known for its expansive private sector, which is now the mainstay of the economy, but it is not unique in this regard. In Qinghe county, Hebei, sometimes called the Wenzhou of the North, 85 percent of financial revenues came from *siying* enterprise in 1994 alone.[21] Moreover, the trend in economic reform is toward privatization. In 1996 officials in Suzhou, home of the much-touted "Sunan model" of collectivist industry, had begun selling off their TVEs to individuals and groups. Officials, entrepreneurs, and ordinary citizens were pronouncing the Sunan model a failure and praising the Wenzhou model.[22] Moreover, the Fifteenth Party Congress in September 1997 scrupulously avoided the term privatization, but indicated that the bulk of state-owned enterprises are to be leased, merged, or transformed into stockholding companies.

While the private sector has grown and changed rapidly, there is considerable confusion and controversy regarding the actual size of the private sector. Observers agree, however, that the official figures significantly understate the real size and significance of the private economy in China today.[23] There is a lack of clarity in the classification and registration of the township and village enterprises, much of which is intentional obfuscation by both entrepreneurs and officials and some of which is the result of new hybrid forms that are difficult to classify as either public or private. In either case confusion reflects the political risks and economic disadvantages of doing private business and the ongoing bias against the pursuit of private interest, as local officials themselves will often quite readily admit. Collective enterprises are more likely to get tax breaks, bank loans, land-use rights, and import-export powers than private enterprises. Politically, private business owners run the risk of being denounced and having their assets confiscated by the party-state. During periods of renewed ideological fervor, private business large and small has come under attack for speculation, profiteering, tax evasion, sale of fake goods, pornography, and other social ills.

In the face of the backlash following the June 4, 1989, Tiananmen crackdown, the number of those registered in the private sector actually fell for the first time since 1978; numbers did not recover until Deng Xiaoping's visit to southern China in 1992 and the subsequent Fourteenth Party Congress gave new life to economic reform. A frenzy of business activity followed, as many public employees began to dive into the sea *(xiahai)* of business. Nevertheless, the ideological ambivalence toward private business interests continued.

Business owners and local cadres who see private business as a source of local revenue, jobs, and economic growth have, therefore, used various subterfuges to obscure or shift the focus from the private nature of private enterprises. Others have found innovative ways to combine public and private. One well-known ploy is the "red hat" firm, or "fake collective." These enterprises pay an administrative fee to a public agency in exchange for the right to use the collective name.[24] Since tax breaks and other incentives for foreign investment are considerable, there are also a growing number of "foreign hat" *(yang mao)* or "fake joint venture" *(jia hezi)* firms in which an entrepreneur uses the name of a relative living in Hong Kong or overseas to establish a joint venture firm. In some cases entrepreneurs themselves obtained permanent resident status in Hong Kong and then returned to their hometown to do business as a foreign-invested firm.[25] These types of firms are not included in the statistics on the private economy.

While fake collectives do allow entrepreneurs to avoid certain economic costs and political risks, they present risks of their own. In some cases entrepreneurs have found themselves charged with economic crimes such as embezzlement or misuse of public funds when they have used enterprise profits for personal use.[26] In other cases fake collectives have been confiscated and entrepreneurs have found themselves dismissed from their positions by the collective with which they have been associated. In these cases the agency has claimed that although the entrepreneur/director provided the capital for the firm, because the enterprise is registered as a collective and has benefited from tax breaks or other favorable policies, the firm is public and the agency has the power to replace the manager should they decide to do so.[27]

Another example is the "share-holding cooperatives" *(gufen hezuo qiye)*, which first emerged in the mid-1980s. Such enterprises are officially considered public and therefore socialist. Some clearly are public, such as those in which shares are held in common by permanent residents of the township or village and decisionmaking authority is vested in the local government or government agency. Others represent a hybrid form of ownership, with significant shares being held both by public agencies and by private individuals or firms. Finally, many are actually private firms that were established or bought with private capital by a small number of relatives or friends or, in some cases, by only one person. Share-holding cooperatives began in Wenzhou in the mid-1980s and spread to other areas. They have become a widespread if sometimes controversial formula for restructuring, and often privatizing, collective and small state-owned enterprises.[28] In 1995 Wenzhou, which is known nationally for its expansive private sector, had only 3,989 *siying* enterprises but approximately 47,000 share-holding cooperatives. According to some estimates at least two thirds of the share-holding cooperatives in Wenzhou are actually private in nature.[29]

Although the share-holding cooperative is an institutional innovation that seeks to clarify property relations, expand the scale, and standardize the management of rural enterprises and family businesses, it began as an effort to co-opt official socialist vocabulary by repackaging private as public. A reformist official from Wenzhou states outright that the term "cooperative" was selected intentionally to satisfy the political requirements of doing business in a socialist system. "The cooperative label bestows a collective status on the share-holding firms and makes them legally part of the mainstream socialist public system. Thus their development is not limited." In contrast, the development of *siying* enterprises is made difficult by the fact that they are considered exploitative and can only be a "supplement" to the public economy.[30]

The difficulty of doing private business and the increasing numbers of hybrid firms have given rise to a realm of the economy that has become known as the "people-managed economy" *(minying jingji)*. The term emerged in the mid-1980s when local officials in Wenzhou and elsewhere undertook an effort to "rectify names," whereby all private and quasi-private operations were renamed in a way that was in keeping with socialist norms. Thus *siying* and *geti* enterprises were grouped with share-holding, contracted, and other hybrid firms under the label *minying* or "people-managed." Neither private nor fully public *(gong)* nor state *(guojia)*, the term *min* has a socialist pedigree and in the PRC is clearly associated with "the people" and thus with the public good. In the Maoist period, *min*, as in "people-run schools" *(minban xuexiao)*, was used to depict the revolutionary self-reliance of the local peasants, and did not involve personal profit, private wage labor, or exploitation.[31] Although Deng greatly reduced the significance of the Maoist vision for the definition of the public good, the revolutionary heritage continues to inform the political vocabulary. The current use of the terms *minying* and cooperative began as an effort to identify the entrepreneurial initiative and private interests with the public good and public spiritedness and to gain control of the naming process that is critical to public discourse in China.[32]

The Public Debate on the Role of the Private

The debate on the role of private business that has continued unabated since the initiation of economic reform reveals considerable division and ambivalence over the nature and role of private business. If the public good is defined as the realization of socialist goals and socialism is identified with public property, then what is the role of private business in China? There seem to be three answers to this question that emerge as a part of public debate. The first of these is the moderate position, which has attempted to find a middle ground between reformers and hard-liners and has been the official party position until recently. According to this view, private business is a necessary supplement *(biyao buchong)* to the public economy that functions to stimulate production, enliven the market, expand employment, and help satisfy the needs of the people. Although necessary, as a characteristic of the primary stage of socialism, its role has been seen as both marginal and transitional. The public "socialist" sector is to remain dominant, the mainstay of the economy *(gong-youzhi weizhu)*. Indeed, the efforts to legitimize the private sector initially were focused on its smallness and marginality, which made it seem harmless and also left it outside of the socialist economy.[33] In this moderate view individual entrepreneurs who rely primarily on their own labor are socialist workers, but the larger *siying* entrepreneurs are not.

As part of the Tiananmen Square crackdown in 1989, the party issued Document Number Nine, officially barring *siying* owners from entering the party because they were not part of the proletariat and their income derived from exploitation.[34] Thus, although private business owners were officially seen as contributing to the public good, they had interests that were in opposition to the ultimate goals of the state and "the people." Private entrepreneurs therefore continued to have an unclear and somewhat precarious political status, no longer enemies but not full-fledged members of "the people." As the official position this view lacked ideological coherence and satisfied few observers.

The reformers, a second voice in the debate, argue that the official explanation of the private sector no longer conforms with Chinese reality and limits the potential of the private sector to act as an engine of growth at a time when the public sector is flagging. They assert that the private economy is already and should be more than just a supplement *(buchong)* to the socialist economy, and is a "necessary component" *(zucheng bufen)* and an "organic part" *(youjiti bufen)* of the national economy and of socialism with Chinese characteristics. While sometimes admitting that *siying* enterprises engage in the extraction of surplus value, and therefore exploitation, and recognizing the problems of corruption, supporters of the private economy typically point to the harmony of interests shared by workers, employers, the state, and society. Such accounts point to the jobs created, taxes paid, and money donated to charitable causes by private business. Private entrepreneurs and the new rich are presented as patriotic and hard-working innovators who enrich not only themselves but whole communities. These reformers argue for a more flexible understanding of socialism and the public interest. Not unlike reformers in the late Qing dynasty, they make the claim that the private is not inimical to the public but is a necessary part of it.[35]

The third position in the debate is that of the hard-liners, who, like the reformers, argue that the official justification of the private sector does not comport with the economic and political realities. They use Maoist rhetoric to argue that private enterprise is a "candy-coated bullet" undermining socialism, which is identified with the state-run enterprises. While Deng Xiaoping's expedition to the South in 1992 reinvigorated reform and momentarily quieted these hard-line critics, a new and vitriolic attack on the private sector and the reform process as a whole began in 1995. Most prominent in this attack was the "Ten-thousand-word document" *(wanyanshu)*, written by Li Yanming of the Chinese Academy of Social Science's Institute of Political Science, and closely associated with the leftist ideologue Deng Liqun, who led earlier campaigns against bourgeois liberalization. The document calls into question the entire reform process and warns against the emergence of a new capitalist class. It argues that private business has undermined the public economy and that, in some areas where it has become the main source of public revenue, local governments serve the interest of private business to the detriment of the public good.[36] The hard-line analysis feeds on public anger over corruption and concerns about the growing gaps in wealth that can only widen as unemployment rises. These same concerns can be seen in the call to build a "socialist spiritual civilization" that was the centerpiece of the party plenum report in the fall of 1996.[37]

This hard-line critique of reform lost ground at the Fifteenth Party Congress in September 1997, where Jiang Zemin sought to initiate a new round of reform. Although Jiang reiterated the official position that public ownership must be dominant, he argued for an "all-round understanding" of the public sector, which includes not just state and collective enterprises but also those of mixed ownership. Moreover, in recognition of the fact that a growing number of localities and sectors are dominated by private business, he noted that there might legitimately be differences in some areas and suggested that public sector dominance should be understood in terms of quality rather than just in terms of quantity.[38]

The party clearly hopes that the private sector will absorb the unemployment that will result from the reform of state enterprises. Jiang's report adopted the language of the reformers and broke with earlier official formulations in referring to the nonpublic economy as an "important component part of the socialist market economy." The Fifteenth Party Congress did little to resolve the ideological problems that the growing private sector presents for party ideology. Although the debate will continue, it is clear that private business has not only been permitted to function but is increasingly seen as a way to serve the public good. In legitimizing private economic activity the party has rather tentatively invited private business owners into the political community.

Private Business in the Political Community

Forums for discussion and debate on public issues are at least symbolically important features of the public realm. Those excluded from participation in public forums can hardly be seen as full-fledged members of the political community. In recent years a small but increasing number of private business owners have become members of the people's congresses and the Chinese people's political consultative committees (CPPCC) at every level in China. Business owners are typically selected through their participation in United Front organizations such as the Industrial and Commercial Federation (*gongshangye lianhe hui*), which is a corporate member of the PPCC, or the Democratic National Construction Association, one of the eight so-called democratic parties, which is set aside for private business owners. In 1993 over 5,400 *siying* entrepreneurs had been selected as representatives in the people's congresses at the county level or above, and 8 representatives were selected to the Eighth National People's Congress; there were 8,600 private business owners selected to the rather less influential CPPCCs at the county level and above and 23 at the national level.[39]

When discussing the improvement in their social status and the growing influence of private entrepreneurs, many of those interviewed noted the election of entrepreneurs to the people's congresses. While the people's congresses have been passive assemblies with only marginal powers, the inclusion of private entrepreneurs after many years of exclusion and denigration is a clear statement on the part of the party-state that private business owners are now part of the political community. Moreover, as Murray Scot Tanner shows, the people's congresses have become more active in recent years, and they have the formal power to select the chief executive at each level of government.[40] With this in mind, business owners in some counties have organized themselves informally to promote their own candidates for nomination and election as people's congress deputies.[41] Others have attempted to buy votes to get themselves elected to village and township governments and even party committees. In one village a private business owner arranged a kind of write-in campaign and paid voters ten yuan for a vote. His announcement was simple: "If everyone will vote for me, I will give you even more money."[42] This type of action reveals the influence and confidence of private business owners in areas along the east coast, where the private sector is becoming a major element in the economy.

While participation in the people's congresses signals increased status for private entrepreneurs, the party remains the central organ of political power in China. *Getihu,* as part of the "working people," are now permitted to enter the party; *siying* business owners were refused admission after 1989. The policy created resentment even among some who did not want to join because it was seen as evidence of ongoing and unfair bias.[43] Moreover, although the party now refused to admit *siying* business owners, those who had been recruited before 1989 remained, and party members continued to establish private and quasi-private businesses. In 1995, 17.1 percent of *siying* business owners were party members.[44] Even as the party was refusing legally registered private entrepreneurs who might want to join, it vigorously recruited the directors of successful share-holding firms who considered their firms private and did not want to join the party. Some entrepreneurs who hold the controlling (and sometimes the only) interest in successful share-holding cooperatives and who define themselves unambiguously as private business owners found that they could not refuse local cadres' efforts to recruit them into the party. The local cadres wrote up the applications and even paid the dues for these entrepreneurs.[45]

Such cases reflect the difficulty the party organization faces at the local levels when confronted with the newly emergent stratum of business owners who offer a model of success counter to the basic ideological principles of the party. To include them is clearly problematic in principle, because to do so might create a communist party led by "exploiters." Yet to ban them is to allow a potentially powerful group to remain outside of the party and become more difficult to co-opt and control. This problem becomes more acute as social categories lose their previously firm attachment to the formal hierarchy of state employment and public authority.

Public Associations and Private Interests

Having made concessions to the existence of potentially powerful private businesses, the CCP has sought to co-opt and control them by setting up new business associations. These associations in part reflect changing institutional arrangements and ideological adjustments that move China away from Leninism and in the direction of authoritarian state corporatism.[46] Corporatism resonates with

China's traditional conception of an organic society wherein particularistic needs and identities were harmonized by the state. Under Chinese state corporatism, the party-state remains the guardian of the public good that transcends the private interests of individuals, groups, and classes. In contrast with Leninism, the public good is no longer identified with the interests of the proletariat but with the strength of the nation. Private interests and class distinctions are recognized as natural and attempts are made to harmonize rather than eliminate them through state-led negotiations with state-licensed, hierarchically organized associations. These associations are meant to occupy an intermediary realm between state and society, though in authoritarian situations they often become dominated by the state. Citizens participate in political life not through political campaigns, political study sessions, or other public displays of loyalty. Rather they are to pursue private interests, make claims against the state, influence the formulation of public policy, and work to promote the public good primarily through participation in these associations. Associations are not only policy advocates; they also execute public duties. The major organizations set up to represent and oversee the private sector are the Self-Employed Laborers Association *(geti laodongzhe xiehui)*, the Private Enterprise Association *(siying qiye hui)*, and the Industrial and Commercial Federation (ICF).

In the mid-1980s, the party-state set up the Self-Employed Laborers Association (SELA) as a mass organization or a transmission belt for individual operators in keeping with the Leninist tradition. Though officially considered a "nongovernmental" or "people's" *(minjian)* organization, the SELA is an arm of the Bureau of Industrial and Commercial Administration (BICA), the state agency responsible for the licensing and regulation of business. SELA cadres are at the same time BICA officials and work in its individual and private enterprise section. After the formal legalization of the *siying* economy, the BICA in some localities established a Private Enterprise Association (PEA) for the *siying* owners, who tended to see themselves as distinct from the smaller individual operators. The mission of the SELA is to educate the self-employed regarding party policy, law, and proper business practices while protecting their legal rights and interests.[47] Officials sought to make the SELA the equivalent of the public unit for these individual entrepreneurs who were left unitless by virtue of being self- employed. Like the public work unit, the SELA combined political, economic, and social functions. It policed market places, attempted to enforce the one-child policy, and organized study sessions to study new laws, party policy, and even Lei Feng. It also organized product fairs in addition to charity drives, speech contests, and sports competitions.[48] Such activities are meant to improve the reputation and raise the social position of the self-employed.[49]

In addition to these activities, the SELA claims to act as an advocate for individual entrepreneurs who have trouble with other government agencies or find themselves in difficulty because of illness or injury. Organization publications and cadres at the local and provincial level proudly discuss the ways in which they aid their members. While examples of such actions are often provided, the actual extent of them is unknown.[50] Some owners became activists in the organization, taking on formal posts such as "board member" *(lishi)* or "vice association director" *(fuhuizhang)*, attending meetings, participating in association activities, and even helping to implement the one-child policy. Such a strategy bestows a quasi-official status and allows the cultivation of personal connections with the authorities.[51] For most, however, membership means nothing more than obtaining a license and paying the requisite fee.[52]

A separate but overlapping official organization to represent the interests of private business is the ICF. In a somewhat confusing arrangement the ICF is also called the Chinese Chamber of Commerce *(shanghui)*. ICF officials explained that they are one organization with two signboards *(yitao renma liangkuai paizi)*. ICF is the name for domestic consumption, while chamber of commerce is typically used for international activities because that is a name more familiar to their counterparts in other countries.[53] Originally created in the 1950s as the officially administered mass organization for private business owners operating under the auspices of the party's United Front Department, the ICF stopped functioning after the "transformation to socialism" was completed late in that decade. It was revived along with the offices of the United Front in 1977, and since 1991 the focus of the ICF has been on private businesses.

The 1993 ICF constitution characterizes the function of the organization as that of a bridge *(qiaoliang)* between nonpublic business owners and the state. Officials and publications of the ICF also describe the organization as a bridge or a family *(niangjia)*.[54] Most members are successful *siying* enterprises and indeed, the ICF seeks out high-profile, successful private enterprises of some scale as members.[55] The central task of the ICF is to protect the legal rights and interests of private business. The organization will, for example, represent business owners in conflicts with other government offices and at times offer legal support to members whose property has been confiscated by local authorities.[56] The ICF also offers other services such as technical and management training classes and consultation. In some areas the ICF has organized mutual aid societies *(huzhu jijinhui)* and people-run credit unions *(minying xinyongshe)* among private enterprises in order to help private businesses gain access to much-needed credit.[57] The ICF in many towns and cities has begun to organize trade associations (*tongye gonghui* or *hangye-hui*) at the city and district level.[58]

While many of these associations seem to do little more than publish a newspaper and collect donations for charities, some of them have taken on quasi-public functions to protect the interests of their members. The Light Manufacturers Association in Lucheng district, Wenzhou, for example, has established a system to register and protect the design and production of new products developed by light manufacturers operating in the prefecture, all of which are private or quasi-private businesses. In at least one case the association board of directors, all entrepreneurs, with the backing of the security bureau and BICA, carried out a raid on a factory that was in violation of the new product protection rules. Several entrepreneurs in other industries in Wenzhou pointed to the association as an example of a business association that actually did something to protect the private interests of its members.[59] Finally, in a controversial move, the ICF in many regions has set up enterprises of its own. These are justified as a self-reliant approach to the problem of limited funding and a way to come to understand the workings of the socialist market economy so as to better serve its constituency.[60]

As organizations set up by the party-state to oversee and advocate for the private sector and act as an intermediary between private businesses and the state, there is an overlap in the functions of the ICF and the SELA/PEA. One difference is that most members of the SELA are part of the small-scale petty commodity sector, while the ICF tends to cater to somewhat larger and more profitable private firms. Moreover, the SELA as a part of the BICA has the backing of a governmental regulatory agency that can license and close down enterprises. ICF officials distinguished themselves from the SELA by saying the latter was part of a licensing and management organization while the ICF was a voluntary association without any management function.[61] One ICF official noted, "we are not the government; we do not manage (guanli), we offer guidance (yindao) and reflect (fanying) their opinions."[62] It is likely that this lack of direct regulatory and licensing power makes the ICF more attractive as a professional association. In the recent survey of siying entrepreneurs, 77 percent were members of the ICF; only 43.7 percent and 24.6 percent, respectively, were members of the PEA and SELA.[63]

From these descriptions it appears that the ICF, if not the SELA, might be a vehicle through which private business owners could air their views, pursue their interests and help shape public policy and public opinion. Though the ICF is said to be a popular or civic (minjian) rather than a state (guanfang) organization, it is not and does not claim to be independent of the state. As an organization that attempts to act as a bridge between private business interests and the party-state, the ICF might come to occupy that intermediary third realm between public and private. Its role is reminiscent of the Qing dynasty chambers of commerce which, like the ICF, were set up by the state to promote private interests as well as undertake public duties which were a function of the new legitimacy of private business. However, the ICF has not yet regained the prestige and power of the Qing chambers of commerce, though some ICF cadres and members express the hope that it will.[64]

Members give the ICF mixed reviews at best, and few see it as playing an important role.[65] A noodle-stand owner who had taken an active role in both the SELA and the ICF admitted to being frustrated. Even as a leader in both organizations and a people's congress deputy, he found himself unable to get the attention of either the city or the district governmental leaders when the district made a decision to eliminate a popular local market. "They just ignored me. I am supposed to be a bridge but how can I be a bridge when no one comes to meet me from the other side?"[66] Several entrepreneurs stated that the ICF was empty *(kongde)*.[67] Others said that the ICF has a useful role in that it provides a channel through which to network and exchange information with other entrepreneurs as well as government officials.[68] Another noted that the ICF becomes important when one gets into trouble with local government officials.[69] Finally, a few entrepreneurs stated that while the ICF did not play the role that it should, the problem was with the entrepreneurs themselves. Private business owners have a low level of organizational consciousness and are more concerned about making money than with trying to promote group interests.[70]

The current reality brings the ICF closer to the Nationalist era chambers of commerce than to those of the late Qing. Joseph Fewsmith argues that the GMD set up the chambers of commerce precisely so that they would not function. Indeed, state corporatist structures are typically the product of an authoritarian state, meant to preempt societal interests and tame them so that they do not pose a threat to the regime and its interpretation of the national interest.[71] A difference with the Nationalist period worth noting, however, is that while the GMD was seeking to expand the role of the state and deny private interests, the emerging state corporatist structures of the PRC are part of a process that sets new limits on party-state power, grants legitimacy to private interests, and creates more space for extra-bureaucratic action. It is, all the same, an authoritarian arrangement. Thus it is not surprising that entrepreneurs believe the role of the ICF to be limited and find the indirect and private strategies of cultivating personal connections and social networking to be a more effective channel for pursuing private interests and influencing the behavior of public officials at the local level. According to one BICA official, an appropriate name for the private economy is "connection economy" *(guanxi jingji)*.[72] To the extent that they were previously administrative or enterprise cadres themselves, as many owners were, they are in a particularly good position to work the system, with many well-located contacts, access to information, and an already established reputation. In this way private interests influence public policy as it is implemented locally.

The indirect influence of business interests on public policy may be felt in some localities more significantly, though still indirectly, through the structural power of business in the local economy. On this, Deng Liqun, the ideological hard-liner, would agree with Charles Lindblom, the pluralist theorist, when he argues that in areas where private business is a major provider of jobs and revenues, private business gains a privileged position from the government because the economic security and consequently the social stability of the whole community is dependent on them.[73] Thus in spite of the fact that business owners in Wenzhou or Qinghe county may not engage in collective action and may seek to affect public policy only defensively in a covert and particularistic manner, their influence is felt in a more powerful way through their structural position in the local economy. Such structural influence is localized in pockets in eastern China and is in its early stages, but it does mean that private business does not have to be organized or popular to exert influence. This is why many local governments seek to absorb enterprises that are generators of jobs and revenues locally either by taking over "fake collectives" or by becoming share-holding partners.

Most business owners are far less concerned with influencing public policy than with cultivating the role of private citizen—working, playing, and raising families. Especially for thirty-five- to fifty-year-old urbanites, life as a private citizen presents a stark contrast with their history as politically mobilized youth. One marketing survey found not only that the most successful private bosses spend over eleven hours a day working, but also that they are in the vanguard of the consumer frenzy that China has experienced in the 1990s. In 1995 they were in the top 7 percent in consumer expenditures.[74] Private business owners buy homes, cars, and brand-name clothes and frequent China's expensive restaurants and trendy tea houses where they negotiate business deals and expand their personal networks. They also spend a large amount of money on tuition to ensure that their children have access to the educational opportunities that many of them did not have. While increased income is one obvious motivation for undertaking private business, many private owners say that self-actualization is a primary goal in starting up a business.[75] Successful private entrepreneurs provide an alternative channel for success in a society where the CCP was once the only vehicle for social mobility.

Conclusion

The economic reform and the rise of private business that has accompanied it have resulted in a struggle to redefine private interests as part of, rather than in opposition to, the public good. Although the party itself has remained divided on the direction of reform, the expansion of the private economy seems inevitable. The public good is no longer identified with revolutionary public spiritedness or the Communist vision but rather with a more instrumental notion of material well-being and national power. Reformers see private entrepreneurialism as an important force in the realization of these public goals. The elaboration of a coherent ideological explanation for the emergence and enrichment of a new business class, however, has been hindered by the ongoing commitment to Marxism-Leninism, which rejects not just private property but private interests. The party is left without a moral vision that justifies its own position. The movement in the direction of a state corporatist solution to the dilemma is evident in China today and becomes more salient as the party moves toward privatization of the state sector. The organic theory of state and society, the acceptance of "natural" inequalities among people, and the effort to establish corporate organizations as intermediaries between the private and the public are evidence of an authoritarian corporatism that resonates well with Chinese traditions. CCP efforts to institutionalize an intermediary realm, however, have been out-paced by the more informal and often illicit merger of public and private in the form of clientelism and corruption. While the power of private business is at best fragmentary and indirect, there are signs that private business owners are becoming influential private citizens in specific local communities within the shifting exchange between public and private.

13 | The Emergence of Politically Independent Intellectuals

In the post-Mao era the close, sometimes critical, relationship of the politically engaged older intellectuals with the state has resembled more that of their principled literati ancestors and less that of the persecuted and cowed intellectuals of the Mao years (1949–1976). Although members of this over-fifty generation were among the most persecuted under Mao, when the Deng Xiaoping leadership asked for their help and advice at the start of the reform era, they quickly responded, sometimes with criticism. The younger generation, those in their late teens and twenties, whose members were too young to have experienced the Cultural Revolution (1966–1976), were more like their May Fourth predecessors in their search to absorb the new international intellectual and cultural trends and go abroad to study, especially to the United States and Europe. Like their older counterparts, however, they too sought to offer advice to the government, especially to help China recapture its one-time greatness.

A small but important segment of the middle generation of intellectuals, the Cultural Revolution generation, whose members were in their thirties and forties in the post-Mao era, resembled its East European counterparts during the Communist era. Members of this group have engaged in more independent political activity than either the older or younger generations. Their behavior has evolved more from their own experiences in the Cultural Revolution and its aftermath than from any direct contact or conscious emulation of East European intellectuals or even Western intellectuals. All three generations share certain attitudes, particularly the belief that only intellectuals can bring about political change. Nevertheless, the politically engaged intellectuals of the Cultural Revolution generation have led and participated in more activities independently of the state than has any intellectual generation in the PRC.

Similarities with the Confucian Literati

Despite the continuance of a Leninist political structure, China's move to the market, the accompanying devolution of power, the opening to the outside world, the loosening of controls over personal activities, and Deng Xiaoping's pragmatic leadership have made possible a more open intellectual environment than at any time since 1949. As in most of China's premodern history, a de facto intellectual autonomy has developed in academia, the arts, and popular culture. If anyone in these areas dares to challenge the leadership or the government's authority directly, the state, as in the imperial period, retains the will and capacity to intervene forcefully to put down the challenge. But as long as intellectuals remain within the limits of their discipline, they have been left largely alone.

The cultural fever that has gripped the intellectual community since the mid-1980s involves reappraisals of China's history and culture and comparisons with the West. The reappraisals resemble past literati attempts to deal with China's problems by reinterpreting history and revising ideology. Like Confucian literati, post-Mao intellectuals regard themselves as responsible for defining and maintaining moral norms for the political leadership as well as for the population at large. Through personal political contacts and articles in the official and semi-official newspapers and journals that emerged in the Deng era, they sought to act as the conscience of society, as they were unable to do under Mao, but as their predecessors had done until 1949. In addition to their roles as advisors and spokespersons for the leadership, intellectuals, as in traditional times, have been appointed to high positions in government, academia, the media, and the cultural sphere. Under the auspices of various political patrons, they have assumed the leadership of important policy-making institutes and have also headed professional federations, replacing the party hacks of the Mao era. Furthermore, they have organized associations and societies, which have more autonomy than the federations but are still under the patronage of the party and serve as links between party and society.

The traditional premodern style of cooperation between the intellectuals and the government, severed in the Mao era, resumed with Deng Xiaoping and his successor, Jiang Zemin. Like their literati predecessors, as intellectuals have served and advised the political leadership, they have been drawn into the policymaking process by their political patrons, each group seeking to use the other for its own political purposes. Such political-intellectual alliances have been held together in some cases by formal linkages but, for the most part, by shared political views and values that have woven a variety of informal intellectual and political networks rather than by purely organizational ties. In the reformist camp, one group of intellectuals, primarily in the over-fifty group, and their disciples, revised ideology under the patronage of party general secretary Hu Yaobang (1980–1987);[1] another network, of younger reformist intellectuals, proposed economic reforms under the patronage of prime minister and then party general secretary Zhao Ziyang (1980–1989).[2]

As Zhao sought to strengthen his position vis-à-vis the party elders and hold on to Deng's support in the late 1980s, he also patronized another group of relatively younger intellectuals who advocated "neo-authoritarianism." They rejected the East European approach of simultaneously implementing political and economic reforms, in favor of an emphasis on economic modernization modeled on the four little tigers of East Asia. The neo-authoritarians argued that, because of the low education level of China's populace and the lack of democratic traditions and consciousness, the introduction of democratic reforms would cause chaos. They called instead for rapid market reforms, economic decentralization, and the nurturing of a middle class, all guided by a strong authoritarian regime. Eventually, they contended, these economic reforms and the development of a middle class would lead to political reforms.

In the 1980s, intellectuals discussed policy matters relatively freely among themselves and at conferences. They published their views and conducted debates publicly in newspapers, journals, and books. But their ability to do this, as in traditional times, was determined by political patronage. Like their literati forebears, there were no laws to protect them; if their patrons were purged, as were Hu Yaobang in January 1987 and Zhao Ziyang in May 1989, or if their patrons changed their minds, as was the case with Deng Xiaoping, their advice was rejected.

Other intellectual networks expressed the ideas of the more conservative party elders, such as those connected with the late Chen Yun and Hu Qiaomu. In the 1980s, the intellectuals in the more conservative networks were drawn from old literary and ideological groups formed in Yan'an in the 1940s and the early 1950s and were shaped by Mao's ideology. By the late 1980s and early 1990s a number of intellectuals from the post–Cultural Revolution generation had joined these conservative networks. Some had drifted from a reformist to a conservative position, particularly after the June 4, 1989, military crackdown on the Tiananmen Square demonstrators. After the suppression—either by imprisonment, exile, or silencing—of the reformist intellectuals and the neo-authoritarians, associated with the deposed Zhao Ziyang, neo-conservativism and rising nationalism became the dominant intellectual trend of the mid-1990s.

The neo-conservatives differed from the neo-authoritarians in their desire to turn the clock back on decentralization and openness to the outside world; they wanted to reinstitute more centralized controls over the economy and intellectual life. There were also differences between the neo-conservatives of the post–Cultural Revolution generation and the more conservative party elders, such as Deng Liqun and his spokespersons in the 1990s. Whereas the older group was more interested in ideological and class issues, the younger group was more nationalistic than ideological. The younger generation was also more concerned with China's competition with the West and more interested in recapturing China's once powerful position in the world than in achieving ideological goals. Rather than invoking Marxism-Leninism, they emphasized finding inspiration in China's traditional culture, especially those elements that supported authoritarian rule.

In the 1990s, therefore, although discussions among colleagues with a variety of views were still relatively free, the ability of reformist intellectuals to express themselves publicly was quite limited. The neo-conservatives, who had the patronage of the leadership, had more access to the public media in the early 1990s, but by the late 1990s, as Jiang Zemin sought to follow a middle course, their access to public forums was also limited.

Similarities with the May Fourth Generation

The pluralistic intellectual atmosphere of the post-Mao era, made possible by China's opening to the outside world and move to the market, has been comparable to the pluralism of the early decades of the twentieth century. As the imposed ideological uniformity and cultural sterility of the Mao years faded away, intellectuals, like their May Fourth predecessors, began to explore all kinds of new ideas and to question the orthodox ideology. In the 1980s, they sought intellectual inspiration from the West and from their ethnic brethren and cultural cousins in East Asia. They interacted with Western intellectuals and overseas Chinese intellectuals, especially from Hong Kong and Taiwan, the majority of whom were Western-trained. As China's intellectuals became involved in international exchanges to a greater extent than at any other time in their history, China's cultural world became globalized.

Like the late Qing literati and the May Fourth generation, most post-Mao intellectuals have been rationalists in the tradition of the Enlightenment. Nevertheless, a substantial minority, particularly those in the arts, have questioned this approach. Nonconformist artists, writers, and poets have been prominent on the cultural scene and were especially so in the early Deng years. Their Cultural Revolution experience led them to question whether there could be any rational or political solutions to China's complex problems. After the destructiveness of the Cultural Revolution, they viewed reality as absurd and senseless and concluded that the arts should not be used for pragmatic or political goals. They are cultural iconoclasts who express their detachment from society through their art; they have sought out new and experimental ways to express their aesthetic and individual visions. Though ostensibly apolitical, their conscious effort to depict images that have no ideological content or to detail everyday life has been in itself a political statement against a society that has been so highly politicized. Thus the cultural and intellectual atmosphere of the post-Mao era has been diverse, multidimensional, and stylistically experimental. It has incorporated a variety of cultural sources, traditional and modern, Chinese and Western.

Despite the party's periodic efforts to regain control over intellectual and cultural discourse, the intellectuals and artists of the post-Mao era have developed a degree of autonomy from party manipulation. Along with the local elites in the coastal and urban areas, the move to the market and international contacts, as in the late nineteenth and early twentieth centuries, has made them less dependent on the state, economically as well as intellectually. By the 1990s this more open, diverse climate had moved beyond the coastal areas and urban areas, where it had been contained earlier in the century, to the countryside and hinterland through modern means of communications such as telephone, television, computers, faxes, film, and e-mail.

Intellectuals have taken advantage of the party's loosening grip to fill the public space vacated by the state with informal salons, study groups, journals, and think tanks.[3] A variety of intellectual and cultural associations have emerged—official *(guanban)*, semi-official *(banguan)*, and nonofficial *(minban)*—which are managed by their members. The semi-official groups have government connections of some sort, but they are looser than the government federations and associations. Their leaders have usually held concurrent posts in the sponsoring unit, and their financial support has come either from the state or their own revenues or both. They generally have had political patronage that protects them, but this has weakened their ability to act as pressure or interest groups on their own. Nevertheless, in association with their political patrons, they have been able to exert political clout, as in the case of the semi-official *World Economic Herald* in the 1980s. Officially attached to the Shanghai Academy of Social Sciences, this newspaper was able to advocate radical economic reforms because it had the patronage of Zhao Ziyang and his associates.

Although nonofficial groups, like the semi-official organizations, must be formally registered with an official unit *(danwei)*, they have been completely independent financially and their sponsoring unit has had little influence over their actions. While most nonofficial groups of intellectuals have been ostensibly apolitical, their discussions of philosophy, history, literature, or the environment have been implicitly political. In the late 1980s, however, some nonofficial groups became explicitly political. Among such groups, those formed by members of the Cultural Revolution generation were most directly involved in devising a new, more independent relationship between the intellectuals and the state. Even though most of these groups were suppressed after June 4, 1989, the ways in which they were able to establish their independence and exert influence in the late 1980s may be the prototypes for others trying to do the same thing in the future.

Politically Engaged Intellectuals of the Cultural Revolution Generation

The experience of the Cultural Revolution generation has diverged from that of the traditional literati and the elite intellectuals of the Mao and Deng eras as well as from the generation that came of age in the post-Mao period. Unlike the others, the education of this generation, born after 1949, was interrupted by Mao's 1966 summons to rebel against authority. Most initially became Red Guards, following Mao's orders to question and overthrow bureaucratic and intellectual authorities, sometimes violently.

When Mao in the late 1960s condemned these activities, carried out in his name, and sent the Red Guards to farms and factories to reform themselves through labor, he provoked profound disillusionment not only with his leadership but also with the ideology and the political system that had given the Chairman the power to manipulate their lives. This experience of their formative years left them bereft of belief, a loss somewhat akin to their late Qing literati predecessors' loss of faith in Confucianism. At the same time, their rebellion against authority engendered in members of this generation a questioning spirit, a search for new values, and an openness that was close to that of their May Fourth predecessors.

Those of the Red Guard generation shared with the intellectual elite a Confucian sense of responsibility for the fate of society and the May Fourth belief that they were the agents of national salvation. Like their forebears, they, too, saw themselves as in charge of the moral well-being and enlightenment of the leadership as well as of the populace in general, and they placed their faith in a rationalist approach to problems. They also shared the older intellectuals' aspirations. Initially they too sought positions in the official intellectual establishment—the universities, institutes, and bureaucracy. They, too, wanted to publish articles in the official media, set up officially approved journals, and convene conferences to spread their ideas.

There have been various congeries of politically engaged intellectuals in this generation, with different emphases. Some have had connections with high officials. One such group in the 1980s, "Toward the Future," organized by Jin Guantao and his wife, Liu Qingfeng, former scientists, advocated applying a scientific approach to social issues. Another group of younger intellectuals published articles in a popular journal for China's youth, *Reading (Dushu)*. Though more independent than the intellectual networks under political patronage, their approach was the traditional one of educating both the leaders and the people about the need for reform.

In the 1980s other members of the Cultural Revolution generation engaged in practices their elders and contemporaries would not deign to be associated with, such as participating in demonstrations, entering local elections, allying with people outside the establishment, and setting up think tanks without any high-level official patronage. The most prominent and effective group of this genre formed around Chen Ziming and Wang Juntao, who were to be charged in 1990 with being the "black hands" behind the 1989 Tiananmen Square demonstration. They shared with their elders and Cultural Revolution colleagues the rationalist approach and Confucian concern for education and moral improvement, but they also believed that the development of an orderly society and good government could no longer depend merely on enlightening the leaders and educating the public. They stressed building new political institutions as necessary for political reform. One way they sought to achieve this goal was to establish a truly independent, politically engaged organization, with its own independent financial base, that could exert political influence without interference from patrons or the state.

While the intellectual elite of the older generation and other Cultural Revolution intellectuals continued to use ideological revisions, political discourse, and high-level patronage to press for change from the top down, much in the tradition of their literati predecessors, Chen, Wang, and their ex–Red Guard associates sought to bring about political change from the bottom up with methods they had been exposed to in the Cultural Revolution. The group that formed around them shared not only their views but also their Cultural Revolution experience in Red Guard groups, labor reform camps, and prisons. They demonstrated against Mao and the Gang of Four during the April 5, 1976, movement and participated in the Democracy Wall movement of the late 1970s. Like their elders and successors, they initially wanted to join official associations and think tanks, but because of their past activities, they were rejected. As a result, they sought to build their own institutions.

They acquired a number of their political skills during the Cultural Revolution—publishing pamphlets, making speeches, and mobilizing mass support. The dismantling of the party apparatus and chaos in the Cultural Revolution left a vacuum that made it possible for some Red Guards to form their own study groups, where they could discuss political issues relatively freely. Although the party apparatus was reconstituted in the post-Mao era, it was not as tightly and cohesively run as it had been before the Cultural Revolution. These Red Guards therefore continued practices they had acquired in their formative years.

The nonestablishment stance of Chen, Wang, and their associates was not one they would have chosen for themselves. It was shaped by their experiences in the Cultural Revolution and under the post-Mao leadership, when they were forced to fend for themselves. Coming from official and intellectual families, Chen and Wang had not envisaged a grass-roots approach to politics in the early years of the Deng era; it was forced on them by the leadership's refusal to give them positions in the official establishment or to listen to their proposals because of their past political activities. As one of Chen Ziming's prosecutors was to tell him before his trial in 1991: "If you had not been imprisoned in 1975, you would have become a manager of a chemical company or an engineer."[4]

As it became increasingly clear by the mid-1980s that Chen and Wang would not achieve official status, their concept of the intellectual's relationship with the state gradually changed. Although they sought to bring about change within the existing system, they believed it was also necessary to take initiatives and participate in activities outside the establishment to make this possible. They therefore worked with people outside as well as inside the party-state. As their group gained stature in the late 1980s, they also linked up with semi-official and even establishment intellectuals—but not at the expense of their own grass-roots approach.

Consequently, though he espoused some Confucian values, Chen Ziming rejected the Confucian ideal of the "scholar-official." In the early 1980s he began criticizing the concept that the "one who studies becomes an official."[5] He urged intellectuals to separate themselves from officials and to assert their independence, hitherto a rare act in the People's Republic. He and his associates attempted to practice what they preached. In the process they also planted the seeds for a civil society in China, but their version differed from that of their East European counterparts, who saw civil society in opposition to the state. Chen and others still retained the traditional Chinese view of state and society as not in opposition, but as mutually interdependent and working together, though in their separate ways. Chen's written statement after he was sentenced to thirteen years in prison encapsulates this view: "I believe that the relationship between government and the stratum of intellectuals needs to be radically changed. The two must develop independently, recognize the common areas in their goals, each shoulder particular responsibilities, each accord the other respect, contending but not clashing, cooperating but remaining independent of each other."[6] His view of civil society was very much one with Chinese characteristics.

The Makings of Independent Intellectuals

In some ways, Chen Ziming is typical of the Cultural Revolution generation of intellectuals. He was born into an intellectual family, which had been educated for several generations at Peking University; his father's generation had joined the party underground while there. Unlike his father, Chen's education was interrupted at age sixteen, when he was sent to Inner Mongolia. There, for the next six years, he learned about farming and medicine as a barefoot doctor. On his own, he also studied Western philosophy, including Montesquieu, as well as Marxist theory. While in Inner Mongolia, he became aware of the persecution of Mongols, the bitter poverty of the countryside, and the arbitrary tyranny of the local party cadres. In 1970, when he was appointed head of a production brigade of educated youth, he held late-night talks with its members about the injustices and lack of accountability in China's political system.[7]

He returned to Beijing in 1974 and was admitted to Beijing Chemical Industry College, but he was imprisoned in 1975 because of his criticism of the Gang of Four in correspondence with a friend. Just before his transfer to a labor reform camp, he was allowed to visit his family in Beijing. His visit coincided with the April 5, 1976, demonstration against the Cultural Revolution, which he joined. He quickly assumed a leadership role when he was pushed forward by the crowd to negotiate with the authorities for the release of protestors who had been arrested. His future political partner, Wang Juntao, the son of a leader of the Military and Political Academy, also made his political debut in the April 5 demonstration, leading his high school class to Tiananmen Square and composing a poem for the occasion. After the party suppressed the demonstration, Wang was imprisoned and Chen continued on to the labor reform camp without the camp authorities' knowing about his activities on April 5. Thus both men early on had shown their leadership abilities in a mass demonstration and had been imprisoned.

Released shortly after Mao's death, Chen and Wang appeared to have bright prospects in highly prized scientific fields at prestigious institutions. Chen entered the Academy of Sciences and Wang enrolled in Peking University's physics department, after taking the exams with the most competitive entering class in the history of the

People's Republic. Wang was also admitted into the Communist Youth League and rose to be an alternate member of its Central Committee, a sure path to party membership and officialdom. Yet when the Democracy Wall movement suddenly exploded in late 1978, Chen and Wang joined in and published one of the most influential journals of the movement, *Beijing Spring (Beijing zhichun)*. Their journal was relatively conservative and mainstream in its call for change within the political system and in its stress on economic reform. It stood in sharp contrast to Wei Jingsheng's journal, *Exploration (Tansuo)*, which asserted that China could not reform as long as the party remained in power and which attacked Deng Xiaoping as a potential dictator.

Beijing Spring attracted a core of fellow Red Guards and prison and labor camp mates who were to stay together as a group until the crackdown almost a decade later on June 4, 1989. Typical of its members was Min Qi. Although he did not come from an elite family like Chen and Wang, he had been imprisoned in the Cultural Revolution for criticizing Lin Biao and, like Chen, he was sent to Inner Mongolia. He, too, while visiting relatives in Beijing participated in the April 5, 1976, demonstration. In 1979 he joined the staff of *Beijing Spring* as its theory editor. Even though Min Qi was admitted by examination in 1985 to the Academy of Social Sciences and became editor of its official journal, *Social Sciences in China (Zhongguo shehui kexue)*, he remained close to the *Beijing Spring* group. When the group set up its own independent think tank in late 1986, he became its chief administrator.[8]

By contrast, Yan Jiaqi, who had early contacts with the *Beijing Spring* group, is an example of an intellectual reformer who took the establishment route. He published an article in *Beijing Spring*'s first mimeographed issue under a pseudonym and another article in the final issue under a different pseudonym. Unlike the others at *Beijing Spring*, however, Yan had not only been admitted into the party as a provisional member in October 1978 but was also invited to Hu Yaobang's important Theory Conference, which sought to make ideology more relevant to the economic reforms. Although Yan agreed with the views of the *Beijing Spring* group, he did not want to do anything that would jeopardize his becoming a full member of the party. In early 1979, at the time of the Theory Conference, he broke off contact with Chen and Wang's group and later was to become the head of the Political Science Institute at the Academy of Social Sciences.[9]

Despite their nonofficial activities, Wang and Chen did not eschew the establishment route and, like their intellectual elders, they remonstrated with the political leaders to get their ideas accepted. In spring 1979 Wang and one of *Beijing Spring*'s editors went to Hu Yaobang's home for an interview, and much to their surprise, Hu engaged them in a vigorous debate. Wang urged Hu not to sentence Wei Jingsheng for his criticisms; Hu, however, urged Wang not to talk merely in generalities about reform, and asked him to specify reform strategies. At that time, unprepared for such a question, Wang could not reply. Hu cautioned Wang that in two thousand years of Chinese history, reformers had rarely succeeded, lacking both the correct strategy and the patience; he pleaded with Wang to keep this in mind. Wang, as well as Chen, disregarded Hu's advice, and they were both subsequently banned by the establishment.[10]

Local Elections, 1980

After Deng Xiaoping suppressed the Democracy Wall movement in spring 1979, Chen and Wang next sought to achieve their political goals in 1980 by organizing and participating in the relatively democratic elections held for the first time to select deputies to the local people's congresses. With Deng's tacit approval, students took the initiative to conduct multicandidate elections to the local congresses in the university areas, principally in Beijing, Shanghai, and Changsha in Hunan. Although the local congresses had little real power, former Red Guards and Democracy Wall activists, who had been silenced by the closure of Democracy Wall, seized the opportunity to work for reform by running in these elections. Again they used the skills of speech making, pamphlet writing, organization building, and group mobilization that they had acquired in the Cultural Revolution and the Democracy Wall movement to conduct their election campaigns.

Beijing was one of the last places to vote. The first pilot election was held in April at Fudan University in Shanghai. Chen's brother, who attended Shanghai's Tongqi University at the time, informed Chen about the Fudan elections. Although the authorities were generally supportive, when one of the candidates at Hunan Teachers College in Changsha, Liang Heng, criticized the party directly during the election campaign in October, the party interfered, provoking a hunger strike and class boycott.

Despite the party's subsequent annulment of the vote in Changsha and the imprisonment of Wei Jingsheng and other leading Democracy Wall activists, Chen, Wang, and scores of other candidates participated eagerly in the Beijing local elections in November–December 1980. Still believing in Deng Xiaoping's promises of reform, they were encouraged by Deng's August 18, 1980, speech in which he attributed Mao's destructive policies to the political system that had given its leaders unlimited powers. The Beijing Party Committee was also fairly open at that time and supported the local elections, and the universities helped by providing duplicating materials, paper for posters, and space for debates.

Normal life on the Peking University campus came to a virtual halt for six weeks in late 1980 as twenty-nine candidates, most of whom had participated in the Democracy Wall movement, pasted up their posters around the campus, distributed leaflets, and conducted opinion polls. Over ten student-run newspapers sprang up overnight to report on the election campaigns. At several large meetings, the candidates presented their views according to set procedures pertaining to time limits, responses, and speaking order, all of which had been agreed upon by them and their staffs without official input. Even though party investigative commissions, the *People's Daily*, and other media journalists came to observe and question the candidates, and the Ministry of Civil Affairs was in charge of the overall election, the campaigns and meetings were conducted in a relatively free and orderly atmosphere.

Wang was a candidate at Peking University and Chen contested a seat to represent the Academy of Sciences, where he was chair of the graduate student association. Both men took Deng's speech and theorist Liao Gailong's subsequent call for some system of checks and balances as license to talk about political reform. Their speeches, therefore, went beyond the party's advocacy of economic reforms. In one of his campaign speeches, Chen declared that "the party should not be allowed to substitute for the nation's laws."[11] In another speech he pointed out that "only with elections can we have politicians who are close to the people . . . and only with elections can we have a check on corrupt officials."[12] Chen later observed that the views they expressed in the 1980 election campaigns were motivated by the desire to prevent another Cultural Revolution.[13]

With his classmates in the Peking University physics department as his campaign committee, Wang Juntao ran on a platform calling for both political reform and economic reform, including the establishment of a system of separation of powers. Though he stayed close to Deng's August 18 themes, Wang was the only candidate at Peking University to offer a sustained critique of the party's thirty-year rule and to criticize Mao directly. He condemned the Anti-Rightist Campaign and the Great Leap Forward as well as the Cultural Revolution and praised the victims of Mao's persecution, such as Liu Shaoqi and Peng Dehuai. Before the party's official acknowledgment of Mao's mistakes in June 1981, Wang called Mao "not a real Marxist," and asserted that Mao's unlimited power had "grievously damaged China's development."[14]

In the first round of voting, six thousand Peking University students cast their votes in an orderly fashion in a secret ballot. Even though philosophy graduate student Hu Ping and Wang were the top vote getters, because neither of them received 50 percent of the total vote, there was a run-off. Wang was an eloquent debater, but because of his public denunciation of Mao, he lost the election to Hu Ping, who had run on a platform of freedom of speech. Nevertheless, Wang's defeat did not lessen his efforts for political reform. In one of his election speeches, he had declared: "My reason for running as a candidate is to try to promote China's political democratization. Whether or not I am elected, I will continue to struggle toward this lofty goal for the rest of my life."[15]

Although Chen Ziming easily won at the Academy of Sciences, his victory, and those of the other elected unofficial candidates in 1980, were short-lived; elections to local congresses in urban areas were discontinued soon after. Nevertheless, their participation in a democratic process, along with their Cultural Revolution experience, had a profound impact on the candidates and their supporters. Without any party guidance, they had worked out procedures among themselves for conducting debates and campaigns, which virtually all of them had followed. They learned how to negotiate, compromise, and abide by a set of rules. A number of them, particularly Chen and Wang, were to put these skills to use by building their own organizations and by negotiating with people in and out of the establishment.

Building an Independent Base

Although Wang's position in the Youth League was a virtually sure channel to party leadership, he let his membership lapse by not paying his dues, a rare act at that time.[16] Such an act was not even contemplated by the older elite intellectuals, who sought to hold on to their party registration at all costs, no matter how badly the party treated them. The elite considered party membership and access to the leadership the only way to influence policy. By contrast, as the party continued to ignore their reform ideas, Wang and Chen began searching for ways to put their political ideas into practice outside the party establishment. Soon after graduation both men left the positions to which they had been assigned and attempted to win support for the setting up of a civil service based on merit in place of the prevailing nomenclature system.

Although a civil service was a traditional Chinese institution, in the People's Republic, where appointments were based on political criteria, it was a revolutionary proposal. Chen and Wang studied the personnel systems in China's imperial period, Japan, Taiwan, and the West and presented their proposals for such a civil service system to the authorities a number of times without any response. Wang went to Wuhan in the mid-1980s to look for a college administrator who would establish a program to train civil servants at their institution. While there, Wang drew around him a circle of associates who had similar aims. No administrator, however, was willing to carry out their ideas.

In the meantime, in response to the party's encouragement of market activities, Chen and his wife, Wang Zhihong, in the mid-

1980s established two correspondence schools in Beijing to train people in administrative skills. These schools proved to be very lucrative.[17] But unlike some of their former Red Guard colleagues, who also became rich in China's emerging market economy, none of their profits went into enriching themselves. They continued to live frugally and put virtually all of their profits into establishing the Beijing Social and Economic Research Institute (SERI), the first nonofficial social science think tank in Beijing. Chen realized early on that in order to be ideologically and politically independent, one must be financially independent. His political goals may have been idealistic, but his methods were pragmatic. Moreover, he was not above using connections *(guanxi)* to, for example, get his think tank officially registered with a unit of the Beijing city government.

Nevertheless, Chen and his colleagues sought to maintain their autonomy at all costs. With repeated rebuffs from the authorities to their proposals, Chen concluded that they "must work outside the party" to achieve their goals.[18] Most of the researchers he gathered around him at SERI had endured the travails of the Cultural Revolution and imprisonment with him, had helped him to publish *Beijing Spring,* or were from Wang's Wuhan contacts. Unable to find positions at official institutes and forced to fend for themselves, they sought to use their think tank to reform the political system so that they as well as others could take independent political positions.

In 1988 Chen bought the *Economic Weekly* from its semi-official sponsor, the Chinese Federation of Economic Associations. Because it already came with an official registration, Chen did not need to register it. An editor of the *Workers' Daily* became its editor, and Wang was its major columnist. They transformed this journal from a pedestrian trade magazine into a forum for a broad range of topics that soon rivaled the highly regarded *World Economic Herald.* Whereas the *Herald* was more a mouthpiece for the reform views of Zhao Ziyang and his network, the *Economic Weekly* was unattached to any official faction or specific view of reform. It published articles by members of both Hu Yaobang's and Zhao Ziyang's networks as well as by nonestablishment intellectuals, and it included discussions on a broad range of topics from Confucianism to the May Fourth movement. Even more than the *Herald,* the *Economic Weekly* became a forum for contending, sometimes opposing views, still a rare occurrence in the same paper in post-Mao China.

Although their political stance was relatively moderate, Chen and Wang's efforts to establish intellectual institutions outside the control of the party-state were radical in both the traditional and the Chinese Communist context. In addition to the *Economic Weekly*, SERI had its own publishing house, which printed translations of Western books and original works by Chinese reformers. It also established a public opinion polling organization, utilizing experts trained in the newest methods, as an alternative to the party's official opinion polls. Its poll results, published in the party's media, revealed a body of opinion that sometimes differed from that presented by party propaganda. Chen and Wang also organized conferences, funded independent research projects on sensitive political subjects, and established ties with researchers in Beijing's universities and institutes.

By the late 1980s, like their counterparts in Eastern Europe and the Soviet Union, Chen and Wang had built a network of independent organizations that attracted hundreds of professors, graduate students, and well-known intellectuals. SERI had achieved such prominence that even intellectuals associated with Hu Yaobang's and Zhao Ziyang's intellectual networks, who had earlier kept their distance, now wrote for the *Economic Weekly*. More significant, several asked Chen to help them set up their own publications, as they too began to seek more independence from the party in the late 1980s. Interaction between political activists in nonofficial think tanks and the intellectual elite was another profound change in China's intellectual community. Although such joint activities were most prominent in Beijing and Shanghai, similar coalitions were forming all over the country.

Contacts with Workers and Other Classes

Initially Chen and Wang adopted the intellectuals' elitist stance toward the workers. Even though by 1987 Chen had concluded that intellectuals could achieve political reforms only in coalition with other social groups, he specified allying with industrialists, rural entrepreneurs, and reform officials, but not with workers or farmers.[19] The student protestors in the Tiananmen Square 1989 demonstration revealed a similar elitism when they literally locked arms to keep the workers from participating in their protest. Although the students talked about sending delegations to factories to link up with workers, as their May Fourth predecessors had done, few did so. In addition to their elitism, Chen and his associates, like the students, were very much aware of the fact that since 1980 the leadership's greatest fear was the formation of a Solidarity-like coalition between intellectuals and workers. Chen, Wang, and those associated with them did not want to do anything that would provoke the leadership's retaliation and put an end to their independent activities.

When the 1989 spring demonstrations erupted following Hu Yaobang's death on April 15, several members of SERI, particularly Liu Gang, a physics graduate student at Peking University, and Chen Xiaoping, a teacher of constitutional law at the College of Politics and Law, helped organize the student marches to Tiananmen Square and the student memorial meeting there for Hu on April 22. A former student of the politically controversial astrophysicist Fang Lizhi, Liu Gang had assisted Peking University students in setting up democratic salons in 1988 to discuss political issues. At that time he became acquainted Wang Dan, the future co–student leader of the 1989 demonstrations. While most intellectuals generally sympathized with the student protestors, and for the first time in the history of the People's Republic, elite intellectuals marched in the square in support of the students, they still had little influence over them.

Although they did not try to dissuade several of their SERI associates from participating, Chen and Wang played no visible role in the early stages of the 1989 demonstration. They had become disillusioned with the efficacy of protests and feared that as in the past, the 1989 protest would evoke a reaction from the party elders and a retreat from the reforms. Initially, they kept their distance. It was only on May 13, when Zhao Ziyang's ally Yan Mingfu asked Chen and Wang to try to persuade the student leaders to end the hunger strike and leave the square before Gorbachev's visit on May 16, that they were thrust directly into the events. They agreed to help because they feared that if the situation were not soon defused, there would be a violent crackdown.

Unlike most intellectuals, they had influence with the student leaders through their SERI colleagues. But they had no contact with the workers and the millions of ordinary Beijing residents and students from the provinces who also had joined the demonstration by mid-May. In fact, at a conference of the All-China Federation of Trade Unions on May 15, Chen opposed encouraging workers to join the student movement because of his fear of provoking retaliation.[20]

Nevertheless, several of their SERI associates had made contact with the workers in the square during the demonstrations and had offered advice to the first nonofficial workers' union, the Beijing Workers Autonomous Federation, BWAF, which was organized in mid-May and led by a worker, Han Dongfang. The most helpful was Li Jinjin, the son of a Public Security Bureau official and a member of Wang Juntao's circle of Wuhan friends.[21] Li had served in the army and, after the Cultural Revolution, received an undergraduate law degree. He then enrolled in the graduate law program at Peking University, where he was elected chair of the graduate student association. He and a few other colleagues trained in law tried to ensure that the BWAF adhered to the letter of the law so as to avoid provoking the authorities. Li drafted the BWAF's inaugural statement: "Our old unions were welfare organizations. But now we will create a union that is not a welfare organization but one concerned with workers' rights."[22] When martial law was enforced on May 20, the BWAF formally appointed Li as its legal counselor.

The imposition of martial law finally led Chen and Wang for the first time to make common cause with the workers. They urged students and Beijing residents to join with workers "in joint pickets" to put pressure on the leadership to find a peaceful resolution to the stand-off between the demonstrators and the party. They supported the efforts of the NPC Standing Committee member Hu Jiwei and the Stone Company think-tank head Cao Siyuan to convene an emergency meeting of the NPC to deal with the martial law order through constitutional means. "This crisis cannot be resolved on the streets," Wang asserted at a meeting on May 19. "We need to bring

democracy off the streets and into the Great Hall of the People."
Chen added: "If the government is to be persuaded to enter into
another round of dialogue and negotiation, it must talk to representatives of all social sectors."[23] And that now included workers.

Beginning on May 20, Chen and Wang convened meetings with
the leaders of the various autonomous federations that had been
formed during the demonstrations, including the BWAF. On May 23
they linked these federations into a united group, the Joint Liaison
Group of All Circles in the Capital to Protect and Uphold the Constitution. On May 25 this group described itself as a "mass organization" of workers, intellectuals, cadres, students, peasants, and business people, whose immediate goal was "to mobilize the masses from
all sections of the community to do everything possible to resist
martial law."[24] For the first time in the People's Republic, a group of
intellectuals had overcome its members' elitism and fear of joining
with workers and appeared to be moving toward a coalition with
workers and other social groups in political action.

They supported several BWAF initiatives. When Han Dongfang
had called for a general strike in sympathy with the protestors,
Chen put out feelers to Zhu Houze, acting head of the official
All-China Federation of Trade Unions. Although some of Zhu's
aides appeared to support the idea, Zhu drew back at the last min-
ute.[25] When three workers were arrested on May 29, and Han led a
group of BWAF members to the offices of the Beijing Public Security
Bureau to demand their release, hundreds of students rushed over
from the square in an unprecedented show of support for the workers. As legal advisor to the BWAF, Li Jinjin asked the police for the
legal justification for their detention.[26] That evening the student
leaders allowed the BWAF to hold a press conference on the steps
of their headquarters at the People's Monument to report on the
arrests of the three workers, but the students let only Li speak, not
Han Dongfang. The three workers were released on May 31.

Despite increased contacts and cooperative efforts, however, there
were tensions between Han and the SERI intellectuals. At a May 26
meeting, Han had charged: "You theoreticians can go on acting as
the brains of the movement and students can give it its emotional
spark. But unless the workers are the main force, the struggle for

democracy will never succeed. I hear you talking a lot about the 'citizens' [*shimin*] who are out on the streets, when what I think you mean is 'workers' [*gongren*]. I don't know if that's a deliberate evasion on your part, but it's important to call these people by their true name."[27] Han considered Chen and Wang's efforts to resolve the stand-off peacefully "unrealistic."[28]

When the original student leaders, Wang Dan and Wu'er Kaixi, went into hiding in late May and Chen and Wang's entreaties to leave the square fell on deaf ears, the Joint Liaison Group gradually dwindled to the core of SERI associates—Chen, Wang, Liu Gang, Chen Xiaoping, and a handful of others. Despite the failure of the coalition to achieve any results, its very existence and the continuing stream of workers joining the demonstration along with the students, now coming from all over the country, perhaps more than any other factors, provoked the party leaders to launch the military crackdown on June 4. The specter of a Solidarity-like coalition of intellectuals and workers, which the leaders had feared since 1980, was finally materializing and had to be broken up.

Shortly after the June 4 crackdown, Chen and Wang went into hiding, and on June 10 police and soldiers burst into SERI's offices and seized manuscripts, files, and computer disks. On June 19, Wang and Chen headed the list of the "black hands" who "incited, organized and directed the counterrevolutionary riot in Beijing."[29] Not surprisingly, the charges against them included their efforts to form a coalition with other social groups, specifically with the workers. Equally important were their efforts to establish an organization outside the party's control. It was not their ideas, which even by comparison with some of the elite intellectuals were comparatively moderate, but their actions in forming an independent political base that had made them anathema to the party. They were captured in 1990 and in 1991 were each sentenced to thirteen years in prison. As the price of President Clinton's delinking China's most favored nation treatment from human rights issues, Chen and Wang were released in 1994. Wang went into exile in the United States, but Chen was rearrested in 1995. He was then released to house arrest in late 1996.

Even though politically independent intellectuals in China can no longer establish their own think tanks or hold public forums, the coalition building between intellectuals and other groups, especially with workers, continues underground. The fact that the party since the mid-1990s has broken up such coalitions all over the country and placed their leaders, worker and intellectual alike, in labor reform camps without trials is evidence that the coalitions begun in the 1989 demonstrations persist in the 1990s.

The Significance of Politically Independent Intellectuals

It would be wrong to discount the impact of Chen, Wang, and the SERI group because they and the politically engaged independent intellectuals they represented have been suppressed and the institutions they sought to build have been crushed. Despite their failure and their small numbers, they signify the beginning of a genuine change in the relationship between China's intellectuals and the state in the post-Mao era. Unquestionably, their behavior and beliefs have had much in common with both those of the traditional literati and the elite intellectuals in the People's Republic: they remonstrated with their leaders to change their political ways; they sought to join the political establishment; they continued to see themselves as members of the vanguard that speaks for others and tells the truth. Yet, unlike other intellectuals, they rejected political patronage, built an independent cohesive political organization, and participated in political activities with people outside as well as inside the establishment. They had the makings of a proto-political party.

Like their East European counterparts in the 1980s, they demonstrated that pressure outside the party-state can influence and undermine an entrenched regime. Yet, unlike them, they were unable to bring down the party-state and help establish a new government. Despite the loosening up and devolution of the party's power that accompanied the economic reforms, China's party-state is much stronger than its former counterparts in Eastern Europe. Moreover, unlike East European intellectuals and even their May Fourth predecessors in the 1920s and 1930s, Chen, Wang, and their associates did not link up with the emerging merchant class and workers in political action until just briefly before the June 4 crackdown. They lacked the broad-based social support enjoyed by their East European brethren that might have helped them succeed.

Perhaps most important, unlike East European societies, China lacked the civil society that might have aided their efforts.[30] As several historians have pointed out, a public sphere existed in late nineteenth- and early twentieth-century China.[31] Gentry rule in the local areas and new types of entrepreneurial activity created a relatively autonomous society alongside the central state. Mary Rankin, William Rowe, and David Strand have described the establishment in the public sphere of chambers of commerce, citizens' groups, city councils, and gentry associations. Similar "zones of de facto autonomy" emerged with Deng's economic reforms, in which the devolution of central control allowed for a bottom-up process of forming embryonic autonomous associations.[32]

Although similar associations have multiplied and engaged in a myriad of activities in the post-Mao era, they have not yet developed into a community of citizens that can freely organize politically and establish a space for political activity outside the party-state. The SERI group came closest to creating this space. Despite the emergence of all kinds of semi-autonomous and even autonomous groups, in order to survive after June 4, these groups have had to be explicitly apolitical. Consequently, without any laws to protect them and without the backing of a broad social base or a civil society as in Eastern Europe, politically independent groups cannot function openly.

Nevertheless, the example of Chen, Wang, and their SERI associates will not be lost on future generations of intellectuals. In retrospect, their role seems closer to that of the dissidents of the former Soviet Union than to East European dissidents. Chen and Wang's Soviet counterparts were also relatively few in number; they did not have a civil society to support them, nor did they have much contact with other social classes. They, too, were silenced, put in prison camps, or exiled. Although they were able to build underground organizations, some in coalition with workers, as is happening now in China, they were unable to organize politically and publicly until the late 1980s, just before the fall of the Soviet Union. If China's party-state unravels as the former Soviet Union did, will China also be as bereft of intellectual and political leadership as Russia is with the collapse of the Soviet Union? True, China has a very different culture and history, but unlike its Confucian and East Asian neighbors, it has not allowed an opposition to organize that can assume leadership if and when the party-state unravels.

China, however, is very different today from even the former Soviet Union. In some ways it is much more open and connected to the outside world, especially economically. Its intellectuals are in contact with their international colleagues. Yet its political culture, in which intellectuals' highest calling is to enter government service, is so deeply embedded that the majority are likely to continue to work in the established political order and to continue to beg the regime to reform itself. Nevertheless, a minority of the Cultural Revolution generation, who came to believe that they could help their country more by being independent of the state and at times in opposition to the state, now exists. Their assertion of relative independence in the late 1970s and 1980s has had a profound influence on their politically engaged countrymen, whether they advocate liberal democracy, decentralization of political power, or a virulent form of nationalism. For independent political actors to reemerge and survive, they will need much more support from Chinese society than they had in the 1980s, and they will need laws to protect their independence if they are to have an impact on policymaking. And that may be a long time in coming.

ELIZABETH J. PERRY

14 | Crime, Corruption, and Contention

Contentious politics, in the form of tax riots, industrial strikes, street demonstrations, and the like, have become a prominent feature of the post-Mao social landscape. The relaxation of political controls, combined with the unsettling effects of economic change, has given rise to a remarkable explosion of collective resistance. The 1989 uprising was only the most dramatic in a series of mass protests that have racked China in recent years. In outward appearance, at least, many of these contemporary movements bear an uncanny resemblance to popular protests of bygone days. Public denunciations of inflation and corruption, "moral economy" demands for a subsistence wage, and sectarian religious beliefs—all of which figure centrally in contemporary movements—hark back to late imperial and Republican precedents. Do we see here a simple resurrection of pre-Communist patterns, in stark contrast to the top-down mobilization that characterized the Maoist era? Has China returned to traditional modes of popular contention after a Communist detour that led, in the end, nowhere? And is such widespread protest likely to have consequences as revolutionary as those of the late Qing and Republican periods?

This chapter will consider some of the varieties of popular contention that have erupted in China in the late twentieth century, with an eye to the question of continuity and change. We will ask whether the resemblance to early twentieth-century exemplars is more than superficial, and whether or not protest repertoires have been fundamentally altered by the influence of nearly fifty years of socialism.

Denunciations of Inflation and Corruption

Few accusations served more thoroughly to discredit previous Chinese regimes than charges of dereliction in curbing official corruption and providing for mass welfare. Following the Opium Wars of the mid-nineteenth century, in which the Qing dynasty was humiliated by foreign powers, criticisms of the ruling elite often ignited a nationalistic determination on the part of protestors to replace inept leaders with a stronger state apparatus. At the turn of the twentieth century, the luxurious lifestyle of the Manchu rulers, combined with widespread economic distress, activated Sun Yatsen and his followers to overthrow the imperial system. Nearly half a century later, popular indignation about galloping inflation and the blatant graft of Guomindang bureaucrats helped in turn to topple the Nationalist regime.

Comparable concerns, albeit without the nationalist fire of earlier times, have resurfaced in the protests of the post-Mao era. Allegations of official malfeasance and mismanagement of the economy figured prominently in the Tiananmen uprising of 1989. Subsequent protests have echoed these grievances. For example, in June 1995 dozens of entrepreneurs rallied outside the Guangdong provincial government offices to complain about cadres charging exorbitant fees. Timed to coincide with the arrival in Guangzhou of the commissioner of the Independent Commission against Corruption (a Hong Kong government agency) for talks about strengthening anti-corruption measures, the protests ended with the arrest of a number of demonstrators.[1] Marches in Shanghai have also been sparked by anger over corruption. In 1990, according to Public Security Bureau statistics, city authorities received fifty-six applications for marches and demonstrations (*youxing shiwei*), up 115 percent from the previous year. While seventeen of these protests concerned disputes over housing or property rights, twenty-two were ignited by a sense of bureaucratic injustice or of outrage toward officials on the part of ordinary citizens.[2]

The low esteem in which government agents are now held can be seen in the widespread violence directed against representatives of state authority. For instance, in June 1994 about a dozen legal personnel and policemen in Shanghai were assaulted by peddlers and their friends and relatives after the authorities launched a search for counterfeit goods at a local market:

> Local peddlers who came in motorcycles and cars . . . blocked the court vehicles and used bricks to break the windows of police cars and watermelons to block their exhaust pipes. They hit and kicked law enforcement officials and even threw people into a river. They took away a detained person and forcibly seized 50 cases of fake products which were to be used as material evidence. Those law offenders even demanded an exchange of hostages. Public security personnel of Lishui city who came upon the scene stopped their car to rescue the law enforcement officials, but they, too, were beaten up.[3]

It is no secret that the forces of law and order suffered a precipitous decline in popular prestige, at least among urban dwellers, following the deployment of soldiers and tanks in June 1989. Anonymous attacks on state agents have escalated of late, perhaps as retribution for the government's draconian repression of the Tiananmen uprising: "The State Council recently admitted that instances of snipers taking potshots at soldiers and policemen have become commonplace on the outskirts of Wuhan, Xi'an, Chengdu, and Beijing. On three days in May of 1994, nine such incidents occurred, resulting in eleven casualties and five explosions."[4]

As the 1989 uprising graphically illustrated, concerns about official malfeasance are shared by some state cadres. The participation of propaganda, security, and union officials in the Tiananmen demonstrations was an indication of the depth of disenchantment within the party-state apparatus. Despite a series of widely publicized campaigns against corruption, public concern with this issue is accelerating. In June 1994, more than 4,000 cadres (3,700 of whom were party members) in Inner Mongolia joined a petition drive demanding:

> (1) immediate measures to curb inflation; (2) a stop to purchasing cars and distributing luxurious houses; (3) immediate increases in allowances to grass-roots cadres and retired cadres in order to guarantee their living standards; (4) making public the investigation and handling of the corrupt officials and abusers of power in the party and government leading bodies of the autonomous region in order to redress the grievances of the general public.[5]

While the commotion in Inner Mongolia was in part an expression of resentment by basic-level cadres against the privileges enjoyed by their superiors, the perception that party and government agents are tainted by corruption is widespread. Unlike the Maoist period, when it was generally assumed that cadres served at some personal cost, today's popular wisdom holds that cadre status facilitates personal enrichment through graft.

In some cases, the disgust with inflation and corruption has dovetailed with separatist tendencies:

> Over 1,000 and over 2,000 people assembled and marched in Urumqi, capital of Xinjiang Uyghur Autonomous Region, on 26 and 28 April [1994] respectively. Marchers assembled at the People's Park, Nanmen Stadium, and the railway station and then went to People's Square . . . to urge the government to protect the working class's interests, curb inflation, and crack down on corrupt bureaucrats. Some of the marchers even shouted the separatist slogan of "long live Xinjiangstan."[6]

In the "between-plan-and-market" economic system that has developed under the reforms, state officials enjoy special access to the low-interest loans, resources, and personal contacts that enable commercial and industrial development. As pivotal figures mediating between hungry investors and scarce resources, cadres are highly susceptible to the temptations of bribery and embezzlement.

Private entrepreneurs are not the only source of bribes, of course. A researcher with the Central Commission for Discipline Inspection recently noted that "collective bribery" (in which public funds are used) accounts for a rapidly growing proportion of all criminal bribery cases.[7] State investment agencies and banks are the principal targets of collective bribery, as enterprises seek funds with which to expand their activities. Organization and personnel departments are also major beneficiaries of collective bribes, as units struggle to secure official positions for some of their employees. The involvement of state officials on the giving as well as the receiving end of these transactions creates a complicated pattern of relationships that is not easily eradicated by even the best efforts of the Discipline Inspection Commission. Reportedly, administrative posts are even up for bid, with the going rate varying by the benefits to be derived from the position in question.

Scholarly studies concur in stressing the growth in corruption—in frequency, scale, and complexity—during the post-Mao era. This is not to suggest, of course, that official wrongdoing was absent during the earlier years of the PRC. Indeed, although the 1950s are often remembered in retrospect as the golden days of the new regime, a large-scale movement against corruption was launched in the cities only two years after the Communists took power. The Three and Five Antis Campaign of 1951–52 targeted first cadres (for corruption, waste, and bureaucratism), and then private entrepreneurs (for bribery, tax evasion, theft of state assets, cheating in labor and materials, and stealing state economic information) in an initiative intended to eliminate a range of infractions not unlike those condemned in contemporary campaigns. A decade later, the Four Cleans Campaign (intended at first to rectify problems with account books, public granaries, collective property, and work-point evaluations) subjected rural cadres to intensive scrutiny for alleged malpractices. The result, according to Richard Baum, was "the most intensive purge of rural party members and cadres in the history of the Chinese People's Republic."[8] The stage was thereby set for the Cultural Revolution, in which charges of bureaucratism and corruption were often hurled with impunity at authorities in city and countryside alike. Moreover, recent memoirs chronicling the extravagant lifestyle of top officials during the height of these Maoist campaigns reveal a scandalous pattern of elite decadence.[9]

Yet, important as these PRC precedents are, they do not fully anticipate recent developments. In the fall of 1993, Deputy Procurator-General Liang Guoqing acknowledged that corruption was "worse than at any other period since New China was founded in 1949. It has spread into the Party, government, administration and every part of society, including politics, economy, ideology and culture."[10]

Explanations for the escalation of corruption in the reform period vary, depending in part on the particular time period under consideration. Alan Liu, analyzing corruption cases from the years 1977 to 1980, highlights residual problems from the Maoist system: promotion of false models in emulation campaigns, illegal imprisonment and torture by lower cadres, disparity between the wealth of public institutions and the generally low living standard in society, a severe shortage of consumer goods, and so forth.[11] Jean Oi, examining cases in the Chinese countryside through the 1980s, emphasizes the redistribution of power among rural cadres under the reforms. In particular, she argues that peasants have become more vulnerable to arbitrary action by a wider array of local authorities: "Cadres who hold power over peasants are no longer limited to team leaders. . . . Clerks at the cooperative store, at the toll stations, at the gas stations, license bureaus, procurement stations, etc. are now all in a position to engage in illegal activity that will directly affect the economic well-being of individual peasants."[12] Local cadres, Oi contends, have been taking advantage of the economic reforms to enrich themselves at the expense of the peasantry.

Gordon White, focusing on the 1990s, explains the rampant corruption as a by-product of a new class, created through a merger of officialdom and business. He speaks of the emergence of a "new, post-communist bourgeoisie" generated by dual trends: "on the one hand, a stratum of economic influentials is rising in the 'private' sector aided by connections with state officials and foreign (mainly overseas Chinese) business and, on the other hand, state officials are attempting to convert their power into control over economic assets, transforming political into economic capital."[13] White suggests that the wave of corruption currently washing over China may be a transitional phenomenon, likely to recede (in perhaps ten to fifteen years) as a truly private class of business entrepreneurs forms and the state is reorganized along more limited, civil service lines.[14]

Much of the scholarly debate has revolved around the issue of whether Chinese-style corruption plays a beneficial or deleterious role in economic development.[15] More important from the perspective of contentious politics, however, is the level of tolerance for "corruption" (which is itself a highly subjective term) among the populace at large. The fact that charges of official wrongdoing have been a central factor in mass protests suggests that corruption is a politically incendiary issue, regardless of any "objective" economic benefits it may bring. In an opinion poll conducted by the Chinese Academy of Social Sciences in 1987, nearly 84 percent of the respondents from thirty cities cited corruption as the social problem that most disturbed them. A similar survey carried out the following year identified "embezzlement and bribe taking" as the most pervasive social crime.[16]

As Richard Levy has documented, different groups of Chinese elites offer competing interpretations of the causes of, and solutions to, corruption. Whereas conservatives blame the new entrepreneurs and democracy activists indict the party-state system, reformers (like many Western analysts)[17] point to imperfections in China's still rudimentary market economy. Despite such differences, Levy concludes that elite discourse concurs in marginalizing the role of the masses.[18] Opening the political system to democratic electoral participation by ordinary citizens is not seriously entertained as a remedy for corruption by any of the parties to this debate.

Nevertheless, although excluded from elite proposals, the Chinese masses have certainly not been silent on the matter. According to a top-level government report, the Chinese countryside witnessed some 1.7 million cases of resistance in 1993, of which 6,230 were "disturbances" (naoshi) that resulted in severe damage to persons or property. Many of these incidents were evidently directed against official malfeasance of one sort or another. Among the so-called disturbances, 830 involved more than one township and more than 500 participants; 78 involved more than one county and over 1,000 participants; and 21 were long-lasting events that enlisted more than 5,000 participants. In the course of these confrontations, a total of 8,200 township and county officials were injured or killed, 560 county-level offices were ransacked, and 385 public security personnel lost their lives. The following year showed a further escalation. In just the first four months of 1994, rural areas saw 720,000 protests, of which more than 2,300 were serious "disturbances" that caused injury or death to nearly 5,000 township and county government personnel. The report noted with alarm that "in some villages, peasants have spontaneously founded organizations of various types, including religious or armed organizations, to replace the party and government organizations. They have established taxation systems on their own."[19]

Although information on the mentality of the protestors is extremely limited, charges of corruption appear to figure prominently. Anger over injustices in tax collection is evidently heightened by perceptions of a degenerate leadership class, prone to extravagant self-indulgence. This is an old theme in rural tax resistance, but it seems to have taken a new twist in the contemporary period. In particular, the rhetoric of class exploitation that was so pervasive during the Maoist era has bequeathed a tool of criticism for contemporary protestors as well.[20] For example, during a series of tax riots that occurred in Jiangsu's Shuyang county in 1990–91, the farmers' slogans revealed resentment at the gap between their own impoverished living standards and the luxurious privileges enjoyed by cadres. The language was reminiscent of Cultural Revolution posters: "Eels and turtles, every cadre likes to eat; but each mouthful is the peasants' flesh and blood."[21]

Metaphors of exploitation, often with a Chinese gastronomic flavor,[22] are symptomatic of a general tendency to frame political criticism in terms of Maoist class discourse. In early 1993, some 2,000 peasants from seven villages in southern Anhui rallied against the government's use of IOUs (in lieu of payment for agricultural products) with banners that read: "All power to the peasants!" "Down with the new landlords of the 1990s!"[23] The "collective action frames" that evidently resonate among today's militants thus differ substantially from those of pre-Communist rebels.[24]

The condemnation of official corruption in class terms is seen in recent protests by city dwellers as well. This was evidenced in a manifesto issued by the Beijing Workers Autonomous Federation at the height of the Tiananmen uprising in May 1989:

We have carefully considered the exploitation of the workers. Marx's *Capital* provided us with a method for understanding the character of our oppression. We deducted from the total value of output the workers wages, welfare, medical welfare, the necessary social fund, equipment depreciation and reinvestment expenses. Surprisingly, we discovered that "civil servants" swallow all the remaining value produced by the people's blood and sweat! The total taken by them is really vast! How cruel! How typically Chinese! These bureaucrats use the people's hard earned money to build luxury villas all over the country (guarded by soldiers in so-called military areas), to buy luxury cars, to travel to foreign countries on so-called study tours (with their families, and even baby sitters)! Their immoral and shameful deeds and crimes are too numerous to mention here.[25]

Another indication of the attraction of class analysis to contemporary Chinese workers was seen in Beijing in the summer of 1992, when an informal group calling itself the "Association of Sanitation Workers and Staff" announced a strike by the city's street sweepers and janitors. If this nonstate organization implied a nascent civil society, its rhetoric nevertheless harked back to the language of the Cultural Revolution. Big-character posters in the eastern district of Beijing showed that even the humblest of China's workers had absorbed some lessons from decades of Communist education in exploitation and class struggle:

We are the masters of society. The honchos depend on our hard work to stay alive, but all they show us is their butt ugly scowling faces. They take all the credit and the rewards and the biggest pay envelopes, while we workers get paid less. We are the ones sweeping the streets and cleaning up the city. Where do the honchos get off acting like lords?

We say to our fellow workers, comrades-in-arms, brothers and sisters throughout the city: We cannot put up with this any longer. We are people, too. We cannot be mistreated by these honchos. All of the workers and staff at Eastern District Sanitation Team No. 1 are uniting to recover the money that those blood suckers and parasites have taken from us workers. We are taking back whatever has been embezzled from us. We are going to show those honchos that the working class is not to be trifled with, that the working class is the master of society, that it is a class with lofty ideals. We are going to make every social class and every prominent person sit up and take notice of the ones with the lowest social position, the ones everyone looks down upon, the ones everyone regards as smelly; the sanitation workers who sweep the streets!

Officials are so cocky and proud. They go everywhere in cars, and bark out what they want to eat, like chicken, duck, fish, squid rolls, swallow's nest soup. . . . The gnawed bones they throw out are the compensation that we, the working class, get. In today's socialist society, can we the working class allow them to treat us this way?[26]

In short, the accusations of official malfeasance—albeit a staple of popular protest from imperial days to the present—are framed differently in the wake of decades of Maoist propaganda. Although government leaders have been reluctant to employ class rhetoric since Deng Xiaoping declared class labels abolished back in 1979, rank-and-file critics of the reforms have found such language a powerful weapon in making sense of their problems.

Moral Economy Claims

A second theme that runs through the discourse of contemporary protest also has an ancient pedigree. The Mencian notion of a ruler's responsibility to provide for the livelihood of his subjects established a classical foundation for the belief in a general right to subsistence. The socialist experience has reinforced and reshaped this traditional value.

In the 1990s, moral economy claims have been especially pronounced in strikes of industrial workers.[27] This distinguishes the current scene from the Republican era, when "reactive" protests against the advancing state were concentrated in the countryside. The largest rural tax riot in contemporary China, which occurred in Sichuan's Renshou county in 1993, was only superficially in the moral economy tradition. Sparked by exorbitant extractions that required the farmers to turn over some 20 to 30 percent of their net income to the state, the movement might appear at first to be a classic case of "reactive" protest against state initiatives of the type often seen during China's Republican era (1911–1945).[28] In fact, however, the Renshou farmers did not make their claim on the basis of notions of customary rights. Instead, led by a former soldier well schooled in interpreting bureaucratic rules, the protestors pointed out that the excessive levies stood in violation of a recent central directive that stipulates a 5 percent ceiling on the tax level. Demanding refunds for the extra taxes and fees remitted over the previous several years, the Renshou peasants claimed that "according to the regulations announced by the central authorities, we have already paid taxes and levies up to the year 2000!"[29]

In contrast to the Renshou case, workers at state-owned industrial enterprises—faced with the promulgation of a new bankruptcy law and reform of state industry—have frequently employed the language of moral economy in resisting the threat to their once iron rice bowls. Alongside the familiar claim to subsistence is a reminder that workers are supposed to reign supreme in a socialist society. Expectations that the industrial proletariat should enjoy special treatment under socialism were heightened during the Cultural Revolution. Yao Wenyuan's slogan, "the working class must lead in everything," translated into a privileged position for workers in the form of Mao Zedong propaganda teams, workers' theory troops, worker ambassadors, and the like.[30] Today, while the once scorned capitalist class enjoys a new lease on life, workers see their own economic and political advantages slipping away.

Industrial strife has escalated at a rapid rate since 1986. Thousands of arbitration committees have been established to handle the growing number of factory disputes. By the end of 1993, more than 60,000 disputes had been reviewed by these committees.[31] That year, arbitration committees dealt with some 11,400 labor disputes—nearly double the figure of the previous year.[32] In just the first quarter of 1994, the number stood at 3,104 cases—almost three times the figure reported during the same period of the year before.[33] Since only a fraction of the disputes are officially recorded,[34] we can assume a remarkably high level of strife.[35]

In the incidents about which we know some details, it is clear that workers often respond to aspects of the reforms—for example, the threatened closure of inefficient state enterprises—with a mixture of protest repertoires reflecting both Communist and pre-Communist influences. Take the case of the Chongqing Knitting Factory, which announced in November 1992 that it was declaring bankruptcy and that its 3,000 workers would have to seek alternative employment on their own. Moreover, retired workers were to be reduced to monthly stipends of only 50 yuan—in contrast to their original levels of 150 to 250 yuan. To protest these injustices, a petition movement was launched:

> The retired workers who led the demonstration procession knelt down before the armed policemen, pleading tearfully that they only wanted to lodge a petition to be able to receive their original pensions and only hoped for the right of subsistence. . . . The retired workers said that the pensions represented the work accumulation they had made in the past decades and belong[ed] to part of the surplus value they had created. . . . Workers on the job said: We just worked according to orders, and business losses were caused by mistakes in the economic plan for guiding production; the blame should not be placed on the workers. The state should be responsible for the future of the workers and should provide them with jobs and training, thus guaranteeing workers' basic right of life.[36]

While claims based on production of surplus value and mistakes in the economic plan reflect obvious Communist influence, the act of kneeling to present one's petition to the government authorities came from the prerevolutionary protest repertoire.[37]

As the current reforms roll back the initiatives of the Maoist era, workers react to the loss of "traditional" guarantees with moral-economic indignation. Labor strife has been especially acute in Liaoning and in Sichuan province, where a number of military enterprises were established during the Cultural Revolution as part of the "third front" program to relocate defense industries in the interior.[38] A report in 1995 noted:

> Workers in Liaoning and Sichuan often took to the streets and staged demonstrations to express their resentment. They called for "being able to get food for survival." . . . In Chongqing, Sichuan

more than ten cases of worker demonstrations happened in this period [early 1995]. In at least four of the events, over 1,000 people participated in the demonstrations, while others involved several hundred or some 100 participants.[39]

Workers at military enterprises in the northern industrial city of Shenyang have marched on government offices to protest against wretched living conditions, the city's mayor [Zhang Rongmao] said yesterday . . . Soft-hearted officials of the Liaoning province capital could not turn away requests for subsidies and money for salaries, creating a new burden on the city treasury. Zhang said, "It is not our responsibility, but the people are ours. They must at least be able to eat."[40]

As workers contrast their current predicament with the relative economic security that they enjoyed during the Maoist era, it is hardly surprising that they should turn to Cultural Revolution slogans to press their case:

In a few areas, flaunting the banner of defending Marxism-Leninism-Mao Zedong Thought and taking advantage of problems existing and arising in the current process of construction and reform, underground organizations instigated cadres and the masses to slow down their work and go on strike and organized activities to overturn existing policies. They made open appeals to party members to step forward bravely to "rescue our party" and of [sic] "down with the old-line capitalist advocate Deng Xiaoping." Party members and three types of persons in the Cultural Revolution were in these extremist organizations.

In the latter half of last April [1994], over 5,000 workers and staff in the iron and steel capital Anshan (most were workers and staff of Anshan Iron and Steel works) took 120 cars to march around the urban district and shouted such slogans as "workers as masters of the state," "protecting workers' class interests," "down with the newborn bourgeoisie," "yes to socialism, no to capitalism" and "long live the working class."[41]

In an ironic reversal of Karl Marx's model (which exerted a central influence on scholarship in the moral economy tradition), the capitalist advance in China today comes as a postscript—rather than a prelude—to communism. As a consequence, those most nostalgic for the status quo ante are not peasants harking back to the sureties of the traditional order, but a proletariat anxious to cling to the fast-disappearing securities of socialism.

Sectarian and Secret Society Connections

One of the distinctive features of pre-Communist collective violence in China was the key role played by religious sects and criminal secret societies. Such groups became a major target of the draconian campaign to suppress counterrevolutionaries carried out in the immediate aftermath of the 1949 Communist victory. Indeed, until recently most observers assumed that sects and secret societies had been effectively eradicated from the Chinese landscape. The resurgence of such entities in recent years is perhaps the most surprising feature of contentious politics under the reforms. Disparaged as "feudal remnants" by the authorities, these groups have not been entirely immune to Communist influences.

Although only in the post-Mao period has the revival of folk religion attracted widespread attention, a surprising number of sectarian organizations sprang to life again during the Cultural Revolution decade. Despite (or perhaps because of) the Red Guards' virulent attacks on the "Four Olds" (old customs, habits, culture, and thinking), popular religion seems to have enjoyed something of a surreptitious resurgence during that tumultuous period.[42]

In view of the temporal overlap, it is perhaps not surprising that many of the contemporary movements espouse certain Maoist values. Take the case of the Heavenly Soldiers Fraternal Army (*tianbing dizijun*), which recruited thousands of followers from some 120 villages. Declaring himself a reincarnation of the Jade Emperor, the leader practiced shamanistic rituals of spirit possession and exorcism. His disciples pledged to fight for a new, divine regime free from social classes, authorities, grades and ranks, and the like.[43] The commitment to rid China of all forms of inequality seems an obvious throwback to Cultural Revolution rhetoric. In another intriguing resistance movement, a twenty-nine-year-old peasant leader claimed to be Mao Zedong's son who had come to lead a rural uprising. The would-be Mao penned treatises on the "thirty great relationships" (Mao Zedong had limited himself to ten) and assumed the titles of party chairman, military commission chair, state chairman, political consultative conference chair, and premier. The imposter also sent letters to various government offices praising the radical ideas of the Gang of Four, attacking Deng Xiaoping's market socialism, and calling for armed rebellion, student boycotts, and workers' strikes.[44]

A common feature of today's rebel organizations is the promulgation of a constitution, party program, and party regulations—in obvious imitation of the Communist Party exemplar.[45] Even in what would appear to be the most "traditional" of peasant uprisings, the slogans have a distinctly "modern" ring to them. Take the case of a rebellion which got under way in the mid-1980s along the Yunnan-Guizhou border after its leader claimed (in the manner of Hong Xiuquan, commander of the Taiping Rebellion, the enormous millenarian uprising that rocked China in the mid-nineteenth century) that he had dreamed of an old man with a white beard who lent him a sacred sword. The contemporary insurgents slaughtered a chicken and swore a blood oath in the ancient manner of Chinese rebels, but alongside the age-old slogan of "Steal from the rich to aid the poor," they emblazoned their battle banners with new mottos: "Support the left and oppose the right!" and "Down with birth control!"[46]

The syncretism of these recent movements is surely due in part to the quasi-religious dimensions assumed by the cult of Mao during the Cultural Revolution. The political rituals of that era helped to blur the distinction between older forms of worship and new Communist practices. As Anita Chan and her co-authors describe Cultural Revolution routines in one South China village:

> Before every meal, in imitation of the army (where the Mao rituals were reaching extraordinary proportions), Chen Village families began performing services to Mao. Led by the family head, they intoned in unison a selection of Mao quotations; sang "The East is Red"; and as they sat to eat they recited a Mao grace.[47]

Similarly, in his memoir of the Cultural Revolution, Liang Heng describes how his father—an urban intellectual sent down to the countryside for "reeducation"—conveyed city rituals to his new peasant neighbors. After converting an old ancestor-worship shrine into a place of adulation for Mao Zedong,

> he put up fresh posters of Chairman Mao and [Defense Minister] Lin Biao wearing soldiers' uniforms . . . "Fellow countrymen," he announced to the fascinated crowd, "from now on we are going to be like the people in the city. In the morning we are going to ask for strength, in the evening make reports" . . . Then he turned to face the Great Helmsman and the Revolutionary Marshal and bowed, with utmost gravity, three times to the waist. There was a general titter of nervous laughter. Father looked so serious, and the peasants had never seen anyone bow to anything except the images of their own ancestors. But they were eager learners, for they loved Chairman Mao. At last they had an earnest teacher to show them how to express their love.[48]

The lasting impact of these religious observances can be seen in the remarkable nostalgia for Mao Zedong that has swept the Chinese countryside in the 1990s. In Mao's home province of Hunan, a monastery dedicated to the deification of the Chairman has attracted tens of thousands of pilgrims in recent years. The devotees, who come from as far away as Guangxi, Jiangxi, Guangdong, and Fujian, undertake a three-day fast before the journey to demonstrate their piety. Once at the monastery,

> some pray for the safety and harmony of family members while others ask Mao to cure chronic diseases. [Members of] the latter group are given a glass of "holy water" after their prayers. Those who feel Mao has listened to their prayers thank him for the kindness received.[49]

Of even greater concern to government authorities than the return and reshaping of popular religion is the rapid growth of criminal secret societies. According to official statistics, China was home to 500 criminal gangs in 1990. By 1992, the figure had risen to 1,800 and by 1995 had mushroomed to nearly 11,000. Membership is estimated at close to a million people, with each year seeing about a doubling in size.[50] The gangs engage in drug smuggling, trafficking of people, gambling and prostitution rings, robbery and extortion, and so on. Many observe age-old practices (for example, initiation rituals in which new recruits drink the blood from a slaughtered chicken, use of fictive kinship nomenclature, and so on). Some also have explicitly political agendas. The gangs are active in both urban and rural areas. In Hunan's Yiyang county alone, as many as 250 gangs are currently in operation.[51]

The historian Cai Shaoqing has categorized the contemporary gangs into five types.[52] The first, and most common, are fundamentally economic in orientation. These are concentrated in cities, especially in coastal areas where the economy is more developed, and along transport routes. The second type Cai refers to as "feudal hegemonic." In these organizations, local ruffians—often grass-roots cadres—carry out criminal initiatives to enhance their own local authority. Recently one such group was suppressed in a township of Yucheng county, Henan. Led by the deputy head of the township, the gang was composed mostly of local cadres in the legal and security fields. A third variety are urban youth gangs. Similar in composition and activities to their counterparts around the world, such groups are a rapidly growing phenomenon in China. As the baby-boomers of the Cultural Revolution come of age, delinquency rates have soared. Thus, although China's overall crime rate is still extremely low by international standards, its rate of juvenile delinquency ranks toward the top of all countries reported.[53] A fourth type of secret society is overtly political in its aims. Hunan's Plum Flower Party, Shanghai's Chinese Socialist Radical Party (which allegedly planned terrorist attacks against Communist Party officials), and Guangxi's Black Dragon Gang (which drew up a namelist of over one hundred party cadres targeted for assassination) are examples of organizations explicitly committed to the overthrow of the Chinese Communist Party. Fifth, there are Chinese branches of international crime syndicates that engage in cross-border drug smuggling, counterfeiting, illegal sales of automobiles and antiques, and the like. Some of these groups offer martial arts services as bodyguards or "hit men" against specified victims. Juvenile delinquents in China have been favored targets of recruitment by international criminal organizations.[54]

Because of its proximity to Hong Kong and Macau, Guangdong

province harbors an exceptional number of internationally affili-
ated gangs. A Hong Kong $10 million jetfoil robbery and the mur-
ders of Hong Kong businessmen in Shenzhen are among the more
spectacular crimes committed by these organizations.[55] Violence between rival gangs has also become a cause for concern in the Pearl
River Delta:

> A dramatic shoot-out involving rival triads in Shenzhen has left one
> dead and one seriously injured. More than 30 police fought a
> two-hour gun battle against one triad gang, capturing three of its
> members while another three escaped. . . . Guangdong police have
> requested stepped up cooperation with their counterparts in Hong
> Kong and Macau in the fight against triads, most of which are
> thought to have links to the two territories. . . . The incident took
> place in the middle of a 100-day anti-crime campaign in the special
> economic zone. In the first 50 days of the campaign, police re-
> ported the break-up of 418 criminal organizations and arrested
> 2,870 suspects.[56]

Cai attributes the remarkable escalation in gang activities to several factors attendant upon the reforms: the dramatic increase in
population mobility, the high level of surplus labor and unemployment, the lack of widely shared moral values (with the result that
young people are looking for any means to get rich quickly), and
the intermingling of traditional Chinese practices and outsider
influence.[57] To this list we might append a few additional factors.
Growing income disparities, between city and countryside as well
as between rich and poor in both sectors, provide a source of disaf-
fection and an opportunity for predatory criminal activity.[58] Moreover, in wealthy and impoverished areas alike, criminal elements
have taken advantage of new market opportunities to gain access to
private industrial and commercial resources.[59] These independent
financial bases promise to render government efforts at repression
increasingly difficult.

The Pivotal Role of Nationalism

Contentious politics in the contemporary era have certain marked
similarities to pre-Communist patterns. As in imperial and Republi-

can days, charges of official corruption and economic misconduct have energized popular protests in city and countryside alike. Moreover, in contrast to the Maoist era, these public outbursts were not primed by injunctions from the top leadership. Although a substantial number of high officials have shown sympathy for the public criticisms, they are not acting in concert with a centrally instigated campaign against bureaucratism as was the case during the Three and Five Antis, Hundred Flowers, Four Cleans, and Cultural Revolution. Cries for "moral economic" justice, as well as religious and secret-society trappings, further distinguish the recent unrest from Maoist-sponsored mobilization efforts and reinforce the impression that age-old beliefs and behaviors have again seized control of the Chinese popular imagination.

Yet these protests in today's China are not a pure recycling of old traditions, unsullied by Communist influences. The past half-century has left an identifiable imprint on repertoires of collective action. While the fact that local cadres have actually led many of the recent protests may explain some of the reliance on Maoist rhetoric and symbolism,[60] it is obvious that such modes of expression have substantial popular appeal. Arguments based upon class analysis resonate to those—for example, workers at state enterprises or farmers in the poorer areas of the countryside—who feel left behind in the reform scramble. One could simply dismiss their claims as the obsolete language of dying classes. The fact that the PRC still presumes to be a socialist regime gives such claims considerable force, however. Despite the official disavowal of class labels, the authorities have proved remarkably responsive to arguments framed in class terms.

Perhaps the most significant way in which contentious politics have been altered by the Communist experience is the decline of Han nationalism as a central theme in popular protest. For a century following the humiliation of the Opium Wars, nationalistic concerns were key ingredients in rural and urban struggles alike. The Taipings' indictment of the Manchu "devils," the Boxers' antagonism toward foreigners and foreign religion, the Triads' involvement in the 1911 Revolution, the May Fourth resistance to Japanese incursions, and the May Thirtieth denunciation of both Japanese and British imperialism all demonstrated the tremendous power of nationalism as a rallying cry. The Communist victory was aided in no small measure by the CCP's popular image as a staunchly patriotic force capable of defeating Japanese militarism while (in stark contrast to the GMD) remaining outside the orbit of U.S. imperialism.

Since Chairman Mao's historic proclamation in the fall of 1949 that the Chinese people had finally "stood up," the PRC has done a notable job of controlling the nationalist issue. The flare-up in the Taiwan Straits in 1996, sparked by Taiwan's first direct election of a president, was one in a long series of incidents in which the PRC authorities have moved aggressively to lay claim to the mantle of Chinese nationalism.

Despite some small-scale student demonstrations against growing Japanese influence in the mid-1980s, for the most part the government has not proved vulnerable to popular criticism on the issue of Chinese nationalism.[61] When the issue of nationalism *has* served as a principal motivation for popular protest in recent days, it has been among separatists in Tibet and Xinjiang, rather than among Han Chinese.

Unrest in the autonomous regions has certainly escalated under the reforms and the attendant loosening of central controls; influenced no doubt by global trends, protests in those regions are often accompanied by demands for political independence based upon claims of religion and ethnic identity. In April 1990, for example, an armed rebellion in the Kizilsu Kirgiz Autonomous Prefecture of Xinjiang province issued a "Sacred War Law and Regulations" that read:

> The purpose of the sacred war is to kill the heathens, oppose the heathens, and use our hands and language to rebuff them. We should use weapons and horses to deal with Allah's and your enemy. You should practice shooting, and Muslim women should also fight. . . . All people of the Turkish nationality, unite. Long live the great East Turkistan![62]

Government authorities charged the rebels with forming a "counter-revolutionary organization" known as the Islamic Party of East Turkistan, which plotted to establish a Republic of East Turkistan in which Islam would triumph over Marxism-Leninism.[63] Separatist sympathies were nothing new in Xinjiang,[64] but they have intensified during the reform era. This latest expression was evidently related to recently promulgated regulations banning the unauthorized construction of new mosques and Koranic schools.[65]

At the same time that this revolt was under way in Xinjiang, hundreds of monks in Tibet vacated their monasteries to protest the government's expulsion of dozens of senior monks and nuns from religious centers in and near Lhasa. The removal was seen as an attempt to undermine the traditional Tibetan educational system.[66] Price hikes on kerosene and gasoline—the main fuels in Lhasa— led to large-scale demonstrations against inflation. The economically motivated protest soon turned into a rally in support of Tibetan independence.[67] In the end, thousands of Tibetans rampaged through the city center, stoning Chinese shops that had remained open for business. The influx of Han entrepreneurs into Lhasa has been a serious grievance of the local population for years, with Tibetans accusing the Chinese of having stolen their jobs.[68]

Although ethnic disturbances are alarming to the Chinese authorities, especially in light of the breakup of the former Soviet Union, they do not pose a commensurate threat inasmuch as minority nationalities constitute less than 10 percent of the PRC population. Nevertheless, they do inhabit large, geopolitically significant regions of the country. Moreover, if China should prove unable to retain control over such sizable and symbolically significant areas as Tibet, Xinjiang or Inner Mongolia, the stage would be set for Han Chinese patriots to accuse the regime of a failure to fulfill its national mandate. Under these circumstances, the specter of breakaway movements in the new economic powerhouses of China proper—the Pearl River Delta, the Yangzi Delta, the Northeast—is not beyond the realm of possibility.

In view of the stunning rapidity with which Communist societies have fragmented across eastern Europe, one would be foolhardy to dismiss parallel possibilities in China. To date, the ability of the Beijing authorities to stay on top of the nationalism issue has rendered such a scenario remote. But the explosion of protests in Taiwan and Hong Kong over Japan's long-standing occupation of the disputed Senkaku Islands (Diaoyutai) in the mid-1990s suggests the latent volatility of nationalism as a mobilizational frame. The fact that the PRC authorities felt compelled to clamp down on anti-Japanese student protests in Shanghai and Beijing indicates the potentially subversive nature of this issue. A leader of the 12,000 protesters in Hong Kong put it bluntly: "The People's Liberation Army only attacks its own people. Why the hell don't they fight outsiders?" Or, as a message on a Fudan University computer notice-board queried shortly before the message-board was shut down, "Could it be that criticizing Japan endangers the leadership of our party?"[69]

Crime, corruption, and popular contention will surely increase in scale and frequency as the reforms continue to generate painful uncertainties and inequalities. If past history is a reliable guide to China's future, then whether or not protestors are able to tap into the moral force of nationalism may well decide whether their criticisms prove as destabilizing to the regime as their forebears' initiatives earlier in this century. The linkage of official corruption and malfeasance to the inflammatory charge of selling out the Chinese nation—a deadly combination for both the Qing and the GMD—has until recently been quite muted, despite the obvious excesses of the open-door policy. Whether this continues to be so in the years ahead will likely determine the revolutionary potential of contentious politics in the PRC.

Conclusion

RICHARD BAUM
ALEXEI SHEVCHENKO

15 | The "State of the State"

Like nature, Sinology abhors a vacuum. Given the sheer variety and magnitude of systemic changes that have occurred in the post-Mao era, it is hardly surprising that there should be substantial controversy over how best to characterize China's evolving institutional landscape. With Leninist regimes everywhere collapsing or undergoing radical reconfiguration, a profound "paradigm gap" has arisen. Does the reforming Chinese political economy more closely resemble communism, capitalism, or Confucianism? feudalism, federalism, or neo-fascism? corporatism or civil society?

Bereft of a theoretical compass, with no ready-made, off-the-shelf models available to fill the void left by the demise of the old Leninist order, more and more scholars have entered the paradigm sweepstakes. The result has been a wild profusion of new labels, accompanied by intense competition for shelf space in the morphological marketplace. Recent contenders for taxonomic hegemony include: "nomenclature capitalism,"[1] "bureaucratic capitalism,"[2] "capitalism with Chinese characteristics,"[3] "capital socialism,"[4] "incomplete state socialism,"[5] "local market socialism,"[6] "*danwei* socialism,"[7] "socialist corporatism,"[8] "corporatism Chinese style,"[9] "local state corporatism,"[10] "state-socialist corporatism,"[11] "symbiotic clientelism,"[12] "Confucian Leninism,"[13] "Leninist patrimonialism,"[14] "market-preserving federalism,"[15] "institutional amphibiousness,"[16] and "bureaupreneurialism."[17] In a field not normally known for its fertile heuristic imagination, this profusion of colorful labels and neologisms seems rather remarkable.

To a considerable extent, the current state of taxonomic anarchy stems from three inescapable facts of reform. First, the "de-totalization" of the Leninist state is without historical precedent. Second, China's reforming institutional landscape is complex and polymorphous, rendering attempts broadly to classify emergent forms and functions hazardous at best. And third, the institutional landscape is itself in a state of flux, presenting observers with a continuously moving target.

In some ways the problem is redolent of the parable of the blind men and the elephant: analysts probing different parts of China's reforming political anatomy often produce substantially dissimilar sketches of the body politic. Even in cases where the same (or similar) part of the elephant's anatomy has been touched, there are often significant differences of interpretation. Further compounding this difficulty is the absence of a standardized conceptual vocabulary.

This chapter represents a preliminary effort to describe China's elephant at this stage of the reforms. It seeks to make sense of China's shifting political-economic landscape and to establish a context for assessing the disparate analytical perspectives and empirical findings that appear in the literature generally and in the essays in this volume in particular. After reviewing some of the more prominent academic disputes concerning the impact of reform on key structures of power and authority in the PRC, the chapter explores various patterns of post-reform accommodation between state and society. It then considers aggregate changes in state capacity, concluding with an overall assessment of the "state of the state" in the post-reform era.

Of Principals and Agents

Central-Local Relations

One of the more intractable controversies in the recent literature concerns central-local relations. While virtually everyone agrees that fiscal and administrative decentralization in the 1980s gave provincial and subprovincial governments broad discretionary authority to raise and allocate revenues, major differences remain over just how independent of their higher-level "principals" these erstwhile local "agents" have actually become. At one extreme, it has been argued that the reforms have so skewed the balance of fiscal and administrative power in favor of the provinces that Beijing has lost effective control over much of the country's economic life.[18]

At the other extreme, it has been argued with equal vigor that decentralization has neither diminished Beijing's extractive capacity (expressed as the ratio of central government revenues to GNP) nor undermined China's unitary political system (measured by the degree of central control over key provincial appointments).[19] A third interpretation holds that "central leaders have not so much 'lost' control as they have chosen not to exercise it because provincial officials are a powerful bloc in the process of selecting top Communist Party leaders."[20] Yet a fourth view holds that the entire issue of center versus province has been improperly framed, since (a) it is not a zero-sum game; and (b) "it is quite crude to use . . . a temporary drop in the center's share of resources . . . as *the* indicator of the relative power of center vs. localities."[21]

The theory of rising provincial autonomy and incipient rebelliousness achieved a certain prominence at the end of the 1980s, when a group of provincial governors, led by Guangdong's Ye Xuanping, successfully resisted the central government's repeated attempts to replace the existing system of contractually fixed provincial remittances with a system of uniform direct taxes, a change that would have tilted the fiscal balance sharply in Beijing's favor.[22] It was also in this period that local governments in many areas, facing the prospect of fiscal starvation induced by Beijing's austerity drive of 1988, ignored central exhortations to curtail expansion of local credit, investment, and construction, while at the same time erecting a series of protective trade barriers against products from other areas.[23] As a result of such local defiance there were widespread references in the Chinese media to the rise of "feudal princeling economies" *(zhuhou jingji)* as well as a spate of oblique—and sometimes not so oblique—warnings of a possible economic breakup of the country.[24]

Reports of the center's demise proved premature. Confounding the warnings of alarmists, Beijing not only weathered the fiscal crisis of 1988–1991 but emerged with its political authority largely intact. This was demonstrated rather convincingly in the aftermath of Deng Xiaoping's *nanxun* (southern tour) undertaken early in 1992 in the wake of the collapse of the Soviet Union to drum up support for the fading leader's program of accelerated economic reform and "opening up." Deng's promotional tour triggered a nationwide credit and investment binge, pushing retail prices up by almost 30 percent in less than a year. The central government stepped in to cool things down, and under the firm hand of Vice Premier Zhu Rongji, in 1993–94 Beijing successfully curtailed local bank loans and commercial credit, reduced interfirm debt, and adopted new uniform tax and banking laws that effectively strengthened Beijing's fiscal and financial authority. Although Zhu's determination to play hardball with provincial leaders was leavened somewhat by his agreement to make side payments to those provinces most adversely affected by the partial recentralization of fiscal authority, in the end Beijing prevailed and the provinces fell into line—but not before some of the more stubborn provincial leaders were removed or reshuffled.[25] In similar fashion, despite strong opposition from the southern coastal provinces, the National People's Congress early in 1996 voted to terminate the system of preferential tax and investment benefits enjoyed by China's special economic zones—benefits that had ostensibly widened the income and development gap between coast and interior. Turning the interior's long-smoldering envy and resentment to its own tactical advantage, Beijing succeeded in cobbling together a legislative majority to counter the powerful regional interests of the southern coast.[26]

In addition to their impact on the central-local balance of power, the reforms of the 1980s arguably improved the central government's ability to collect, process, and coordinate policy-relevant information. One of the principal structural advantages enjoyed by market societies over command economies are the former's more widely distributed (and more highly autonomous) mechanisms for monitoring local market signals and gathering and evaluating policy feedback. Because of built-in informational rigidities in command economies, and because lower-level officials in Leninist systems have a strong incentive to lie to their superiors, hiding assets and under-estimating capacity, the quality of information available to leaders in such systems is generally poor.[27] Another, related weakness of China's prereform command economy stemmed from the vertical insularity of its bureaucratic structures. With each central ministry gathering and processing its own proprietary information, overall coordination of policy planning and implementation was difficult at best. As Yasheng Huang has noted, the independent, parallel proc-essing of information within the Chinese system often meant that "there was no central attempt to coördinate the activities of the various bureaucracies."[28]

The economic and administrative reforms of the 1980s served to decentralize, de-monopolize, and de-insulate the collection, process-ing, and dissemination of information in China. Central bureaucra-cies lost proprietary control over information resources and man-agement; quasi-autonomous professional societies began churning out a wide variety of technical publications; and a plethora of new policy research centers—China's first "think tanks"—began provid-ing the central government with independent policy input and analysis.[29] At the same time, bureaucratic incentives designed to promote interagency policy consultation and coordination within the government were significantly enhanced, thereby at least par-tially overcoming traditional barriers to the flow of ideas, informa-tion, and expertise. As Nina Halpern has pointed out, the net result was more and better information and—at least arguably—a higher capacity for policy coordination at the center.[30]

The above considerations surely do not "prove" the center's con-tinued potency. Nevertheless, they suggest that reform has not re-duced the central government's political role to that of a mere spectator. As Dorothy Solinger has persuasively argued, it is incor-rect to understand decentralization as a set of uniform policies that have benefited equally—and at Beijing's expense—all China's re-gions, provinces, and localities. On the contrary, decentralization has conferred different benefits and burdens upon different territo-rial units, including the center, at different points in time. And within the new decentralized administrative order, Beijing arguably remains the foremost redistributor, regulator, and policy coordinator, thereby continuing to play a decisive role in the determination of "who gets what, when, and how."[31] The fact that central-provincial (and provincial-local) relations have increasingly been marked by bilateral bargaining and compromise rather than unilateral command and coercion reflects the changing structure of China's post-reform political economy. It does not, however, imply either irreversible imperial impotence or the imminent implosion of political power at the center.

Of Power and Property Rights

An examination of the relationship between administrative authority and property rights helps to explain how the reform process has altered the balance between center and locality. The downward transfer of fiscal responsibility and property rights has enhanced the bargaining power of local governments. Under reforms enacted in the 1980s local governments were required to assume substantially greater responsibility for meeting their own budgetary (and extrabudgetary) needs. To help meet those needs, governments at each level were granted residual property rights over state-owned enterprises within their jurisdiction. With the demise of mandatory central planning and top-down budgeting, enterprise residuals became a principal source of funds for governments at each level.[32]

While local governments had a clear incentive to maximize the inflow of revenues from the enterprises under their jurisdiction, they had an equally strong incentive to minimize the outflow of revenues upward to the next higher level. Since both revenue flows—from enterprises to local governments and from local governments to higher levels—were subject, under the new economic system, to bilateral "fixing" through negotiated contracts, the net result was an ongoing multilevel game characterized by "polymorphous bargaining."[33]

In order to curb the tendency toward "particularistic contracting" that was inherent in this multilevel bargaining game,[34] the central government early in 1994 enacted a new uniform tax law fixing the enterprise profit tax at 33 percent and imposing a flat 17 percent value-added tax (VAT) on manufactured goods. Revenues from the profit tax were to be apportioned between the center and localities on a 60:40 basis (a reversal of the 40:60 ratio of the early 1990s); proceeds from the VAT were to be distributed between center and localities at a fixed ratio of 3:1.[35] While it is too soon confidently to assess the full impact of the new tax system, initial reports suggest that the center has experienced considerable difficulty in collecting its share of the revenue pie.

The Growth of the Local State

As one moves farther down the hierarchy of local government, formal distinctions between property rights and administrative rights tend to become blurred. At the rural township and village levels, where state-owned enterprises are few, where the vast majority of nonagricultural firms are small, and where the grip of the central state is relatively weak, the distinction becomes almost meaningless—a situation that has led one observer to speak of "local governments *as* industrial firms."[36] In some cases entire villages have been legally reorganized into profit-making commercial corporations.[37] To date such cases have been sparsely documented, but they suggest a growing trend toward the fusion of political and economic power at the basic levels.

In addition to blurring the lines between political and economic authority, the downward transfer of property rights and fiscal responsibility has prompted local governments everywhere to expand their organizations and staff. Indeed, the proliferation of bureaucratic agencies is one of the most remarkable unintended consequences of China's economic reforms.[38] Bureaucratic expansion has taken place both horizontally (under local territorial jurisdictions, or *kuai*) and vertically (under higher-level functional jurisdictions, or *tiao*). Horizontally, governments at each level, faced with the need to raise extra-budgetary funds to finance local activities and projects, have added scores of administrative cadres—and in some cases whole new departments—to enhance their revenue-collecting potential.[39]

To make up for revenues lost as a result of fiscal decentralization and the decollectivization of agriculture, local rural governments have been forced to engage in economic diversification and creative financing. To fund new activities (and to continue to pay for old ones) a variety of fees, levies, and surcharges have been imposed on local residents. Standard exactions at the village level have included the *tiliu* (village reserve fund) and the *tongchou* ("consolidation fund"). In addition to such regular levies, numerous irregular "contributions" have been exacted. One of the more innovative forms of ad hoc contribution is the *dabiao,* or "reaching standards levy." In some townships and villages, residents have been required to subsidize more than forty different *dabiao* services—including militia training, school construction, old-age home construction, pest control, newspaper subscription, and insurance purchase.[40] Sometimes the exactions become so onerous that farmers rebel. In Renshou county, Sichuan, local government demands for excessive highway repair contributions resulted in riots involving more than 10,000 people.[41]

The horizontal expansion of local fee-collecting agencies has been paralleled by a vertical expansion of functional offices and staffs at the provincial and subprovincial levels. Vertical (branch) expansion generally results from the creation of new state regulatory agencies or the expansion of existing ones. At the *xiang* level, for example, branch departments of at least fifteen regulatory agencies are currently staffed by county-level cadres.[42] Owing largely to staff increases in these functional departments, the total number of budgeted *guojia ganbu* (state cadres) at the county level and above has increased dramatically.[43]

"Tiao" vs. "Kuai"

While the parallel processes of horizontal and vertical staff expansion have jointly contributed to the mushrooming costs of local state administration, each has its own distinctive organizational logic. Vertical branch agencies, or *bumen* (departments), enjoy political and budgetary support from higher levels, while horizontal staffs, as agents of the local *zhengfu* (government), generally rely on local resources. While it is not always clear at any given time just who has the upper hand in this modified recapitulation of the classic *tiaotiao* versus *kuaikuai* dualism of the 1950s and 1960s, it is reasonably clear that one goal of the reformers—to eradicate the conflicting particularisms of *tiao* and *kuai*—has not been achieved.[44]

At the basic levels of the rural township and village, the balance of power between *zhengfu* and *bumen* has generally been weighted in the latter's favor. Each department of the county government maintains a corresponding branch office at the township level. These offices are staffed by agents of the county government, a fact that places the township in a relationship of administrative dependency vis-à-vis the county. According to David Zweig, such dependency "demonstrates the continuing role of bureaucratic authority as a determinant of resource allocations," thus supporting the conclusion that, for subcounty governments, "vertical authority remains more powerful than horizontal ties."[45] This view is evidently shared by many village and township officials, who tend to be openly envious of the superior resources commanded by county agencies. As one *xiang* cadre put it, "*bumen* eat meat; *zhengfu* gnaw on the bones."[46]

Above the township level, however, the balance of power is frequently reversed. At the county level, local governments are empowered to formulate their own development plans and blueprints, set specific economic performance targets, and macro-manage local enterprises, for example, by providing investment incentives and other forms of preferential treatment (including the leveraging of bank loans) to assist local "key" projects. County governments also enjoy privileged access to a wide variety of fiscal and administrative assets, including a 30 percent residual share of local industrial taxes.[47]

Similar advantages accrue to municipal-level governments. In his study of post-reform urban administration, David Wank notes that the resources controlled by urban governments include "previously unpriced assets such as . . . publicly owned real estate . . ., access to financial capital, permission to trade in restricted products, . . . and advantages in the handling of routine administrative procedures that confer competitive advantage."[48] In addition, both county and municipal governments have created a number of cross-sectoral territorial "committees" and "commissions" to regulate and coordinate activities—such as local commerce, external trade, and pollution control—that previously fell under the jurisdiction of specialized branch agencies of the central or provincial government. Such cross-sectoral committees further extend and amplify the reach of the local territorial state.[49]

The Role of the Party

As might be expected, where village and township governments have become actively involved in promoting entrepreneurial activities, the political and ideological work of local party branches has generally been downgraded vis-à-vis their economic role. For example, in the village of Qiaotou, Zhejiang, in the highly commercialized suburbs of Wenzhou municipality, the party secretary reported that his "most important work is to make the economy grow."[50] In Daqiuzhuang village, near Tianjin, Nan Lin observes that "party organization and functions are subsumed under the economic system. . . . [T]he existence of the party apparatus is absolutely nonessential."[51]

Albeit anecdotally, these examples suggest that marketization and fiscal decentralization have made the creation and appropriation of wealth the principal measures of effective local state agency. A cadre's value is increasingly measured by his or her ability to generate—and successfully tap into—new revenue streams. In the process, the organizational identity and functions of local party cadres have been profoundly altered. In general, it appears that where party secretaries have successfully adapted to new commercial and entrepreneurial roles, local party branches have been transformed into agencies of dynamic economic growth. Where party secretaries have been inept or slow to adapt, or where entrepreneurial initiative has been seized by others, party organs have tended to atrophy.[52] In either case, local cadres no longer bother to carefully mask their *enrichissez-vouz* mentality. As one village party secretary in Heilongjiang put it when queried about his motives for assuming a local leadership role: "Society has changed now. Who cares about the party and the state? Even top leaders in Beijing are only interested in getting rich. . . . Why am I doing this job? Simple—for money. I was not interested in the title of party secretary, but I do like the salary of 3,000 yuan per year."[53]

Under such circumstances it is hardly surprising that the Chinese Communist Party should be facing a profound identity crisis as a result of the reform process. In the countryside there have been widespread reports of organizational demoralization and decay, lack of new recruits, and even the dissolution of village party branches.[54] By 1994 Beijing officials were reporting that party organizations had effectively ceased functioning in almost half of China's villages.[55] In some cases, the decline of party life was accompanied by a revival of prerevolutionary kinship associations and long-dormant clan feuds;[56] in other cases, the erosion of party morale occurred in conjunction with a resurgence of "feudal superstitions" and religious rites. Whatever the cause, the party's traditional dominance over local socioeconomic organization and activity has been significantly attenuated.[57]

Even in those villages where party cadres have played a proactive leadership role in the post-reform economy, they are now subject to more stringent performance monitoring and feedback from the local populace. Kevin O'Brien and Lianjiang Li note that because state extractions have become more visible and more contentious under the reforms, village cadres have often been forced to implement unpopular policies with fewer (and often blunter) instruments available to persuade reluctant inhabitants. With the extraction process increasingly transparent, with market information more readily available, and with farmers better able to calculate and express their own interests, the authority of village leaders has been rendered more conditional—and more problematic. O'Brien and Li thus conclude that "Even without meaningful democratization, structural changes . . . appear to be enabling villagers to say 'no' more often and with greater effect."[58] In a similar vein, Bernstein and Solinger note that in the aftermath of a series of violent rural disturbances in 1992–93, the central government began to encourage farmers to assert their rights and voice their grievances against despotic or corrupt local officials.[59] And Yunxiang Yan observes that "after the reforms, . . . village cadres have gradually come to depend more on support from below than recognition from above."[60]

Of Entrepreneurs, Patrons, Predators, and Developers

Although local autonomy has visibly increased at both the basic (township and village) and the intermediate (county and municipal) levels, decentralization has failed to produce a uniform pattern of local governmental participation in the economy.[61] Jean Oi notes that "The Chinese model . . . holds a number of useful general lessons about reform. . . . The first is that one cannot make broad assertions about government intervention and markets."[62] In some cases, local state agents have "taken the plunge" *(xiahai)* and become directly involved in profit-making activities, for example, by setting up or spinning off their own enterprises or becoming joint venture partners.[63] In other cases, state agents (or agencies) have formed clientelist ties with local entrepreneurs, using bureaucratic connections to negotiate favorable start-up loans, secure business licenses, procure inputs, appoint enterprise managers, and otherwise preferentially assist their local clients.[64] In still other cases, local governments have played a more indirect economic role, helping to plan, finance, and coordinate local projects, investing in local infrastructure, and promoting cooperative economic relations with external agencies. Through such intervention, local governments develop a friendly economic environment while remaining bureaucratically neutral and avoiding the formation of particularistic ties to "preferred" enterprises and clients.[65] In a corporatist variant of this pattern, local government agencies play a major role in licensing and regulating (that is, "incorporating") secondary associations in the private sector, including commercial, industrial, and occupational groups.[66]

Officials in some areas have assumed neither direct entrepreneurial and clientelist roles nor indirect developmental ones, engaging instead in simple predation. Unlike the other three modes of local state involvement in the economy, predation—defined as the use of the state apparatus to extract and distribute unproductive rents—is geared neither to the reproduction of wealth nor to the expansion of local economic activity, but to the maximum appropriation of existing, extractable surplus. The literature of the late 1980s and early 1990s is rich with examples of naked predation by local state agents—collectively dubbed "patrimonial bureau-preneurs" by Xiaobo Lu.[67] In the countryside, such predation typi-cally takes the form of opportunistic township and village officials exacting exorbitant (and often illegal) user fees, levies, and fines from an increasingly overburdened peasantry.[68] Much of this preda-tory behavior has been the result of individual cadres exploiting their official positions to enrich themselves; but some of the appro-priation has been institutional in nature, involving excessive exac-tions by local officials on behalf of their cash-starved state agencies.[69] In urban areas, the municipal bureaucrats' imposition of taxes and fees and the extortion of funds, factory goods, food products, and other "gifts" from local entrepreneurs had became so commonplace by the early 1990s that, in the view of one observer, "the currently prevalent form of revenue seeking . . . threatens to turn local gov-ernment into successive layers of leeches battening on the blood of caged enterprises."[70] While the metaphor may be a bit lurid, the problem is real enough.

These four modes of local state economic involvement—en-trepreneurial, clientelist, developmental, and predatory—can be represented schematically in matrix form, using two key variables. The first variable (the horizontal axis in Figure 15.1) indicates whether the state agency is strongly oriented toward the goal of increasing economic output and productivity. The second variable (the vertical axis in Figure 15.1) indicates whether state agencies (or

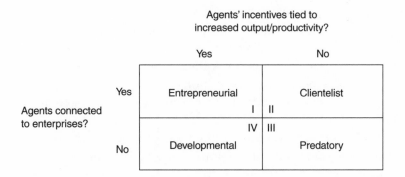

Figure 15.1 Typology of state agency involvement in local economic activity

agents) have a vested interest in the financial success of particular enterprises and clients.[71]

Each of these four principal modes of local state economic involvement arose as a calculated response to the advent of marketization and the downward transfer of fiscal and administrative authority. Marketization and decentralization meant that local governments were increasingly left to their own devices. Saddled with new fiscal and administrative responsibilities and armed with new residual property rights, local officials scrounged for resources and scavenged for revenues as best they could. The resulting pattern of local state behavior varied widely from place to place. Indeed, the fiscal creativity and resourcefulness of local governments in this regard has been one of the more notable by-products of the reform era.

Of Corporatism and Civil Society

The post-Tiananmen literature on China's reforms has been more or less evenly divided between narratives of local governmental dynamism and development, on the one hand, and tales of local bureaucratic corruption and decay, on the other.[72] Only rarely has the attempt been made to reconcile or conjoin these divergent narratives.[73] It is to this task that we now turn.

As state agencies at every level have struggled to adjust to the exigencies of marketization and decentralization, new forms of state-societal interaction have emerged. As noted earlier, the very novelty of these emergent structures, and the striking variation in their local characteristics, have resulted in a profusion of colorful new classificatory schemes and labels. What many (if not most) of these scholarly taxonomies have in common is their concern with describing and analyzing new borderline institutions that are at once both public and private in nature, serving to bridge the gap between state and society.

Dorothy Solinger was among the first to recognize the new hybrid pattern of state-society interactions. In 1990 she noted that far from simply retreating gracefully in the face of a relentlessly advancing civil society, the state proactively encircled, enmeshed, and incorporated the various new economic and social forces unleashed by reform. In the effort to shape and control these new social forces, however, the state has itself been partially coopted and reshaped:

> [Economic reform in China has not] hewed out any sharp and novel borderline between the "state" and a distinctive sphere of "society" among its subjects. . . . No "repluralization" can be said to have issued from some genuine formation of a "private" realm truly separate from the still enveloping "public" one for those who make their lives in the marketplace. Instead, the essential economic monolith of the old party-state now shapes official and merchant alike; both have become dependent, mutually interpenetrated semi-classes, even as both share a new kind of dependence on the state.[74]

As Solinger suggests, the idea of state-dependent interpenetration, which lies at the heart of most corporatist models, tends to conflict with the idea of an autonomous, self-organizing civil society.[75] The civil society concept enjoyed widespread intellectual currency in comparative communist studies in the 1980s, when it was employed to analyze the emergence (or revival) of opposition groups within the Soviet bloc.[76] Imported into Chinese studies at the end of the decade, the civil society concept was utilized to assess the prospects for pluralistic group formation and intellectual/professional autonomy in the reform era. In the aftermath of the 1989 Tiananmen debacle, however, the weakness of China's emergent *pouvoirs intermédiaires* and the historical absence of a meaningful "public sphere" were frequently cited as key factors contributing to the inability of pro-democratic forces to regroup and reassert themselves after June 4.[77]

Insofar as the idea of civil society connotes a protected public space where the state neither penetrates nor dominates private social and economic exchanges, it tends to come into conflict with the type of state-dependent interpenetration described by Solinger. This helps to explain the rising popularity of corporatist models in the gloomy aftermath of June 4. Indeed, in much of the post-Tiananmen literature, corporatism and civil society are juxtaposed in yin/yang fashion, as two obverse and inherently contradictory sides of the reformist coin in China.[78]

The principal attraction of corporatist models is their ability simultaneously to acknowledge the pluralizing socioeconomic changes induced by market reforms and the continued dominance of the Leninist party-state. Whereas civil society models frequently assume the existence of relatively autonomous intermediate associations and social forces that restrict the scope of state penetration, corporatism posits the existence of clear limits imposed by the state upon society, with the state setting both the terms of secondary group existence and the permissible limits of member activity.[79]

Proponents of the corporatist paradigm generally agree that the relaxation of centralized state economic and administrative controls in the reform era has provided a certain amount of social space for the segmentation—and legitimation—of societal interests. While the state continues to define the terms and conditions of its engagement with society, state control is exercised indirectly—through cooptation, coordination, and "interest licensing"—rather than directly, through vertical command. What has emerged, therefore, is a hybrid form of state-societal interdependence that is less firmly state-driven and state-dominated than the "organized dependency" model of the Maoist era, but more highly regulated and regimented than the civil society model.[80]

While proponents of the corporatist paradigm tend to agree on these general points, they differ among themselves on a number of issues, including the nature of local state involvement in the economy; the degree of operational autonomy enjoyed by local intermediate associations; and the future potential for an embryonic civil society to grow within the womb of the corporate state. Generally speaking, corporatists who view local state intervention in the economy as "entrepreneurial" in nature (see Figure 15.1, quadrant I) tend to see the grip of the central state on its local agents being profoundly altered—and substantially attenuated—by the latter's direct involvement in profit-making activity. Using the term "capital socialism" to describe the entrepreneurial activities of local governments, Frank Pieke observes that under this particular mode of corporatism,

[t]he market does not replace the bureaucracy. Instead, through personal transactions, the bureaucracy enters the market. . . . Local communist cadres gradually become part of a new . . . capital socialist elite whose power derives equally from their [personal] networks, political position, and control over the means of production . . . [For them], continued reform means freedom and autonomy to operate on the market. The more powerful and entrenched in local society capital socialist actors become, the less they will need the party and its national government.[81]

Somewhat perversely, the rise of such entrepreneurial corporatism augurs neither the continued potency of the central party-state nor the emergence of a pluralistic civil society, but rather the proliferation of quasi-autonomous (and potentially corrupt) local economic empires.[82] Indeed, this would seem to be the lesson of the "United Corporation" of Daqiuzhuang village, Tianjin—a prototype of freewheeling entrepreneurial corporatism whose rise to national prominence in the 1980s was accompanied by the virtual atrophy of its Communist Party organs and by reports of flagrant corruption and racketeering by its village chief.[83]

Where local state involvement in the economy is clientelist rather than entrepreneurial in nature (see Figure 15.1, quadrant II), corporatism takes the form of indirect manipulation of entrepreneurs by officials—and vice versa. In this variant, which David Wank calls "symbiotic clientelism," entrepreneurs depend on local governments for licenses, tax benefits, access to resources, protection from predators, and so forth; officials get kickbacks, favors, jobs for relatives, and access to profits, inter alia. Such particularistic exchanges are the essence of the clientelist mode of corporatism.[84] As one entrepreneur put it: "Everything depends on personal ties (*guanxi*). If you have good ties with officialdom, everything is easy to deal with. If you do something wrong, your friends in the relevant bureau will see that the matter is forgotten. But if your ties are bad, then officialdom will make trouble for you even if you've done nothing wrong."[85] In this model of corporatism, the informal ties that bind individual bureaucratic patrons to particular entrepreneurial clients tend to operate at the expense of the more formal regulatory and supervisory functions of local government. Consequently, symbiotic clientelism undermines the institutional authority of the state—but without necessarily presaging the rise of an autonomous civil society.

There is another, less particularistic mode of local corporate clientelism that does not intrinsically weaken the state. The advent of urban reform in 1984 brought with it the rapid proliferation of new intermediate associations, including occupational groups, commercial alliances, and professional societies. To receive official recognition and protection, urban groups such as the Individual Laborers' Association, the China Enterprise Management Association, and the Chamber of Commerce, to name just a few, first had to seek approval from the vertical branch agencies *(tiao)* that regulated their particular spheres of activity; they then had to apply for formal affiliation with the relevant department of the local government *(kuai)*. While such bureaucratic cooptation is open to possible corruption, recent field research has shown that the process of "interest licensing" tends to reinforce the regulatory authority of the local state while at the same time opening up a certain "social space" within which the rights and interests of group members can be advanced.[86]

A distinctive "developmental" variant of bureaucratic incorporation (see Figure 15.1, quadrant IV) has also been identified. In Jean Oi's model of "local state corporatism," rural governments *(kuai)* at the county and township levels play major roles in coordinating and directing the operations of economic enterprises within their jurisdictions.[87] Among other activities, they guarantee loans, establish credit ratings, allocate resources and raw materials, grant tax relief, create channels to outside suppliers and end-users, hire and fire managers, and engage in lobbying with higher authorities—much in the manner of corporate boards of directors. Though they have a claim to enterprise residuals (and hence an interest in profit maximization and productivity), they neither own the enterprises nor participate directly in running them. Rather, they create a regulatory environment that facilitates local economic growth. In this respect, rural governments are ostensibly engaged in a form of public-private cooperation that "brings China closer to the successful developmental state model of the East Asian NICs [newly industrializing countries]."[88] One significant difference, however, lies in the fact that, whereas in the East Asian NIC model the central state plays the principal coordinating and regulatory roles, in China local governments do so.

While marketization and decentralization have clearly strengthened the hand of local state agencies and pushed (or pulled) them into a variety of creative new partnerships with entrepreneurs and other emerging societal forces, the reform-induced empowerment of local state agents appears to have shortened the span—and narrowed the scope—of central state hegemony. Vivienne Shue thus argues that the "thickening" of local statehood has been accompanied by a partial "thinning" of central statehood.[89] In other respects, noted earlier, however, the capacity of the central state appears substantially undiminished—and in some cases actually enhanced—as a consequence of economic reform. Examples include Beijing's control over key provincial personnel assignments; a stable ratio of central revenues to GNP; and the central government's improved capacity to gather information, respond to market signals (and other environmental cues), and coordinate policymaking and implementation.

Clearly, both the shape and the role of the state have changed in post-reform China, as has the nature of its relationship(s) to society. But what of overall state efficacy and capacity? To invoke Charles Lindblom's vivid metaphor, post-reform Chinese leaders have deliberately exchanged some of the unified command power of a strong (but clumsy and insensitive) thumb for the heightened responsiveness of sensitive (but relatively fragile and delicate) fingers.[90] The exchange has not been complete, however; China has not simply transformed itself, willy-nilly, from a command-based to a market-based society and polity. Old structures persist; new ones emerge slowly, between the cracks. Accommodation and adaptation occur continuously, leading to fresh organizational and institutional syntheses. The transformation of the state, and of its relations with society, has been anything but simple and straightforward.

Of State Capacity

In a situation of partially dispersed decisionmaking, partially diluted central authority, partially corporatized local government, and partially marketized exchange relations, how are we to assess the overall potency of the partially transformed Chinese state? Following Gabriel Almond and G. Bingham Powell, we begin by identifying five dimensions of state capacity: extractive, regulative, distributive, symbolic, and responsive.[91] Modifying the Almond-Powell schema to reflect the shifting contours and configurations of the post-reform Chinese state, we distinguish between central and local state capabilities, focusing on changes in the five dimensions of state capacity at each level. The results are presented in Table 15.1.

Although the heuristics of state capacity are undoubtedly easier to assay than its concrete empirical measurement, the picture that emerges from Table 15.1 is nonetheless instructive. Perhaps the most significant conclusion to be drawn is that while overall state capacity may have changed only marginally, with gains in some areas offset by losses in others, the nature, shape, and distribution of state power have changed appreciably. For example, while governments at both the central and the local levels are clearly far less intrusive than before, micro-managing fewer areas of socioeconomic and cultural life, they have arguably become more adept at macro-management—in effect, governing less but governing more effectively. Moreover, significant increases in the state's extractive capability at the subprovincial level suggest that the resources needed to accomplish successful macro-management are accessible to government, albeit on a more decentralized basis. Nevertheless, a clear decline in the state's symbolic/normative capacity under the reforms, clearly visible during the 1989 Tiananmen disturbances, suggests that an incipient "crisis of faith" could prove troublesome to the regime in the event of increased rural unrest or a sharp rise in urban unemployment. Such a danger could be exacerbated by the cumulative, adverse distributional effects of rising income disparities between coast and interior, urban and rural areas, "bureaupreneurs" and ordinary citizens.

The State of the State

"Generally speaking, the most perilous moment for a bad government is when it seeks to mend its ways."[92] Written with reference to the regime of Louis XVI in prerevolutionary France, de Toc-

Table 15.1 Changes in local and central state capacity under reforms

	Local state	Central state
Extractive capacity	*Gains:* sharp increase in fiscal resources and revenues; improved tax monitoring and collection capacity. *Losses:* significant rise in corruption and fiscal predation.	*Gains:* small net increase in central revenues; increasing standardization and routinization of fiscal mechanisms. *Losses:* significant gap between taxes assessed and taxes actually collected.
Regulative capacity	*Gains:* interest licensing supplants local state micro-management; corporatist cooptation replaces organized dependency. *Losses:* scope of state-regulated behavior narrowed.	*Gains:* macroeconomic regulation supplants microeconomic management. *Losses:* bilateral central-local bargaining replaces hierarchical command; sphere of state planning restricted.
Distributive capacity	*Gains:* increased local responsibility for social services, infrastructure. *Losses:* growing gap between rich and poor; redistribution of wealth favors cadres and entrepreneurs.	*Gains:* preferential tax and investment policies stimulate rapid coastal development. *Losses:* reduced central responsibility for social services and infrastructure; rising regional differentials in economic growth and income.
Symbolic capacity	*Gains:* negligible. *Losses:* CCP ideology increasingly irrelevant in everyday life; "feudal superstition" and family loyalties rise; "get rich quick" mentality pervades.	*Gains:* economic growth shores up sagging regime prestige. *Losses:* corruption reduces CCP legitimacy; "four cardinal principles" widely ignored; alternative values, norms, and cultural symbols readily available to citizens.
Responsive capacity	*Gains:* entrepreneurs, merchants form secondary associations; rural grievance procedures institutionalized; village assemblies articulate peasant interests. *Losses:* corporatist cronyism and clientelism rise sharply.	*Gains:* consultative role of NPC strengthened; high-profile anticorruption drive launched. *Losses:* prosecution of high-level malfeasance episodic, noninstitutionalized; no regime tolerance of autonomous interest groups or NGOs.

queville's words resonate strongly today, in the age of "waning communist states." To rescue their endangered regimes, Leninist elites in the 1980s introduced a variety of within-system reforms. Yet few survived. In this respect, the Chinese government's narrow escape from the debacle of June 4, 1989, only serves to underscore the ostensible anomaly of an individual organism surviving in an era of mass species extinction.

In assessing the effects of economic reform upon state power and efficacy in China, the traditional, dichotomous zero-sum formulations—state versus society, central versus local, plan versus market—have not proved very helpful. It is more useful, we believe, to focus on the changing modes and patterns of interaction between state and society, cadres and entrepreneurs, higher and lower levels, *tiao* and *kuai*. It is the *reconfiguration* of state power, rather than its aggregate increase or decrease, that is crucial.

As noted earlier, reform policies have not produced uniform patterns of interaction between state agencies and emerging (or renascent) socioeconomic forces. We found, for example, that local governments have responded in four distinct ways to reform-induced alterations in fiscal and administrative incentive structures (see Figure 15.1). The existence of significant variation in patterns of local governmental response to central policies, in turn, strongly suggests the relevance of path-dependent modes and models of adaptation and accommodation.[93]

Local states and societies have "interpenetrated" one another in different ways in the course of reform. In the process of mutual accommodation and adaptation, state agents and societal forces have actively (if unwittingly) transformed both themselves and each other. Such mutually transformative accommodation lies at the very heart of China's post-reform political experience. Physicists refer to such systemic transformations as "renormalized states"—a most suitable appellation.

In light of the process of state-society interpenetration, it is helpful to reassess the utility of traditional "totalitarian" descriptions of state power in pre-reform China. Clearly, the Chinese state was never wholly insulated from the demands of society, or of its own cadres; nor were lower levels of the party-state always fully or faithfully responsive to upper levels. Kenneth Jowitt's model of Soviet "neo-traditionalism" seems particularly relevant insofar as it sharply illuminates some of the key organizational and behavioral precursors of the corporatist phenomena so widely observed in post-reform China.[94]

In Jowitt's view, the erosion of the prereform Leninist state's organizational integrity can be traced to a growing disconnect between the organizational imperatives of the central *apparat* and the particularistic interests and behavioral orientations of the *apparat*'s locally deployed agents. Absent the use (or threat) of terror to enforce cadre compliance, and absent an overriding transformative societal agenda, local agents of the post-Stalinist state were free (as long as they fulfilled their quantitative output targets) to become patrons who protected their local clients in exchange for payment of goods, services, and loyalty. In this manner, what had once been taken as a sign of totalitarian potency—that is, the state's capacity for ubiquitous intervention in the affairs of society—gradually showed the effects of significant particularistic distortion, displacement, and decay. In such a situation, as Vivienne Shue has noted, local networks of personal relations and reciprocal obligations became substitute vehicles for the "normal" institutions of everyday associational life; at the same time, departmentalism and deception became key defensive strategies adopted by local state agents to lessen their dependence on the center.[95]

For Jowitt, the neo-traditional pattern of Soviet rule was ultimate proof of the degeneration of the Leninist polity. For students of China, however, the lesson has been less clear-cut and unambiguous. On the one hand, China scholars have accepted that the growth of clientelist ties reflects a loss of what Michael Mann has termed "infrastructural power" (defined as "the capacity of the state actually to penetrate civil society, and to implement logistically political decisions throughout the realm");[96] on the other hand, however, neo-traditionalism can also be seen as a "basic means of holding organization together."[97]

Applying Jowitt's insight to the Chinese *danwei*, Walder demonstrated how, in the absence of widespread terror and mass ideological enthusiasm, the concentration of distributional decisions in the hands of local party-state agents permitted the Leninist state to achieve its goal of penetrating society via a system of organized dependency (or "principled particularism") involving the exchange of material benefits for individual compliance:

> [I]n an unintended way this partial "corruption" of the system promotes social stability by creating personal loyalties and obligations among a minority of workers that run parallel to formal leadership ties. . . . [H]idden by a façade of conformity . . . this complex web of personal loyalty, mutual support, and material interest creates a stable pattern of tacit acceptance and active coöperation for the regime that no amount of political terror, coercion, or indoctrination can even begin to provide.[98]

With the exception of diehard devotees of the totalitarian and civil society models, an emerging consensus has begun to form around the idea that post-Mao reforms have blurred and softened, rather than clarified and sharpened, the boundaries and distinctions between state and society. Theoretically, the drive for greater economic efficiency (which was the principal motive for within-system reform in virtually all Leninist regimes) operates to undermine state hegemony. This is so because departures from central planning, pricing, and administration create something which mono-organizational systems have great difficulty coping with—*alternatives*. The emergence of a legalized nonstate sector breaks the foundation of organized dependency by creating alternative sources of income, market information, and material satisfaction for the new stratum of merchants and entrepreneurs as well as for local state officials, thereby rendering them less dependent on higher-level authorities.[99]

Yet, as the Chinese case demonstrates, the commercialization of everyday life does not necessarily entail a wholesale departure from prereform patterns of neo-traditionalism. Indeed, David Wank has argued that the institutional logic of prereform patron-client ties has actually been reinforced, rather than counteracted, by the growing commercialization of exchange relations. In his view, the organized dependency of the prereform socialist *danwei*, characterized by the particularistic exchange of nonmonetized benefits (such as loyalty, conformity, or personal services) for bureaucratic protection and favoritism, has been largely supplanted by the symbiotic clientelism of the neo-corporatist marketplace, in which the benefits accruing to each side in the exchange have become increasingly commercialized and monetized.[100]

Proponents of corporatist models generally acknowledge that one important effect of interest licensing by agents of the local state has been to preempt autonomous interest articulation by new *pouvoirs intermédiaires*. But they disagree on the implications of this fact. The more optimistic corporatists tend to view the existence of small, scattered patches of public space reserved for the pursuit of private interests as an important discontinuity with the Leninist past and a potential opening wedge in the "destatization" of the polity.[101] Corporatist skeptics and pessimists, on the other hand, see the emerging private and collective sectors not as emergent enclaves of civil entrepreneurship but as captives (or adjuncts) of the Leninist political economy, complementing—but not competing with—the administratively managed economy.[102] Some pessimists further argue that the putative appearance of tiny islands of socioeconomic autonomy within the emerging post-reform political configuration reflects not an authentic empowerment of society but the heightened fusion of state and society, marked by ever tighter, ever more interpenetrative alliances between officials and entrepreneurs.[103]

The pessimistic corporatist interpretation of the reinvented Chinese state is based on a belief that the country's Leninist heritage remains an insurmountable obstacle to meaningful sociopolitical transformation. In this view Leninism is the regime's "original sin," inevitably distorting and corrupting each nascent sprout of civil society. By definition, societal forces cannot be empowered through collaboration with a Leninist regime. The more likely outcome of such unholy collusion is a reversion to primitive predatory patrimonialism, a new variation on the old Chinese Communist tale of the "rent collection courtyard"—and the very antithesis of civil society.[104]

Pessimists tend to discount the possibility that it is the very interpenetration of entrepreneurs and local officials—the fluid, self-organizing, co-dependent dualism of the emerging corporatist state—that has provided the modicum of social stability needed to keep China moving (more or less) forward on the developmental path while preventing the country from slipping back into purer, more regressive forms of patrimonial predation. That is, the absence of independent, self-assertive secondary associations, rather than posing an insuperable obstacle to the "peaceful evolution" of the post-reform polity may actually facilitate such evolution by helping to reduce the potentially enormous frictional costs of a zero-sum, winner-take-all confrontation between state and society, autonomy and domination.[105] In this connection, the twin concepts of organizational "entwinement" and proto-institutional "embeddedness" may prove instructive. As elaborated by Kevin O'Brien, entwinement involves a strategy of voluntary cooptation—that is, the attempt by new social forces to acquire value and identity by working in harmony with, and subordinating themselves to, established centers of state power. Through a strategy of entwinement, new social forces and organizations can, over time, embed themselves in the political system, acquiring viability and legitimacy within their recognized spheres of competence; and this is possible even—or especially—in political environments characterized by sharply limited organizational autonomy, minimal permissible policy conflict, and low formal institutionalization.[106] While the idea of embeddedness shares with the concept of institutionalization an appreciation for increased organizational complexity and competence, it differs from the latter in that it downplays the importance of self-organization and the existence of autonomous, well-defined boundaries, stressing instead the opportunistic accommodations to power that frequently characterize the early stages of organizational development in authoritarian systems.[107] O'Brien thus notes:

> Although institutionalization ultimately reduces the role of individuals and hardens boundaries, embeddedness typically hinges on extraorganizational power. . . . In an organization seeking to become embedded, the agents of change seek proximity to existing centers of power (i.e., entwinement) rather than distance. . . . They realize that independence at this point means irrelevance and that future development demands sensitivity to existing power relations.[108]

Under conditions of the Leninist party-state's continuing monopolization of political power, it is not merely expedient but also strategically optimal for newly emerging social forces and would-be *pouvoirs intermédiaires* to tie their fortunes to the local state, allowing themselves to be coopted. The process of entwinement transforms both parties to the transaction. The local state is not immune from societal influence, and vibrant social forces may be able to appropriate or otherwise make use of bits and pieces of the protean state to suit their own purposes. Moreover, the party-state itself may be strengthened by the new corporatist arrangements, becoming more highly responsive to, and invigorated by, its increased exposure to society's demands and interests. The state thus "reinvents" itself in the process of regulating social forces and secondary associations. It is in this sense that the new corporatist relationship between state and society has been described as "mutually empowering."[109]

Such a co-evolutionary process will not necessarily be pleasing to Western eyes. The reinvented Chinese state is likely to be at least moderately illiberal and undemocratic, more neo-conservative than pluralistic; in places, it may even be downright decadent and despotic. But as Samuel Huntington reminds us, in rapidly modernizing countries with weakly institutionalized political structures the *degree* of government generally counts for more than the *form* of government.[110]

As China continues to change shape, certain key questions loom large: Will the existing system be able to survive the travails of high-speed (but alarmingly uneven) economic growth and social mobilization? Will it, in the process, promote the formation of a broad middle class—the only known source of that vital modicum of political stability needed to achieve a successful post-authoritarian transition? And if a middle class does emerge, will it be so dominated by bureaucrat-capitalists and other corporate-state collusionists as to preclude the eventual development of a vigorous, free-standing bourgeoisie?

Given the existence of substantial reform-induced social stresses—rising crime rates, massive rural emigration, rampant corruption, widening polarization of wealth, and so on—the answers to these and other important questions remain elusive. Certainly the rapid growth, increased complexity, and reduced capacity for hierarchical command that have characterized China's reform era political economy will continue to pose serious challenges to Beijing's leaders in the future.[111] Given the probability of high societal stress, an institutionalized capacity for flexible response may be essential to prevent centrifugal forces from overtaxing the system's adaptive capacity.

One way to strengthen this capacity would be to further devolve decisionmaking powers from Beijing to the provinces, in a type of de facto federalism. Incipient signs of such a devolution of power have already been detected, e.g., in the greater legislative scope and initiative currently being exercised by provincial people's congresses[112] and in the "market-preserving federalism" that has informally evolved in the economic sphere.[113] In these respects, China has already begun to change shape, albeit only informally and extra-constitutionally.[114]

Absent a formal reconstitution of the Chinese polity, which Beijing's leaders have been extremely loath to initiate, it remains to be seen whether China's existing policymaking structures and procedures—variously characterized as "fragmented authoritarianism,"[115] "management by exception,"[116] and "muddling through"[117]—can cope proactively with the stressful side effects of marketization, urbanization, and regional economic differentiation. There are, after all, no historical precedents for the successful, self-induced institutional transformation of a Leninist system under Communist Party auspices—let alone a system as vast and heterogeneous as China's. While the outcome thus remains problematical, the appearance of diverse new institutional forms and fluxes at the intersection of state and society in China poses a compelling challenge to the scholarly imagination in the post-totalitarian era.

Notes

Contributors

Notes

1. Dynamic Economy, Declining Party-State

1. Deng Xiaoping, "We Shall Speed Up Reform," June 12, 1987, in *Selected Works of Deng Xiaoping (1982–1992)* (Beijing: Foreign Languages Press, 1994), p. 236.

2. Based on Deng Xiaoping, "Our Magnificent Goal and Basic Policies," in *Selected Works of Deng Xiaoping (1982–1992)*, p. 86.

3. "China's Lost Savings," *Asian Wall Street Journal*, editorial, March 21–27, 1997, p. 10.

4. Deng Xiaoping, "On the Reform of the System of Party and State Leadership," August 18, 1980, in *Selected Works of Deng Xiaoping (1975–1982)* (Beijing: Foreign Languages Press, 1984), p. 316.

5. Li Lianjiang, presentation at the conference on "Elections on Both Sides of the Straits," Fairbank Center, Harvard University, May 8, 1997.

6. Yasheng Huang, presentation at the conference on "Unintended Consequences of the Post-Mao Reforms," Fairbank Center, Harvard University, September 1996.

7. Tony Saich, "Most Chinese Enjoy More Personal Freedom than Ever Before," *International Herald Tribune*, February 1–2, 1997, p. 6.

8. Tony Saich, "Changing Party/State-Society Relations," manuscript, p. 12.

9. Gordon White, Jude Howell, and Shang Xiaoyuan, *In Search of Civil Society* (Oxford: Clarendon Press, 1996), p. 213.

10. Jean Oi, "Fiscal Reform and the Economic Foundation of Local State Corporatism in China," *World Politics*, 45, no. 1 (October 1992); Jonathan Unger and Anita Chan, "Corporatism in China: A Developmental State in an East Asian Context," in Barrett L. McCormick and Jonathan Unger, eds., *China after Socialism* (Armonk, N.Y.: M. E. Sharpe, 1996), pp. 95–129; and Margaret Pearson, "The Janus Face of Business Associations in China:

Socialist Corporatism in Foreign Enterprises," *Australian Journal of Chinese Affairs,* no. 31 (January 1994).

11. Christopher Nevitt, "Private Business Associations in China: Evidence of Civil Society or Local State Power," *China Journal,* no. 36 (July 1996).

12. Patrick Tyler, "China Migrants: Economic Engine, Social Burden," *New York Times,* June 29, 1994.

13. Xing Zhigang, "Disparity in Assets Widening," *China Daily,* January 8, 1997, p. 3.

14. Alan Piazza and Echo H. Liang, "The State of Poverty in China: Its Causes and Remedies," paper presented at the conference on "Unintended Social Consequences of Chinese Economic Reform," Harvard School of Public Health and Fairbank Center, May 23–24, 1997.

15. Arthur Kleinman and A. Cohen, "Psychiatry's Global Challenge," *Scientific American* (March 1997).

16. Lucian Pye, remarks at the conference on "Unintended Consequences of the Post-Mao Reforms," Fairbank Center, Harvard University, September 1996.

17. Geremie Barmé, presentation at the conference on "Unintended Consequences of the Post-Mao Reforms," Fairbank Center, Harvard University, September 1996.

2. China's Transition in Economic Perspective

1. Barry Naughton, *Growing out of the Plan: Chinese Economic Reform, 1978–1993* (New York: Cambridge University Press, 1995).

2. This strategy was most clearly articulated by reformers in the Czech Republic and Poland, but was also the objective of some of the radical reformers in the former Soviet Union, such as those behind the Shatalin plan. Vaclav Klaus, subsequently the Czech prime minister, was an articulate exponent of this view.

3. Lawrence J. Lau, Yingyi Qian, and Gerard Roland, "Reform without Losers: An Interpretation of China's Dual-Track Approach to Reform," photocopy, Stanford University, October 1997.

4. "Russia Survey," *The Economist,* July 12, 1997, p. 5. Despite the large concentrations of economic power emerging in Russia, the boast is probably not literally true.

5. The turning point in 1991 is particularly distinct because of cyclical factors. The slowdown of the economy during 1989–90 means that agriculture actually absorbed *more* labor during those years than it did in previous years, and the subsequent recovery showed a more distinct change. The long-run shift is quite clear in any case.

6. I define "private sector" here in a way that excludes publicly owned rural enterprises, that is, those collectives at the township or village level. The definition is thus substantially narrower than the frequently used category of "nonstate" employment. Private sector includes registered urban private and individual enterprises, foreign-invested enterprises, and "rural" nonagricultural workers, excluding those in township and village cooperatives. Many of these "rural" nonagricultural workers are in fact working in urban areas. For additional explanation and sources of data, see Barry Naughton, "China's Emergence and Future as a Trading Nation," *Brookings Papers on Economic Activity*, 2 (1996), esp. pp. 281–286.

7. Department of Overall Planning and Wages, Ministry of Labor and Department of Population and Employment Statistics, State Statistical Bureau, *Zhongguo laodong tongji nianjian 1996* (China labor statistical yearbook) (Beijing: Zhongguo tongji chubanshe, 1996), pp. 290–297; State Statistical Bureau, *Zhongguo tongji zhaiyao 1997* (China statistical abstract) (Beijing: Zhongguo tongji chubanshe, 1997), p. 32.

8. Yanjie Bian and John R. Logan, "Market Transition and the Persistence of Power: The Changing Stratification System in Urban China," *American Sociological Review*, 61 (1996): 739–58; Deborah S. Davis, "Urban Catch-up: Impact of Greater Marketization on Job Mobility," photocopy, Yale University, June 1996.

9. Conversely, if the opportunity to push ahead with reforms in the near future is missed, the aging of China's population, which sets in after about 2005, will start to make further changes more and more difficult.

3. Elite Politics

1. For contrasting views of China's future, see William H. Overholt, *The Rise of China* (New York: W. W. Norton, 1993); James Miles, *The Legacy of Tiananmen: China in Disarray* (Ann Arbor: University of Michigan Press, 1996); Chalmers Johnson, "Nationalism and the Market: China as a Superpower," Japan Research Institute, Working Paper no. 22 (July 1996); Edward Friedman, *National Identity and Democratic Prospects in Socialist China* (Armonk, N.Y.: M. E. Sharpe, 1995); and Richard Baum, "China after Deng: Ten Scenarios in Search of Reality," *China Quarterly*, no. 145 (March 1996).

2. The literature on democratic transition takes the role of political elites in negotiating or resisting political change to be one of the central variables. See Guillermo O'Donnell and Philippe C. Schmitter, *Transitions from Authoritarian Rule: Tentative Conclusions about Uncertain Democracies* (Baltimore: Johns Hopkins University Press, 1986).

3. Andrew Walder, "China's Transitional Economy: Interpreting Its Signifi-cance," *China Quarterly*, no. 144 (December 1995): 976.

4. See Peter B. Evans, Dietrich Rueschemeyer, and Theda Skocpol, eds., *Bringing the State Back In* (New York: Cambridge University Press, 1985).

5. Douglass C. North, *Institutions, Institutional Change, and Economic Perform-ance* (New York: Cambridge University Press, 1990).

6. Joel S. Migdal, Atul Kohli, and Vivienne Shue, eds., *State Power and Social Forces: Domination and Transformation in the Third World* (New York: Cam-bridge University Press, 1994).

7. X. L. Ding, *The Decline of Communism in China: The Legitimacy Crisis, 1977–1989* (New York: Cambridge University Press, 1994).

8. This proposition is controversial within the China field, but this is not the place to defend or develop it. Suffice it to say, this approach does not conflict with a bureaucratic politics approach, which deals with a different level of the political system. For an elegant restatement and elaboration of the winner-take-all approach, see Tang Tsou, "Chinese Politics at the Top: Factionalism or Informal Politics? Balance-of-Power Politics or a Game to Win All?" *China Journal*, no. 34 (July 1995): 95–156.

9. Zou Dang [Tsou Tang], *Ershi shiji Zhongguo zhengzhi: cong hongguan lishi yu weiguan xingdong jiaodu kan* (Twentieth-century Chinese politics: Viewed from the perspective of macro-history and micro-actions) (Hong Kong: Oxford University Press, 1994).

10. Li Zehou and Liu Zaifu, *Gaobie geming: Huiwang ershi shiji Zhongguo* (Fare-well to revolution: Looking back on twentieth-century China) (Hong Kong: Cosmos Books, 1995), p. 85.

11. Zhengyuan Fu, *Autocratic Tradition and Chinese Politics* (New York: Cam-bridge University Press, 1993).

12. Tang Tsou, "Prolegomenon to the Study of Informal Groups in CCP Politics," in Tang Tsou, *The Cultural Revolution and Post-Mao Reforms: A Historical Perspective* (Chicago: University of Chicago Press, 1986), p. 99.

13. Li and Liu, *Gaobie geming*, p. 23.

14. It has often been noted that much of Hua Guofeng's economic program was formulated by Deng Xiaoping before Deng was purged again in 1976. Politics might have taken a different course if the oil wells that were being madly dug in 1978–1980 in support of Hua's economic program had struck oil, but they did not. In the event, Deng adopted a different approach to economic development. On China's efforts to strike oil, see Barry Naughton, *Growing out of the Plan: Chinese Economic Reform, 1978–1993* (New York: Cambridge University Press, 1995), pp. 70–74.

15. The obvious comparison is to the early 1960s when efforts to sum up the lessons of the Great Leap Forward could not be articulated in ideological terms because Mao was still alive.

16. Much has been written, in both Chinese and English, about the discussion on practice as the sole criterion of truth. See Michael Schoenhals, "The 1978 Truth Criterion Controversy," *China Quarterly*, no. 126 (June 1991): 243–268; Merle Goldman, *Sowing the Seeds of Democracy: Political Reform in the Deng Xiaoping Era* (Cambridge: Harvard University Press, 1994), pp. 35–41; Wu Jiang, *Shinian zhi lu* (The course of ten years) (Hong Kong: Mirror Post Cultural Enterprises, 1995); Ruan Ming, *Deng Xiaoping diguo* (The Deng Xiaoping Empire) (Taibei: Shibao chuban gongsi, 1991); and Su Shaozhi, *Shinian fengyu: Wengehou de dalu lilunjie* (Ten years of storms: The mainland's theoretical circles after the Cultural Revolution) (Taibei: Shibao chuban gongsi, 1996), pp. 38–78.

17. Frederick C. Teiwes, "The Paradoxical Post-Mao Transition: From Obeying the Leader to 'Normal Politics,'" *China Journal*, no. 34 (July 1995): 55–94.

18. Deng Xiaoping, "Zenyang huifu nongye shengchan" (How can agricultural production be restored?), in *Deng Xiaoping wenxuan (1938–1965)* (The selected works of Deng Xiaoping, 1938–1965) (Beijing: Renmin chubanshe, 1983), p. 305. Over the years, the colors of the cats changed to black and white as Deng's aphorism was repeated, but, as Deng might say, the color of the cats does not matter.

19. Lowell Dittmer, "Chinese Informal Politics," *China Journal*, no. 34 (July 1995). It should be noted that the "game to win all" and informal politics do not exist on the same level. After all, the term "game to win all" suggests the nature of the game being played, whereas informal politics are merely one of the ways of playing the game. Other means of playing the game could be elaborated.

20. Joseph Fewsmith, "Formal Structures, Informal Politics, and Political Change in China," in Lowell Dittmer and Haruhiro Fukui, eds., *East Asian Informal Politics in Comparative Perspective* (New York: Cambridge University Press, forthcoming).

21. Kenneth Jowitt, *The Leninist Response to National Dependency* (Berkeley: Institute of International Studies, University of California, 1978).

22. Ezra Vogel, "From Friendship to Comradeship: The Change in Personal Relations in Communist China," *China Quarterly*, no. 21 (January–March 1965): 46–60.

23. See, for instance, Pang Song and Han Gang, "Dang he guojia lingdao tizhi de lishi kaocha yu gaige zhanwang" (A historical investigation of the party's and the state's leadership structure and the outlook for reform), *Zhongguo shehui kexue* (Chinese social science), no. 6 (November 10, 1987).

24. Communiqué of the Third Plenary Session of the Eleventh Central Committee. There were a number of important decisions that followed from this change. Intellectuals, who had been denounced as the "stinking ninth

category" during the Cultural Revolution, were now regarded as "part of the working class." In addition, the party made formal decisions to remove the label from landlords and to reaffirm the role of the "national bourgeoisie."

25. Belatedly published as Hu Qiaomu, "Act in Accordance with Economic Laws, Step Up the Four Modernizations," Xinhua, October 5, 1978, translated in Foreign Broadcast Information Service, *Daily Report–China* (hereafter cited as FBIS-Chi), October 11, 1978, pp. E1–22.

26. On such conflict in the sciences, see H. Lyman Miller, *Science and Dissent in Post-Mao China: The Politics of Knowledge* (Seattle: University of Washington Press, 1996).

27. "Xuyan" (Preamble), *Zhonghua renmin gongheguo xianfa* (Constitution of the People's Republic of China), in Zhonggong zhongyang wenxian yanjiushi, ed., *Shierda yilai zhongyao wenxian xuanbian* (Important documents since the Twelfth Party Congress), 3 vols. (Beijing: Renmin chubanshe, 1986), 1: 219.

28. Tang Tsou, "Reflections on the Formation and Foundations of the Communist Party-State," in Tsou, *The Cultural Revolution and Post-Mao Reforms*, pp. 313–315.

29. See especially Ding, *The Decline of Communism in China.*

30. Shaoguang Wang, "The Politics of Private Time: Changing Leisure Patterns in Urban China," in Deborah S. Davis et al., eds., *Urban Spaces in Contemporary China* (New York: Cambridge University Press, 1995), pp. 149–172.

31. Jean Oi, *Rural China Takes Off: The Institutional Foundations of Economic Reform* (Berkeley: University of California Press, 1999).

32. Barry Naughton, "Implications of the State Monopoly over Industry and Its Relaxation," *Modern China*, 18, no. 1(1992): 14–41.

33. "Guanyu dangnei zhengzhi shenghuo de ruogan zhunze" (Guiding principles for political life within the party), in Zhonggong zhongyang wenxian yanjiushi, ed., *Shiyijie sanzhong quanhui yilai zhongyao wenxian xuandu* (Selected readings in important documents since the third plenary session of the eleventh Central Committee), 2 vols. (Beijing: Renmin chubanshe, 1987), 1: 163–184.

34. Melanie Manion, *Retirement of Revolutionaries in China: Public Policies, Social Norms, Private Interests* (Princeton: Princeton University Press, 1993).

35. Hong Yung Lee, "China's New Bureaucracy?" in Arthur Lewis Rosenbaum, ed., *State and Society in China: The Consequences of Reform* (Boulder, Colo.: Westview Press, 1992), p. 56. See also Hong Yung Lee, *From Revolutionary Cadres to Party Technocrats in Socialist China* (Berkeley and Los Angeles: University of California Press, 1991).

36. Lee, "China's New Bureaucracy?" p. 67.

37. Yasheng Huang, *Inflation and Investment Controls in China: The Political Economy of Central-Local Relations during the Reform Era* (New York: Cambridge University Press, 1996), p. 119.

38. This is so in its control functions, but there is an important difference between the Chinese bureaucracy and Weber's model of legal-rational authority. As Huang notes, the central authorities are able to keep such tight control over the bureaucracy because of the stress on "ideological conformity." See ibid.

39. Chen Yun, "Tiba peiyang zhongqingnian ganbu shi dangwu zhi ji" (Promoting and cultivating young and middle-aged cadres is an urgent task at present), *Chen Yun wenxuan (1956–1985)* (Selected works of Chen Yun, 1956–1985), (Beijing: Renmin chubanshe, 1986), pp. 262–266.

40. For a classic statement of the conservative position on party building, see Chen Yeping, "Have Both Political Integrity and Ability, Stress Political Ability: On Criteria for Selecting Cadres," *Renmin ribao*, September 1, 1991, trans. FBIS-Chi, September 6, 1991, pp. 26–31.

41. On the Theory Conference of January–April 1979, see Goldman, *Sowing the Seeds of Democracy*, pp. 47–61. See also Su, *Shinian fengyu*, pp. 80–117.

42. Joseph Fewsmith, *Dilemmas of Reform in China: Political Conflict and Economic Debate* (Armonk, N.Y.: M. E. Sharpe, 1994), esp. chap. 3.

43. "Decision of the Central Committee of the Communist Party of China on Reform of the Economic Structure," Xinhua, October 20, 1984, trans. FBIS-Chi, October 22, 1984, K1–19. This decision endorsed the creation of a "socialist planned *commodity* economy." The term "commodity economy" had implications that had long been resisted by conservatives within the party. Obviously, the decision of the Fourteenth Party Congress in 1992 to endorse the creation of a "socialist *market* economy" went an important step further. See Jiang Zemin, "Political Work Report," Beijing Central Television, trans. FBIS-Chi (supplement), October 13, 1992, pp. 23–43.

44. Joseph Fewsmith, "Institutions, Informal Politics, and Political Transition in China," *Asian Survey*, 36, no. 3 (March 1996): 230–245.

45. Fewsmith, *Dilemmas of Reform in China*, pp. 219–220.

46. Joseph Fewsmith, "Reaction, Resurgence, and Succession: Chinese Politics since Tiananmen," in Roderick MacFarquhar, ed., *The Politics of China*, 2d ed. (New York: Cambridge University Press, 1997), chap. 6.

47. Gao Xin and He Pin, *Zhu Rongji zhuan* (A biography of Zhu Rongji) (Taibei: Xin Xinwen wenhua chuban, 1993), pp. 231–232.

48. Fewsmith, "Reaction, Resurgence, and Succession," pp. 505–508.

49. Minxin Pei has stressed the difficulty of this dual transition. See *From*

Reform to Revolution: The Demise of Communism in China and the Soviet Union (Cambridge: Harvard University Press, 1994).

50. This is the major thesis of Li and Liu, *Gaobie geming.*

51. Ding Xueliang, *Gongchanzhuyihou yu Zhongguo* (Post-communism and China) (Hong Kong: Oxford University Press, 1994), p. xxii.

52. Adam Przeworski, *Democracy and the Market: Political and Economic Reforms in Eastern Europe and Latin America* (New York: Cambridge University Press, 1991), p. 37, and Axel Hadenius, ed., *Democracy's Victory and Crisis* (Cambridge: Cambridge University Press, 1997).

53. Adam Przeworski et al., *Sustainable Democracy* (Cambridge: Cambridge University Press, 1995).

54. Yossi Shain and Juan J. Linz, eds., *Between States: Interim Governments and Democratic Transitions* (Cambridge: Cambridge University Press, 1995), pp. 10–14, and Juan J. Linz and Alfred Stepan, *Problems of Democratic Transition and Consolidation: Southern Europe, South America, and Post-Communist Europe* (Baltimore: Johns Hopkins University Press, 1996), pp. 16–37.

55. Lee, *From Revolutionary Cadres to Party Technocrats in Socialist China,* pp. 402–408.

56. Ding, *The Decline of Communism in China.*

57. Pei, *From Reform to Revolution,* p. 49.

58. Andrew G. Walder, "The Quiet Revolution from Within: Economic Reform as a Source of Political Decline," in Andrew G. Walder, ed., *The Waning of the Communist State* (Berkeley: University of California Press, 1995), p. 3.

59. Barry Naughton, "Fiscal and Banking Reform: The 1994 Fiscal Reform Revisited," in Maurice Brosseau, Kuan Hsin-chi, and Y. Y. Kueh, eds., *China Review, 1997* (Hong Kong: Chinese University Press, 1997), p. 255.

60. Ibid., p. 262.

61. Huang, *Inflation and Investment Controls in China.* For a contrary interpretation, see Jia Hao and Lin Zhimin, eds., *Changing Central-Local Relations in China: Reform and State Capacity* (Boulder, Colo.: Westview Press, 1994).

62. Cheng Xiaonong, "Weichi wending yu shenhua gaige: Zhongguo mianlin de jueze" (Maintaining stability and deepening reform: A choice confronting China), *Dangdai Zhongguo yanjiu,* nos. 1 and 2 (1995), trans. in "Wang Shaoguang Proposal (II)," *Chinese Economic Studies,* 28, no. 4 (July–August 1995): 88–125.

63. On the military, see Richard H. Yang and Gerald Segal, eds., *Chinese Economic Reform: The Impact on Security* (London: Routledge, 1996).

64. Xiao Gongqin, "Dongya quanwei zhengzhi yu xiandaihua" (Asian authoritarian politics and modernization), in *Zhanlüe yu guanli,* no. 2 (1994).

65. Shain and Linz, *Between States.*

66. William P. Alford, *To Steal a Book Is an Elegant Offense: Intellectual Property Law in Chinese Civilization* (Stanford: Stanford University Press, 1995), pp. 9–29.

67. William P. Alford, "Seek Truth from Facts—Especially When They Are Unpleasant: America's Understanding of China's Efforts at Law Reform," *Pacific Basin Law Journal,* 8 (1990): 182. Quoted in Stanley Lubman, "Introduction: The Future of Chinese Law," *China Quarterly,* no. 141 (March 1995): 2.

68. William P. Alford, "Tasseled Loafers for Barefoot Lawyers: Transformation and Tension in the World of Chinese Legal Workers," *China Quarterly,* no. 141 (March 1995): 35.

69. Donald C. Clarke, "The Execution of Civil Judgments in China," *China Quarterly,* no. 141 (March 1995): 65–81.

70. Minxin Pei, "Creeping Democratization in China," in Larry Diamond, Marc F. Plattner, Yun-Han Chu, and Hung-mao Tien, eds., *Consolidating the Third Wave Democracies: Regional Challenges* (Baltimore: Johns Hopkins University Press, 1997), p. 216.

71. Jean Oi, "Fiscal Reform and the Economic Foundations of Local State Corporatism in China," *World Politics,* 45, no. 1 (1992): 99–126.

72. Jonathan Unger and Anita Chan, "Corporatism in China: A Developmental State in an East Asian Context," in Barrett L. McCormick and Jonathan Unger, eds., *China after Socialism: In the Footsteps of Eastern Europe or East Asia?* (Armonk, N.Y.: M. E. Sharpe, 1996); David Wank, "Private Business, Bureaucracy, and Political Alliances in a Chinese City," *Australian Journal of Chinese Affairs,* no. 33 (January 1995); and Christopher Earle Nevitt, "Private Business Associations in China: Evidence of Civil Society or Local State Power?" *China Journal,* no. 36 (July 1996): 26–45.

73. Ding, *The Decline of Communism in China.*

74. Peter Evans, *Embedded Autonomy: States and Industrial Transformation* (Princeton: Princeton University Press, 1995).

75. Luo yi ning ge er [pseud. for Wang Shan], *Disanzhi yanjing kan Zhongguo* (Looking at China through a Third Eye) (Taiyuan: Shanxi renmin chubanshe, 1994), p. 61.

76. Lowell Dittmer and Lu Xiaobo have found an *increase* in personal politics even as *danwei* become more formal in their structure. See "Personal Politics in the Chinese *Danwei* under Reform," *Asian Survey,* 36, no. 3 (March 1996): 246–267.

77. Nationalist sentiment was given expression in the much-talked-about book *Zhongguo keyi shuo bu* (The China that can say no) (Beijing: Zhonghua gongshang lianhe chubanshe, 1996), which spawned a cottage industry

of similar books. It should be noted that the Chinese government subsequently banned such books and offered criticism in books such as Xiao Fang, ed., *Zhongguo ruhe miandui xifang* (How China should face the West) (Hong Kong: Mingjing chubanshe, 1997). For a more historical treatment of nationalism, see Jonathan Unger, ed., *Chinese Nationalism* (Armonk, N.Y.: M. E. Sharpe, 1996).

78. See, for instance, Song Taiqing, *Zhongguo shidai: Ershiyi shiji da yuyan* (The age of China: A great prediction for the twenty-first century) (Guiyang: Guizhou renmin chubanshe, 1993).

79. Michel Oksenberg, "China's Confident Nationalism," *Foreign Affairs*, 65, no. 3 (Winter 1987).

80. Przeworski et al., *Sustainable Democracy*, p. 61.

81. Li Zehou, *Zhongguo jindai sixiangshi lun* (History of modern Chinese thought) (Beijing: Renmin chubanshe, 1979) and Li Zehou, *Zhongguo xiandai sixiangshi lun* (History of contemporary Chinese thought) (Beijing: Dongfang chubanshe, 1987). See also Vera Schwarcz, *The Chinese Enlightenment: Intellectuals and the Legacy of the May Fourth Movement of 1919* (Berkeley: University of California Press, 1986).

82. Wu Guoguang and Zheng Yongnian, *Lun zhongyang-difang guanxi* (On central-local relations) (Hong Kong: Oxford University Press, 1995).

83. This proposition follows the lines of the suggestions for readjusting central-local relations contained in Wang Shaoguang and Hu Angang, *Jiaqiang zhongyang zhengfu zai shichang jingji zhuanxing zhong de zhudao zuoyong* (Strengthen the guiding functions of the central government during the transition to a market economy) (Shenyang: Liaoning renmin chubanshe, 1993), trans. as "Wang Shaoguang Proposal," *Chinese Economic Studies*, 28, nos. 3 and 4 (May–June and July–August 1995).

84. Tang Tsou, "Political Change and Reform: The Middle Course," in Tsou, *The Cultural Revolution and Post-Mao Reforms*, p. 241.

85. Li and Liu, *Gaobie geming*, p. 4.

4. Party-Military Relations

The views expressed in this essay are those of the author and are not to be construed as those of the National War College, the National Defense University, the Department of Defense, or any other agency of the United States Government.

1. There is an extremely rich social science literature covering the field of civil-military relations in the various milieu of advanced industrial states, the militaries of developing countries, and in Marxist-Leninist states. Within this field are such significant contributions as Samuel P. Hunt-

ington, *The Soldier and the State* (Cambridge: Harvard University Press, 1957); Bengt Abrahamsson, *Military Professionalism and Political Power* (Beverly Hills, Calif.: Sage Publications, 1972); Morris Janowitz, *The Professional Soldier* (New York: Free Press, 1971); Claude E. Welch, Jr., ed., *Civilian Control of the Military: Theory and Cases from Developing Countries* (Albany: State University of New York Press, 1976); Eric A. Nordlinger, *Soldiers in Politics: Military Coups and Governments* (Englewood Cliffs, N.J.: Prentice Hall, 1977); and Dale Herspring and Ivan Volgyes, eds., *Civil-Military Relations in Communist Systems* (Boulder, Colo.: Westview Press, 1978). There is no attempt in this brief essay to survey the various approaches and paradigms used in this extensive and diverse field of social science research. For an extremely useful analysis of the consequences of this diversity in the analysis of party-military relations in China, see Richard J. Latham, "China's Party-Army Relations after June 1989: A Case for Miles' Law?" in Richard H. Yang, ed., *China's Military: The PLA in 1990/1991* (SCPS Year Book, National Sun Yat-sen University, Taiwan; distributed by Westview Press, Boulder, Colo., 1991), pp. 103–124.

2. My use of the concept *military ethic* is taken from Abrahamsson, *Military Professionalism and Political Power,* p. 63.

3. For an excellent overview of these early years and the divisive issues raised in the process of creating a party-army, see Harlan W. Jencks, *From Muskets to Missiles: Politics and Professionalism in the Chinese Army, 1945–1981* (Boulder, Colo.: Westview Press, 1982), pp. 37–68.

4. See Ellis Joffe, *Party and Army: Professionalism and Political Control in the Chinese Officer Corps, 1949–1964* (Cambridge: Harvard University Press, 1967), for a detailed analysis of this period.

5. Beijing Domestic Service, February 22, 1983, in Foreign Broadcast Information Service, *Daily Report–China* (hereafter FBIS-Chi), no. 037, February 23, 1983, p. K30.

6. Bai Changqin, "My Views on Technical Equipment for Mobile Forces," *Jiefangjun bao,* December 2, 1989, in FBIS-Chi, no. 248, December 28, 1989, p. 26.

7. Jun Ping, "The Army and People Unite as One to Thoroughly Put Down the Rebellion," *Jiefangjun bao,* June 19, 1989, in FBIS-Chi, no. 131, July 11, 1989, p. 44.

8. "Why We Cracked Down: Two Conversations," *U.S. News & World Report,* March 12, 1990, p. 54.

9. For a detailed analysis of this campaign, see David Shambaugh, "The Soldier and the State in China: The Political Work System in the People's Liberation Army," *China Quarterly,* no. 127 (September 1991), esp. pp. 551–568.

10. For an analysis of this issue, see Harlan W. Jencks, "Civil-Military Relations in China: Tiananmen and After," *Problems of Communism*, 40 (May–June 1991): 15–17; and Latham, "China's Party-Army Relations after June 1989," pp. 111–113.

11. There were numerous reports of a letter to the Martial Law Command in Beijing opposing the imposition of martial law and the use of deadly force by the PLA against the demonstrators. This letter was allegedly signed by seven senior retired officers. Surviving Marshals Nie Rongzhen and Xu Xiangqian also reportedly opposed martial law and the use of violence by the armed forces to restore order. See, for example, Robert Delfs, "The People's Republic," *Far Eastern Economic Review*, 144, no. 22 (June 1, 1989): 14.

12. Ibid.

13. "Deng Talks on Quelling Rebellion in Beijing," *Beijing Review*, no. 28, July 10–16, 1989, in FBIS-Chi, no. 131, July 11, 1989, p. 15 (emphasis added).

14. Ibid.

15. Shi Shanyu, "Never Lose the 'Lifeline,'" *Jiefangjun bao*, August 5, 1989, in FBIS-Chi, no. 162, August 23, 1989, 42.

16. Tokyo, Kyodo, January 18, 1990, in FBIS-Chi, no. 012, January 18, 1990, pp. 23–24.

17. Tai Ming Cheung, "Rank Insubordination," *Far Eastern Economic Review*, 147, no. 5 (February 1, 1990): 22.

18. Lieutenant General Li Lianxiu, the PAP commander since 1984, was replaced by Major General Zhou Yushu, commander of the Twenty-fourth Group Army. General Zhou received two new deputies: the PAP chief of staff Wang Wenli, and the deputy commander of the elite Fifteenth Group Army (Airborne) Zuo Yinsheng. Elements of both the Twenty-fourth and Fifteenth Group Armies played major roles in suppressing the Beijing demonstrations.

19. Liu Guohua, "At an All-Army Political Work Meeting, Yang Baibing Explains 'Several Questions on Strengthening and Improving Army Political Work in [the] New Situation,'" *Jiefangjun bao*, December 19, 1989, in FBIS-Chi, no. 18-supplement, January 26, 1990, p. 33.

20. Ibid.

21. Chi Haotian, "Strive to Raise the Leadership Level of the Party Committees and Ensure the Party's Absolute Leadership over the Army," based on his speech to party committee members organized by the headquarters of the PLA General Staff Department (n.d.), *Qiushi*, no. 2, January 16, 1990, in *Joint Publications Research Service Report—China* (hereafter JPRS-CAR), no. 024, March 29, 1990, pp. 1–9.

22. Ibid., p. 1.

23. See "Text of Peng Zhen Report" on the revised constitution of the PRC

to the Fifth Session of the Fifth National People's Congress, November 26, 1982, in FBIS-Chi, no. 235, December 7, 1982, p. K43.

24. See David Shambaugh, "China's Commander-in-Chief: Jiang Zemin and the PLA," in C. Dennison Lane, Mark Weisenbloom, and Dimon Liu, eds., *Chinese Military Modernization* (New York: Kegan Paul International, 1996), pp. 219–220.

25. Lin Jiangong, "Refuting the Advocacy of 'Separating the Army from the Party,'" *Jiefangjun bao*, November 21, 1989, in FBIS-Chi, no. 245 (supplement), December 7, 1989, pp. 6–8.

26. Chi Haotian, "Strive to Raise," p. 3.

27. *Wen wei pao* (Hong Kong), December 22, 1989, in FBIS-Chi, no. 13 (supplement), January 19, 1990, p. 1.

28. *Jiefangjun bao* contributing commentator, "Take the Guarantee of Being Forever Politically Qualified as a Fundamental Task—Discussing the Strengthening of the Political Building of Our Army," April 10, 1990, in FBIS-Chi, no. 86, May 3, 1990, pp. 40–47.

29. Ibid., p. 46.

30. Ibid., p. 24.

31. Commentator's article, "Fundamental Basis for Conducting Ideological and Political Education among Soldiers in [the] New Situation," *Jiefangjun bao*, March 12, 1990, in FBIS-Chi, no. 70, April 11, 1990, p. 33.

32. General Political Department, "Some Questions Concerning the Strengthening and Improvement of Political Work in the Army under the New Situation," Beijing, Xinhua, February 27, 1990, in FBIS-Chi, no. 40, February 28, 1990, p. 23.

33. Ibid., p. 24.

34. Bai Xuan, "Unswervingly Uphold the Party's Absolute Leadership of the Army," *Jiefangjun bao*, December 19, 1989, in FBIS-Chi, no. 23 (supplement), February 2, 1990, p. 17.

35. Ibid., p. 38.

36. Shambaugh, "The Soldier and the State in China," pp. 566–567.

37. My analysis of Jiang Zemin's efforts to establish his personal status within the PLA draws heavily on Shambaugh, "China's Commander-in-Chief," especially pp. 215–231.

38. Ibid., pp. 221–226.

39. Zhang Jianzhong, "Ideological and Political Work in the Course of Strengthening Military Training," *Jiefangjun bao*, March 24, 1993, in FBIS-Chi, April 1, 1993, pp. 37–39.

40. "'Excerpts' of speech by Jiang Zemin at the Central Military Commission's rank-conferring ceremony in Beijing on 8 June," Beijing, Xinhua, June 8, 1994, in FBIS-Chi, no. 111, June 9, 1994, pp. 32–34.

41. Ibid., p. 33.

42. Ibid., p. 34.

43. Ibid.

44. For a lengthy discussion of this decision, see Tang Wu and Zhu Ruiqing, "Central Military Commission Promulgates Decision on Further Augmenting Party Building in the Army," *Jiefangjun bao,* January 7, 1995, in FBIS-Chi, January 31, 1995, pp. 15–22.

45. Ibid., p. 17.

46. Ibid.

47. Ibid.

48. Ibid.

49. Shambaugh, "China's Commander-in-Chief," p. 226.

50. David S. G. Goodman, "Corruption in the PLA," in Gerald Segal and Richard H. Yang, eds., *Chinese Economic Reform: The Impact on Security* (London: Routledge, 1996), pp. 35–52.

51. See, for example, Thomas J. Bickford, "The Chinese Military and Its Business Operations: The PLA as Entrepreneur," *Asian Survey,* 34, no. 5 (May 1994): 460–474.

52. Liu Huaqing and Zhang Zhen, "Carrying Forward Fine Traditions Is a Major, Strategic Issue of Our Army's Construction under the New Situation," *Renmin ribao,* July 26, 1993, in FBIS-Chi, July 27, 1993, pp. 22–25.

53. Ibid., pp. 24–25.

54. Ellis Joffe, "The PLA and the Economy: The Effects of Involvement," in Segal and Yang, eds., *Chinese Economic Reform,* pp. 11–35.

55. This section draws heavily on Ellis Joffe, "Party-Army Relations in China: Retrospect and Prospect," *China Quarterly,* no. 146 (June 1996): 299–314.

56. For a thorough analysis of generations in the PLA leadership, see Michael D. Swaine, *The Military and Political Succession in China: Leadership Institutions and Beliefs* (Santa Monica, Calif.: RAND, 1992).

57. See Michael D. Swaine, *The Role of the Chinese Military in National Security Policymaking* (Santa Monica, Calif.: RAND, 1996), for a careful analysis of the PLA's roles and influence in various "arenas" of Chinese foreign and defense policy.

58. On the concept of *guardianship,* see Samuel P. Huntington, *Political Order in Changing Societies* (New Haven: Yale University Press, 1968), pp. 225–233.

59. On the "hundred years of humiliation" and its formative role in Chinese patriotism *(aiguozhuyi),* see Michael H. Hunt, *The Genesis of Chinese Communist Foreign Policy* (New York: Columbia University Press, 1996).

60. For a discrete analysis of factions within the PLA, see June Teufel Dreyer, "The New Officer Corps: Implications for the Future," *China Quarterly,* no. 146 (June 1996), esp. pp. 329–332.

5. The National People's Congress

1. Kevin J. O'Brien, *Reform without Liberalization: China's National People's Congress and the Politics of Institutional Change* (New York: Cambridge University Press, 1990), pp. 4–5.

2. Regrettably, Western scholars know virtually nothing about the internal leadership politics of this 1979 decision to undertake a very limited electoral liberalization, including whether or not the decision sparked much serious debate among the broad reformist majority at that time. It is consequently difficult to say with any certainty how much support there might be for further electoral reform, now that virtually all the principals of the 1979 decision have died.

3. *Selected Works of Deng Xiaoping [1975–1982]* (Beijing: Foreign Languages Press, 1984). Issues of "democracy" are addressed on pp. 155–158, with the need for accelerated lawmaking work discussed on pp. 157–158. Deng argues that "These laws should be discussed and adopted through democratic procedures," but does not mention the people's congresses in this context.

4. In order to help draft the laws that would provide stability and continuity to democracy, the plenum communiqué stated that "from now on, lawmaking work should be placed on the important agenda of the National People's Congress and its Standing Committee." While the communiqué endorsed greater independence for judicial and procuratorial offices, it said nothing about greater legislative independence for the NPC. See "Zhongguo gongchandang di shiyijie zhongyang weiyuanhui di sanci quanti huiyi gongbao" (Communiqué of the Third Plenary Meeting of the Eleventh Central Committee of the Chinese Communist Party), in *Shiyijie sanzhong quanhui yilai zhongyao wenxian xuandu (shangce)* (Selected Important Documents since the Third Plenum of the Eleventh Central Committee (first volume)) (Beijing: Renmin chubanshe, 1987), pp. 1–14, esp. p. 11.

5. Peng Zhen served as chairman of the NPC's Legislative Affairs Committee from 1979 until 1983, when he succeeded Marshal Ye Jianying as Standing Committee chairman. Peng, in turn, was succeeded by Wan Li as chairman in the spring of 1988. Qiao Shi replaced Wan as chairman in 1993, and continued to hold the post until Li Peng took over as chairman in 1998.

6. For a detailed discussion of Peng Zhen's views and role in building up the NPC during the 1950s, see Murray Scot Tanner, *The Politics of Lawmaking in Post-Mao China: Institutions, Processes, and Democratic Prospects* (New York: Oxford University Press, 1998), chap. 4.

7. Pitman B. Potter, "Foundation and Emblem of PRC Elite Legal Culture: Peng Zhen in the Deng Era," paper presented to the annual meeting of the Association for Asian Studies, Honolulu, April 1996, pp. 12, 17–21.

8. In addition to Potter, the role of party "elders" and their view of the NPC as a conduit for their influence is discussed in Murray Scot Tanner, "Organizations and Politics in China's Post-Mao Law-Making System," in Pitman B. Potter, ed., *Domestic Law Reforms in Post-Mao China* (Armonk, N.Y.: M. E. Sharpe, 1994), pp. 58, 72, 74–78.

9. Potter, "Peng Zhen in the Deng Era," pp. 22–23.

10. Peng Zhen, "Jiaqiang minzhu yu fazhi jianshe, jiaqiang renda changweihui gongzuo" (Strengthen the construction of democracy and the legal system, strengthen the work of the NPC Standing Committee), speech at an NPC/Standing Committee (NPC/SC) delegates' work meeting, June 27, 1986, available in Peng Zhen, *Lun xin shiqi de shehuizhuyi minzhu yu fazhi jianshe* (On the construction of socialist democracy and the legal system in the new period) (Beijing: Zhongyang wenxian chubanshe, 1989), pp. 324–331, or in NPC Standing Committee General Office Research Office, ed., *Zhonghua renmin gongheguo renmin daibiao dahui wenxian ziliao huibian, 1949–1990* (Collection of documents of the PRC National People's Congress, 1949–1990) (Beijing: Zhongguo minzhu fazhi chubanshe, 1990), pp. 601–603.

11. Wan Li, "Making Decisionmaking More Democratic and Scientific Is an Important Part of Reforming the Political System," *Renmin ribao*, August 15, 1986, p. 1.

12. The two speeches are Wan Li, "Wan Li zai qijie quanguo renda changweihui dishisanci huiyi shang de jianghua" (Wan Li's speech at the Thirteenth Meeting of the Seventh NPC Standing Committee), March 15, 1990; and Jiang Zemin, "Guanyu jianchi he wanshan renmin daibiao dahui zhidu" (On maintaining and perfecting the People's Congress system), March 18, 1990, both in NPC Standing Committee General Office Research Office, ed., *Zhonghua renmin gongheguo renmin daibiao dahui wenxian ziliao huibian, 1949–1990*, pp. 622–625. NPC advisors have confirmed in interviews that the two men were engaged in a debate at this time over NPC-party relations.

13. An excellent example is Qiao Shi, "Zai shoudu gejie jinian renmin daibiao dahui chengli sishi zhounian dahui shang de jianghua" (Speech at the meeting of all groups in the capital to celebrate the fortieth anniversary of the establishment of the National People's Congress), *Renmin ribao*, September 16, 1994, p. 1. See also David Kwan, "Qiao Says NPC Must Clear All Party Decisions," *South China Morning Post*, September 16, 1994, p. 13; "NPC Celebrates 40th Anniversary," Beijing, Xinhua News Agency, September 15, 1994; Qiao has discussed these issues in detail in an inter-

view with *Philadelphia Inquirer* reporter Trudy Rubin, "Bringing China under the Rule of Law," December 13, 1996. I am indebted to Merle Goldman for providing me with a copy of the original interview. See also Secretary General Tian Jiyun's speech summarized in the *South China Morning Post,* September 13, 1994, p. 10.

14. *South China Morning Post,* May 23, 1996, p. 10.

15. To the extent that this viewpoint is followed, it creates a dilemma in the relationship between economic and legal development, particularly in Stalinist economies trying to build a legal basis for freer markets. For, as James Feinerman has pointed out, reforming Stalinist economies, unlike those of eighteenth- and nineteenth-century Western states, do not generally use law to regulate already existing market activities; instead they often use law to call into existence and legitimize economic activities that heretofore have been illegal or nonexistent. Laws such as the 1979 Sino-Foreign Joint Venture Law were passed not to codify the state's accumulated experience in how to manage and regulate such ventures; they were passed to create such ventures. Hence, strict adherence to experience-based lawmaking can often be unfeasible or can inhibit the development of the legal basis for the market. James V. Feinerman, "Backwards into the Future," *Law and Contemporary Problems,* 52, nos. 2 and 3 (Spring and Summer 1989): 169–184; and James V. Feinerman, "Economic and Legal Reform in China, 1978–91," *Problems of Communism,* 40 (September–October 1991): 62–75.

16. Interview with NPC Standing Committee Research Office staffer, Beijing, August 1992.

17. See, for example, the official report on the joint NPC–State Council legislative planning meeting reported in FBIS-Chi, June 22, 1992, pp. 38–39. This tension in NPC–State Council relations was also discussed by NPC staffers and advisors interviewed by the author in 1992 and 1995.

18. By the end of Mao's life, virtually all major policy decisions, to the extent that they were codified at all and not simply announced as "Chairman Mao's latest directive," were drafted in the highly authoritative form of CCP Central Committee documents *(zhongfa)* rather than as regulations of the State Council or laws adopted by the NPC. On this point, see Kenneth Lieberthal, *Central Documents and Politburo Politics in China,* Michigan Papers in Chinese Studies, no. 33 (Ann Arbor: University of Michigan Center for Chinese Studies, 1976); see also O'Brien, *Reform without Liberalization,* pp. 61–77.

19. Hu Shikai, "Representation without Democratization: The 'Signature Incident' and China's National People's Congress," *Journal of Contemporary China,* 2, no. 1 (Winter–Spring 1993): 3–34.

20. The organization and process of party leadership over lawmaking is dis-

cussed in O'Brien, *Reform without Liberalization*, pp. 45–49, 158–164; and Murray Scot Tanner, "The Erosion of Central Party Control over Lawmaking," *China Quarterly*, no. 138 (June 1994): 381–403.

21. This is according to a variety of data from interviews and internal party documents; Tanner, "The Erosion of Central Party Control," pp. 393–396; see also O'Brien, *Reform without Liberalization*, pp. 159–160.

22. The document, issued on February 21, 1991, with the classification "secret" (*jimi*), is entitled "Zhonggong zhongyang guanyu jiaqiang dui lifa gongzuo lingdao de ruogan yijian" (Several opinions of the CCP Central Committee on strengthening leadership over lawmaking work). I have discussed the contents of this document in some detail in "The Erosion of Central Party Control," pp. 397–402.

23. For a richly detailed analysis of the attacks on reforms during this period, see Joseph Fewsmith, *Dilemmas of Reform in China: Political Conflict and Economic Debate* (Armonk, N.Y.: M. E. Sharpe, 1994).

24. The NPC positions on the Central Committee *nomenklatura* list have stayed essentially unchanged during the past decade, despite general efforts after Tiananmen to tighten up central control of appointments elsewhere in the system. These positions include the chairman, vice chairmen, and members of the NPC/SC, the secretary and members of the NPC/SC party core group (*dangzu*), the NPC secretary general and deputy secretaries general, and the chairman and vice chairmen of the Legislative Affairs Work Committee and each of the (now) eight special committees under the NPC/SC. See John P. Burns, *The Chinese Communist Party's Nomenklatura System* (Armonk, N.Y.: M. E. Sharpe, 1989), and John P. Burns, "Strengthening Central CCP Control of Leadership Selection: The 1990 *Nomenklatura*," *China Quarterly*, no. 138 (June 1994), esp. p. 476.

25. On the party meetings before these sessions, see Tanner, "The Erosion of Central Party Control."

26. Kevin J. O'Brien and Li Lianjiang, "Chinese Political Reform and the Question of 'Deputy Quality,'" *China Information*, 8 (Winter 1993–94): 20–31; also O'Brien, *Reform without Liberalization*, esp. pp. 63–65, 131–137, and 215–218.

27. O'Brien and Li, "Deputy Quality," pp. 23–29.

28. Ibid., pp. 24–25.

29. Tanner, "Organizations and Politics in China's Post-Mao Lawmaking System," esp. pp. 74–76.

30. Peng Zhen, "Jiaqiang minzhu yu fazhi jianshe, jiaqiang renda changweihui gongzuo."

31. Most of the organizational data in this section are from CCP and NPC internal documents, speeches, and interviews with legislative scholars and

officials. They are discussed in much greater detail in Tanner, *The Politics of Lawmaking in Post-Mao China,* chap. 4.

32. On this period in the NPC, see Dorothy Solinger, "The Fifth NPC and the Process of Policy-Making," *Asian Survey,* no. 12 (December 1982): 1238–1275; Frances Hoar Foster, "Codification in Post-Mao China," *American Journal of Comparative Law,* 30, no. 3 (Summer 1982): 413–414; and O'Brien, *Reform without Liberalization,* pp. 91–109, 125–156.

33. The drafting of these laws is analyzed in Tanner, *The Politics of Lawmaking in Post-Mao China;* see especially chaps. 6, 7, and 8.

34. Peng Zhen, "Jiaqiang minzhu yu fazhi jianshe, jiaqiang renda changweihui gongzuo."

35. On the center's eroding power to force lower-level implementation, see the essays in David M. Lampton, ed., *Policy Implementation in Post-Mao China* (Berkeley: University of California Press, 1987).

36. See, for example, Andrew Nathan, *Chinese Democracy* (New York: Alfred A. Knopf, 1985); Barrett L. McCormick, *Political Reform in Post-Mao China* (Berkeley: University of California Press, 1990); and O'Brien, *Reform without Liberalization.*

37. Nathan, *Chinese Democracy,* and McCormick, *Political Reform,* provide two of the best Western analyses of the 1979 electoral reforms.

38. The data in this paragraph are all derived from my paper "The Post-Deng National People's Congress: How Much Change? How Fast?," presented to the annual meeting of the Association for Asian Studies, Honolulu, April 1996.

39. The laws were the 1986 Enterprise Bankruptcy Law and the 1989 Public Demonstrations Law, both of which were voted down during NPC/Standing Committee sessions preceding those in which their revised drafts were adopted. This information was provided to the author by two advisors to the NPC, both with access to the information, speaking independently in 1995. See Tanner, "The Post-Deng National People's Congress."

40. Kevin J. O'Brien, "Agents and Remonstrators: Role Accumulation by Chinese People's Congress Deputies," *China Quarterly,* no. 138 (June 1994): 359–380.

41. I am indebted to an anonymous reviewer for this information.

42. R. R. Palmer, *The Age of the Democratic Revolutions: A Political History of Europe and America, 1760–1800,* vol. 1: *The Challenge* (Princeton: Princeton University Press, 1959); Kenneth Shepsle, "Representation and Governance: The Great Legislative Trade-off," *Political Science Quarterly,* 103, no. 3 (Fall 1988): 461–484.

43. Jeffrey W. Hahn, ed., *Democratization in Russia: The Development of Legislative Institutions* (Armonk, N.Y.: M. E. Sharpe, 1996), pp. 3–26.

6. The Struggle over Village Elections

This chapter benefited from the help of many Chinese friends and colleagues. For generous financial support, we would also like to thank the Asia Foundation, the Henry Luce Foundation, the John D. and Catherine T. MacArthur Foundation, the China Times Cultural Foundation, the Sun Yat-sen Culture and Education Foundation, the Ford Foundation, and the Pacific Cultural Foundation.

1. For reports on the implementation of the Organic Law, see Zhongguo jiceng zhengquan jianshe yanjiuhui, eds., *Zhongguo nongcun cunmin weiyuanhui huanjie xuanju zhidu* (Beijing: Zhongguo shehui chubanshe, 1994); and Minzhengbu jiceng zhengquan jianshesi, comp., *Quanguo cunmin zizhi shifan gongzuo jingyan jiaoliu ji chengxiang jiceng xianjin jiti he xianjin geren biaozhang huiyi wenjian huibian* (Beijing: Zhongguo shehui chubanshe, 1996).

2. Kevin J. O'Brien, "Implementing Political Reform in China's Villages," *Australian Journal of Chinese Affairs*, no. 32 (July 1994): 33–60.

3. Daniel Kelliher, "The Chinese Debate over Village Self-Government," *China Journal*, no. 37 (January 1997): 67–75. Kelliher also argues (pp. 75–78) that elections are a foreign propaganda bonanza.

4. Melanie F. Manion, "The Electoral Connection in the Chinese Countryside," *American Political Science Review*, 90, no. 4 (December 1996): 736–48.

5. See Susan V. Lawrence, "Village Representative Assemblies: Democracy, Chinese Style," *Australian Journal of Chinese Affairs*, no. 32 (July 1994): 61–68; O'Brien, "Implementing Political Reform," pp. 47–48; Amy B. Epstein, "Village Elections in China: Experimenting with Democracy," in U.S. Congress, Joint Economic Committee, *China's Economic Future: Challenges to U.S. Policy* (Washington, D.C.: Government Printing Office, 1996), pp. 418–419; and Jean C. Oi, "Economic Development, Stability and Democratic Village Self-Governance," in Maurice Brosseau, Suzanne Pepper, and Tsang Shu-ki, eds., *China Review 1996* (Hong Kong: Chinese University Press, 1996).

6. For an account by a participant in the lawmaking process, see Bai Yihua, "Cunweihui zuzhifa de xingcheng ji qi jiben yuanze" (The making of the Organic Law of Villagers' Committees and its basic principles), in Minzhengbu jiceng zhengquan jianshesi nongcunchu, comp., *Cunmin zizhi shifan jiangxi ban shiyong jiaocai* (Shandong: Laixishi niuxibu caiyinchang, 1991), pp. 86–109. For further discussion of the NPC debates, see O'Brien, "Implementing Political Reform," pp. 36–39.

7. See Peng Zhen, "Woguo jumin weiyuanhui cunmin weiyuanhui diwei he zuoyong lieru le xianfa" (The status and role of residents' committees and villagers' committees in our country have been confirmed by the consti-

tution) (Speech at the Fifth Session of the Fifth NPC, December 26, 1982); "Cunmin weiyuanhui zuzhifa shi guojia zhongyao falü zhi yi" (The Organic Law of Villagers' Committees is one of the nation's important basic laws) (Speech at the twentieth group meeting of the Standing Committee of the Sixth NPC, March 16, 1987); "Cunmin weiyuanhui shi nongcun jiceng cunmin de zizhi zuzhi" (Villagers' committees are a rural grassroots autonomous organization of villagers) (Speech at the twentieth group meeting of the Standing Committee of the Sixth NPC, March 18, 1987); and "Qunzhong zizhi shi fazhan shehuizhuyi minzhu de zhongyao yi huan" (Mass autonomy is an important link in the development of socialist democracy) (Speech at the chairmanship meeting of the Standing Committee of the Sixth NPC, November 23, 1987). Excerpts of these speeches can be found in Bai Yihua, *Zhongguo jiceng zhengquan de gaige yu tansuo* (Beijing: Zhongguo shehui chubanshe, 1996), pp. 294–306.

8. Interview, Beijing, November 1993.

9. Peng Zhen, "Fandui qiangpo mingling, jianchi qunzhong zizhi" (Against coercion and commandism, uphold mass autonomy) (Speech at the fifth joint meeting of delegation leaders and members of the Law Committee of the Sixth NPC, April 6, 1987) and "Yao jianchi cunweihui zizhi zuzhi de xingzhi" (The autonomous nature of villagers' committees should be upheld) (Speech at the chairmanship meeting of the Standing Committee of the Sixth NPC, April 9, 1987). For excerpts, see Bai Yihua, *Zhongguo jiceng zhengquan de gaige yu tansuo,* pp. 294–306. For a discussion of Peng's understanding of the relationship of party leadership to democracy and law, see Pitman B. Potter, *From Leninist Discipline to Socialist Legalism: Peng Zhen on Law and Political Authority in the PRC* (Hong Kong: Hong Kong Institute of Asia-Pacific Studies, 1995). Peng's advocacy of villagers' autonomy may be traced to his experiences with "filtered democracy" in Jin Cha Ji (Potter, *From Leninist Discipline,* p. 14), where village elections were first held in 1938. In a report delivered to the Politburo in 1941, Peng explained why and how village elections were conducted and suggested establishing village representative congresses to supervise elected village leaders. See "Report on the Work of the Party and Specific Policies in the Jin Cha Ji Border Region," in Tony Saich, ed., *The Rise to Power of the Chinese Communist Party: Documents and Analysis* (Armonk, N.Y.: M. E. Sharpe, 1996), pp. 1017–1038.

10. Zhao apparently favored establishing village administrative offices nationwide. Peng reportedly said that one of his major disagreements with Zhao was that Peng believed in mass line democracy while Zhao was an elitist. Interviews, Beijing, November 1993, January 1997.

11. Wang Zhenyao and Wang Shihao, "Guanjian zaiyu jishi tiaozheng dang he

guojia yu nongmin de zhengzhi guanxi—Heilongjiang cunji zuzhi jianshe diaocha" (The key is to adjust the political relationship between the party, state, and peasants—an investigation into constructing village-level organizations in Heilongjiang), *Shehui gongzuo yanjiu*, no. 3 (May 1990): 12.

12. Interview, Beijing, November 1993.

13. Interviews, Beijing, November 1993, January 1997.

14. See "Quanguo cunji zuzhi jianshe gongzuo zuotanhui jiyao" (Summary report of the national workshop on constructing village-level organizations), in Minzhengbu jiceng zhengquan jianshesi nongcunchu, comp., *Cunmin zizhi shifan jiangxi ban shiyong jiaocai*, p. 7.

15. For Mao's original statement, see Huang Yanpei, "Yan'an guilai" (Upon returning from Yan'an), in *Bashi nianlai* (Beijing: Wenshi ziliao chubanshe, 1982), p. 149.

16. Bo Yibo, *Ruogan zhongda juece yu shijian de huigu*, vol. 1 (Beijing: Zhonggong zhongyang dangxiao chubanshe, 1991), p. 157.

17. Peng Zhen, "Cunmin weiyuanhui he jumin weiyuanhui shi qunzhongxing zizhi zuzhi" (Villagers' committees and residents' committees are mass autonomous organizations) (Speech at the twentieth meeting of the Standing Committee of the Fifth NPC, April 22, 1982); "Jiji fahui jumin weiyuanhui, cunmin weiyuanhui de zuoyong" (Give full play to residents' committees and villagers' committees) (Speech at the enlarged meeting of the Central Political-Legal Committee, 2 February 1983).

18. Peng Zhen, "Fandui qiangpo mingling"; Peng Zhen, "Yao jianchi cunweihui." On the relationship between elections and rural unrest, see Kelliher, "Chinese Debate," p. 66; Epstein, "Village Elections in China," pp. 415–416.

19. Wang Zhenyao, "Kaizhan nongmin zizhi shifan huodong de yiyi" (The significance of carrying out peasant autonomy demonstration activities), in Minzhengbu jiceng zhengquan jianshesi nongcunchu, comp., *Cunmin zizhi shifan jiangxi ban shiyong jiaocai*, p. 227.

20. See Zhongguo jiceng zhengquan jianshe yanjiuhui zhongguo nongcun Cunmin zizhi zhidu yanjiu keti zu, *Zhongguo nongcun cunmin weiyuanhui de falü zhidu* (Beijing: Zhongguo shehui chubanshe, 1996), pp. 78–79.

21. Interview, Beijing, January 1997.

22. The ministry's report (Zhongguo jiceng zhengquan jianshe yanjiuhui, *Zhongguo nongcun cunmin weiyuanhui de falü zhidu*, pp. 77–78) made it appear that a central leader (that is, Zhao Ziyang) opposed further experiments with village administrative offices. In fact, there are indications that he supported additional test sites. Interview, Beijing, February 1997.

23. The other three provinces are Hainan, Guangxi, and Yunnan. Jean Oi ("Economic Development," p. 137) has noted the dominance of party

secretaries in industrialized villages and comments that "rich Guangdong province is notable for its unenthusiastic response to carrying out the Organic Law."

24. See Wang Zhenyao, "Kaizhan nongmin zizhi shifan huodong de yiyi," p. 225.

25. Interviews, Hebei, October–November 1993. For a discussion of the cadre responsibility system, see Kevin J. O'Brien and Lianjiang Li, "Selective Policy Implementation in Rural China," *Comparative Politics*, forthcoming.

26. See Yang Xuejun and Sun Xinmin, "Lishun xiang zhengfu yu cunmin weiyuanhui zhijian de guanxi" (Rationalize relations between township governments and villagers' committees), in Zhongguo jiceng zhengquan jianshe yanjiuhui, eds., *Shijian yu sikao* (Practice and reflections) (Shenyang: Liaoning chubanshe, 1989), p. 113.

27. See Bao Yonghui, "Cunmin zizhi fuhe bu fuhe Zhongguo guoqing?" (Does villagers' autonomy accord with China's conditions?), *Xiangzhen luntan*, no. 6 (June 1991).

28. Interviews, Hebei, May 1994, December 1995. Reports of rigged village elections can be found in Zhongguo jiceng zhengquan jianshe yanjiuhui, eds., *Shijian yu sikao;* Zhongguo jiceng zhengquan jianshe yanjiuhui, comp., *Shijian yu sikao* (Practice and reflections) (Beijing: Zhongguo shehui chubanshe, 1992); and Zhongguo jiceng zhengquan jianshe yanjiuhui, eds., *Zhongguo nongcun cunmin weiyuanhui huanjie xuanju zhidu.*

29. Interviews, Beijing, October 1993, July 1994, January–February 1997.

30. Interview, Hebei, December 1995. "Leadership" implies nearly total control by a superior over a subordinate—control that extends to personnel appointment and an unquestioned right to issue orders concerning budgets, plans, and administrative decisions. "Guidance" indicates an advice-granting relationship between superiors and subordinates, yet can also include extensive supervision. See Kevin J. O'Brien and Laura M. Luehrmann, "Institutionalizing Chinese Legislatures: Trade-offs between Autonomy and Capacity," *Legislative Studies Quarterly,* 23, no. 1 (February 1998): 91–109.

31. See Zhang Houan, "Cunmin weiyuanhui de xianzhuang, wenti yu duice" (The current situation of villagers' committees, problems and countermeasures), in Zhang Houan, Bai Yihua, and Wu Zhilong, eds., *Zhongguo xiangzhen zhengquan jianshe* (Chengdu: Sichuan chubanshe, 1992), p. 203; Zhang Houan, "Cong xingzhenghua zou xiang zizhi" (From administrativeness move toward autonomy), in Zhongguo jiceng zhengquan jianshe yanjiuhui, eds., *Shijian yu sikao* (Shenyang: Liaoning chubanshe, 1989), p. 128.

32. Interviews, Hebei, October-November, 1993. See also Lu Xiaozhang,

"Qing gei tamen jianqing dian fudan ba" (Please reduce their burden a little bit), *Xiangzhen luntan*, no. 4 (April 1994): 24; interviews, Shandong, July 1994.

33. See Kelliher, "Chinese Debate," p. 78; Manion, "Electoral Connection," pp. 737–738; O'Brien, "Implementing Political Reform," pp. 54–57.

34. Tang Jinsu, "Woguo cunji zuzhi xianzhuang ji duice fenxi" (An analysis of the current situation of our country's village organization and counter-measures), in Zhang Houan, Bai Yihua, and Wu Zhilong, *Zhongguo xiang-zhen zhengquan jianshe*, p. 239. See also the discussion of "recalcitrants" in Lianjiang Li and Kevin J. O'Brien, "Villagers and Popular Resistance in Contemporary China," *Modern China*, 22, no. 1 (January 1996): 28–61.

35. See Lin Chen and Zhang Yun, "Qiancun zhengquan shi zenyang lan diao de?" (How did governance in Qiancun become rotten?), *Banyuetan (neibuban)*, no. 8 (August 1996): 21; Hua Bing, "Tiao longmen de guanjian he zai?" (Where is the key to jump through the dragon's door?), *Xiangzhen luntan*, no. 4 (April 1992): 10–11; and Zhang Chenggong, "Cunzhang si yu chunjie" (Village heads die at spring festival), *Landun*, no. 3 (March 1993): 23–27.

36. Interview, Hebei, October 1993.

37. Amy Epstein ("Village Elections in China," pp. 418–419) argues that boss politics is most common in wealthy villages where, however, elections are not particularly competitive.

38. See Fang Yan, "Shandong sheng Zoucheng shi cunmin weiyuanhui huan-jie xuanju diaocha baogao" (An investigation report on the reelection of villagers' committees in Zoucheng city, Shandong province), unpublished 1993 report of the Ministry of Agriculture, p. 16. Similar sentiments were also expressed in an interview, Hebei, October 1993.

39. Interviews, Hebei, October-November 1993, May and August 1994, December 1995; Beijing, January–February 1997.

40. Interview, Beijing, February 1997.

41. See Zhengdingxian minzhengju, "Shixing cunmin daibiao huiyi zhidu jiakuai nongcun jiceng minzhu jincheng" (Implement the villagers' rep-resentative assembly system, quicken the construction of rural grass-roots democracy), unpublished report, 1991, p. 3.

42. See Bao Yonghui, "Shenhua nongcun dierbu gaige de qiji" (The turning point in deepening the second stage of rural reform), *Xiangzhen luntan*, no. 5 (May 1991): 18. For similar stories, see Wang Zhenyao, "Kaizhan nongmin zizhi shifan huodong de yiyi," p. 298; Interviews, Hebei, October 1993.

43. Bao Yonghui, "Cunmin zizhi fuhe bu fuhe Zhongguo guoqing?" p. 17.

44. See Shao Xingliang et al., "Yi min wei tian" (Regarding the people as

sovereign), *Xiangzhen luntan,* no. 4 (April 1994): 10–11. Survey data from four counties suggest that, when villagers contact officials, about two fifths of all mentions concern elections. M. Kent Jennings, "Political Participation in the Chinese Countryside," *American Political Science Review,* 91, no. 2 (June 1997): 361–372.

45. For more discussion, see Kevin J. O'Brien, "Rightful Resistance," *World Politics,* 49, no. 1 (October 1996): 43–45.

46. See Tian Yuan, "Zhongguo nongcun jiceng de minzhu zhilu" (The pathway to grass-roots democracy in rural China), *Xiangzhen luntan,* no. 6 (June 1993): 3–4.

47. Interviews, Beijing, January–February 1997; Hebei, October–November 1993, August 1994, and December 1995.

48. For a discussion of this dynamic, see Wu Liming, "Shang qian xuanmin taohui xuanju quan" (Nearly one thousand voters regained their right to vote), *Minzhu yu fazhi,* no. 4 (21 February 1996): 4–5.

49. Interviews, Beijing, February 1997; the State Department estimate is found in International Republican Institute, "China's Economic Future: Challenges to U.S. Policy" (Study papers submitted to the Joint Economic Committee, Congress of the United States, August 1996), p. 3; the magazine editor offered his assessment in an interview, Beijing, February 1997.

50. See Gao Zhongyi, "Guanxi wang, baohu san, nanbatian" (Relationship networks, protective umbrellas, and a local bully), *Landun,* no. 11 (November 1994): 4–7; Cheng Tongshun, "Nongcun jiceng xuanju zai changshi zhong jianguan" (Grass-roots rural elections are being perfected through trials), *Zhongguo nongmin,* no. 11 (November 1996): 31; Zhongguo jiceng zhengquan jianshe yanjiuhui, eds., *Zhongguo nongcun cunmin weiyuanhui huanjie xuanju zhidu;* Zhang Houan and Meng Guilan, "Wanshan cunmin weiyuanhui de minzhu zhidu, tuijin nongcun zhengzhi wending yu fazhan" (Perfect the democratic electoral system of villagers' committees, advance rural political stability and development), *Shehuizhuyi yanjiu,* no. 4 (August 1993): 41.

51. Interview, Hebei, October 1993.

52. Interview, Hebei, October 1993.

53. Interviews, Shandong, July 1994.

54. See Epstein, "Village Elections in China," pp. 414–415.

55. Interviews, Fujian, July 1992.

56. Interview, Hebei, October 1993. Kelliher ("Chinese Debate," pp. 73–75) agrees that elected cadres may distribute burdens more fairly, but downplays the practical benefits that village self-government offers.

57. Interviews, Beijing, July 1994.

58. Interviews, Hebei, October 1993; Beijing, February 1997.

59. Interview, Hebei, October 1993. For a similar report, see Deng Baoquan and Zhao Yiyun, "Zengqiang minzhu yishi gaohao cunmin zizhi" (Enhance democratic consciousness, do village autonomy well), in Zhongguo jiceng zhengquan jianshe yanjiuhui, comp., *Shijian yu sikao* (Beijing: Zhongguo shehui chubanshe, 1992), p. 108. On VRAs, see Lawrence, "Village Representative Assemblies," pp. 61–68.

60. Interview, Beijing, February 1997. Jean Oi ("Economic Development," p. 141) has suggested that one weakness of the law is that "it does not include the accountability of the party secretary to the villagers." Daniel Kelliher ("Chinese Debate," p. 84) largely agrees, though he also points out that "concurrent office-holding may lead to popular control over the local Party."

61. Interviews, Beijing, June 1994.

62. See Zhou Ziqing and Zhao Zhenji, "Liangpiao zhi—nongcun dangzuzhi jianshe de youyi changshi" (The two-ballot system—a useful experiment in the construction of rural party organizations), *Xiangzhen luntan*, no. 6 (June 1992): 6–7.

63. Interview, Beijing, December 1995.

64. Interview, Hebei, October 1993.

65. Interview, Hebei, October 1993.

66. On villagers' threatening to vote out cadres who enforce birth control, see Wang Kean, "Cunmin weiyuanhui de xianzhuang yu gaige" (The present situation and reform of villagers' committees), in Zhang Houan, Bai Yihua, and Wu Zhilong, *Zhongguo xiangzhen zhengquan jianshe*, p. 188. On such cadres surviving an election, see Fei Yuncheng, "Minzhu xuanju de linghun" (The soul of democratic elections), *Xiangzhen luntan*, no. 8 (August 1993): 3; Zhongguo jiceng zhengquan jianshe yanjiuhui, eds., *Zhongguo nongcun cunmin weiyuanhui huanjie xuanju zhidu*, pp. 91–92.

67. Fang Yan, "Shandong sheng Zoucheng shi cunmin weiyuanhui," p. 17. Cf. O'Brien, "Implementing Political Reform," pp. 57–58, on "run-away villages." On stories of cadres who enforce a hated policy but go on to win re-election, see Kelliher, "Chinese Debate," p. 74.

68. See Jiang Zemin, *Gaoju Deng Xiaoping lilun weida qizhi, ba jianshe you Zhongguo tese shehuizhuyi shiye quanmian tuixiang 21 shiji* (Hold high the great banner of Deng Xiaoping theory in order to advance the cause of building socialism with Chinese characteristics into the 21st century) (Beijing: Renmin chubanshe, 1997), p. 36; Li Peng, *Zhengfu gongzuo baogao* (Government work report), delivered at the fifth session of the Eighth NPC, March 1, 1997.

69. International Republican Institute, "China's Economic Future," p. 8.

70. See, for example, Yuan Genbo, Helian Xidian, and Yang Jianmin, "Rang

nongmin deng shang zhengzhi wutai chang zhujiao" (Let farmers come on the political stage and play the role of heroes), *Zhongguo minzheng*, no. 9 (September 1996): 4–7.

71. Interviews, Hebei, October-November 1993.
72. Interviews, Beijing, January 1997.

7. Mass Political Behavior in Beijing

The author acknowledges the support of National Science Foundation grant INT-88-14199. I would also like to thank the Opinion Research Center of China for the first survey and the Research Center for Contemporary China of Peking University for the second survey.

1. Seymour Martin Lipset, "Some Social Requisites of Democracy," *American Political Science Review*, 53 (1959): 75. Recently, Francis Fukuyama boldly argues that modernization makes liberal democracy so inevitable that history has been concluded. See Francis Fukuyama, "Capitalism and Democracy: The Missing Link," *Dialogue*, 2 (1993): 2–7.

2. Karl Deutsch, "Social Mobilization and Political Development," *American Political Science Review*, 53:3 (1961): 493–514; Lipset, "Some Social Requisites of Democracy"; James Coleman, "Conclusion: The Political System of Developing Areas," in Gabriel A. Almond and James Coleman et al., eds., *The Politics of the Developing Areas* (Princeton: Princeton University Press, 1960); Alex Inkeles and David Smith, *Becoming Modern: Individual Change in Six Developing Countries* (Cambridge: Harvard University Press, 1974); Jan F. Triska and Paul M. Cocks, eds., *Political Development in Eastern Europe* (New York: Praeger, 1977); Samuel Huntington and Joan M. Nelson, *No Easy Choice: Political Participation in Developing Countries* (Cambridge: Harvard University Press, 1976). For a recent reevaluation of the thesis, see Ross E. Burkhart and Michael S. Lewis-Beck, "Comparative Democracy: The Economic Development Thesis," *American Political Science Review*, 88 (December 1994): 903–910.

3. For a discussion of the impact of government output on political participation, see Myron Weiner, "Political Participation: Crisis of the Political Process," in Leonard Binder et al., *Crises and Sequences in Political Development* (Princeton: Princeton University Press, 1971), pp. 173–175.

4. Ibid., p. 44.

5. Increased requirements for training labor, increased opportunity for social mobility, and the expansion of formal education will lead to a change in the social structure—that is, the pyramidal class structure associated with peasant and peasant-worker societies gives rise to a more diamond-

shaped structure—the middle stratum expands and eventually becomes the majority class as greater numbers of citizens become members of the educated white-collar class. See Norman H. Nie, G. Bingham Powell, Jr., and Kenneth Prewitt, "Social Structure and Political Participation: Developmental Relationships, Part I and Part II," *American Political Science Review*, 63, nos. 2–3 (1969): 362.

6. Although the postulates of the culturalist approach lead to the expectation of political continuity, the "idea that rapid, large-scale contextual changes are personally disorienting and culturally disruptive is hardly new." See Harry Eckstein, "A Culturalist Theory of Political Change," *American Political Science Review*, 82, no. 3 (September 1988): 796.

7. Cultural change usually manifests itself in two ways—changes in psychological orientation and changes through generational replacement. Increases in level of education, media access, and wealth may gradually transform people's orientation toward political objects. Furthermore, because the consequences of evolving economic and social structures do not fall equally on a population, new cohorts with relatively short memories and open minds are more vulnerable and susceptible to the effects of change brought about by the process of modernization. With new generations gradually replacing older ones, the political culture of a society may also be altered.

8. Gabriel A. Almond and Sidney Verba, *The Civic Culture: Political Attitudes and Democracy in Five Nations* (Princeton: Princeton University Press, 1963); Robert A. Dahl, *Who Governs?* (New Haven: Yale University Press, 1961), pp. 282–301; Lester Milbrath and M. L. Goel, *Political Participation: How and Why Do People Get Involved in Politics?* 2nd ed. (Chicago: Rand McNally, 1977).

9. See Lianjiang Li and Kevin J. O'Brien, "Villagers and Popular Resistance in Contemporary China," *Modern China*, 22, no. 1 (January 1996): 28–61; Kevin J. O'Brien, "Rightful Resistance," *World Politics*, 49, no. 1 (October 1996): 31–55.

10. For the situation of trade unions, see Anita Chan, "Revolution or Corporatism? Workers and Trade Unions in Post-Mao China," *Australian Journal of Chinese Affairs*, no. 29 (January 1993): 31–61; on women's associations, see, among others, Stanley Rosen, ed., "Women and Politics in China (I)," *Chinese Law and Government*, 26, no. 5 (1993): 3–87.

11. For example, Gordon White argues that "successful industrialization remakes society and lays down the economic basis of a new form of 'civil society' which serves both to limit the power of the state and provides the political impetus for democratization." See Gordon White, "Democratization and Economic Reform in China," *Australian Journal of Chinese Affairs*,

no. 31 (January 1994): 81; see also Gordon White, *Riding the Tiger: The Politics of Economic Reform in Post-Mao China* (Stanford: Stanford University Press, 1993); William Overholt, *The Rise of China: How Economic Reform Is Creating a New Superpower* (New York: W. W. Norton, 1993).

12. Vivienne Shue, "State Power and Social Organization in China," in Joel S. Migdal, Atul Kohli, and Vivienne Shue, eds., *State Power and Social Forces* (New York: Cambridge University Press, 1994), pp. 65–88; Dorothy J. Solinger, *China's Transition from Socialism: Statist Legacies and Market Reforms, 1980–1990* (Armonk, N.Y.: M. E. Sharpe, 1993).

13. The differing views of Gordon White and Barrett McCormick on how China can best establish a prosperous democracy touch on this issue. While White believes the transition is irresistible given economic development, McCormick argues that the experiences of the socialist countries in Eastern Europe and the Soviet Union show that "dictatorship of a particularly severe sort can last decades past industrialization." See White, "Democratization and Economic Reform in China," p. 81, and Barrett L. McCormick, "Democracy or Dictatorship?: A Response to Gordon White," *Australian Journal of Chinese Affairs,* no. 31 (January 1994): 108.

14. The interviews were conducted by students of the sociology and statistical departments of the People's University. A total of 941 interviews were scheduled and 757 were completed, which represents a response rate of 80 percent. The most important reason for survey nonresponse was no contact. Refusals were rare. The potential bias due to survey nonresponse can be ignored.

15. The survey was conducted by students from the Department of Political Science of Peking University. A total of 1,198 interviews were scheduled in the second survey and 895 were completed, a response rate of 74.1 percent.

16. According to Kish, a survey population must be defined in terms of (1) content, (2) units, (3) extent, and (4) time. The population of the first survey is thus defined as (1) all persons, (2) in family units, (3) in eight urban districts of Beijing, and (4) in 1988. The first three elements of the second survey are the same as in the first one; the last element differs. For discussion, see Leslie Kish, *Survey Sampling* (New York: John Wiley & Sons, 1965), p. 7.

17. The only exception is the study of the relationship between economic development and unconventional political participation in Western democracies. See M. Kent Jennings et al., *Continuities in Political Action: A Longitudinal Study of Political Orientations in Three Western Democracies* (Berlin: Walter de Gruyter, 1989).

18. For comparison, the average salary figures used here are based on the

constant price of 1979 RMB. The 1988 average salary figure comes from the Statistical Bureau of Beijing, *Beijing tongji nianjian, 1989* (Beijing: Zhongguo tongji chubanshe, 1989), pp. 476, 439, and the 1996 figure comes from the *Beijing tongji nianjian, 1997* (Beijing: Zhongguo tongji chubanshe, 1997), pp. 87, 332.

19. For per capita living space in 1988, see *Beijing tongji nianjian, 1989*, p. 549. For data of 1996, see *Beijing tongji nianjian, 1997*, p. 392.

20. The figure includes pork, beef, mutton, and fish and other sea food. For 1988 figures, see *Beijing tongji nianjian, 1989*, p. 568. For 1995 figures, see *Beijing tongji nianjian, 1996*, p. 412.

21. If we were to measure the difference monetarily, we would find that the gap between rich and poor actually increased, reflecting the fact that the rich became richer. Here it is more important to determine whether people are able to keep body and soul together and no longer worry about basic needs so that they have extra time and energy to be concerned about politics and public affairs. For this purpose, the items measured in the figure are more appropriate.

22. Economic development usually brings about a cluster of social changes—exposure to mass media, changes in residence, increases in education, and increases in general level of income. Empirically, the impact of urban residence and income on political participation cannot be confirmed. See Nie, Powell, and Prewitt, "Social Structure and Political Participation, Part I and Part II." Studies of participation in many other societies, including advanced democracies, further demonstrate that income has only a marginal role in mobilizing people to participate in politics. For example, Wolfinger and Rosenstone show that as long as people can take care of their basic needs, the impact of income is negligible. See Raymond Wolfinger and Steven J. Rosenstone, *Who Votes?* (New Haven: Yale University Press, 1980), pp. 23–26.

23. Tianjian Shi, *Political Participation in Beijing* (Cambridge: Harvard University Press, 1997), p. 215.

24. Weiner, "Political Participation," pp. 166–167.

25. Philip E. Converse, "Change in the American Electorate," in Angus Campbell and Philip E. Converse, eds., *The Human Meaning of Social Change* (New York: Russell Sage Foundation, 1972), pp. 263–337; George Balch, "Multiple Indicators in Survey Research: The Concept 'Sense of Political Efficacy,'" *Political Methodology*, 1 (1974): 1–43; Stephen C. Craig, Richard G. Niemi, and Glenn E. Silver, "Political Efficacy and Trust: A Report on the NES Pilot Study Items," *Political Behavior*, 12, no. 3 (1990): 290.

26. There are two possible explanations for the change. One is that the economic development in China has changed the scope of governmental

activities, making people realize that their lives are now influenced by government decisions at various levels. Another possibility is that the increase in the general level of education has made more people become aware of the impact of government.

27. The figure is reached by adding the total population of the sampled areas together (8,164,000), adjusted for people who did not reach the sampling age at the time of the survey. The figure is then multiplied by .017, which is the percentage difference between the people who claimed to have engaged in strikes in 1996 and in 1988.

28. Further analysis shows that the decline in voting turnout is due to voter apathy and ignorance.

29. Sidney Verba, Norman H. Nie, and Jae-on Kim, *Participation and Political Equality: A Seven-Nation Comparison* (New York: Cambridge University Press, 1978), pp. 73–74.

30. Shi, *Political Participation*, pp. 39–42.

31. Verba, Nie, and Kim, *Participation and Political Equality*, pp. 51–52.

32. The scales are composed of simple additions of respondents' answers to questions in both surveys asking about people's involvement in alternative participatory activities.

33. The grouping of different participatory acts is determined by the result of the exploratory factor analysis.

34. Channels of appeal are easily accessible to ordinary citizens. Relatively little initiative is required to take action in this category. Neither the regime nor bureaucrats oppose people who express their opinions through these channels, and there is little risk associated with them. Shi, *Political Participation*, p. 120.

35. Different from acts belonging to the appeals mode, acts in this category are usually done in a confrontational manner—participants are trying to coerce local officials to take care of their interests. By enlarging the scope of conflict, they try to bring other actors into the struggle to change the balance of power between themselves and decisionmakers.

36. Another way to contact officials is through *guanxi*, or instrumental-personal ties. A major difficulty facing participants in any society is how to overcome the hierarchical relationship between themselves and government officials. Through a "subtle form of reciprocation bordering on bribery" people can turn the hierarchical relationship between themselves and government officials into one of exchange. See Andrew G. Walder, *Communist Neo-Traditionalism* (Berkeley: University of California Press, 1986), pp. 179–186. Since *guanxi* has to be cultivated and bribery must be skillfully managed for bureaucrats to accept it, activities in this category are difficult. Moreover, a great deal of initiative is required for people to

gamble what they have in hand for something they may get in the future. Because all the acts in this mode are outlawed by the authorities, there are substantial risks associated with them, although it is the bureaucrats rather than participants who bear the risks.

37. Resistance is a difficult act and requires great initiative on the part of participants. By withdrawing support for bureaucrats and damaging their ability to fulfill their functional role as leaders, participants can also put pressure on local bureaucrats to grant concessions. Since none of these acts is permitted by the authorities, engaging in them usually puts participants in confrontation with not only bureaucrats but also the regime. Risks associated with resistance are high.

38. For discussion of the method, see, among others, J. H. Goodnight, *Tests of the Hypotheses in Fixed-Effects Linear Models*, SAS Technical Report R-101 (Cary, N.C.: SAS Institute, 1978), and J. H. Goodnight and W. R. Harvey, *Least-Squares Means in the Fixed-Effects General Linear Models*, SAS Technical Report R-103 (Cary, N.C.: SAS Institute, 1978).

39. I focus on appeals and adversarial activities here because of limitations of space. But another reason for me to drop cronyism, resistance, and protests is the relatively lower number of people who reported engaging in such acts.

40. See Shi, *Political Participation*, pp. 79–81, 116–117, 235–237.

41. As Almond and Powell argue, "Some interest articulation involves only a citizen and his family, as when a veteran writes his congressman for help in getting his benefits approved, or when a homeowner asks the local party precinct leader to see if she can have her driveway snow-plowed regularly. These narrow, personal demands on the political system are called parochial contacts." See Gabriel A. Almond and G. Bingham Powell, Jr., eds., *Comparative Politics Today: A World View*, 2d ed. (Boston: Little, Brown and Company, 1980), p. 54.

42. People are now more likely to go through trade unions, their local people's congresses, and higher-level governmental organizations to challenge the decisions of local bureaucrats and even general government policy. When a person seeks out deputies to people's congresses, he is unlikely to resolve issues of policy implementation, but more likely to express his opinion on the policy itself.

43. Zehra F. Arat, *Democracy and Human Rights in Developing Countries* (Boulder, Colo.: Lynne Rienner Publishers, 1991), p. 52.

44. For example, even though authorities in China strictly prohibited people from participating in strikes and demonstrations after 1989, the survey indicates that an increasing number of people have become involved in such activities to express their opinions.

45. Guillermo O'Donnell and Philippe Schmitter, eds., *Transitions from Authoritarian Rule: Tentative Conclusions about Uncertain Democracies* (Baltimore: Johns Hopkins University Press, 1986), pp. 15–37.
46. Kevin J. O'Brien, "Implementing Political Reform in China's Villages," *Australian Journal of Chinese Affairs*, no. 32 (July 1994): 33–59.

8. The Changing Role of Workers

1. The works on the Polish events of 1979–1989 are voluminous. See, for example, Timothy Garton Ash, *The Polish Revolution: Solidarity, 1980–82* (London: Jonathan Cape, 1983); Jadwiga Staniszkis, *Poland's Self-Limiting Revolution* (Princeton: Princeton University Press, 1984); and Alain Touraine et al., *Solidarity: The Analysis of a Social Movement, 1980–81* (Cambridge: Cambridge University Press, 1983). For an account of the growing alienation of workers from the state in the Soviet Union, see Walter Connor, *The Accidental Proletariat* (Princeton: Princeton University Press, 1991). It is not my contention that workers played the central role in the downfall of any of the Leninist regimes in Eastern Europe except Poland. The growing discontent of workers, however, helped deprive other regimes of the confidence that they could rely on the support of this supposedly "leading class." As a result, the ability of these regimes to withstand the other pressures and crises that beset them in the 1980s weakened.
2. For details on these trends in the Soviet Union, see Connor, *Accidental Proletariat*.
3. There is not space here to develop these parallels with Marxist analysis fully. It might be noted, though, that Poland's distinctiveness in having a dedicated intelligentsia helping to form the emerging consciousness of the working class and direct it against the state also fits the Marxist framework, although that intelligentsia opposed rather than supported socialism.
4. See the discussion in Jeanne L. Wilson, "The 'Polish Lesson': China and Poland, 1980–1990," *Studies in Comparative Communism*, 23, no. 2 (1990): 259–280.
5. The preceding statistics are drawn from Andrew Walder, "The Remaking of the Chinese Working Class, 1949–1981," *Modern China*, 10, no. 1 (1984): 3–48. The figures given for nonstate industrial employment include managerial, technical, and office personnel, and not just workers. For state industrial firms Walder gives the total employment (worker and employee) as 34 million in 1981. If one can assume that the proportions of workers versus employees in urban collective enterprises are the same as

in state industry and that all of the temporary personnel are working in state firms, then one would conclude that China at the time had close to 55 million urban workers, with about 77 percent of these employed in state firms.

6. For details on such practices, consult American Rural Small-scale Industry Delegation, *Rural Small-scale Industry in the People's Republic of China* (Berkeley: University of California Press, 1977), pp. 51–54.

7. Jack Potter at one point argued that the absence of private property and the utilization of work points meant that China's commune members should be considered rural proletarians, rather than peasants. See his article "From Peasants to Rural Proletarians: Social and Economic Change in Rural Communist China," in Jack Potter, ed., *Peasant Society* (Boston: Little, Brown, 1967). In retrospect this contention seems misleading, since there was very little that was proletarian about the nature of China's rural organization at the time, even in commune-run factories.

8. Andrew Walder cites a figure of only 320,000 self-employed individuals in the Chinese urban economy in 1979. See Walder, "Remaking of the Chinese Working Class," p. 21.

9. Originally in the 1950s collective enterprises were conceived as operating as independent financial units, able to reward their employees at various levels depending upon their profitability. By the 1970s, however, collective enterprises were almost as bound by official regulations governing their wages and fringe benefits as were state enterprises. As a result, their levels of compensation often approached but were somewhat inferior to those in comparable state firms, and their level of provision of fringe benefits was also less complete and generous. The smallest collective firms provided little except modest wages to their employees, but very large collective firms often provided compensation and benefits not that inferior to state firms.

10. Here I am emphasizing the other side of the coin from Walder in his article "The Remaking of the Chinese Working Class." By stressing the various lesser subtypes of workers in the Mao era, including rural factory workers, temporary workers in urban firms, and those employed in neighborhood workshops, Walder highlights the castelike segmentation of the Chinese working class of that era. If one discounts village factory workers, as I do here, and then considers the dominance of state and large collective firms, then the similarities in the condition of workers in the Mao era are highlighted.

11. Andrew Walder cites figures showing that the average industrial firm in China had grown from 24 employees in 1949 to 125 employees in 1956 (Walder, "Remaking of the Chinese Working Class," p. 8). By the end of

the Mao era the figure had grown to 405 employees in state industrial firms and 134 employees in the average urban collective enterprise (ibid., p. 35).

12. In the Soviet Union university graduates were, like their Chinese counterparts, subject to mandatory state assignment to an initial job. The frequent Soviet press criticism of evasion of this obligation (as in the high percentage of agricultural college graduates who secured urban jobs), however, suggests a less rigid bureaucratic allocation system than in Mao-era China. Individuals with lower levels of education and college graduates who had completed initial job assignments were under no obligation to remain at the same workplace indefinitely.

13. These features have been stressed by Andrew Walder as leading to a quasi-feudal dependency of employees on their superiors. See his book *Communist Neo-Traditionalism* (Berkeley: University of California Press, 1986). Walder also points out another contrast—there was no counterpart in the Soviet Union to China's category of urban collective firms. In an earlier study I pointed out that there was no counterpart in the Soviet Union to the regular political study and group criticism among ordinary employees as practiced in China. See my book *Small Groups and Political Rituals in China* (Berkeley: University of California Press, 1974).

14. The terms used here were made famous by Albert Hirschman, in his book *Exit, Voice, and Loyalty* (Cambridge: Harvard University Press, 1970). For an application of these categories to explain the enforced display of loyalty within Chinese work units, see Gail Henderson and Myron Cohen, *The Chinese Hospital* (New Haven: Yale University Press, 1984).

15. See the comments on worker loyalty in various systems in Anita Chan, "Chinese Enterprise Reforms: Convergence with the Japanese Model?" in Barrett McCormick and Jonathan Unger, eds., *China after Socialism* (Armonk, N.Y.: M. E. Sharpe, 1996). For a set of insightful essays comparing the Chinese *danwei* with work organizations in pre-1949 China, in Japan, and in the former Soviet Union, see Xiaobo Lu and Elizabeth J. Perry, eds., *Danwei: The Changing Chinese Workplace in Historical and Comparative Perspective* (Armonk, N.Y.: M. E. Sharpe, 1997).

16. See the discussion in Walder, "Remaking of the Chinese Working Class," pp. 40–42. By this claim Walder means that post-1949 changes weakened the potential for proletarian self-consciousness and opposition to other classes. See, however, the contrary view presented in Elizabeth Perry, "Labor's Battle for Political Space: The Role of Worker Associations in Contemporary China," in D. Davis et al., eds., *Urban Spaces in Contemporary China* (Cambridge: Cambridge University Press, 1995).

17. The 1994 edition of the yearbook *Zhongguo nongcun tongji nianjian* (Chi-

nese rural statistical yearbook), published by the Chinese Statistical Publishing House in Beijing, provides a total of 72.6 million employees in rural industrial firms at the township level and below in 1993, out of a total of rural nonagricultural employment in that year of 123.5 million. No comprehensive statistics are available on what percentage of these employees are workers, but a survey of 3,000 TVEs yielded an estimate of 80.7 percent of total employment composed of workers, which would yield a worker-only total of about 58 million. These figures were kindly provided to me by Samuel Ho, personal communication. It should be noted that other sectors beyond manufacturing that are excluded from these totals, such as construction, also contain workers, so that the actual total of proletarians operating in China's countryside is higher than this figure.

18. This position is advanced particularly by Jean Oi in her article "The Role of the Local State in China's Transitional Economy," *China Quarterly*, no. 144 (December 1995): 1132–1149.

19. See, for example, the account in Kate Xiao Zhou, *How the Farmers Changed China* (Boulder, Colo.: Westview Press, 1996). Some part of the disagreement here may involve a focus on number of firms versus share of industrial output. Since privately owned firms tend to be smaller than collectively owned TVEs, the former may be more numerous but still less important in the overall economy than the latter.

20. Since 1993 China's Ministry of Agriculture has been encouraging TVEs to transform themselves into stock-holding cooperatives. See David D. Li, "Ambiguous Property Rights in China—Three Analytical Perspectives," *Davidson Window*, Winter 1997, p. 7. Presumably when this happens, if shares are held by local governments, management, and employees, the mixed nature of the TVE form in terms of property rights is further accentuated.

21. The miserly support of the state for rural development and also changes in local finance regulations mean that local industrial enterprises can become cash cows to support much else in the village, and villages without meaningful nonagricultural firms have great difficulty funding schools, public welfare, and everything else.

22. Jean Oi, personal communication.

23. See David Peetz, "China's New Labour Law: Forging Collective Bargaining from the Rusting Iron Rice Bowl," in Lo Chi Kin, Suzanne Pepper, and Tsui Kai Yuen, eds., *China Review 1995* (Hong Kong: Chinese University Press, 1995).

24. See, for example, the accounts provided by Anita Chan, "The Emerging Patterns of Industrial Relations in China," *China Information*, 9, no. 1 (1995): 36–59; Dorothy Solinger, "The Chinese Work Unit and Transient

Labor in the Transition from Socialism," *Modern China*, 21, no. 2 (1995): 165–168. Both Chan and Solinger stress that these conditions are common to both TVEs and many foreign-owned and joint venture firms, a point to which I will return below.

25. TVEs may also be more able than state firms to engage in tax evasion and other activities that will keep them competitive even if they do not operate very efficiently.

26. For details on the motivations of migrants who go to work in rural firms, see Ching-kwan Lee, "Production Politics and Labour Identities: Migrant Workers in South China," in Kin, Pepper, and Tsui Kai Yuen, eds., *China Review 1995*.

27. Figures cited in Lora Sabin, "New Bosses in the Workers' State: The Growth of Non-State Sector Employment in China," *China Quarterly*, no. 140 (December 1994): 946.

28. Alternative estimates provided by ibid., p. 968.

29. See the discussion in Deborah Davis, "Urban Catch-up: Impact of Greater Marketization on Job Mobility," *China Journal*, forthcoming. However, I have been unable to find figures comparing urban private manufacturing firm wages with state and collective firm wages, as opposed to wages in the overall sectors.

30. On the general process of new, private sector firms emulating state firms in providing a range of fringe benefits, see the discussion in Corinna-Barbara Francis, "Reproduction of *Danwei* Institutional Features in the Context of China's Market Economy: The Case of Haidian District's High-Tech Sector," *China Quarterly*, no. 147 (1996): 839–859.

31. See the discussion in Sabin, "New Bosses in the Workers' State," and in Dorothy Solinger, "The Floating Population Enters Urban Labor Markets," photocopy.

32. See the discussion in Dorothy Solinger, "The Floating Population Enters Urban Labor Markets," and by the same author, "The Impact of the Floating Population on the Danwei: Shifts in the Pattern of Labor Mobility Control and Entitlement Provision," photocopy.

33. See Sabin, "New Bosses in the Workers' State," p. 946. A 1995 source gives a figure of 6 million workers in the entire foreign-funded sector, with 76 percent of this total attributable to Hong Kong and Taiwan firms. See Chan, "The Emerging Patterns of Industrial Relations in China," p. 47.

34. This major distinction between two types of foreign firms and two patterns of industrial relations is stressed by both Anita Chan and Dorothy Solinger. See their works cited in notes 32–33. Japanese-owned firms in China appear to be a hybrid that fits the pattern of Western firms more than of Asian firms.

35. In particular, the culture of dependency on enterprise party officials described by Andrew Walder is somewhat muted in these firms. See the discussion in Margaret Pearson, "Breaking the Bonds of 'Organized Dependence': Managers in China's Foreign Sector," *Studies in Comparative Communism*, 25, no. 1 (1992): 57–78.

36. See, for example, the ethnographic details provided in Ching Kwan Lee, "Engendering the Worlds of Labor: Women Workers, Labor Markets, and Production Politics in the South China Economic Miracle," *American Sociological Review*, 60, no. 3 (1995): 378–397.

37. See the discussion in Anita Chan, "Trade Union and Collective Bargaining in South China," photocopy, 1995. Chan and others note, however, a variety of signs of increased efforts by local and national level leaders of the All-China Federation of Trade Unions to promote the interests of workers and call attention to industrial abuses.

38. In recent years, however, Russia has increasingly moved toward privatizing state enterprises, signaling a switch toward the first reform strategy.

39. Nicholas Lardy, personal communication. Overall employment in state and collective firms in China's urban areas increased from 74.5 million and 20.5 million in 1978 to 108.9 million and 36.2 million in 1992 (figures from Sabin, "New Bosses in the Workers' State," p. 946). These figures, however, include all types of state and collective employment, not simply industrial firms or the workers within them.

40. Obviously the precision with which these three periods are distinguished represents an oversimplification. Many of the changes that took hold during one stage were already occurring, at least on an experimental basis, earlier. Furthermore, large numbers of firms dragged their heels and were slow in implementing the changes that I locate in a particular period. My periodization here is intended simply to crudely differentiate different dominant trends.

41. See the discussion in Anita Chan, "Chinese Enterprise Reforms: Convergence with the Japanese Model?" and Wenfang Tang and William L. Parish, "The Changing Social Contract: Chinese Urban Life under Reform," chap. 7 (Labor-Management Relations), manuscript. Some sources state that *dingti* job replacement was not formally discontinued until 1986. However, we have an account of the practice still being followed at the end of the decade. See Chih-yu Shih, *State and Society in China's Political Economy* (Boulder, Colo.: Lynne Rienner, 1995), p. 129.

42. The press during this period carried accounts of numerous instances of reformist managers in firms experimenting with smashing the iron rice bowl being physically attacked and in some cases killed by their workers. See the discussion in my article "Social Trends in China: 1984," in S. Goldstein, ed., *China Briefing 1984* (Boulder, Colo.: Westview Press, 1984).

43. See the discussion in Lowell Dittmer and Lu Xiaobo, "Personal Politics in the Chinese Danwei under Reform," *Asian Survey*, 36, no. 3 (1996): 246–267.

44. See the discussion in Andrew Walder, "Wage Reform and the Web of Factory Interests," *China Quarterly*, no. 109 (1987): 22–41; Tang and Parish, "The Changing Social Contract."

45. Athar Hussain and Juzhong Zhuang, "Impact of Reforms on Wage and Employment Determination in Chinese State Enterprises, 1986–1991," photocopy, 1994, cited in Margaret Maurer-Fazio, "Labor Reform in China: Crossing the River by Feeling the Stones," *Comparative Economic Studies*, 37, no. 4 (1995): 111–123.

46. As noted earlier, according to official figures, there were only 8.4 million employed in urban private firms and 2.8 million in foreign or joint-venture firms in 1992, in comparison with 36.2 million in collective firms and 108.9 million in state firms (these are all comprehensive figures, rather than figures on industrial workers in each sector). However, at least the private employment figures contain a substantial undercount, as discussed earlier. See the discussion in Sabin, "New Bosses in the Worker's State."

47. See the discussion in Alex Inkeles, C. Montgomery Broaded, and Zhongde Cao, "Causes and Consequences of Individual Modernity in China," *China Journal*, no. 37 (1997): 31–62. Prof. Inkeles earlier directed surveys of the modernization of attitudes in other developing countries. See Alex Inkeles and David H. Smith, *Becoming Modern* (Cambridge: Harvard University Press, 1974). A chapter on the culture of workers in a recent monograph strikes a similar note, concluding, "their attitude toward the factory is shockingly passive." See Shih, *State and Society*, p. 130.

48. However, Chapter 7, by Tianjian Shi, suggests that changes during the 1990s may be energizing urbanites into less fatalistic ways of thinking. My stress on this continuity in urban work experiences also comes from my own research on unrelated topics dealing with urban family life. In a survey conducted in urban areas of Chengdu, Sichuan, in 1987, I found little sign that the sort of individual variation in attitudes and behavior by educational level, income, or other socioeconomic status traits that exists in market societies was visible among my respondents. See the discussion in my papers "Wedding Behavior and Family Strategies in Chengdu," in D. Davis and S. Harrell, eds., *Chinese Families in the Post-Mao Era* (Berkeley: University of California Press, 1993); and "From Arranged Marriages to Love Matches in Urban China," in Chin-chun Yi, ed., *Marriage Formation and Dissolution: Perspectives from East and West* (Taipei: Academia Sinica, 1995).

49. Figures cited in Wenfang Tang and William L. Parish, "Social Reaction to Reform in Urban China," *Problems of Post-Communism*, 43, no. 6 (1996):

35–47. In a related analysis, Tang and Parish review surveys from 1991–92 which show that the level of dissatisfaction with a variety of features of the work environment was greater for workers in state and collective firms than for their counterparts in TVEs or foreign firms. See Tang and Parish, "The Changing Social Contract," fig. 7.5.

50. See my chapter, "The Social Sources of the Student Demonstrations," in A. Kane, ed., *China Briefing 1990* (Boulder: Westview, 1990). See also the discussion in Andrew Walder and Gong Xiaoxia, "Workers in the Tiananmen Protests: The Politics of the Beijing Workers' Autonomous Federation," *Australian Journal of Chinese Affairs*, no. 29 (1993): 1–30.

51. For example, in January 1992 state enterprises were given new freedom to hire new employees without consulting a municipal labor plan or obtaining the approval of their superiors. See *People's Daily*, January 15, 1992, p. 3, cited in Davis, "Urban Catch-up."

52. See, for example, Dittmer and Lu, "Personal Politics," n. 23. See also James B. Stepanek, "China's Enduring State Factories: Why Ten Years of Reform Has Left China's Big State Factories Unchanged," in Joint Economic Committee, ed., *China's Economic Dilemmas in the 1990s* (Armonk, N.Y.: M. E. Sharpe, 1992), pp. 440–453.

53. See the discussion in Dorothy Solinger, "China's Urban Transients in the Transition from Socialism and the Collapse of the Communist Urban Public Goods Regime," *Comparative Politics*, 27, no. 2 (1995): 127–147; see also Ramon Myers, "The Socialist Market Economy in the People's Republic of China: Fact or Fiction?" Morrison Lecture in Ethnology, Australian National University, 1994.

54. *China Daily*, May 2, 1996, cited in Davis, "Urban Catch-up," p. 5. For a verifying case study, see Minghua Zhao and Theo Nichols, "Management Control of Labour in State-owned Enterprises: Cases from the Textile Industry," *China Journal*, no. 36 (1996): 1–21. Of course, as noted earlier, simply reclassifying a worker from permanent to contract status has little meaning if contracts are automatically renewed without regard to performance.

55. Zhongguo Xinwen She news bulletin, Beijing, July 31, 1996, translated in *Summary of World Broadcasts*, FE/2680, S1/3, August 2, 1996. The bulletin lists a total of 64.7 million contract workers, 11.92 million temporary workers, and 134.98 million permanent workers. The 36 percent figure is based on a combination of temporary and contract workers.

56. These changes are reviewed in Davis, "Urban Catch-up."

57. On these changes, consult ibid.; Dittmer and Lu, "Personal Politics," and Pearson, "Breaking the Bonds." In cases of an employee wanting to switch jobs from one state firm to another, refusal by superiors may still have

some impact, with transfer of the employee's personnel dossier *(dang'an)* to the new unit being necessary. Because the *dang'an* system is lacking in private and foreign firms, however, individuals can and do simply ignore the refusal of superiors and leave.

58. See the discussion in Maurer-Fazio, "Labor Reform in China." Most of this kind of competition involves managerial and technical personnel, of course, not production workers.

59. See the discussion in Davis, "Urban Catch-up," in which figures from a small sample of Shanghai families display this heightened labor mobility, but for sons more than daughters. One study indicated, however, that industrial workers in the 1990s were still less likely to have changed jobs than industrial white-collar employees or personnel in nonindustrial enterprises. The average industrial worker studied in 1992–93 had changed jobs only 0.4 times over a lifetime, compared with rates from 0.64 to 3.01 for other kinds of personnel. See Feng Tongqing, "1992–1993 Zhongguo zhigong qingkuang" (Status of Chinese workers and employees in 1992–1993), *Shehui yanjiu,* no. 3 (1993): 14–24, cited in Davis, "Urban Catch-up."

60. See the general discussion of this trend in Solinger, "The Chinese Work Unit and Transient Labor in the Transition from Socialism," and "The Floating Population Enters Urban Labor Markets."

61. See the case study discussed in Zhao and Nichols, "Management Control of Labour."

62. Examples of high employment of migrants in textile firms in some cities come from Solinger, "The Floating Population Enters Urban Labor Markets," pp. 67–68. The 1995 overall figure comes from *Summary of World Broadcasts,* May 22, 1995, cited in Maurer-Fazio, "Labor Reform in China," n. 4.

63. The details and exceptions are discussed in Solinger, "The Chinese Work Unit and Transient Labor," pp. 161–165.

64. *People's Daily,* July 17, 1993, cited in Solinger, "The Floating Population Enters Urban Labor Markets," pp. 72–73.

65. Quoted in Maurer-Fazio, "Labor Reform in China," n. 7. In 1997 Vice Premier Wu Bangguo stated that the current national figure for layoffs from state and urban collective enterprises was more than 9 million, that stopped or reduced wage payments affected another almost 11 million, while more than 2 million pensioners were receiving no or reduced pensions. See Xinhua News Service Bulletin, Beijing, May 28, 1997, translated in *Summary of World Broadcasts,* FE/2950, June 20, 1997, p. S1–2. These figures indicate that more than 10 percent of all adult urbanites in China are affected, far higher than the 3 percent unemployment rates

usually cited in official statistics. Outside observers give estimates of the proportion of urban workers affected by dismissals and layoffs in 1997 that are substantially higher—20 percent or more. See Tang and Parish, "The Changing Social Contract," chap. 7, p. 5.

66. Agence France Press dispatch, Beijing, September 8, 1996, reported that China's total urban industrial work force at the end of June 1996 stood at 146.9 million, down 2.17 million from the end of 1995, with state-owned enterprises accounting for 53 percent of the decline. I am grateful to Anita Chan for supplying this reference.

67. "Scientific management" refers to the industrial engineering schemes developed by F. W. Taylor in the United States early in the twentieth century, which were designed to use time and motion studies to scientifically calculate how to get each worker to maximize production output. The fact that Lenin praised Taylorism provided legitimacy for subsequent efforts to enforce such schemes in Soviet and Chinese factories, even as Taylorism was denounced by Western specialists on industrial relations.

68. See the discussion of this last variant in Zhao and Nichols, "Management Control of Labour," and in Feng Tongqing, "Workers and Trade Unions under the Market Economy," *Chinese Sociology and Anthropology*, 28, no. 3 (1996): 28–30.

69. See the discussion in Solinger, "China's Urban Transients in the Transition from Socialism," and in Davis, "Urban Catch-up."

70. These examples come from the cases of Henan cotton plants described in Zhao and Nichols, "Management Control of Labour." See also Feng, "Workers and Trade Unions under the Market Economy."

71. These examples come from Tang and Parish, "The Changing Social Contract," p. 7.

72. A version of this argument is advanced in Tang and Parish, "The Changing Social Contract." Some analysts trace the effort to enhance managerial control back to the reforms launched in 1984. See the discussion in Wang Shaoguang, "From a Pillar of Continuity to a Force for Change: Chinese Workers in the Movement," in Roger DesForges, Luo Ning, and Wu Yen-bo, eds., *Chinese Democracy and the Crisis of 1989* (Albany: SUNY Press, 1993), pp. 177–190.

73. Two recent doctoral theses provide rich data on these changes. See Julia S. Sensenbrenner, "Rust in the Iron Rice Bowl: Labor Reform in Shanghai's State Enterprises, 1992–1993," Ph.D. dissertation, Johns Hopkins University, 1996; Rebecca M. Matthews, "Where Do Labor Markets Come From? The Emergence of Urban Labor Markets in the People's Republic of China," Ph.D. dissertation, Cornell University, 1998.

74. One available account stresses that the ultimate objective of the sort of reforms reviewed in this chapter is to "eliminate the boundaries of ownership type and to bring all the enterprises in the country under the same legal umbrella." See Feng Tongqing and Zhao Minghua, "Introduction," in Feng, "Workers and Trade Unions under the Market Economy," p. 4.

75. In 1992 there were 62 million employed in rural industrial firms (38 million in collective and 24 million in private firms) in comparison with 64 million in state and urban collective industrial firms. Figures cited in Samuel P. S. Ho, "Rural Non-Agricultural Development in Post-Reform China: Growth, Development Patterns, and Issues," *Pacific Affairs*, 68, no. 3 (1995): 360–391.

76. See the details provided in the following accounts: Tang and Parish, "The Changing Social Contract"; Feng, "Workers and Trade Unions under the Market Economy"; and Perry, "Labor's Battle for Political Space." Technically, the right to strike was eliminated from the Chinese constitution in 1982, but going on strike was not made a crime. As a result of this ambiguity, leaders of industrial protests for the most part are subject to dismissal from their jobs, but not to arrest. This distinction was explained to me by Anita Chan, personal communication.

77. See the discussion in Peetz, "China's New Labour Law."

78. Here the contrast with the South Korean government's attempt to force through policies weakening job security in that country's factories is indicative. Following widespread strikes by South Korean labor unions, that country's president in early 1997 backed down and agreed to reconsider the unpopular measures.

79. See the discussion in Perry, "Labor's Battle for Political Space."

80. However, if the state should shift from its present stance of accommodating and trying to institutionalize mechanisms for resolving industrial conflicts back toward its prior prohibitive stance, the potential for local industrial grievances to translate into challenges against the state will be enhanced.

81. An internal document called the "Ten Thousand Character Statement," drafted by conservative elements within the Chinese elite in 1995, states the matter in these terms: "At least a considerable number of workers and impoverished peasants feel that the party represents the interests of those who have knowledge, capability, and wealth rather than their interests. . . . The estrangement between the communist party on the one hand and the working class and impoverished peasants on the other is likely to leave the party in an isolated and helpless position at a critical moment as the Communist Party of the Soviet Union was during the 'August 1991 incident.'" Quotation from *Summary of World Broadcasts*, FE/2718 S1/7, Sep-

tember 16, 1996. I am grateful to David Shambaugh for providing me with a copy of this document.

9. Farmer Discontent and Regime Responses

1. On imputing interests, see Kay Schlozman and John T. Tierney, *Organized Interests and American Democracy* (New York: Harper & Row, 1989), p. 19.
2. See Joseph Fewsmith, *Dilemmas of Reform in China: Economic Debate and Political Conflict* (Armonk, N.Y.: M. E. Sharpe, 1994), for an analysis of how major leaders use academic surrogates to argue their positions.
3. Schlozman and Tierney, *Organized Interests and American Democracy*, p. 391.
4. Zhongguo xinwen she (ZXS), Beijing, March 20, 1994, Foreign Broadcast Information Service, *Daily Report–China* (FBIS), no. 55–1994, p. 20, remark made by Xing Bensi, deputy head of the Central Party School.
5. *Nongmin ribao* (NMRB), Apr. 2, 1988, and NMRB editorial, Nov. 17, 1988.
6. *Asiaweek,* April 1, 1988, p. 39.
7. See Lianjiang Li and Kevin O'Brien, "The Politics of Lodging Complaints in Rural China," *China Quarterly,* no. 143 (September 1995): 756–783.
8. See Li Rui, *Lushan huiyi shilu* (The real record of the Lushan meetings) (Beijing: Chunqiu and Changsha: Hunan jiaoyu chubanshe, 1989), pp. 216ff.
9. Tyrene White, "Postrevolutionary Mobilization in China: The One-Child Policy Reconsidered," *World Politics,* 43, no. 1 (October 1990): 55.
10. For an overstated but compellingly argued view of how unorganized peasants outfoxed the regime on this issue, see Kate Xiao Zhou, *How the Farmers Changed China: Power of the People* (Boulder, Colo.: Westview Press, 1996), chap. 7.
11. NMRB, September 11 and 12, 1989. The paper seems to have lowered the emotionalism of its headlines but did not cease to advocate agrarian causes.
12. See Jean C. Oi, *Rural China Takes Off: The Institutional Foundations of Economic Reform,* (Berkeley: University of California Press, 1999). See also Cheng Li, "Huaxi Village: A 'Mini-Singapore' in China," *Institute of Current World Affairs,* March 1995. For a case of despotic rule in China's richest village, Daqiuzhuang, in Tianjin, see Xinhua, Beijing, August 27, 1993, FBIS, no. 169, pp. 20–21.
13. "Authoritative figures' forum: Properly handle contradictions among the people under new conditions," *Banyue tan,* no. 6, March 23, 1993, FBIS, no. 75, pp. 18–19.
14. *Renmin ribao* (RMRB), November 4, 1987.
15. *Guangming ribao* (GMRB), November 12, 1991, FBIS, no. 232, p. 29.

16. Song Guoping, "Lun Zhongguo tese de tuanti zhengzhi" (On China's special group politics), *Zhengzhi yu falü*, no. 3 (1995): 23–28. Song quotes Philippe Schmitter's work at some length.

17. Cf. Steven Goldstein, "The Political Foundations of Incremental Reform," *China Quarterly*, no. 144 (December 1994): 1123–1125, and Jonathan Unger and Anita Chan, "Corporatism in China: A Developmental State in an East Asian Context," in Barrett L. McCormick and J. Unger, eds., *China after Socialism* (Armonk, N.Y.: M. E. Sharpe, 1996), pp. 95–129.

18. Xinhua, Beijing, January 12, 1988, FBIS, no. 13, p. 25.

19. NMRB, April 12, 1988, March 28, 1989, and April 28, 1990; Li Xiuyi, "Guanyu shiban 'nongmin xiehui' de ruogan wenti" (Several questions with regard to the experimental establishment of farmers' associations), *Zhongguo nongcun jingji*, no. 6 (1992): 15–16.

20. See Daniel Kelliher, *Peasant Power in China: The Era of Rural Reform, 1979–1989* (New Haven: Yale University Press, 1992), chaps. 2 and 3, as well as Kate Xiao Zhou, *How the Farmers Changed China*, chap. 3.

21. See, for instance, Wan Li, in RMRB, December 23, 1982, FBIS, no. 2, 1993, p. K-5, and Deng Liqun, RMRB, November 6, 1982, FBIS, no. 216, pp. K-7ff.

22. See David Zweig, "Context and Policy in Policy Implementation: Household Contracts and Decollectivization, 1977–1983," in David Lampton, ed., *Policy Implementation in Post-Mao China* (Berkeley: University of California Press, 1987), pp. 255–283.

23. Dali L. Yang, *Calamity and Reform in China: State, Rural Society, and Institutional Change since the Great Leap Forward* (Stanford: Stanford University Press, 1996), p. 122.

24. See Fewsmith, *Dilemmas of Reform*, p. 23; also Zou Qiming, "Baochan daohu yuanqi, zhenglun, he fazhan" (The origin, dispute over, and development of contracting to the household), *Nongye jingji congkan*, no. 4 (1981): 49.

25. Yang, *Calamity and Reform*, pp. 260–261.

26. Ibid., p. 130; Chen Yun in Central Committee Documents Research Department, eds., *Sanzhong quanhui yilai* (Since the Third Plenum), vol. 1 (Beijing: Renmin chubanshe, 1982), p. 74; Chen Yizi, *Zhongguo: Shinian gaige yu bajiu minyun* (China: Ten years of reform and the democracy movement of 1989) (Taipei: Lianjing chubanshe, 1989), p. 2, 20–22; Wang Lixin, "Life after Mao Zedong: A Report on Implementation of Major Chinese Agricultural Policies in Anhui Villages," *Kunlun*, no. 6 (December 1988) in Joint Publications Research Service (JPRS) CAR-89-79, July 28, 1989, p. 33.

27. Xinhua, Beijing, October 5, 1979, FBIS, no. 208—Supplement no. 32, p. 6.

28. See the central documents in *Sanzhong quanhui yilai*, vol. 1, pp. 542–549 and Zweig, "Context and Policy," p. 263.

29. Interview with former assistant to top-level official, 1988, New York.

30. On HRS adoption as a criterion of adherence to the political line, see Du Runsheng in RMRB, September 16, 1982; Wan Li in RMRB, December 23, 1982; and RMRB Commentator, January 23, 1983.

31. For examples of severe criticism of privatization, see *Zhongguo nongmin bao*, October 11, 1981; RMRB Commentator, October 31, 1981; and *Nanfang ribao*, November 20, 1981.

32. Chen Yun, December 22, 1981, in *Sanzhong quanhui yilai*, vol. 2, pp. 1057–1058.

33. Wu Xiang and Zhang Changyou, RMRB, April 9, 1980, and Wu Xiang, RMRB, November 5, 1980.

34. Fewsmith, *Dilemmas of Reform*, pp. 34–39.

35. Chen Yizi, *Shinian gaige*, pp. 34–39.

36. Chen Yizi, *Shinian gaige*, pp. 28, 37–38.

37. RMRB editorial, May 14, 1980, FBIS, no. 97, p. L-2.

38. Radio Chengdu Commentator, January 3, 1981, FBIS, no. 5, p. Q-1; Wan Li in RMRB, November 23, 1982; Sun Xianjian and Pei Changhong, *Hongqi* (Red Flag), no. 9 (1983): 21–24; and RMRB Commentator, April 22, 1983, FBIS, no. 80, p. K 8.

39. Zhang Tao, ed., *Zhongguo nongcun sishi nian* (Forty years of the Chinese village) (Henan: Zhongyuan nongmin chubanshe, 1989), p. 176.

40. This is the theme of the later chapters of Daniel Kelliher's book, *Peasant Power in China*.

41. NMRB, May 15, 1996, FBIS, no. 147, July 30, 1996, p. 39.

42. Xinhua, Beijing, December 9, 1987, FBIS, no. 237, p. 18, quoting from a discussion by agricultural economists convened by *Jingji ribao*.

43. See, for example, "Do Not Forget to Take Agriculture as the Foundation," *Liaowang*, Beijing, Commentator, no. 6, February 10, 1986, FBIS, no. 38, p. K-6, and Han Jun, "Use of Intensified Reform Methods to Solve the Problems That Rural Villagers Face—An Interview with Minister of Agriculture Liu Jiang," *Zhongguo jingji wenti* (ZJW), no. 11, November 20, 1993, JPRS-CAR-94-012, February 16, 1994, p. 23.

44. See George P. Brown, "Rural Reforms and the Sunan Model," paper presented at panel on "Chinese Rural Development: Regional Variation in Politics and Economy in Five Coastal Areas," Association for Asian Studies, April 1992.

45. A. R. Khan, K. Griffin, C. Riskin, and R. W. Zhao, "Household Income and Its Distribution in China," *China Quarterly*, no. 132 (December 1992): 1029–1061.

46. Terry Sicular, "Grain Pricing: A Key Link in Chinese Economic Policy," *Modern China,* 14, no. 4 (October 1988): 470–478.

47. NMRB, October 20, 1988, November 17, 1988, and March 31, 1989. The article in the last issue is entitled "Zou chu guoku kan minqing" (Go past the state granary and look at popular feelings).

48. Zonghe jihua si, nongye bu, "Guanyu nongmin fudan de diaocha" (Investigation of peasant burdens), *Nongye jingji wenti* (NJW), no. 2 1990, p. 58. In Gansu, burdens took 6.8 percent of household net per capita incomes; in Zhejiang, 4.2 percent.

49. Sometimes grain collectors relied on public security forces to ensure delivery. See Bao Yonghui and Li Xinrui, "Shenhua nongcun di erbu gaige de qiji" (The deepening turning point of the second stage of rural reform), *Neicun cankao,* no. 19 (August 3, 1991): 5, and also Zhang Suofei, "Hope of Democratic Development in China's Rural Areas," *Minzu yu fazhi,* no. 7 (July 1991) in JPRS-CAR-91–067, p. 2.

50. Interview, NMRB editors, August 1994.

51. NMRB, September 12, 1988.

52. NMRB, March 25, 1989.

53. "Zhengque kandai shichang liangjia shangzhang wenti" (Correctly examine the rise of the grain market price), *Liaowang,* Beijing, no. 8 (February 23, 1987): 23, and Zonghe jihua si, "Guanyu nongmin fudan," p. 60.

54. See, for example, Zheng Ying, "Dalu minzhong saodong cibiluo" (Mainland people stage more and more disturbances), *Jiushi niandai* (The nineties) July 1988, pp. 38–40, on a county-level riot caused by officials' reneging on the purchase of garlic.

55. Liu Huazhen, "Qie ji buyao weibei nongmin de yiyuan" (Always remember not to violate peasant wishes), NJW, no. 6 (1989): 10.

56. NMRB, March 31, 1989.

57. Xinhua, Beijing, March 19, 1988, FBIS, no. 54, p. 63.

58. *Deng Xiaoping wenxuan* (Selected works), vol. 3 (Beijing: Foreign Languages Press, 1993), p. 238. Deng used the phrase "yi jun tu qi," an army suddenly appearing from nowhere.

59. RMRB, January 8, 1984, FBIS, no. 17, January 25, 1984, p. K-9.

60. Xinhua, Beijing, September 23, 1985, *Summary of World Broadcasts, Far East* (SWB/FE), no. 8065/C/1 (B), September 25, 1985. In 1990 Chen, in a conversation with Deng Xiaoping, reiterated his concerns about grain. Deng reportedly "listened a bit impatiently." *Chengming,* no. 11 (1990): 17.

61. NMRB, April 4, 1990, report on a State Council response to inquiries by the NPC.

62. ZXS, Beijing, July 6, 1993, FBIS, no. 128, pp. 34–35, and Lu Yu-sha, "Wan

Li Delivers Speech, Expressing Worry about Peasant Rebellion," *Tangtai* (Contemporary Times), Hong Kong, no. 25 (April 15, 1993): 13–14, FBIS, no. 72, p. 43.

63. NMRB, April 7, 1988.

64. *Jingji ribao,* October 19, 1988, JPRS-CAR-88–79, December 14, 1988, pp. 59–60.

65. Xinhua, Beijing, March 25, 1989, FBIS, no. 58, p. 20.

66. The preceding is based on *Nongmin ribao,* April 3, 1989; March 28 and April 4, 1990; March 28, April 1, and April 3, 1991; April 1, 1992; March 31, 1993.

67. See "Text of Document Circulated among Senior Party and Government Officials Earlier this Month," *South China Morning Post* (SCMP), May 31, 1989, FBIS, no. 103, p. 35.

68. Beijing Television Service, June 19, 1989, FBIS, no. 120, p. 40.

69. Wang Hsiao-chun, "Looking Forward to the 14th Congress," *Kuang chiao ching,* no. 231, December 16, 1991, FBIS, no. 234, p. 25. The Eighth Central Committee Plenum also pointed out that in the late 1980s agriculture had been neglected, causing "setbacks" in the "country's political and economic situations." See *Ta kung pao,* November 25, 1991, FBIS, no. 227, pp. 25–26.

70. RMRB–Overseas edition, January 27, 1993.

71. Sichuan Government Information Office, in *Zhongguo xinwen she,* Beijing, June 12, 1993, FBIS, no. 112, pp. 28–29; Jung Sheng, "Great Impact of Agricultural Issue—Tracking Incident of Peasant Riots in Sichuan's Renshou County," *Hsin pao,* Hong Kong, June 10, 1993, FBIS, no. 111, pp. 10–15.

72. SCMP, Hong Kong, March 23, 1993, FBIS, no. 54, p. 46, and Xinhua, Beijing, March 17, 1993, FBIS, no. 51, pp. 15–26.

73. Lu Yu-sha, "Wan Li Delivers Speech."

74. RMRB–Overseas edition, January 27, 1993.

75. *Zhonghua renmin gongheguo guowuyan gongbao* (PRC State Council Bulletin), no. 18, September 2, 1993, pp. 850–857.

76. The law and interpretation are in Luo Yousheng and Sun Zuohai, eds., *Zhonghua renmin gongheguo nongye fa shiyi* (Explanation of the PRC Agricultural Law) (Qinhuangdao City: Zhongguo zhengfa daxue chubanshe, 1993), pp. 61–68.

77. Cf. the author's "Ideology and Rural Reform: The Paradox of Contingent Stability," in Arthur L. Rosenbaum, ed., *State and Society in Contemporary China* (Boulder, Colo.: Westview Press, 1992), pp. 143–165.

78. NMRB Commentator, February 9, 1988, FBIS, no. 32, pp. 16–18; NMRB Commentator, December 18, 1989, and NMRB, Editorial Department, September 14, 1990.

79. Zhou Qiren, "Jiating jingying zai faxian" (The reappearance of family management), *Zhongguo shehui kexue*, no. 2 (1985) esp. pp. 33–44. See also Zhang Luxiong in *Guangming ribao*, July 2, 1984, FBIS, no. 139, pp. K7–9, and Wu Zhan, RMRB, November 10, 1989.

80. For the politics of this period, see Richard Baum, *Burying Mao* (Princeton: Princeton University Press, 1994), part 4.

81. In Ningxia, a group of farmers wrote to the provincial newspaper inquiring about recollectivization. Their letter was published by RMRB. See *Ningxia ribao*, November 18, 1989, FBIS, no. 239, pp. 41–43.

82. NMRB, March 19, 1990; NMRB, March 21, 1990, and NMRB Commentator, October 4, 1990, FBIS, no. 207, p. 40.

83. NMRB, March 2, 1990.

84. Chen Xiwen, "Wending jiben zhengce shi shenhua nongcun gaige de qianti" (Stabilizing basic policy is the premise for deepening of reform), NJW, no. 6 (1991): 5.

85. NMRB, April 20, 1995, FBIS, no. 123, June 27, 1995, pp. 70–73.

86. Roy L. Prosterman, Tim Hanstad, and Li Ping, "Can China Feed Itself?" *Scientific American*, November 1996, pp. 90–96.

87. See RMRB Commentator, October 22, 1995, FBIS, no. 209, pp. 61–63; Wen Jiabao, "Guanyu xin shiqi de nongmin wenti," *Qiushi* (Seeking Truth), no. 24 (1995): 2–9; and Jiang Zemin's speech in Henan province, Xinhua, Beijing, July 15, 1996, FBIS, no. 137, pp. 5–10.

88. Editorial Department, "Issues in Current Rural Economic Reform and Development," NJW, no. 10, October 23, 1991, in JPRS-CAR-009, February 26, 1992, p. 43.

89. Yang Yongzhe, "The Trend of China's Agricultural Development and Measures to be Adopted," speech at meeting of NMRB provincial reporters, NMRB, May 21, 1993, FBIS-Chi no. 113, pp. 38–45. See also NMRB Commentator, December 23, 1992, and Lu Rongshan, "Lun shichang nongye de ruozhixing yu zhengfu baohu" (The weakness of agriculture in the market and government protection), *Shehui kexue zhanxian*, no. 4 (1995): 93–103.

90. Xinhua, Beijing, September 14, 1995, FBIS, no. 179, p. 16.

91. Xinhua, Beijing, February 1, 1996, FBIS, no. 25, February 6, 1996, p. 61. See also RMRB Commentator, October 22, 1995, FBIS, no. 209, pp. 61–63, and Jiang Zemin's speech in Henan, Xinhua, July 15, 1996, FBIS, no. 137, pp. 5–10.

92. NMRB, May 15, 1996, FBIS, no. 147, July 30, 1996, pp. 38–39, and Frederick Crook, "Grain Galore," *China Business Review*, 24, no. 5 (September–October 1997): 12.

93. RMRB–Overseas edition, May 7, 1996.

94. Reports on outbreaks appeared in the Hong Kong press. A summary is in

Li Zijing, "Sisheng wushiwan nongmin kangzheng" (Resistance by 500,000 farmers in four provinces), *Chengming* (August 1997): 19–21.

95. The edict was published in RMRB, April 1, 1997.
96. See Li and O'Brien, "The Politics of Lodging Complaints."
97. On Renshou, see Jung Sheng, "Great Impact," and for Hunan, see *Ming pao,* November 8, 1996, SWB/FE/2765/G/4, November 9, 1996.
98. Daniel Kelliher, "The Chinese Debate over Village Elections," *China Journal,* no. 37 (January 1997): 1–24.
99. See note 20 and the author's "Proposals for a National Voice for Agricultural Interests: A Farmers' Association," paper prepared for conference on "Rural China: Emerging Issues in Development," East Asian Institute, Columbia University, March 31–April 1, 1996.
100. NMRB, March 23, 1989.
101. NMRB, March 19, 1993, citing remarks made by Wang Yushao, deputy head, State Council Development Research Center.
102. NMRB, March 28, 1989, and NMRB, April 4, 1990.

10. China's Floating Population

This chapter draws on material in chapter 7 of Dorothy J. Solinger, *Contesting Citizenship: Peasant Migrants, the State, and the Logic of the Market in Urban China,* © 1999 The Regents of the University of California, used by permission of the University of California Press.

1. F. W. Mote, "The Transformation of Nanking, 1350–1400," in G. William Skinner, ed., *The City in Late Imperial China* (Stanford: Stanford University Press, 1977), pp. 101–153, esp. pp. 102, 103, 114, and 117.
2. Alejandro Portes and Alex Stepick, *City on the Edge: The Transformation of Miami* (Berkeley: University of California Press, 1993), pp. 8, 210, 213.
3. Sulamith Heins Potter and Jack M. Potter, *China's Peasants: The Anthropology of a Revolution* (Cambridge: Cambridge University Press, 1990), pp. 296–310; and Tiejun Cheng and Mark Selden, "The Origins and Social Consequences of China's *Hukou* System," *China Quarterly* (hereafter *CQ*), no. 139 (September 1994): 644–668. See also "Huji yanjiu" ketizu ("Household Registration Research" task force), "Xianxing huji guanli zhidu yu jingji tizhi gaige" (The present household registration management system and economic system reform), *Shanghai shehui kexueyuan xueshu jikan* (Shanghai Social Science Academy Academic Quarterly) (hereafter SH), no. 3 (1989): 81–91; and Ding Shuimu, "Huji guanli yu shehui kongzhi—xianxing huji guanli zhidu zaiyi" (Household registration management and social control—Another opinion on the present household management system), *SH,* no.3 (1989): 26–29. Relevant regu-

lations are "Directive on Establishing a System for Registration of Permanent Households," Guowuyuan fazhiju, Zhonghua renmin gongheguo fagui huibian bianji weiyuanhui, bian (State Council Legal System Bureau, Editorial Committee of the Compendium of legal documents of the People's Republic of China, eds.), *Zhongguo renmin gongheguo fagui huibian* (Compendium of Legal Documents of the People's Republic of China) (hereafter *Compendium*), vol. 1 (Beijing: Falü chubanshe, 1956), pp. 197–200, and translated in Zhang Qingwu, "Basic Facts on the Household Registration System," *Chinese Economic Studies*, 22, no. 1 (1988): 103–106; "Criteria for the Demarcation of Urban and Rural Areas," in *Compendium*, vol. 2 (Beijing: Falü chubanshe, 1956), pp. 411–417; and "Regulations on Household Registration in the People's Republic of China," in *Compendium*, vol. 7 (Beijing: Falü chubanshe, 1958), pp. 204–216, translated in Zhang, "Basic Facts," pp. 87–92.

4. Wang Feng, "The Breakdown of a Great Wall: Recent Changes in Household Registration System in China," paper presented at the International Conference on Migration and Floating, Cologne, Germany, May 2–4, 1996, pp. 5–6; and Dali Yang, *Calamity and Reform in China: State, Rural Society, and Institutional Change since the Great Leap Famine* (Stanford: Stanford University Press, 1996), p. 108.

5. Kam Wing Chan, *Cities with Invisible Walls: Reinterpreting Urbanization in Post-1949 China* (Hong Kong: Oxford University Press, 1994).

6. Dali L. Yang, "Reforms, Resources, and Regional Cleavages: The Political Economy of Coast-Interior Relations in Mainland China," *Issues and Studies*, 27, no. 9 (1991): 44. See also Nicholas R. Lardy, *Economic Growth and Distribution in China* (Cambridge: Cambridge University Press, 1978).

7. "Huji yanjiu," p. 87; and Jeffrey R. Taylor and Judith Banister, "China: The Problem of Employing Surplus Rural Labor," CIR Staff Paper 49 (Washington, D.C.: U.S. Bureau of the Census, Center for International Research, July 1989), p. 26.

8. Hu Yinkang, "The Reform of Household Registration Regulations and the Needs of Economic Development," *Shehui kexue* (Social science), no. 6 (1985): 37, cited in Judith Banister, "Urban-Rural Population Projections for China," CIR Staff Paper 15 (Washington, D.C.: U.S. Bureau of the Census, Center for International Research, March 1986), p. 9.

9. *Guowuyuan gongbao* (State Council Bulletin) (hereafter *GWYGB*), no. 26 (447), (November 10, 1984) pp. 919–920.

10. The document, in *Renmin ribao* (People's Daily), September 8, 1985, p. 4, translated in U.S. *Foreign Broadcast Information Service* (hereafter FBIS), September 12, 1985, pp. K12–14, is discussed in Judith Banister and Jeffrey R. Taylor, "China: Surplus Labor and Migration," *Asia-Pacific Popula-*

tion Journal, 4 (no year): 14, and in "Huji yanjiu," p. 88. This new card was to be distinguished from the "temporary domicile card" *(zhanzhu zheng),* which was meant for anyone planning to stay at least three months for unstated reasons, not necessarily for work.

11. Taylor and Banister, "China: The Problem of Employing Surplus Rural Labor," p. 27. Even before this measure legalized such purchases, they were taking place: according to Tian Xueyuan, "Reform and Opening Gives the Urbanization of Population a New Vitality," *Zhongguo renkou kexue* (Chinese population science) (hereafter *ZRK*), no. 3 (1988): 17.

12. FBIS, June 18, 1993, p. 27. See "Ordinance of the People's Republic of China on the Trial Implementation of the Resident Identity Card" (dated April 6, 1984), *GWYGB,* no. 8 (429), (May 5, 1984) pp. 246–247.

13. FBIS, December 15, 1989, p. 31. See "Circular of the Public Security Ministry of the People's Republic of China on Implementing the Use and Inspection System of the Residents' Identification Card throughout the Country," dated September 8, 1989, *GWYGB,* no. 17 (598), (October 11, 1989) pp. 653–657.

14. Alan P. L. Liu, "Economic Reform, Mobility Strategies, and National Integration in China," *Asian Survey* (hereafter *AS*), vol. 31, no. 5, p. 395 (May 1995).

15. These are "Provisional Regulations on the Management of Temporary Labor in State-Owned Enterprises," (dated October 5, 1989) in *GWYGB,* no. 19 (600), (October 23, 1989) pp. 714–716; and "Provisions on Employing Contract Workers from among the Peasants by State-Owned Enterprises," *GWYGB,* no. 28, (October 18, 1991) pp. 1001–16.

16. "Huji yanjiu," 87, states that from 1978 to 1987, there are records of 10,165,000 such people, though there are no statistics for the years 1979 and 1981. This means that nationwide, an average of 1,270,000 peasants were hired legally in state firms per year. See also Jeffrey R. Taylor, "Rural Employment Trends and the Legacy of Surplus Labour, 1978–86," *CQ,* no. 116 (December 1988): 743.

17. Michael Korzec, "Contract Labor, the 'Right to Work,' and New Labor Laws in the People's Republic of China," *Comparative Economic Studies,* 30, no. 2 (Summer 1988): 125–126.

18. R. J. R. Kirkby, *Urbanisation in China: Town and Country in a Developing Economy, 1949–2000 A.D.* (London: Croom Helm, 1985); and Chan, *Cities with Invisible Walls.*

19. Cheng Li, "Surplus Rural Laborers and Internal Migration in China: Current Status and Future Prospects," *AS,* 36, no. 11 (1996): 1122–1145, citing the research of Wuhan University demographer Gu Shengzu.

20. Dutton introduction, in Zhang, "Basic Facts," p. 15; and Kirkby, *Urbanisation in China*, p. 32.

21. Michel Oksenberg and James Tong, "The Evolution of Central-Provincial Fiscal Relations in China, 1971–1984: The Formal System," *CQ*, no. 125 (March 1991): 1–32; and Shaoguang Wang, "The Rise of the Regions: Fiscal Reform and the Decline of Central State Capacity in China," in Andrew G. Walder, ed., *The Waning of the Communist State: Economic Origins of Political Decline in China and Hungary* (Berkeley: University of California Press, 1995), pp. 87–113.

22. See Zhang Qingwu, "A Preliminary Probe into China's Floating Population," *Renkou yu jingji* (Population and economy) (hereafter *RKYJJ*), no. 3 (1986): 4.

23. Judith Banister, "China's Population Changes and the Economy," in U.S. Congress, Joint Economic Committee, *China's Economic Dilemmas in the 1990s: The Problems of Reforms, Modernization and Interdependence*, vol. 1 (Washington, D.C.: U.S. Government Printing Office, 1991), p. 235.

24. Beijing City People's Government Research Office, Social Section, "A Comprehensive Report on the Question of the Floating Population in Eight Big Cities," *Shehuixue yanjiu* (Sociology research), no. 3 (1991): 22.

25. See Hu Teh-wei and Elizabeth Hon-Ming Li, "Labor Market Reforms in China," paper presented at the Center for Chinese Studies, Spring Regional Seminar, University of California, Berkeley, April 11, 1992, p. 49.

26. Feng Lanrui and Jiang Weiyu, "A Comparative Study of the Modes of Transference of Surplus Labor in China's Countryside," *Social Sciences in China*, 9, no. 3 (September 1988): 73.

27. Wuhan shi laodongju bian (Wuhan City Labor Bureau, ed.), *Chengshi wailai laodongli guanli* (The Management of Outside Urban Labor) (Wuhan: Wuhan chubanshe, 1990), p. 106.

28. See Xue Muqiao, "Some opinions on urban labor and employment problems," in Bao Ji, ed., *Zhongguo dangdai shehui kexue mingjia zixuan xueshu jinghua congshu*, 8: *Xue Muqiao xueshu jinghua lu* (A collection of selected scholarly works by China's modern social science masters, vol. 8: A collection of scholarly works by Xue Muqiao) (Beijing: Beijing shifan xueyuan chubanshe, 1988), pp. 405–411 (cited in Lora Sabin, "New Bosses in the Workers' State: The Growth of Non-State Sector Employment in China," *CQ*, no. 140 (December 1994): 948.

29. Cui Lin, "The Development of the Tertiary Sector and the Question of Urban Population," *RKYJJ*, no. 1 (1989): 46.

30. See Zhang Qingwu, "A Preliminary Probe," p. 4.

31. Cindy C. Fan, "Economic Opportunities and Internal Migration: A Case

Study of Guangdong Province, China," *Professional Geographer,* 48, no. 1 (1996): 28–45.

32. Wang Feng and Zuo Xuejin, "Rural Migrations in Shanghai: Current Success and Future Promise," paper prepared for presentation at the International Conference on Rural Labor Migration in China, Beijing, June 25–27, 1996, p. 8, states that migrants in Shanghai in late 1995 were earning more than three times what they earned at home.

33. In 1985 the per capita income of the rural population was 497 yuan in the east, 343 in the center, and 355 in the west; by 1990 it had changed to 812 yuan in the east, 538 in the center, and only 497 yuan in the west (see Zhongguo tongxunshe, April 1, 1993, reprinted in FBIS, April 5, 1993, p. 42); at the end of 1994, the differences had widened even more: eastern ruralites were taking in 1,617 yuan per year, central China rural residents 1,087, and westerners only 856, on the average (see *Eastern Express,* March 25–26, p. 7, in FBIS, March 27, p. 3). See Yang Xiaoyong, "The Flow of Migrant Labor and the Development of China's Urban and Rural Economy," *RKYJJ,* no. 5 (1995): 27, for a slightly different index.

34. Dorothy J. Solinger, "China's Urban Transients in the Transition from Socialism and the Collapse of the Communist 'Urban Public Goods Regime,'" *Comparative Politics,* 27, no. 2 (January 1995): 127–146.

35. Andrew G. Walder, *Communist Neo-Traditionalism: Work and Authority in Chinese Industry* (Berkeley: University of California Press, 1986), pp. 48–56.

36. Chan, *Cities with Invisible Walls,* p. 131.

37. *China Daily* (hereafter *CD*), *Business Weekly* (January 10, 1993), in FBIS, January 11, 1993, p. 8.

38. Li Ruojian, "Structural Defects versus Migrant Population in the Especially Big Cities in China," *RKYJJ,* no. 4 (1996): 44.

39. In two 1995 surveys, one in Dongguan, in the Pearl River Delta, and one in Jinan, an average of 81 percent of the respondents were informed of job opportunities by relatives and friends before they migrated (Xin Meng, "Regional Wage Gap, Information Flow and Rural-Urban Migration," presented at the International Conference on the Flow of Rural Labor in China, Beijing, June 25–27, 1996, p. 20).

40. Li Mengbai and Hu Xin, eds., *Liudong renkou dui da chengshi fazhan de yingxiang ji duice* (The influence of the floating population on big cities' development and countermeasures) (Beijing: Jingji ribao chubanshe, 1991), p. 251; and Cheng Ke, "The Problem of Large Cities' Floating Population and Policy Measures," *Chengxiang jianshe* (Urban-rural construction) (Beijing), 5 (1988): 17.

41. Wang Ju, Shi Chongxin, and Song Chunsheng, "Beijing's Mobile Population: Current Status, Policy," *RKYJJ,* no. 4 (1993), translated in Joint Publications Research Service (hereafter JPRS)-CAR-93–091, p. 46 (De-

cember 29, 1993); see also *CD,* January 21, 1995, p. 3, in FBIS, January 23, 1995, p. 74; and Shi Xianmin, "Beijingshi getihu de fazhan licheng ji leibie fenhua: Beijing xichengqu getihu yanjiu" (The Categorization and Development History of Beijing City's Private Entrepreneurs: Research on Beijing Xicheng District's Private Entrepreneurs), *Zhongguo shehui kexue* (Chinese social science), no. 5 (1992): 36. I am grateful to Thomas Heberer for sending this to me.

42. Shi, "Beijingshi," p. 38.

43. *CD,* July 30, 1991, p. 6.

44. Ge Xiangxian and Qu Weiying, *Zhongguo mingongchao: "Mangliu" zhen-xianglu* (China's tide of labor: A record of the true facts about the "blind floaters") (Beijing: Zhongguo guoji guangbo chubanshe, 1990), p. 97.

45. Street interviews, Tianjin, May 1992.

46. Liu Bingyi, "Floating 'City People,'" *Qing chun* (Youth), no. 6 (1989): 31; Min Kangwu, "A Village in the Capital," *China Focus,* 3, no. 8 (1995): 4; and Jean Philippe Beja and Michel Bonnin, "The Destruction of the 'Village,'" *China Perspectives,* no. 2 (1995): 22.

47. By way of comparison, in the catering trade, only 75 percent of the employees were outsiders; in other services, 60 percent; and in repairs, only 44 percent. Li Yu and Tang Bu, "Floating Population among the Beijing Urban Individual Proprietors," *Shehuixue yanjiu* (Sociology research), no. 2 (1988): 21, 22. Li and Hu, *Liudong,* p. 41, have the same figure of over 90 percent for employees, for 1989.

48. Li and Hu, *Liudong,* p. 358.

49. Xiang Biao, "How to Create a Visible 'Non-State Space' through Migration and Marketized Traditional Networks: An Account of a Migrant Community in China," presented at European Science Foundation workshop on "European Chinese and Chinese Domestic Migrants," Oxford, July 3–5, 1996.

50. Li and Hu, *Liudong,* p. 358; interview, August 5, 1994.

51. Xiang, "How to Create," p. 16.

52. Min, "Village"; interview, August 5, 1994. Xiang, "How to Create," p. 15, states that there were interest rates charged among relatives, but that they ran in the range of 2 to 3 percent.

53. The reference is to *sanlai yibu* firms. The *sanlai* or "three imports" are the materials, the patterns, and the equipment; the *yibu* or "one compensation" stands for compensatory trade. This term is best simply translated as processing enterprises.

54. Wang Zhiwang and Jiang Zuozhong, "One Million 'Migrants' Go to the Pearl River," *Nanfang chuang* (hereafter *NFC*) (South window), no. 5 (1988): 29.

55. Ge and Qu, *Zhongguo mingongchao,* pp. 139–140. For a story on Bijie as a

poverty prefecture, and as part of a special state program to help such places, see FBIS, June 26, 1996, p. 30.

56. Interview, Wuhan Social Science Academy, September 17, 1990; and in Wuhan, May 30, 1992 and Tianjin, June 15, 1992; see also Hu Xiaobo, at conference on "China and Constitutionalism: Cross-National Perspectives," sponsored by the Center for the Study of Human Rights, the Center for Chinese Legal Studies, and the East Asian Institute, Columbia University, April 30, 1993.

57. A maid hired in a spontaneous market might land a salary as high as 200 yuan in that city's unofficial markets (interview, Tianjin Women's Federation, June 15, 1992).

58. Huang Bicheng, Liu Yong, and Peng Shaoci, "A Report from Changsha Labor Market," *SH*, no. 3 (1988): 16; interview at labor exchange, Nanjing, May 17, 1992; and FBIS, April 11, 1989, p. 46.

59. Chai Junyong, "Floating Population: The Puzzle in Urban Management," *SH*, no. 10 (1990): 9; *CD*, July 30, 1991, p. 6; Zeng Jingwei, "Big Cities' 'Trash Collectors,'" *NFC*, no. 1 (1988): 24; Liu Hantai, "Zhongguo de qigai qunluo" (China's beggar community), *Wenhui yuekan* (Cultural monthly), no. 10 (1986): 198, 205–210; FBIS, October 17, 1994, p. 80 (from Zhongguo xinwenshe); and interview, June 10, 1992, Tianjin's public security office.

60. Lincoln Kaye, "Conflicts of Interest," *Far Eastern Economic Review*, August 4, 1994, p. 26.

61. Zeng, "Big Cities' 'Trash Collectors,'" p. 25 says that "those not in a *bang* are excluded and get low incomes." Huang Ruide, "The Next Generation among the Floaters," *NFC*, no. 9 (1989): 21, writes of a father collecting junk with his twelve-year-old son, who does this job in lieu of school.

62. Thus, he states, "the modern question of citizenship is structured by two issues": the first of these has to do with social membership or, one might say, with the definition of community; the second concerns the allocation of resources, broadly conceived (Bryan S. Turner, "Contemporary Problems in the Theory of Citizenship," in Bryan S. Turner, ed., *Citizenship and Social Theory* (London: SAGE Publications, 1993), p. 2).

63. Yasemin Nuhoglu Soysal, *Limits of Citizenship: Migrants and Postnational Membership in Europe* (Chicago: University of Chicago Press, 1994), p. 119; Elizabeth Meehan, *Citizenship and the European Community* (London: SAGE Publications, 1993), p. 22. On p. 4, Meehan refers to the matter of citizenship as "the question of who inside a regime has entitlements and the territorial basis of inclusion."

64. See Gail Hershatter, *The Workers of Tianjin* (Stanford: Stanford University Press, 1986).

65. Interview, Tianjin Housing Bureau, June 19, 1992; and with Gu Shangfei, New York, February 14, 1994; and Xu Xue-qiang and Li Si-ming, "China's Open Door Policy and Urbanization in the Pearl River Delta Region," *International Journal of Urban and Regional Research,* no. 1 (1990): 56, though they note exceptions in the towns of the Pearl River Delta.

66. JPRS-CAR-93–091, p. 53; Xu and Li, "China's Open Door Policy."

67. Xiang, "How to Create," p. 4.

68. Ibid., pp. 16, 22, 34; Beja and Bonnin, "The Destruction," p. 22.

69. Linda Wong, "China's Urban Migration—The Public Policy Change," *Pacific Affairs,* 67, no. 3 (1994): 335–355.

70. As of 1982, the state owned 82.3 percent of the floorspace in cities nationwide (28.7 percent by city housing bureaus and 53.69 percent by enterprises or other work units). Kirkby, *Urbanisation in China,* p. 166. Yok-shiu F. Lee, "The Urban Housing Problem in China," *CQ,* no. 115 (1988): 397, puts a date of 1981 on these data. In Tianjin in 1992, 60 percent of the housing was city-owned and 32 percent unit-owned, according to the Housing Bureau, interview, June 19, 1992.

71. Interview, Tianjin Housing Bureau, June 19, 1992.

72. Wang and Zuo, "Rural Migrations in Shanghai," p. 9.

73. Olga Lang, *Chinese Family and Society* (New Haven: Yale University Press, 1946), p. 84; Hershatter, *Workers of Tianjin,* chap. 3.

74. Li Cheng, "Tidal Wave of Migrant Laborers in China, Part II," *Institute of Current World Affairs,* CL-10 (1994): 12, 14; idem, "Under Neon Lights: Street People in Shanghai," CL-16 (Shanghai: Institute of Current World Affairs, 1994), p. 3. See also Zhongguo xinwenshe (China News Agency), March 15, 1995, in FBIS, March 16, 1995, p. 64 (4,000 to 5,000 were sleeping in Guangzhou's streets during the Spring Festival that year).

75. Mobo C. F. Gao, "On the Sharp End of China's Economic Boom—Migrant Workers," *Human Rights in China* (Spring 1994): 13.

76. *Liaowang,* no. 48 (1995): 20–23, in FBIS, February 12, 1996, p. 23.

77. Zhao Minghua and Theo Nichols, "Management Control of Labour in State-Owned Enterprises: Cases from the Textile Industry," *China Journal,* no. 36 (July 1996): 1–21, throws even this option into question, as of the early and mid-nineties.

78. Alejandro Portes and Ruben G. Rumbaut, *Immigrant America: A Portrait* (Berkeley: University of California Press, 1990), p. 21.

79. Interview, Gu Shangfei, New York, February 14, 1994; and JPRS-CAR-93–091 (December 29, 1993), from *RKYJJ,* no. 4 (1993): 45; Xiang, "How to Create," p. 16; Min, "Village," p. 4; Yuan Yue et al., *Luoren—Beijing liumin de zuzhihua zhuangkuang yanjiu baogao* (The exposed—A research report on the condition of the organization of migrants in Beijing) (Beijing:

Beijing Horizon Market Research and Analysis Company, 1995), pp. 16–18, 24.

80. *Zhengming* (Contend) (hereafter *ZM*), no. 151 (May 1990): 26–27.

81. Reinhard Bendix, *Nation-Building and Citizenship: Studies of Our Changing Social Order* (New York: John Wiley & Sons, 1964), pp. 102, 87.

82. Victor Yuan, Shouli Zhang, and Xin Wang, "Self-Organize: Finding Out the Way for Migrants to Protect Their Own Rights," June and July, 1996, Beijing and Oxford, p. 1.

83. In mid-1996, the State Education Commission decreed that most school-age children of migrants could attend local schools as "temporary students," in exchange for enrollment fees, a practice that had already been followed for some years anyway (Xinhua, June 6, 1996, in FBIS, same date, p. 22).

84. Ibid.

85. Zhao Yaqin, "Floating Population and Compulsory Education," *Renmin jiaoyu* (People's education), no. 380 (June 1996): 16–17, in FBIS, no. 159, 1996 (received on Internet, no page). I am grateful to June Dreyer for sending me this article.

86. *Liaowang*, in FBIS, February 12, 1996, p. 22; Yang Zhonglan, "Come and Gone Overnight," *SH*, no. 134 (1996): 40–41, in FBIS, May 30, 1996, p. 33.

87. Dede Nickerson, "Migrant Workers Said 'Flocking' to Beijing," *South China Morning Post*, November 16, 1992, p. 10, in FBIS, November 16, 1992, p. 38. An official from the Tianjin Markets Section of the Industrial and Commercial Management Office of the city held that children were not permitted to go to school without a *hukou* (interview, June 22, 1992).

88. The Zhejiang village had established its first kindergarten as early as 1988 (Xiang, "How to Create," p. 16); by 1995, it had a nursery school and five kindergartens there (Min, "Village," p. 4); interview with Gu Shangfei, New York, February 14, 1994. Wong ("China's Urban Majority") states that temporary dwellers organized makeshift schools in Guangzhou and Shenzhen in the early 1990s, but does not indicate whether these were kindergartens or at a higher level. In late 1997 Haidian district approved the first migrant school in Beijing.

89. Jian Xinhua, "The Urban Floating Population: Problems and Solutions," *Zhongguo renkoubao* (Chinese Population News), July 8, 1996, p. 3, in FBIS, July 8, 1996.

90. Xiang, "How to Create," p. 34.

91. Yuan Yue et al., *Luoren*, p. 16.

92. Xiang, "How to Create."

93. Ming Lei, "The 'Zhejiang Village' of Beijing That I Have Seen," *ZM*, no. 2 (1994): 25; Zhu Suhong, "Chengshizhong de nongmin: Dui Beijingshi

zhanzhu nongcun renkou de yanjiu" (Peasants in the city: An investigation of the peasant population temporarily living in Beijing) (M.A. thesis, Beijing University, Department of Sociology, 1992), p. 22; JPRS-CAR-93-091, p. 45; Min, "Village," p. 4; Xiang, "How to Create," p. 29; interview Gu Shangfei, February 14, 1994.

94. Though, according to recent research, even among city residents the power of the *danwei* was receding by the mid-1990s. See Lowell Dittmer and Lu Xiaobo, "Personal Politics in the Chinese *Danwei* under Reform," *AS*, 36, no. 3 (March 1996): 246–267.

95. In Guangzhou, city officials attempted on several occasions to wipe out "shack villages" (or what might be called shantytowns), beginning in 1989 (interview, Guangzhou Urban Automated Planning Center, May 11, 1992). In Beijing, the city government restricted people from Zhejiang to the outskirts of town; but could not prevent their construction of a huge and versatile community. Even the city government's effort to wipe out Zhejiang village in November 1995 (Beja and Bonnin, "The Destruction") was largely erased within a few months as the original residents gradually returned (information from Li Zhang).

96. Wang Chunguang, "Communities of 'Provincials' in the Large Cities: Conflicts and Integration," *China Perspectives,* no. 2 (November-December 1995): 18.

97. Zhu Suhong, "Chengshizhong de nongmin," pp. 23, 30, 36–42.

98. T. H. Marshall, *Sociology at the Crossroads and Other Essays* (London: Heinemann, 1963), pp. 72–74.

99. Xiang, "How to Create," has a somewhat different, but very detailed and compelling, analysis with the same conclusion.

11. The New Middle Class

1. R. M. Glassman, *China in Transition: Communism, Capitalism and Democracy* (New York: Praeger, 1991), provides an explicit example. The most famous recent general work on "convergence" of this kind is Francis Fukuyama, *The End of History and the Last Man* (London: Penguin, 1992).

2. James S. Cotton, "The Limits of Liberalisation in Industrializing Asia: Three Views of the State," *Pacific Affairs*, 64 (1991): 311.

3. Richard Robison and David S. G. Goodman, "The New Rich in Asia: Economic Development, Social Status, and Political Consciousness," in Richard Robison and David S. G. Goodman, eds., *The New Rich in Asia: Mobile Phones, McDonalds, and Middle-class Revolution* (London: Routledge, 1996), provides a survey of the concept of the "middle classes."

4. Unless otherwise indicated all statistics are official PRC statistics derived

from the State Statistical Bureau's *Zhongguo tongji nianjian* (China statistical yearbook) or *Shanxi tongji nianjian* (Shanxi statistical yearbook), both of which are published annually, and related publications.

5. Localism and the encouragement of local competition can occur without constitutional change. See, for example: G. Montinola, Y. Qian, and B. R. Weingast, "Federalism, Chinese Style—The Political Basis for Economic Success in China," *World Politics*, 48 (October 1995): 50.

6. The information on and examples of China's new middle classes presented here are derived from a project to investigate the emergence of political communities and the negotiation of identity in Shanxi province, North China, during 1996–1998. As part of that project, approximately one hundred cadres, officials, managers, entrepreneurs, intellectuals, and professionals are interviewed each year. The project is supported by a research grant from the Australian Research Council. Similiar, earlier research in the 1990s elsewhere in China (Hainan, Guangdong, and Zhejiang provinces) is reported in "New Economic Elites" in R. Benewick and P. Wingrove, eds., *China in the 1990s* (London: Macmillan, 1995), p. 132; and "The People's Republic of China: The Party-state, Capitalist Revolution, and New Entrepreneurs," in Robison and Goodman, eds., *The New Rich in Asia*, p. 225.

7. *Renminbi* (people's currency) (RMB); there are 8.3 yuan (dollar) RMB to US$1 (October 1997).

8. Zhonghua renmin gongheguo guojia tongjiju ed., *Zhongguo tongji nianjian 1997* (China statistical yearbook 1997) (Beijing: Zhongguo tongji chubanshe, 1997), p. 42.

9. Victor Nee, "Organisational Dynamics of Market Transition: Hybrid Forms, Property Rights, and Mixed Economy in China," *Administrative Science Quarterly*, 37, no.1 (1992): 237.

10. Dorothy J. Solinger, *From Lathes to Looms: China's Industrial Policy in Comparative Perspective, 1979–1982* (Stanford: Stanford University Press, 1991).

11. Dorothy J. Solinger, "Urban Entrepreneurs and the State: The Merger of State and Society," in Dorothy J. Solinger, *China's Transition from Socialism: Statist Legacies and Market Reforms, 1980–1990* (Armonk, N.Y.: M. E. Sharpe, 1993), p. 256.

12. "Shanxi fazhan tuopin zhudao chanye" ("Shanxi develops the backbone industries to shake off poverty") in *Shanxi ribao* (Shanxi daily), October 9, 1996, p. 1. The fifty counties have just over 11 percent of the provincial population, and thirty-five of these counties obtain poverty support from the central government.

13. On patterns of provincial development, see David S. G. Goodman, ed., *China's Provinces in Reform: Class, Community, and Political Culture* (London:

Routledge, 1997); and Feng Chongyi and Hans Hendrischke, ed., *Politics outside Beijing: Region, Identity, and Cultural Construction* (London: Routledge, 1998).

14. David S. G. Goodman, "King Coal and Secretary Hu: Shanxi's Third Modernisation," in Feng and Hendrischke, eds., *Politics outside Beijing.*

15. Donald G. Gillin, *Warlord Yen Hsi-shan in Shansi Province, 1911–1949* (Princeton: Princeton University Press, 1967).

16. Shanxi wenshi ziliao bianjibu, ed., *Shanxi wenshi jingxuan: Yan Xishan longduan jingji* (Selections from *Shanxi wenshi ziliao:* Yan Xishan's monopoly economy) (Taiyuan: Shanxi gaoxiao lianhe chubanshe, n.d.).

17. Interview with Ma Jiajun, deputy director of the Shanxi Provincial Economic and Trade Commission, Taiyuan, July 12, 1996.

18. "Shanxi Jianhang xindai zhanlüe he zhizhu chanye xuanze" (The Shanxi Construction Bank's credit strategy and selection of industries for support), *Touzi daokan* (Investment guide), no. 1, February 1, 1996, p. 9.

19. Statistics as calculated from *Zhongguo tongji nianjian 1997*, pp. 42, 43, 602, 608.

20. S. Young, "Wealth but Not Security: Attitudes towards Private Business in China in the 1980s," *Australian Journal of Chinese Affairs*, no. 25 (1991): 115–137.

21. See also Wang Yonghai, Liu Yaoming, Wang Jikang, Zhang Guilong, "Shanxi Huanhai jituan yougongsi zhongshizhang Liang Wenhai yu tade Huanhai shiye he huanbao zhanlüe" (General manager of the Shanxi Huanhai Group Company, Liang Wenhai, his Huanhai business and environmental strategy), in *Shanxi ribao* (Shanxi daily), September 22, 1996, p. 4.

22. For a biography of Li Anmin, see Liu Liping, ed., *Zhongguo dangdai qiyejia mingdian—Shanxi tao* (Contemporary entrepreneurs in China—Shanxi volume) (Beijing: Gongren chubanshe, 1989), p. 302.

23. Interviewed at the company's Taiyuan office, September 25, 1997.

24. The official PRC definition of the state sector includes those enterprises technically "owned" by the state and subject to the state plan. It does not include all enterprises over which the state has direct control. Many collective sector enterprises that are subject to the market (rather than the plan) are also part of the state, though perhaps in general the collective sector of the economy is best regarded as the local government economy.

25. Interviewed in Yuncheng, September 17, 1997.

26. For contemporary accounts of such enterprises, see, for example, Charles Bettelheim, *Cultural Revolution and Industrial Organization in China: Changes in Management and the Division of Labor* (New York: Monthly Review Press,

1974), esp. section 3, "Transformations in the Social Division of Labor," pp. 69ff; Joan Robinson, *Reports from China, 1953–1976* (London: Anglo-Chinese Educational Institute, 1977), pp. 106ff.

27. Interviewed in Zhaojiabao village, Qingxu, Taiyuan, October 28, 1996.

28. W. A. Byrd and Lin Qingsong, eds., *China's Rural Industry: Structure, Development, and Reform* (New York: Oxford University Press, 1990); Ma Wu, ed., *Jiushi niandai Zhongguo xiangzhen qiye diaocha* (Survey of town and village enterprises in 1990s China) (Hong Kong: Oxford University Press, 1994).

29. Interviewed in Xiaqian, Yangquan, July 11, 1996.

30. Interviewed at Shanxi University, September 28, 1997.

31. The initial and official case against Wu Tong'an may be found in *Shanxi ribao* (Shanxi daily), January 29, 1992.

32. The incident occurred in 1992; the park manager was charged with negligence, but later exonerated. No one was seriously injured in the bridge collapse.

33. "Zhandou de gangwei—shanguang de qingchun: ji Qiaodong paichusuo huji minjing, gongqingtuanyuan Wang Jijun de guangjin shiji" (Battle station—Spring Lightning: Recalling the advanced deeds of Qiaodong police station household registration policeman and CYL member Wang Jijun), *Taiyuan bao* (Taiyuan daily), February 17, 1976, p. 3.

34. See, for example, Keith Forster, "The 1982 Campaign against Economic Crime in China," *Australian Journal of Chinese Affairs*, no. 14 (1983): 1; Stephen K. Ma, "Reform Corruption: A Discussion on China's Current Development," *Pacific Affairs*, 62, no. 1 (1989): 40; Jean-Louis Rocca, "Corruption and Its Shadow: An Anthropological View of Corruption in China," *China Quarterly*, no. 130 (1992): 402.

35. Established by Chen Chuntang in 1985, the former manager of the Taiyuan Bank of Industry and Commerce, as a financial support for the development of Shanxi's heavy industry. This was Shanxi's first experiment in this area. Details may be found in Liu, ed., *Zhongguo dangdai qiyejia mingdian—Shanxi tao*, p. 516.

36. Interviewed in Taiyuan, September 13, 1997.

37. Shanxi's development in 1996 and 1997 is reminiscent of Zhejiang in 1991 and 1992 as reflected both in aggregate statistics and in life on the streets.

38. See in particular Linda Weiss and John M. Hobson, *States and Economic Development* (Cambridge: Polity Press, 1995), esp. pp. 190ff.

39. A significant difference between Shanxi and the more economically developed areas of South and East China is that in the former there are few examples among the new middle classes of the nonworking wife, something of a status symbol elsewhere in the country.

40. Chen Yu, "'Kala' shi fou 'OK'—Taiyuan geting shichang sanmiao" (Is Karaoke o.k.?—An investigation of Taiyuan's song halls), *Beiyue feng* (The Beiyue scene), no. 1 (1996): 41.

41. The significance of this expansion is a little harder to assess in Shanxi than elsewhere. The province, and especially the rural areas around Taiyuan, Linfen, and Yuncheng, has a long history of Christian experience. Catholics have had communities there since 1602, Protestants since the 1870s. There are currently some 400,000 officially recognized Christians in the province.

12. The Rise of Private Business Interests

Research for this paper was carried out with support from the Committee for Scholarly Communication with China and a Research Planning Grant from the National Science Foundation (9520133). I would also like to thank Yao Xianguo, who helped to facilitate my stay at Zhejiang University, Chen Guoquan, Bao Song, and Yu Yuequn, for their able assistance and useful advice in the field, and Merle Goldman, for her comments on an earlier draft.

1. Albert Hirschman, *Shifting Involvements: Private Interests and Public Action* (Princeton: Princeton University Press, 1979).

2. On Confucian and Republican understanding of the public and private see Joseph Fewsmith, *Party, State, and Local Elites in Republican China* (Honolulu: University of Hawaii Press, 1985), pp. 17–36; Mary Backus Rankin, *Elite Activism and Political Transformation in China: Zhejiang Province, 1865–1911* (Stanford: Stanford University Press, 1986), pp. 15–17.

3. Rankin, *Elite Activism*, pp. 15–17.

4. Lowell Dittmer, *The Continuing Revolution* (Berkeley: University of California Press, 1987), pp. 40–43.

5. Gail Henderson and Myron Cohen, *The Chinese Hospital* (New Haven: Yale University Press, 1984), pp. 1–47.

6. Dittmer, *The Continuing Revolution*, p. 78; see also Andrew Walder, *Communist Neo-Traditionalism: Work and Authority in Chinese Industry* (Berkeley: University of California Press, 1986).

7. Deng Xiaoping, "Emancipate the Mind, Seek Truth from Facts and Unite as One in Looking to the Future," in *Selected Works of Deng Xiaoping (1975–1982)* (Beijing: Foreign Languages Press, 1984).

8. For a detailed history of the reemergence of the private sector between 1978 and 1989 see Susan Young, *Private Business and Economic Reform in China* (Armonk, N.Y.: M. E. Sharpe, 1995).

9. *Ta kung pao*, August 13, 1980, translated in Foreign Broadcast Information Service (FBIS), p. 017 (August 15, 1980).

10. Xinhua, August 20, 1980.

11. Zhao Ziyang, "Advance Along the Road of Socialism with Chinese Characteristics—Report Delivered at the Thirteenth National Congress of the Communist Party of China, October 25, 1987," *Beijing Review*, no. 30 (November 9–15, 1987), 23–49.

12. *Renmin ribao* (People's daily), April 4, 1988.

13. National and some local regulations on *siying* enterprises are reproduced in *Zhongguo siying jingji nianjian (1996)* (Chinese private economy yearbook) (Beijing: Zhonghua gongshang lianhe chubanshe, 1996).

14. For example see: "Qu zhengfu youquan baimian jingli ma?" (Does the district government have the right to remove the manager?), *Minzhu yu falü* (Democracy and law), no. 10 (1996): 46; "Guanyu siying jingji de falü wenti" (Regarding the legal problems of the private economy), *Zhongguo gongshang* (China industry and commerce), no. 2 (1995) "Gongmin de hefa quanli shou qinfan" (Citizens' legal rights are violated), *Guangzai* (Brilliance), no. 9 (1995): 19; Huang Yingzhang, "Hebei sheng geti siying fazhan de xiankuang wenti ji duice" (Problems of and approaches to current development of the private sector in Hebei province), *Jingji yanjiu cankao*, no. 90 (June 10, 1995): 33–34.

15. Cai Beihua, "Lun geti jingji" (On the individual economy), *Shehui kexue* (Social science), no. 6 (1980): 15–16.

16. "1995 nian Zhongguo di erci siying qiye chouyang diaocha shuju ji fenxi" (Data and analysis of the second annual sample survey of China's private enterprises), *Zhongguo siying jingji nianjian (1996)*, p. 157.

17. Ibid., pp. 142, 147.

18. Pan Shiyong, "Geti gongshanghu, siying qiyezhu shouru qingkuang fenxi ji zhengce jianyi" (An analysis and policy proposal for the current situation of individual and private business owner income), *Jingji yanjiu cankao*, nos. 13/14 (January 23, 1995): 34–35.

19. "Siying qiyezhu de xiaofei xintai" (The consumer mentality of private enterprise owners), *Zhongguo jingji xinxi* (Chinese economic news), no. 9 (1996): 25; *Zhongguo shichang jingji bao* (Chinese market economy news), March 20, 1996.

20. Xinhua, April 25, 1996, in FBIS, no. 82, April 26, 1996.

21. Huang, "Hebei sheng," p. 31.

22. Interviews, Suzhou, Changzhou, 1996.

23. See Chapter 8 and Lora Sabin, "New Bosses in the Workers' State: The Growth of Non-State Sector Employment in China," *China Quarterly*, no. 140 (December 1994): 944–970.

24. The extent to which collective enterprises are really private businesses in disguise is a subject of debate among scholars in the West. See Chapter 8.

The actual figure is impossible to know and varies considerably from place to place. According to one Chinese report there are estimated to be as many private enterprises wearing red hats as there are legally registered as *siying*. Wu Shuzhi and Chen Yuansheng, "Dangqian siying jingji fazhan-zhong de wenti ji duice" (Problems of and approaches to the developing private economy), *Lilun dongtai* (Theoretical trends), no. 4 (1994): 4. See also Song Hai, "Jia jiti qiyezhu xintai tansuo" (An exploration of the mentality and motivations of fake collective owners), *Zhongguo gongshang* (Chinese industry and commerce), no. 7 (1995): 18–19.

25. Interviews, Changzhou, Suzhou, Wenzhou, Hangzhou, 1996.

26. Interviews, Wenzhou, 1989, 1996.

27. Interviews, Hangzhou, Wenzhou, 1996; see also "Qu zhengfu youquan baimian jingli ma?"

28. This approach has apparently been embraced by the Fifteenth Party Congress. On the history and problems of these firms, see Ma Jinlong, "Wenzhou gufen hezuozhi fazhan qingkuang yanjiu" (Research on the development of the share-holding cooperative system in Wenzhou), manuscript, 1993; Wang Juening, "Xiangcun gufen hezuo qiye lifa de jige wenti" (Several problems regarding the legal status of share-holding cooperative firms), *Hebei xuekan* (Hebei journal), no. 3 (1996): 99–103.

29. Ma Jianhang, "Geti siying jingji yu xiangzhen qiye de fazhan—Wenzhou diqu shehui jingji fazhan diaocha baogao" (Individual and private economy and the development of township and village enterprise—A research report on the social economic development of the Wenzhou region), *Shehui kexue zhanxian* (Social science front), no. 1 (1995): 77–83; "Guamu xiangkan Wenzhou xing" (Looking at Wenzhou with new eyes), *Zhongguo siying jingji nianjian (1996)*, p. 216.

30. Ma Jinlong, "Wenzhou gufen hezuozhi," p. 4.

31. Kristen Parris, "Local Initiative and National Reform: The Wenzhou Model of Development," *China Quarterly*, no. 134 (June 1993): 258.

32. For other attempts to coopt or subvert the dominant discourse, see James Scott, *Domination and the Arts of Resistance* (New Haven: Yale University Press, 1990), p. 102.

33. Young, *Private Business*, p. 25.

34. Huang, "Hebei sheng," p. 26.

35. Shi Chenglin, "Dui 'buchonglun' de zai renshi" (A new look at "supplemental theory"), *Nongye jingji wenti* (Agricultural economic problems), no. 2 (1989): 17; "Siying fazhan yanjiu" (Private enterprise development research) *Jingji yanjiu cankao*, no. 195 (September 12, 1995): 9; Ge Wenyou, "Lun geti jingji yu geti jingying" (On individual economy and individual management), *Jingji kexue* (Economic science), no. 1 (1993): 1–2; Ma

Jianhang, "Geti siying jingji," p. 81; for a review of this debate, see Yi Cheng, "Siying jingji wenti ruogan wenti" (Materials on the problems of the private economy), *Dangdai sichao* (Contemporary thought), no. 1 (1996): 13–17. On Qing dynasty reformers, see Fewsmith, *Party, State, and Local Elites,* and Rankin, *Elite Activism.*

36. This essay was published as "Several Factors Affecting the Security of Our Country," in *Yazhou zhoukan* (Asiaweek), January 14, 1996, pp. 22–28, and is summarized in *China News Analysis,* no. 1572 (November 15, 1996). For similar hard-line analysis, see *Xuexi, yanjiu, cankao* (Study, research, reference), no. 12 (1995): 1–4.

37. *Renmin ribao,* October 14, 1996.

38. Jiang Zemin, "Gaoju Deng Xiaoping lilun weida qizhi, ba jianshe you Zhongguo tese shehuizhuyi shiye quanmian tuixiang ershiyi shiji" (Hold high the great banner of Deng Xiaoping theory, for an all-round advancement of the cause of building socialism with Chinese characteristics into the twenty-first century), *Renmin ribao* (overseas edition), September 9, 1997, p. 2.

39. Zhang Houyi, "Siying qiyezhu qunti zai woguo shehui jiegou zhong de diwei" (The social position of private entrepreneurs as a group in our country), in *Zhongguo siying jingji nianjian (1996),* p. 95.

40. See Kevin J. O'Brien, "Agents and Remonstrators: Role Accumulation by Chinese People's Congress Deputies," *China Quarterly,* no. 138 (June 1994): 359–380, and Chapter 5.

41. Interview, Hangzhou, 1996.

42. "Guard against 'Electoral Bribery' in Rural Areas," *Renmin ribao,* May 21, 1996, translated in FBIS, no. 116, (June 14, 1996).

43. Interview, Fuyang county, Zhejiang, 1996.

44. *Zhongguo siying jingji nianjian (1996),* p. 162.

45. Interviews, Wenzhou, Hangzhou, 1996.

46. Authoritarian state corporatism is distinguished from a more liberal societal corporatism found in West European nations. On this distinction and corporatism generally, see Frederick Pike and Thomas Stritch, eds., *The New Corporatism: Social and Political Structures in the Iberian World* (Notre Dame: Notre Dame University Press, 1974), and Howard Wiarda, *Corporatism and Comparative Politics: The Other Great "Ism"* (Armonk, N.Y.: M. E. Sharpe, 1997). On corporatism in China, see Jonathan Unger and Anita Chan, "China, Corporatism, and the East Asian Model," *Australian Journal of Chinese Affairs,* no. 33 (January 1995): 29–53.

47. Interview, Hangzhou, November 1988. On the SELA, see Ole Bruun, *Business and Bureaucracy in a Chinese City* (Berkeley: Center for Chinese Studies, University of California, 1993), pp. 109–120; Young, *Private Business,* pp. 126–130.

48. Interviews, Hangzhou, Wenzhou, 1989 and 1996.

49. Interviews, Hangzhou, 1996.

50. Interviews, Hangzhou, 1989, 1993, 1996; Wenzhou, 1989, 1996; Ningbo, 1996. BICA publications include *Gongshang xingzheng guanli* (Industrial and commercial administration) and *Zhejiang xingzheng guanli* (Zhejiang industrial and commercial administration).

51. Interviews, Hangzhou, 1989, 1996; Wenzhou, 1989, Ningbo and Suzhou, 1996; Bruun, *Business and Bureaucracy,* pp. 109–120.

52. Interviews, Hangzhou, Wenzhou, 1989, 1996.

53. On the ICF, see also Jonathan Unger, "'Bridges': Private Business, the Government, and the Rise of New Associations," *China Quarterly,* no. 145 (September 1996): 795–819, and Christopher Earle Nevitt, "Private Business Associations in China: Evidence of Civil Society or Local State Power," *China Journal,* no. 36 (July 1996): 25–43.

54. *Niangjia* refers to a married woman's parents or her parents' home. Both terms are often used by ICF cadres and appear often in the articles published by the ICF in *Zhongguo gongshang* (China industry and commerce).

55. Interviews, Hangzhou, Suzhou, Changzhou, 1996.

56. "Guanyu siying jingji de falü wenti," p. 11; interviews, Suzhou, Changzhou, Wenzhou, 1996.

57. Interviews, Suzhou, Wenzhou, 1996.

58. Not all trade associations are under the authority of the ICF. Some have been set up by governmental economic agencies and ministries.

59. *Wenzhou ribao* (Wenzhou daily), July 6, 1994; interviews, Wenzhou, 1996.

60. Interview, Hangzhou, 1996; Zhou Guanglu, "Tantan gongshanglian de huiban qiye" (A Discussion of the ICF's association-run enterprises), *Zhongguo gongshang,* no. 2, pp. 21–33 (1996).

61. Interviews, Hangzhou, Suzhou, Wenzhou, 1996.

62. Interview, Suzhou, 1996.

63. *Zhongguo siying jingji nianjian (1996),* p. 162.

64. Interviews, Suzhou, Changzhou, Wenzhou, 1996.

65. Of fifty-five entrepreneurs interviewed in Zhejiang and Jiangsu in 1996, only two said that the ICF was very useful.

66. Interview, Hangzhou 1996.

67. Interviews, Wenzhou, Hangzhou, Suzhou, 1996.

68. Interviews, Hangzhou, Changzhou, Suzhou, 1996.

69. Interview, Wenzhou, 1996.

70. Interview, Changzhou, Wenzhou, 1996.

71. Fewsmith, *Party, State, and Local Elites,* p. 191.

72. Interview, Suzhou, 1996.

73. Charles E. Lindblom, *Politics and Markets: The World's Political Economic Systems* (New York: Basic Books, 1977), pp. 161–222.

74. "Siying qiyezhu de xiaofei," pp. 25–26.

75. See results of the survey in *Zhongguo siying jingji nianjian (1996)*, p. 158.

13. The Emergence of Politically Independent Intellectuals

1. Merle Goldman, *Sowing the Seeds of Democracy in China* (Cambridge: Harvard University Press, 1994).

2. Joseph Fewsmith, *Dilemmas of Reform in China: Political Conflict and Economic Debate* (Armonk, N.Y.: M. E. Sharpe, 1994).

3. X. L. Ding, *The Decline of Communism in China: Legitimacy Crisis, 1977–1989* (New York: Cambridge University Press, 1994).

4. Chen Ziming, *Chen Ziming fansi shinian gaige* (Chen Ziming's reflections on ten years of reform) (Hong Kong: Dangdai yuekan, 1992), p. 380.

5. Ibid., p. 380.

6. Ibid., p. 382.

7. For detailed background on Chen Ziming and Wang Juntao, see George Black and Robin Munro, *Black Hands of Beijing* (New York: John Wiley and Sons, 1993).

8. For information on Min Qi, see *Pai Hsing* (The People), no. 192, May 16, 1989, pp. 6–8: trans. in JPRS-CAR-89-094, September 6, 1989, p. 4.

9. Yan Jiaqi, *Toward a Democratic China: The Intellectual Autobiography of Yan Jiaqi* (Honolulu: University of Hawaii Press, 1992), pp. 43–44.

10. Author's interview with Wang Juntao.

11. Chen Ziming, *Fansi shinian gaige*, p. 507.

12. Ibid., p. 512.

13. *Pai Hsing*, no. 193, June 1, 1989, pp. 17–19; trans. in JPRS-CAR-89-099, September 27, 1989, p. 30.

14. Hu Ping, Wang Juntao et al., eds., *Kaituo—Beida xueyun wenxian* (Exploration—Peking University student movement materials) (Hong Kong: Tianyuan shuju, 1990), p. 108.

15. Ibid.

16. Author's interview with Wang Juntao.

17. *Wall Street Journal*, February 13, 1991, p. 20, reported that they had an enrollment of 250,000 correspondence students, and tuition had brought in more than two million dollars.

18. Chen Ziming, *Fansi shinian gaige*, p. 381.

19. Ibid., p. 385.

20. Asia Watch China, "Defense Statement of Chen Ziming," *News from Asia Watch*, June 10, 1992, p. 12.

21. Black and Munro, *Black Hands of Beijing*, p. 188. For information about

Han Dongfang, the BWAF, and the activities of Chen and Wang during the Tiananmen demonstration, see pp. 137–242.

22. Ibid., p. 222.
23. Ibid., p. 193.
24. Ibid., pp. 212–213.
25. Ibid., p. 223.
26. Ibid., pp. 229–231.
27. Ibid., p. 223.
28. In a talk at an Asia Watch meeting, 1994.
29. Black and Munro, *Black Hands of Beijing*, p. 265.
30. Discussed in David Kelly and He Baogang, "Emergent Civil Society and the Intellectuals in China," in Robert Miller, ed., *The Developments of Civil Society in Communist Systems* (London: Allen and Unwin, 1992), p. 25.
31. Mary Rankin, William Rowe, and David Strand, "'Public Sphere'/'Civil Sphere' in China?: Paradigmatic Issues in Chinese Studies," *Modern China*, 19, no. 2 (April 1993).
32. Kelly and He, "Emergent Civil Society and the Intellectuals," p. 28.

14. Crime, Corruption, and Contention

My thanks to Nara Dillon and Robyn Eckhardt for research assistance on this paper.

1. Foreign Broadcast Information Service (FBIS), June 15, 1995, p. 55.
2. *Shanghai gong'an nianjian* (Shanghai public security yearbook) (Shanghai: Shanghai renmin chubanshe, 1991), p. 56.
3. *Wenhui bao* (June 29, 1994), p. 2.
4. *Zhengming* (Contention) (June 1994): 9. My thanks to Dorothy Solinger for sharing this report.
5. FBIS, June 6, 1994, p. 20.
6. FBIS, June 6, 1994, p. 19.
7. *Renmin ribao* (People's daily) (January 17, 1996), p. 9.
8. Richard Baum, *Prelude to Revolution: Mao, the Party and the Peasant Question* (New York: Columbia University Press, 1975), p. 130.
9. See, for example, Li Zhisui, *The Private Life of Chairman Mao* (New York: Random House, 1994).
10. Quoted in Gordon White, "Corruption and Market Reform in China," *IDS Bulletin*, 27, no. 2 (1996): 41.
11. Alan P. L. Liu, "The Politics of Corruption in the PRC," *American Political Science Review*, 77, no. 3 (September 1983): 602–623.
12. Jean C. Oi, "Market Reforms and Corruption in Rural China," *Studies in Comparative Communism*, 22, nos. 2/3 (Summer–Autumn 1989): 230.

13. White, "Corruption and Market Reform," p. 45.

14. Ibid., p. 46.

15. Unlike an earlier literature that often associated corruption with economic backwardness, many recent analysts—whether focusing on China or on other newly industrializing countries in East Asia—see rent-seeking accommodations between politicians and businessmen as fueling the engines of economic growth. See ibid., p. 45, for a review of this literature.

16. Ting Gong, *The Politics of Corruption in Contemporary China: An Analysis of Policy Outcomes* (Westport, Conn.: Praeger, 1994), p. 135.

17. See, for instance, Gordon White, *Riding the Tiger: The Politics of Economic Reform in Post-Mao China* (Stanford: Stanford University Press, 1993).

18. Richard Levy, "Corruption, Economic Crime, and Social Transformation since the Reforms: The Debate in China," *Australian Journal of Chinese Affairs,* no. 33 (January 1995): 1–25.

19. FBIS, August 8, 1994, p. 18.

20. Levy points out that class analysis plays an important role in the criticisms of democracy activists and conservatives, but is notably absent from the arguments of reformers—who are at pains to avoid being associated with the Cultural Revolution and the Maoists. See Levy, "Corruption," 1995, p. 20.

21. FBIS, October 28, 1991, p. 55.

22. A common pun in the countryside, rendered by a change in tones, transforms the official slogan "Our party is an experienced and glorious party" into "Our party is experienced in alcohol and large of stomach" *(Women de dang shi jiujing kaoyan weida de dang).* See *Nanyang shangbao* (South Seas Commercial Journal) (September 20, 1993) for this and other peasant witticisms. I am grateful to Lu Xiaobo for this reference.

23. FBIS, September 10, 1993, p. 40.

24. David Snow and Robert Benford define a collective action frame as an "interpretive schemata that simplifies and condenses the 'world out there' by selectively punctuating and encoding objects, situations, events, experiences, and sequences of actions within one's present or past environment." See their "Master Frames and Cycles of Protest," in Aldon D. Morris and Carol McClurg Mueller, eds., *Frontiers in Social Movement Theory* (New Haven: Yale University Press, 1992), pp. 133–155. See also Sidney Tarrow's "Mentalities, Political Cultures, and Collective Action Frames: Constructing Meanings through Action," in ibid., pp. 174–202.

25. Mok Chiu Yu and J. Frank Harrison, eds., *Voices from Tiananmen Square* (Montreal: Black Rose Books, 1990), p. 109.

26. Joint Publications Research Service (JPRS), January 14, 1993, pp. 20–22. In the summer of 1992, Beijing sanitation workers had also put up an

eight-page poster demanding a substantial wage hike, criticizing officials in the sanitation department for corruption, and calling for a general strike. See FBIS, August 11, 1992, pp. 24–25.

27. Although James C. Scott's *The Moral Economy of the Peasant* (New Haven: Yale University Press, 1974) applied the concept to the peasantry of Southeast Asia, E. P. Thompson's original formulation had of course referred to urban rioters and factory artisans in England during the industrial revolution.

28. On "reactive" protests, see Charles Tilly, "Rural Collective Action in Modern Europe," in Joseph Spielberg and Scott Whiteford, eds., *Forging Nations: A Comparative View of Rural Ferment and Revolt* (East Lansing: Michigan State University Press, 1976), pp. 9–40. On Republican period tax unrest, see Elizabeth J. Perry, *Rebels and Revolutionaries in North China, 1845–1945* (Stanford: Stanford University Press, 1980), chap. 5.

29. FBIS, June 11, 1993, p. 13. After paralyzing their county government for the better part of a year, the Renshou protestors received assurances from Beijing of greater efforts to protect farmers against the exactions of unscrupulous local cadres.

30. See Elizabeth J. Perry and Li Xun, *Proletarian Power: Shanghai in the Cultural Revolution* (Boulder, Colo.: Westview Press, 1997), chap. 6.

31. FBIS, August 2, 1994, p. 8.

32. FBIS, July 15, 1994, pp. 12–13.

33. FBIS, September 27, 1994, pp. 62–63.

34. The All-China Federation of Trade Unions estimated a total of 250,000 labor disputes between 1988 and the end of 1993—nearly five times the number brought to arbitration. See *China News Digest* (February 22, 1994).

35. An exceptional year during the Maoist period was 1957, when the Hundred Flowers Campaign generated an impressive outpouring of labor unrest. See Elizabeth J. Perry, "Shanghai's Strike Wave of 1957," *China Quarterly*, no. 137 (March 1994). The Cultural Revolution decade also saw some strike activity, perhaps most seriously in the city of Hangzhou.

36. FBIS, April 6, 1993, p. 67.

37. For the example of a labor movement in the pre-Communist period adopting a similar demeanor, see Elizabeth J. Perry, *Shanghai on Strike: The Politics of Chinese Labor* (Stanford: Stanford University Press, 1993), p. 44.

38. On the Third Front, see Barry Naughton, "The Third Front: Defense Industrialization in the Chinese Interior," *China Quarterly*, no. 115 (September 1988), and Naughton, "Industrial Policy during the Cultural Revolution," in William Joseph et al., eds., *New Perspectives on the Cultural Revolution* (Cambridge: Harvard University Press, 1991).

39. FBIS, May 8, 1995, pp. 42–43.

40. FBIS, March 16, 1995, p. 24.
41. FBIS, June 6, 1994, p. 19.
42. For more on this point, see Elizabeth J. Perry, "'To Rebel is Justified': Maoist Influences on Popular Protest in Contemporary China," paper prepared for the colloquium series of the Yale University Program in Agrarian Studies (November 17, 1995).
43. Li Kaifu, ed., *Xingshi fanzui anli congshu—fangeming zui* (Compilation of criminal cases—counterrevolutionary crimes) (Beijing: Zhongguo Jiancha chubanshe, 1992), p. 180.
44. Ibid., pp. 132–133.
45. Ibid., pp. 139–140, 143, 145, 150, 180.
46. Ibid., pp. 154–155. Anger over the state's family planning programs has figured in a number of rural uprisings. One group, the Humanitarian Lovers of the Way *(renxue haodao)*, began its revival (having been outlawed in 1953) in 1972 and three years later had recruited new followers by preaching Confucian values and martial arts techniques. In the 1980s, its leaders predicted the imminent coming of a messiah and railed against the state's birth control policy. Ibid., p. 182. Kevin O'Brien and Lianjiang Li (forthcoming) also identify opposition to the birth control policy as a central animus in a petition movement they studied in one north China village.
47. Anita Chan, Richard Madsen, and Jonathan Unger, *Chen Village: The Recent History of a Peasant Community in Mao's China* (Berkeley: University of California Press, 1984), p. 170.
48. Liang Heng and Judith Shapiro, *Son of the Revolution* (New York: Vintage Books, 1983), p. 174.
49. *Eastern Express* (October 5, 1995), p. 39.
50. Cai Shaoqing, "Dangdai Zhongguo de heishehui" (Criminal gangs in contemporary China), paper delivered at the University of California, Berkeley China Colloquium, April 18, 1996, p. 1.
51. Ibid.
52. Ibid.
53. Borge Bakken, "Crime, Juvenile Delinquency, and Deterrence Policy in China," *Australian Journal of Chinese Affairs*, no. 30 (July 1993): 34.
54. Shao Daosheng, *Preliminary Study of China's Juvenile Delinquency* (Beijing: Foreign Languages Press, 1992), p. 25.
55. FBIS, March 20, 1996, p. 51.
56. FBIS, January 25, 1995, p. 26.
57. Cai, "Dangdai Zhongguo de heishehui," p. 4.
58. In 1980, as the economic reforms got under way, the ratio of urban to rural incomes stood at 3 to 1. Five years later, it had dropped to just over

2 to 1. But in 1993—because of tax increases, higher prices for agricultural inputs, and reduced state investment in agriculture—the ratio had increased dramatically, to 3.3 to 1. See FBIS, March 30, 1995, p. 32. Within rural areas, as well, the gap was substantial. In early 1995, rural residents in eastern provinces enjoyed an average income (RMB 1,617) that was nearly twice the figure (RMB 856) for those living in western provinces. See FBIS, March 27, 1995, pp. 83–84. In 1994, the top 10 percent of household incomes outstripped the bottom 10 percent by 3.9 times; the previous year, the differential had stood at 3.6. See Pan Gang, "Ruhe kan Zhongguo pinfu chaju lada" (How to interpret China's growing gap between rich and poor), *Shehui xue* (Sociology), no. 1 (1996): 108.

59. This was evident during the Tiananmen uprising, when students received important aid from the Stone Corporation—a private company with close ties to government officials and dissident intellectuals alike. It is also apparent in many of the recent rural incidents in which protest leaders have used proceeds from newly established factories and shops to purchase land, procure weapons, and so on. See Li Kaifu, *Xingshi fanzui anli congshu*, pp. 137, 142. A number of criminal organizations have established their own businesses, especially massage and games parlors, karaoke lounges, dance halls, bath houses, and barber shops. See FBIS, March 20, 1996, p. 51, for government pledges to submit such establishments to "closer scrubbing" [*sic*].

60. See Elizabeth J. Perry, "Rural Violence in Socialist China," *China Quarterly*, no. 103 (September 1985): 414–440, for a discussion of the role of grass-roots cadres in instigating rural violence during the early reform years.

61. Transnational triad outfits, true to the tradition of the 1911 Revolution, did help student activists flee the country after June 4, 1989, but the political agenda of these gangs appears limited at best.

62. FBIS, April 23, 1990, p. 62. See also FBIS, April 11, 1990, pp. 10, 47–48; April 30, 1990, p. 1.

63. This was not the first time in Chinese history that Muslim separatists in this region had attempted to form an independent Republic of East Turkistan. See Linda Benson, *The Ili Rebellion: The Moslem Challenge to Chinese Authority in Xinjiang, 1944–1949* (Armonk, N.Y.: M. E. Sharpe, 1990), for a discussion of a similar effort in the Republican period.

64. Since the 1980s, major ethnic incidents have erupted in Xinjiang on the average of once a year. See FBIS, April 30, 1990, pp. 64–65, for a listing of the largest incidents. This was also not the last rebellion in Xinjiang by independence activists. See FBIS, July 1, 1991, p. 11; December 11, 1991, pp. 28–29; and December 12, 1991, p. 28.

65. FBIS, April 20, 1990, pp. 52–53.

66. FBIS, April 23, 1990, p. 59.
67. FBIS, May 28, 1993, p. 10.
68. FBIS, May 25, 1993, p. 16.
69. "The Perils of Nationalism," *The Economist* (September 21, 1996), pp. 34–35.

15. The "State of the State"

1. Tony Saich, "The Fourteenth Party Congress: A Programme for Authoritarian Rule," *China Quarterly*, no. 132 (December 1992): 1160.
2. Maurice Meisner, "Bureaucratic Capitalism: Some Reflections on the Social Results of the Chinese Communist Revolution," paper presented at the Symposium on "Rethinking the Chinese Revolution," UCLA, November 19, 1994.
3. Dorothy J. Solinger, "Capitalist Measures with Chinese Characteristics," in Dorothy J. Solinger, *China's Transition from Socialism: Statist Legacies and Market Reforms, 1980–1990* (Armonk, N.Y.: M. E. Sharpe, 1993), pp. 126–152.
4. Frank N. Pieke, "Bureaucracy, Friends, and Money: The Growth of Capital Socialism in China," *Comparative Studies in Society and History*, 37, no. 3 (1995): 494–518.
5. Minxin Pei, "Microfoundations of State Socialism and Patterns of Economic Transformation," *Communist and Post-Communist Studies*, 29, no. 2 (1996): 131–145.
6. Nan Lin, "Local Market Socialism: Local Corporatism in Action in Rural China," *Theory and Society*, 24 (1995): 301–354.
7. Peter Nan-shong Lee, "The Chinese Industrial State in Historical Perspective: From Totalitarianism to Corporatism," in Brantly Womack, ed., *Contemporary Chinese Politics in Historical Perspective* (Cambridge: Cambridge University Press, 1991), p. 168. Lu Xiaobo has employed a similar term—"*danwei* regime." See his "'Small Public' vs. 'Big Public': The Danwei Regime and Institutional Corruption," paper presented at the annual meeting of the Association for Asian Studies, Boston, March 24–27, 1994.
8. Margaret Pearson, "The Janus Face of Business Associations in China: Socialist Corporatism in Foreign Enterprises," *Australian Journal of Chinese Affairs*, no. 31 (January 1994): 25–46.
9. Jonathan Unger and Anita Chan, "Corporatism in China: A Developmental State in an East Asian Context," in Barrett L. McCormick and Jonathan Unger, eds., *China after Socialism: In the Footsteps of Eastern Europe or East Asia?* (Armonk, N.Y.: M. E. Sharpe, 1996), pp. 104ff.

10. Jean Oi, "Fiscal Reform and the Economic Foundations of Local State Corporatism," *World Politics*, 45, no. 1 (October 1992): 99–126.

11. Vivienne Shue, "State Power and Social Organization in China," in Joel Migdal et al., *State Power and Social Forces: Domination and Transformation in the Third World* (Cambridge: Cambridge University Press, 1994), pp. 76ff.

12. David L. Wank, "Bureaucratic Patronage and Private Business: Changing Networks of Power in Urban China," in Andrew G. Walder, ed., *The Waning of the Communist State: Economic Origins of Political Decline in China and Hungary* (Berkeley: University of California Press, 1995), pp. 153–183.

13. Edward Friedman, "Confucian Leninism and Patriarchal Authoritarianism," in Edward Friedman, *National Identity and Democratic Prospects in Socialist China* (Armonk, N.Y.: M. E. Sharpe, 1995), pp. 148–187.

14. Barrett L. McCormick, *Political Reform in Post-Mao China: Democracy and Bureaucracy in a Leninist State* (Berkeley: University of California Press, 1990).

15. Gabriella Montinola, Yingyi Qian, and Barry R. Weingast, "Federalism, Chinese Style: The Political Basis for Economic Success in China," *World Politics*, 48 (October 1995): 50–81.

16. X. L. Ding, "Institutional Amphibiousness and the Transition from Communism: The Case of China," *British Journal of Political Science*, 24, no. 3 (July 1994): 293–318.

17. Lu Xiaobo, "Booty Socialism, Bureaupreneurs, and Economic Development: A Study of Organizational Corruption in China," paper presented to the annual meeting of the Association for Asian Studies, Honolulu, April 11–14, 1996.

18. See, for example, Shaoguang Wang, "The Rise of the Regions: Fiscal Reform and the Decline of Central State Capacity in China," in Walder, *The Waning of the Communist State*, pp. 87–113.

19. See Yasheng Huang, "Central-Local Relations in China during the Reform Era," photocopy, 1995; also Dali L. Yang, "Reform and the Restructuring of Central-Local Relations," in David S. G. Goodman and Gerald Segal, eds., *China Deconstructs: Politics, Trade, and Regionalism* (London: Routledge, 1994), pp. 59–98.

20. Susan L. Shirk, "Fragmentation in China and Its International Implications," paper presented at the conference on "The Growth of Chinese Power and Implications for U.S. Policy," Aspen, Colorado, August 20–25, 1995, p. 1.

21. Yang, "Reform and the Restructuring," p. 89.

22. See Peter Tsan-yin Cheung, "The Case of Guangdong in Central-Provincial Relations," in Jia Hao and Lin Zhimin, eds., *Changing Central-Local Relations in China* (Boulder, Colo.: Westview Press, 1994), pp. 207–238.

23. See Christine Wong, "Central-Local Relations in an Era of Fiscal Decline," *China Quarterly*, no. 128 (December 1991): 691–715; Jean C. Oi, "Local Government Response to the Fiscal Austerity Program, 1988–1990," paper presented at the UCLA China Seminar, March 1991; and Andrew Wedeman, "Bamboo Walls and Brick Ramparts: Uneven Development, Inter-Regional Economic Conflict, and Local Protectionism in China, 1984–1991," Ph.D. dissertation, University of California, Los Angeles, 1994, chap. 1.

24. See Maria Hsia Chang, "China's Future: Regionalism, Federation, or Disintegration?" *Studies in Comparative Communism*, 25, no. 3 (September 1992): 211–227; also Shaoguang Wang and Angang Hu, *Jiaqiang zhongyang zhengfu zai shichang jingji zhuanxingzhong de zhudao zuoyong* (Strengthen the central government's guiding role in the shift to a market economy) (Shenyang: Liaoning renmin chubanshe, 1993). For a collection of articles stressing the rising power of provinces vis-à-vis the center, see Jia and Lin, *Changing Central-Local Relations*.

25. The center's unflinching use of its control over approximately 5,000 provincial-level *nomenklatura* positions to reward loyal centralists and remove stubborn localists is discussed in Huang, "Central-Local Relations," pp. 10–16. See also John Burns, "Strengthening Central CCP Control of Leadership Selection: The 1990 *Nomenklatura*," *China Quarterly*, no. 138 (June 1994): 458–491; and Yang, "Reform and the Restructuring," pp. 85–86.

26. Beijing's tactics of "divide and rule" are examined in ibid., p. 86.

27. Charles Lindblom describes this built-in informational incapacity of communist systems in metaphorical terms as a case of "strong thumbs, no fingers." See Lindblom, *Politics and Markets: The World's Political Economic Systems* (New York: Basic Books, 1977), chap. 5 and passim.

28. Yasheng Huang, "Information, Bureaucracy, and Economic Reforms in China and the Soviet Union," *World Politics*, 47, no. 1 (October 1994): 116.

29. See Carol Lee Hamrin, *China and the Challenge of the Future* (Boulder, Colo.: Westview Press, 1990), pp. 75–80; and Joseph Fewsmith, *Dilemmas of Reform in China: Political Conflict and Economic Debate* (Armonk, N.Y.: M. E. Sharpe, 1994), chap. 4.

30. It should be noted, however, that increased information flows do not necessarily ensure enhanced policy performance. See Nina Halpern, "Information Flows and Policy Coordination in the Chinese Bureaucracy," in Kenneth Lieberthal and David M. Lampton, eds., *Bureaucracy, Politics, and Decision Making in Post-Mao China* (Berkeley: University of California Press, 1992), pp. 125–148; also Shue, "State Power and Social Organization," p. 83.

31. See Dorothy Solinger, "Despite Decentralization: Disadvantages, Dependence, and Ongoing Central Power in the Inland—the Case of Wuhan," *China Quarterly*, no. 145 (March 1996): 1–34.

32. See Andrew G. Walder, "Local Governments as Industrial Firms: An Organizational Analysis of China's Transitional Economy," *American Journal of Sociology*. 101, no. 2 (September 1995): 279–80; also Oi, "Fiscal Reform," pp. 102ff.

33. Barry Naughton identifies three sources of polymorphous bargaining relations in the reform era: (1) the diminishing volume of resources directly controlled by the central government; (2) an increase in the range of information, managerial skills, and policy instruments available to central government officials; and (3) the increasing complexity and diversity of bargaining arrangements at each level necessitated by the coexistence of centrally planned, locally controlled, and marketized sectors of the economy. See Barry Naughton, "Hierarchy and the Bargaining Economy: Government and Enterprise in the Reform Process," in Lieberthal and Lampton, eds., *Bureaucracy, Politics, and Decision Making*, pp. 245–279.

34. The term is borrowed from Susan L. Shirk, *The Political Logic of Economic Reform in China* (Berkeley: University of California Press, 1993), chap. 9.

35. See Tsang Shu-ki and Cheng Yuk-shing, "China's Tax Reforms of 1994: Breakthrough or Compromise?" *Asian Survey*, 34, no. 9 (September 1994): 778–779 and passim.

36. Walder, "Local Governments as Industrial Firms" (emphasis added).

37. For a study of one such "corporate village," the notorious Daqiuzhuang village near Tianjin, see Nan Lin, "Local Market Socialism," pp. 316ff.

38. According to official Chinese sources, between 1978 and 1990 the total number of party and state officials increased from 18 million to 33 million, with most of the expansion taking place at local levels. See Ting Gong, *The Politics of Corruption in Contemporary China* (Westport, Conn.: Praeger, 1994), p. 122. The following discussion is based in part on Lu Xiaobo, "Levying on the Peasants: The Politics of Peasant Burden in China," *Journal of Peasant Studies* (July 1997).

39. In Liaoning province, for example, the average number of full-time cadres at the *xiang* (administrative township) level rose from 20 to 70. In one suburban Beijing county there was a thirteen-fold increase in the number of full-time *xiang* officials, with the average number per *xiang* rising from around 12 in the 1960s to more than 160 in 1992. Cited in Lu, "Levying on the Peasants."

40. In Shandong province it was reported that 619 different *dabiao* contributions were exacted in different parts of the province in a single year. See *Banyuetan*, nos. 1 and 11 (1993), cited in ibid.

41. The Renshou riots are discussed in Thomas P. Bernstein and Dorothy J. Solinger, "The Peasant Question for the Future: Citizenship, Integration, and Political Institutions?" paper presented at the conference on "China and World Affairs in 2010," Stanford University, April 25–26, 1996, pp. 23–26. See also James Miles, *The Legacy of Tiananmen: China in Disarray* (Ann Arbor: University of Michigan Press, 1996), pp. 169–173.

42. The fifteen branch agencies are industry and commerce; taxation; public security; land management; environmental protection; post office; banking; grain; cotton; power management; industrial management; road management; farm machinery; veterinary medicine; and water management. See Lu, "Levying on the Peasants."

43. In Gansu province, the number of state cadres increased from 470,000 in 1985 to 700,000 in 1993. See Lu, "Levying on the Peasants."

44. See Jonathan Unger, "The Struggle to Dictate China's Administration: The Conflict of Branches vs. Areas vs. Reform," *Australian Journal of Chinese Affairs*, no. 18 (July 1987): 15–45; and Chien-min Chao, "*T'iao-t'iao* vs. *K'uai-k'uai*: A Perennial Dispute between the Central and Local Governments in Mainland China," *Issues and Studies*, 27, no. 8 (August 1991): 31–46. One key difference between the *tiao-kuai* dualism of the Maoist era and the new *zhengfu-bumen* opposition is that whereas during the Mao years the term *kuaikuai* generally referred to administrative control exercised by party committees, in the reform era major responsibility for territorial policy implementation has been shifted from party committees to local governments.

45. David Zweig, "Urbanizing Rural China: Bureaucratic Authority and Local Autonomy," in Lieberthal and Lampton, eds., *Bureaucracy, Politics, and Decision Making*, p. 335.

46. Another *xiang* cadre lamented that "it is not the functional agencies that serve the government, but the government that serves the agencies." Quoted in Lu, "Levying on the Peasants."

47. For a fairly detailed description of the operations of county-level government in Pengzhe county, Jiangxi, see Zhong Yang, "Withering Governmental Power in China? A View from Below," *Communist and Post-Communist Studies*, 29, no. 4 (December 1996).

48. See Wank, "Bureaucratic Patronage," p. 160.

49. See Gordon White, "Basic-Level Local Government and Economic Reform in Urban China," in Gordon White, ed., *The Chinese State in the Era of Economic Reform: The Road to Crisis* (Armonk, N.Y.: M. E. Sharpe, 1991), pp. 232–234.

50. *Wall Street Journal*, August 13, 1992, cited in Lin, "Local Market Socialism," p. 333.

51. Ibid.

52. Thus, for example, in Xiajia village, Heilongjiang, the party secretary's self-reported strategy for carrying out his official duties was minimalist, consisting largely of "three no's"—"say nothing, do nothing, and offend no one." See Yun-xiang Yan, "Everyday Power Relations: Changes in a North China Village," in Walder, *The Waning of the Communist State,* p. 226. A similar shift in the modal qualities of party secretaries after decollectivization—from political activism to economic instrumentalism—was noted by Chan, Madsen, and Unger in their follow-up study of the effects of economic reform in Chen village, Guangdong. See Anita Chan, Richard Madsen, and Jonathan Unger, *Chen Village under Mao and Deng* (Berkeley: University of California Press, 1992), pp. 315, 320.

53. Quoted in Yan, "Everyday Power Relations," p. 226. In a rural survey conducted in Xiajia village in 1989, Yan found that 54 percent of all local cadres who had been in power on the eve of decollectivization became affluent thereafter, as compared with only 9 percent of ordinary villagers. See ibid., p. 238.

54. In 1991, then Chinese vice president Wang Zhen complained that the party's prestige and vitality in rural areas had fallen to an all-time low. See *South China Morning Post,* March 12, 1991.

55. Cited in Zhao Suisheng, "Political Reform and Changing One-Party Rule in China," paper presented at the annual meeting of the American Political Science Association, Chicago, September 1995, p. 16.

56. On clan organizations "taking over from party branches" in rural areas, see ibid.; also *South China Morning Post,* April 28, 1995. Elizabeth Perry has linked the decline in the morale of rural party organs in some areas to an upsurge in clan-based collective action. See Elizabeth J. Perry, "Rural Collective Violence: The Fruits of Recent Reforms," in Elizabeth J. Perry and Christine Wong, eds., *The Political Economy of Reform in Post-Mao China* (Cambridge: Council on East Asian Studies, Harvard University, 1985), pp. 175–192.

57. Wang Zhen reportedly complained that in rural Hebei, three times as many people had become Catholics in 1990 as had joined the Communist Party. "While words of CCP cadres in the villages have little appeal," he said, "the response to religious figures is overwhelming." See *South China Morning Post,* March 12, 1991.

58. Kevin O'Brien and Lianjiang Li, "The Politics of Lodging Complaints in Rural China," *China Quarterly,* no. 143 (September 1995): 761–762, 781.

59. Bernstein and Solinger, "The Peasant Question for the Future," pp. 12–15, 22–26.

60. Yan, "Everyday Power Relations," p. 227.

61. The following discussion is based loosely on a typology of local state economic involvement suggested by Peter Evans, "Predatory, Developmental, and Other Apparatuses: A Comparative Political Economy Perspective on the Third World State," *Sociological Forum*, 4, no. 4 (1989): 562; Wank, "Bureaucratic Patronage," pp. 153–155; and Marc Blecher, "Development State, Entrepreneurial State: The Political Economy of Socialist Reform in Xinju Municipality and Guanghan County," in White, *Chinese State*, pp. 265–291.

62. Jean Oi, "The Role of the Local State in China's Transitional Economy," *China Quarterly*, no. 144 (December 1995): 1146.

63. Examples of this are noted in Blecher, "Development State, Entrepreneurial State," pp. 280ff.; and Lin, "Local Market Socialism," pp. 312ff.

64. Since this pattern of agency-entrepreneur relations generally involves the particularistic exchange of preferential treatment by officials for financial payoffs, partnerships, or other tangible benefits by entrepreneurs, David Wank ("Bureaucratic Patronage") has labeled it "symbiotic clientelism," to distinguish it from the *danwei*-centered "dependent clientelism" that prevailed in the Maoist period.

65. This pattern comes closest to the Japanese model of a "developmental state." See Evans, "Predatory, Developmental, and Other Apparatuses." For Chinese examples of this pattern of local state involvement, see Blecher, "Development State, Entrepreneurial State," pp. 280ff.

66. On the emerging corporatist structures of local power in urban China, see Chapter 12. See also Oi, "The Role of the Local State"; Unger and Chan, "Corporatism in China," pp. 104–107; Pearson, "The Janus Face of Business Associations," pp. 34ff.; and Ole Odgaard, "Entrepreneurs and Elite Formation in Rural China," *Australian Journal of Chinese Affairs*, no. 28 (July 1992): 98ff.

67. See Lu, "Booty Socialism," p. 4.

68. See ibid.; also Bernstein and Solinger, "The Peasant Question"; Jean Oi, "Partial Market Reform and Corruption in Rural China," in Richard Baum, ed., *Reform and Reaction in Post-Mao China: The Road to Tiananmen* (New York: Routledge, 1991), pp. 143–161; and Andrew Wedeman, "Stealing from the Farmers: Institutional Corruption and the 1992 IOU Crisis," paper presented at the annual meeting of the Association for Asian Studies, Honolulu, April 11–14, 1996.

69. The distinction between individual and institutional predation is discussed in Wedeman, "Stealing from the Farmers," pp. 3–6; and Lu, "'Small Public' vs. 'Big Public,'" pp. 1–4. Examples of institutional predation include, inter alia, local trade protectionism and the imposition of irregular fees,

fines, and other apportionments (the so-called *san luan,* or "three disorders") for the purpose of setting up *danwei* slush funds (*xiaojinku,* or "small treasuries"), used to finance "collective goods" such as extrabudgetary housing construction, the purchase of automobiles, and the holding of banquets and receptions.

70. White, "Basic-Level Local Government," p. 239. See also Connie Squires Meaney, "Market Reform and Disintegrative Corruption in Urban China," in Baum, *Reform and Reaction,* pp. 124–142; and Ole Bruun, "Political Hierarchy and Private Entrepreneurship in a Chinese Neighborhood," in Walder, *The Waning of the Communist State,* pp. 193ff.

71. We are indebted to Steve Krasner for suggesting this matrix configuration.

72. Compare, for example, Oi, "Partial Market Reform" and Lu, "Booty Socialism," with Oi, "The Role of the Local State."

73. Partial exceptions include Wank, "Bureaucratic Patronage"; Bruun, "Political Hierarchy"; and Nevitt, "Private Business Associations." We leave aside for the moment Oi's migration from the "predation" camp (1989) to the "clientelist" camp (1992) to the "developmental" camp (1995).

74. Dorothy Solinger, "Urban Entrepreneurs and the State: The Merger of State and Society," in Arthur Lewis Rosenbaum, ed., *State and Society in China: The Consequences of Reform* (Boulder, Colo.: Westview, 1992), p. 121.

75. A similar point is made by Shue, "State Power and Social Organization," p. 83.

76. See Robert F. Miller, ed., *The Developments of Civil Society in Communist Systems* (Sydney: George Allen and Unwin, 1992); and Kazimierz Poznanski, *Constructing Capitalism: The Re-emergence of Civil Society and Liberal Economy in the Post-Communist World* (Boulder, Colo.: Westview Press, 1992).

77. For debate on this question, see, inter alia, Clemens Stubbe Ostergaard, "Citizens, Groups, and a Nascent Civil Society in China," *China Information,* 4, no. 2 (Autumn 1989): 28–41; Thomas Gold, "The Resurgence of Civil Society in China," *Journal of Democracy,* 1, no. 1 (Winter 1990); and Martin K. Whyte, "Urban China: A Civil Society in the Making?" in Rosenbaum, *State and Society in China,* pp. 77–102.

78. Exceptions to this generalization include Gordon White, who argues that the economic interpenetration of state and society has left sufficient social space for an "embryonic" civil society to emerge, and Martin Whyte, who suggests that the June 1989 crackdown failed fully to quench the flames of China's nascent civil society. See Gordon White, "Prospects for Civil Society in China: A Case Study of Xiaoshan City," *Australian Journal of Chinese Affairs,* no. 29 (January 1993): 63–87; and Martin Whyte, "Urban China: A Civil Society in the Making?"

79. See Philippe Schmitter, "Still a Century of Corporatism," *Review of Politics,*

36, no. 1 (January 1974): 93–96. For an early application of corporatist ideas to the Chinese reform experience, see Jeremy Paltiel, "China: Mexicanization or Market Reform?" in James A. Caporaso, ed., *The Elusive State: International and Comparative Perspectives* (Newbury Park, Calif.: Sage Publications, 1989), pp. 255–278.

80. See, inter alia, Unger and Chan, "Corporatism in China," pp. 104ff.; Lee, "The Chinese Industrial State," p. 155; David Wank, "Private Business, Bureaucracy, and Political Alliance in a Chinese City," *Australian Journal of Chinese Affairs*, no. 33 (January 1995): 69–71; Wank, "Bureaucratic Patronage," pp. 179–181; Oi, "The Role of the Local State," pp. 1146–1149; Shue, "State Power and Social Organization," pp. 76ff.; and Kristen Parris, "Private Entrepreneurs as Citizens: From Leninism to Corporatism," *China Information*, 10, nos. 3/4 (Winter 1995–Spring 1996): 8–9.

81. Pieke, "Bureaucracy, Friends, and Money," pp. 511, 515, 516.

82. A similar trend is noted by Andrew Walder, "The Quiet Revolution from Within: Economic Reform as a Source of Political Decline," in Walder, *The Waning of the Communist State*, p. 15. Maurice Meisner identifies the empire-building tendencies of local cadres as a pathological consequence of post-reform bureaucratic capitalism, while Nan Lin sees it as an outgrowth of local market socialism. Cf. Meisner, "Bureaucratic Capitalism," and Lin, "Local Market Socialism."

83. Lin, "Local Market Socialism," pp. 312ff. In August 1993 the village chief, Yu Zuomin, was sentenced to twenty years in prison for his involvement in the coverup of a murder. See *Far Eastern Economic Review*, 156, no. 37 (September 16, 1993): 16–18; and *Beijing Review*, 36, no. 37 (September 13, 1993): 7.

84. Jeremy Paltiel refers to the symbiotic relations between state officials and entrepreneurs as "Mexicanization." See Paltiel, "China: Mexicanization or Market Reform," p. 257.

85. Quoted in Wank, "Bureaucratic Patronage," p. 158.

86. See Chapter 12; cf. Pearson, "The Janus Face of Business Associations," pp. 44–46; White, "Prospects for Civil Society," pp. 85–87; Parris, "Private Entrepreneurs as Citizens," pp. 27–28; and Mayfair Mei-hui Yang, "Between State and Society: The Construction of Corporateness in a Chinese Socialist Factory," *Australian Journal of Chinese Affairs*, no. 22 (July 1989): 58–60.

87. See Oi, "Local State Corporatism"; and Oi, "The Role of the Local State."

88. Oi, "The Role of the Local State," p. 1148.

89. See Vivienne Shue, "State Socialism and Modernization in China through Thick and Thin," paper presented at the 1988 annual meeting of the American Political Science Association. Similar observations are made by

Shaoguang Wang, "Central-Local Fiscal Politics in China," in Jia and Lin, *Changing Central-Local Relations,* p. 109; and Walder, "The Quiet Revolution from Within."

90. See Lindblom, *Politics and Markets,* p. 65.

91. Gabriel A. Almond and G. Bingham Powell, *Comparative Politics: A Developmental Approach* (Boston: Little, Brown, 1966), pp. 194–203.

92. Alexis de Tocqueville, *The Old Regime and the French Revolution* (New York: Anchor, 1955), pp. 176–177.

93. Path-dependent outcomes are those that are significantly constrained—but not wholly predetermined—by previous institutional choices, ingrained patterns of behavior, and elite decisions. Prior branchings tend to narrow the viable range of present and future pathways, favoring certain outcomes while precluding others. On the uses of path-dependency analysis in the study of reform in Leninist and post-Leninist systems, see David Stark, "Path Dependence and Privatization Strategies in East-Central Europe," in Vedat Melor, ed., *Changing Political Economies: Privatization in Post-Communist and Reforming Communist States* (Boulder, Colo.: Lynne Rienner Publishers, 1994). On path-dependent outcomes in the case of China's reforms, see Shue, "State Power and Social Organization in China"; Blecher, "Development State, Entrepreneurial State"; and Lin, "Local Market Socialism."

94. See Kenneth Jowitt, "Soviet Neotraditionalism: The Political Corruption of a Leninist Regime," *Soviet Studies,* 35, no. 3 (1983): 275–297.

95. Shue, "State Power and Social Organization," pp. 70ff.

96. Michael Mann, "The Autonomous Power of the State: Its Origins, Mechanisms, and Results," in John A. Hall, ed., *States in History* (New York: Basil Blackwell, 1986), p. 113.

97. McCormick, *Political Reform in Post-Mao China,* p. 83.

98. Andrew G. Walder, *Communist Neo-Traditionalism: Work and Authority in Chinese Industry* (Berkeley: University of California Press, 1986), p. 249. Insofar as it allows for individual exceptions, special deals, compromises, and (especially) dissembled compliance, neo-traditionalism is sometimes referred to as "despotism with a human face." See McCormick, *Political Reform in Post-Mao China,* p. 195.

99. Andrew G. Walder, "The Decline of Communist Power: Elements of a Theory of Institutional Change," *Theory and Society,* 23, no. 3 (June 1994): 297–323.

100. Wank, "Bureaucratic Patronage," p. 181.

101. See You Ji, "Corporatization, Privatization, and the New Trend in Mainland China's Economic Reforms," *Issues and Studies,* vol. 31, no. 4 (April 1995): 59–61; M. Yang, "Between State and Society"; Pearson, "The Janus

Face of Business Associations"; and Parris, "Private Entrepreneurs as Citizens."

102. See, for example, Steven M. Goldstein, "China in Transition: The Political Foundations of Incremental Reform," *China Quarterly*, no. 144 (December 1995): 1105–1131; and Lee, "The Chinese Industrial State."

103. See Meisner, "Bureaucratic Capitalism," pp. 91ff.

104. See, for example, Edward Friedman, "Is China a Model of Reform Success?" in Friedman, *National Identity and Democratic Prospects*, pp. 189–207; and McCormick, *Political Reform in Post-Mao China*, pp. 195–196. Interestingly, some pessimistic corporatists view the problem of original sin not in terms of China's Leninist heritage, but rather in terms of the recrudescence of long-dormant prerevolutionary (Confucian) patterns of official-merchant collaboration. See, for example, Meisner, "Bureaucratic Capitalism," pp. 2–8.

105. In this connection it is interesting to note that China has not suffered from the most debilitating type of patrimonial predation—massive "spontaneous privatization"—that afflicted Russia's post-Soviet economy.

106. See Kevin J. O'Brien, "Chinese People's Congresses and Legislative Embeddedness: Understanding Early Organizational Development," *Comparative Political Studies*, 27, no. 1 (April 1994): 99–101.

107. Huntington has postulated four main criteria of institutionalization: adaptability, complexity, autonomy, and coherence. See Samuel P. Huntington, *Political Order in Changing Societies* (New Haven: Yale University Press, 1968), pp. 12–24.

108. O'Brien, "Chinese People's Congresses and Legislative Embeddedness," p. 101.

109. Shue, "State Power and Social Organization," p. 83. A similar notion of ongoing interactive state-societal co-evolution underpins X. L. Ding's concept of "institutional amphibiousness."

110. For many Chinese—top leaders and ordinary citizens alike—this was a primary lesson drawn from the Tiananmen debacle of 1989. See Huntington, *Political Order in Changing Societies*, chap. 1.

111. For a gloomy but well-reasoned prognosis of accelerating post-Deng sociopolitical disarray, see Miles, *The Legacy of Tiananmen*.

112. See Sen Lin, "A New Pattern of Decentralization in China: The Increase of Provincial Powers in Economic Legislation," *China Information*, 7, no. 3 (Winter 1992–93): 27–38.

113. See Montinola, Qian, and Weingast, "Federalism, Chinese Style," pp. 52ff.

114. The Chinese reform economist Chen Yizi has proposed further extending and formalizing these decentralizing changes, though he stops short of calling for full constitutional federalism. See Chen Yizi, "A Realistic Alter-

native for China's Development and Reform Strategy: Formalized Decentralization," *Journal of Contemporary China*, no. 10 (Fall 1995): 81–92. On the putative advantages of full, formal federalism in China, see Arthur Waldron, "China's Coming Constitutional Challenges," *Orbis*, 39, no. 1 (Winter 1995): 27–28 and passim.

115. Kenneth Lieberthal, "The 'Fragmented Authoritarianism' Model and Its Limitations," in Lieberthal and Lampton, eds., *Bureaucracy, Politics, and Decision Making*, pp. 1–30.

116. See Susan L. Shirk, "The Chinese Political System and the Political Strategy of Economic Reform," in Lieberthal and Lampton, eds., *Bureaucracy, Politics, and Decision Making*, p. 69.

117. See Richard Baum, "China after Deng: Ten Scenarios in Search of Reality," *China Quarterly*, no. 145 (March 1996): 157–159.

Contributors

Richard Baum is Professor of Political Science at the University of California, Los Angeles. His latest book is *Burying Mao: Chinese Politics in the Age of Deng Xiaoping* (1994).

Thomas P. Bernstein is Professor of Political Science and a member of the East Asian Institute at Columbia University. His most recent publication is "China: Growth without Political Liberalization," in James W. Morley, ed., *Driven by Growth: Political Change in the Asia-Pacific Region* (1998).

Joseph Fewsmith is director of the East Asian Interdisciplinary Studies Program and Associate Professor of International Relations at Boston University. He is the author of *Dilemmas of Reform in China: Political Conflict and Economic Debate* (1994) and *Party, State, and Local Elites in Republican China* (1985).

Paul H. B. Godwin is Professor of International Affairs in the Department of Military Strategy and Operations at the National War College, Washington, D.C. His most recent publications are "Uncertainty, Insecurity, and China's Military Power," *Current History* (September 1997), and "Force and Diplomacy: China Prepares for the 21st Century," in Samuel S. Kim, ed., *China and the World: Chinese Foreign Policy toward the New Millennium* (1998).

Merle Goldman is Professor of Chinese History, Boston University, and research associate at the Fairbank Center for East Asian Research,

Harvard University. Her most recent publications include *Sowing the Seeds of Democracy in China: Political Reform in the Deng Xiaoping Era* (1994) and (with John K. Fairbank) *China: A New History*, enlarged edition (1998).

David S. G. Goodman is director of the Institute for International Studies, University of Technology, Sydney. His most recent publications include *China's Provinces in Reform: Class, Community, and Political Culture* (1997) and (with Gerald Segal) *China Rising: Nationalism and Interdependence* (1997).

Lianjiang Li is Assistant Professor of Government and International Studies at Hong Kong Baptist University. He has recently published articles in *Modern China* and *China Quarterly* on the response of villages to grass-roots reforms.

Roderick MacFarquhar is Leroy B. Williams Professor of History and Political Science and research associate at the Fairbank Center for East Asian Research at Harvard University. His latest publication is the third and final volume of *The Origins of the Cultural Revolution*.

Barry Naughton is Associate Professor at the Graduate School of International Relations and Pacific Studies, University of California, San Diego. He is the author of *Growing Out of the Plan: Chinese Economic Reform, 1978–1993* (1995), and editor of *The China Circle: Economics and Technology in the PRC, Hong Kong, and Taiwan* (1997).

Kevin J. O'Brien is Associate Professor of Political Science at Ohio State University, and Visiting Associate Professor of Political Science at the University of California, Berkeley, 1997–1999. He is the author of *Reform without Liberalization: China's National People's Congress and the Politics of Institutional Change* (1990).

Kristen Parris is Associate Professor of Political Science at Western Washington University. Her publications include "Renegotiating Chinese Identity: Between Local Group and National Ideology," in Kenneth Hoover, with James Marcia and Kristen Parris, *The Power of Identity: Politics in a New Key* (1997), and "Private Entrepreneurs as Citizens:

From Leninism to Corporatism," *China Information*, 10, nos. 3/4 (1995/1996).

Elizabeth J. Perry is Professor of Government at Harvard University. She is coauthor (with Li Xin) of *Proletarian Power: Shanghai in the Cultural Revolution* (1996) and coeditor (with Lu Xiaobo) of *Danwei: The Changing Chinese Workplace in Historical and Comparative Perspective* (1997).

Alexei Shevchenko is a graduate of the Moscow Institute of International Relations. He is currently working toward a Ph.D. in political science at the University of California, Los Angeles.

Tianjian Shi is Assistant Professor of Political Science at Duke University. He is the author of *Political Participation in Beijing* (1997).

Dorothy J. Solinger is Professor in the Department of Politics and Society at the University of California, Irvine. She is the author of *Contesting Citizenship in Urban China* (1999) and *China's Transition from Socialism* (1993).

Murray Scot Tanner is Associate Professor of Political Science, Western Michigan University. He is the author of *The Politics of Lawmaking in Post-Mao China: Institutions, Processes, and Democratic Prospects* (1998).

Martin King Whyte is Professor of Sociology and International Affairs at George Washington University. His recent works include "The Fate of Filial Obligations in Urban China," *China Journal*, no. 38 (1997), and "The Chinese Family and Economic Development: Obstacle or Engine?" *Economic Development and Cultural Change*, 45 (1996).

Harvard Contemporary China Series